MULTICULTURAL
CURRICULUM

To our mentors
Mowni, Quadir, Ray and Carl and Michael

MULTICULTURAL CURRICULUM

*New Directions
for Social Theory,
Practice, and Policy*

Edited by
Ram Mahalingam
and
Cameron McCarthy

ROUTLEDGE • *New York   London*

Published in 2000 by
Routledge
29 West 35th Street
New York, NY 10001

Published in Great Britain by
Routledge
11 New Fetter Lane
London EC4P 4EE

Printed in the United States of America on acid-free paper.

Library of Congress Cataloging-in-Publication Data

Multicultural curriculum : new directions for social theory, practice, and policy / [edited] by
    Ram Mahalingam and Cameron McCarthy.
        p.   cm.
    Includes bibliographical references (p.   ).
    ISBN 0-415-92013-2.   — ISBN 0-415-92014-0 (pbk.)
        1. Multicultural education—Curricula.   2. Multiculturalism.   3. Critical pedagogy.
    I. Mahalingam, Ram.   II. McCarthy, Cameron.
    LC1099.M816   2000
370.117—dc21   99-42140
                                                                                  CIP

CONTENTS

v

ACKNOWLEDGMENTS

The editors would like to express their gratitude to each member of the dedicated cast of international scholars who contributed their remarkable essays to this volume. We were fortunate to have material support and funding that helped to move *Multicultural Curriculum: New Directions for Social Theory, Practice, and Policy* from the rarefied air of an American Educational Association conference panel in San Francisco to the final fruition that is this book. Ram Mahalingam was able to draw on the material support of a Michigan Society Postdoctoral Fellowship offered to him at the University of Michigan at Ann Arbor. Cameron McCarthy received funding in the form of a University Scholars Fellowship at the University of Illinois at Urbana-Champaign. We are grateful to our sponsors. We would also like to express our profound appreciation to Heidi Freund, Publishing Director at Routledge, for her steadfast support of our book project from the earliest stages of its conception. Finally, this book would not have been possible without the keen research and editorial support of Greg Dimitriadis, Shawn Miklaucic, Craig Robertson, and Marie Leger, our research assistants at the University of Illinois. To them we owe our sincerest thanks.

Introduction

Rethinking Multiculturalism and Curricular Knowledge for the Twenty-First Century

Ram Mahalingam
University of Michigan

Cameron McCarthy
University of Illinois, Urbana-Champaign

It is with a deep sense of responsibility, and an overwhelming sense of concern that we write to you. . . .

Soniaji, you have lived as a daughter-in-law to India for the past 30 years. You have, in your own way, absorbed much of this great country's spirit. You are in the line of many non-Indians who have loved and adopted this country and worked for its benefit. The Congress party which you now lead was the brainchild of a Scotsman, Sir A. O. Hume. The seat you occupy had been once adorned by Annie Besant. It is in this selfless tradition that we see your services to the party and the nation.

Madam president, India is a country with a history and tradition going back thousands of years. It is a confident culture and a proud nation. Above all, it is a country which is self sufficient in every sense of the word. India always lived in the spirit of the Mahatma's words *"Let the winds from all over sweep into my room,"* but again he said: *"I will not be swept off my feet."* We accept with interest and humility the best which we can gather from the North, South, East or West and we absorb them into our soil.

But our inspiration, our soul, our honor, our pride, our dignity, is rooted in our soil, it has to be of this earth. Soniaji, you have become a part of us because you have all along respected this. We, therefore, find it strange that you should allow yourself to forget it at this crucial juncture.

1

It is not possible that a country of 980 million, with a wealth of education, competence and ability, can have anyone other than an Indian born of Indian soil to head its government.

With regards,
Yours sincerely,
P. A. Sangma, Tariq Anwar, Sharad Pawar, New Delhi, India
[emphasis added]

THE PREDICAMENT OF CULTURE

The epigraph above is an excerpt from a letter written on May 16, 1999 by three members of India's Congress Working Committee (CWC) to Sonia Gandhi, an Italian-born daughter-in-law in the Nehru dynasty in India. It was written because Sonia was being primed to become the prime minister of India by a party elite opportunistically preparing for the upcoming general elections. It reflects an important predicament—the need to essentialize one's identity through a search for one's roots, especially when there is a perceived threat to the established social order.

The predicament and tone of the letter exemplify the ambivalence and the apprehensions about multiculturalism discourse throughout the world. For instance, Sangma, Anwar, and Pawar (the "three musketeers" who are signatories to the letter) argue that the essential identity of an Indian can be authenticated only through the claim to birth on India's soil. By no means is the articulation of the link between biology and geography in the formation of an identity, especially a cultural identity, innocuous or apolitical. As noted by Kwame Appiah (1992), the underscored relationship among biology, essences, and geography has several incarnations. The (mis)quote of Mahatma Gandhi suggests that the winds may come from all four directions (i.e., wherever one's social experience lies), but cultural identity is rooted in the soil of one's birthplace. A discursive Foucauldian interpretation of the metaphor would show that in the archaeology of the apparently unshakable ground beneath such identities reside seismic movements, tensions, and contradictions. The appeal to history can often be a frustrating exercise for those who seek facile coherences and simpleminded ethnic essentialisms.

The Gandhian metaphor of Indian identity unswayed by powerful winds coming from different directions struggles to hold within itself some of the most powerful tensions and ambivalences that now haunt ethnocentric discourses in general. There is also the suggestion, too, that multiculturalism is as capricious and as ephemeral as the wind, a passing fad, a mere peripheral influence of various cultures on the core identity of "the" group or "the" nation, be it American, British, Australian, or Indian.

When it is clear that it is not a passing fad, there are three kinds of responses to multiculturalism in the American context. First, when the reform is not seen as a fleeting practice, then the political economy of engaging multiculturalism is manifested in naturalizing the European roots of American identity (Ravitch 1990; Hirsch 1987). Second, multicultural rhetoric is deployed to obfuscate the political economic consequences of globalization. Third, the social production of multiculturalism is elaborated in a pedagogy that is rooted in the essentialized representation of various minority cultures. We will briefly discuss these three "discursive" turns in the monocultural, Eurocentric discourse as a response to multiculturalism. And we will make the case for why we need a paradigmatic shift in the multicultural discourse.

The early Eurocentric response to multiculturalism is similar to the wind metaphor discussed above. The main argument is that the great civilization of Europe has been the "natural" ancestor of Americans. American identity should thus be rooted in European thought and should not be swayed by the winds from the south or east (read, multiculturalism). For example, E. D. Hirsch (1987) argues that the cultural connection to European civilization is the root cause of "our" identities. He insists on a curriculum project of strengthening America's intellectual ties with Europe—as if the ideas (read, cultures) of the third world are in a race with those of Europe, and the winner will surely *be* Europe (see Joseph 1990 for an excellent critique of Eurocentrism in the history of mathematics). The presumed "naturalness" of the lineage between America and Europe has several assumptions about a homogeneous Europe (West 1993). Not withstanding Frantz Fanon's argument that Europe is the invention of the third world, the cultural history that embodies the spirit of the Eurocentrists rests on essentialized, biological roots in an imagined "bounded" community that is anchored in both the ethical and intellectual landscape of dominant American identity. So multiculturalism is designated to represent the marginalized identities, without the burden of their historical past.

The second approach—the rhetoric of multiculturalism—is deployed increasingly in the service of transatlantic corporate interests. While the market potential of the celebration of different "cultures" has been realized (e.g., the marketability of New Age remedies and Eastern herbs), simultaneously, the socioeconomic consequences of the global economy have been masked by a rhetoric of pluralism and multiplicity. Gayatri Spivak (1996) warned of such possibilities in her critique of tokenism in the multicultural world. Fredric Jameson (1998) argues that globalization is a communicational concept that "masks and transmits cultural or economic meanings" (55).

Walter Mignolo (1998) argues that globalization creates a condition that subverts critical strategies and subaltern histories, thus creating "the conditions for spatializing the civilization process and, by so doing, of denying the denial of coevalness as one of the main epistemological strategies of colonial/imperial expansion" (51). We contend that the specific modes of representations of multiculturalism have been at the service of spatializing the civilizations. The apparent "naturalness" of the progression of "Western civilization" implies that "other" cultures are sitting in a historical waiting room, anticipating their "turn" to hitch a ride on the train of globalization as they attempt to move more quickly through the stages of socioeconomic development. To achieve this, globalization needs to locate cultures that are embodied, essentialized, and established within specific geographical boundaries, cultures that need to be rescued from their historical slumber. Thus, globalization simultaneously celebrates different cultures for their market potential while deploying multiculturalism to create "others" who need to be part of the "one world, one solution" of universal consumerism. Creating an essentialized, homogenized representation of culture is crucial to the globalization project. The epistemological and ethical implications are also far reaching.

Interestingly, current anthropological thinking is moving away from the bounded notion of "culture" (Anderson 1983; Dirks, Eley, and Ortner 1994; Rosaldo 1993) the third, essentialist approach to multiculturalism. The notion of culture as bounded in a hermeneutic time seal has been challenged and the hybrid nature of culture(s) has been recognized. Nicholas Dirks, Geoff Eley, and Sherry Ortner (1994) argue that the shift in the notion of culture has been manifested in three different ways:

> At the level of theory the concept of culture has been expanded by Foucauldian notions of discourse, and Gramscian notions of hegemony (on the latter point, the works of Raymond Williams have been partially influential). Both concepts emphasize the degree to which culture is grounded in unequal relationships and is differentially related to people and groups in different social positions. . . . Another core aspect of the concept of culture has been the notion of culture's extraordinary durability. . . . In many cases, timeless traditions turn out to be "invented" and not very long ago at that. . . . Finally a central aspect of culture has been the claim of relative coherence and internal consistency. . . . But an intriguing line of discussion in contemporary critical theory has now posed a major alternative view: culture as multiple discourses, occasionally coming together in large systematic configuration, but more often coexisting within fields of interaction and conflict. (1–2)

In a similar vein, Homi Bhabha (1994) argues that culture is an uneven product and that cultural forms and practices are often elaborated in response to displacement. Bhabha maintains that social marginality and affective experience play pivotal roles in the critical strategies that are deployed as "culture reaches out to create a symbolic textuality" (172). For Bhabha, the idea of culture in the classic, romanticist sense needs to be challenged.

While the essentialized, homogenized, bounded notion of culture has been problematized in anthropology and in critical theory, the notion of culture in the production of multiculturalism—especially in textbooks—is still a romanticized, classical notion of culture. Primarily, multiculturalism is used as a pedagogical device to essentialize cultures. Several enthusiastic proponents of multiculturalism primarily use it as an extension of civic education—that there are other cultures that exist in the world and we should respect them. In a survey of textbooks on multiculturalism (Mahalingam and McCarthy 1999) we found that the "other cultures" are also conveniently homogenized into discrete units such as Asian

Americans, African Americans, Hispanic Americans, and so forth. The relative stability and instability of these cultures and the historical flux and the patterns of variation in their elaboration are rarely discussed. At times, the essentialization of a culture is incarnated in the form of the canonization of its aesthetic and folkloric practices (see Ruth Vinz, "Cautions against Canonizing (An)Other Literature," in this volume).

The challenge is to develop critical strategies for a meaningful praxis that would challenge the essentialist notions of culture now being generated within capitalist globalization. It is imperative to foreground the location of the subject within the multiculturalism discourse. The embodied experiences of marginalized groups should be understood in order to produce a shift in the conception of culture from that of a collection of aesthetic and folkloric objects and practices. Instead, we need to foreground the uneven nature of cultural production and the incompleteness of historically produced identities (Bhabha 1994). Another discursive strategy would be to focus on intersectionality (Crenshaw 1995), looking at the interplay of different identities, such as those "black" and "woman." Kimberlé Crenshaw suggests that the concept of intersectionality might be a useful way to look at the multiply classed and gendered histories of people of color. She argues that intersectionality is a way of exploring the tension between multiple identities and the need to have specific, unified group identities for political mobilization.

Having considered the three kinds of responses of the hegemonic discourse to multiculturalism, we argue that multiculturalism needs a paradigmatic shift in order to achieve its political and egalitarian goals. Our analysis of multicultural textbooks shows that the public production and consumption of multiculturalism is riddled with epistemological, as well as ethical, questions. How culture is conceptualized, and how intellectual and marginalized histories are layered into a bounded notion of culture, is linked to the spatialization of human practices in ways that mask the political and economic ramifications of globalization.

Multicultural Curriculum is the result of our concern that the multicultural project has to move beyond articulating the need for the recognition and the legitimation of cultures. The first wave of multiculturalism had specific political goals to challenge the political and cultural hegemony of Eurocentrism. While succeeding in making its presence felt in educational reform, multiculturalism is in danger of becoming the homogenized "other" of monoculturalism. Multiculturalism creates an ideal foil for the naturalization of the European intellectual legacy, as if it were itself free of internal contradictions or the essentializations of cultures that serve the interests of global capitalism.

On the other hand, we do not suggest a version of an antiessentialist thesis, that which Crenshaw (1995) calls the "vulgarized social construction thesis" (i.e., "since all categories are socially constructed, there is no such thing as say, 'Blacks' or 'women,' and thus it makes no sense to continue reproducing those categories by organizing around them" [375]). Rather, multiculturalism should be seen as a paradigm for a global educational reform where bounded notions of culture, including the notion of "white," are constantly contested and challenged. We need to confront the ethnic absolutism now rampant in education and society with the complex historical record and the living experiences and realities of marginalized subjects. We need to generate critical pedagogical strategies that deeply articulate the embodied experiences of the marginalized. All the contributors to this volume address these concerns in substantive ways. While problematizing various aspects of multiculturalism, contributors also formulate strategies that foreground the transformative potential of the multicultural project. As well, we insist on the need to rescue the best intuitions in multiculturalism from a full-scale corruption and incorporation by the interests of global capitalism. Our contributors include international researchers who are interested in a critical and reflexive approach to multiculturalism. This critical framework is elaborated in opposition to the homogenizing tendencies of the state or right-wing politics and the aggressive appropriation of pluralism by insatiable corporate interests.

THE CHAPTERS

Multicultural Curriculum is divided into three sections. Section 1 foregrounds theoretical critiques of mainstream forms of multiculturalism. In section 2, contributors present empirically based analyses of the complex issues involved in multicultural classroom practice. In section 3 the political and the policy imperatives of multiculturalism are discussed.

Steve Fuller and Mary Coffey begin the theory section with powerfully analytical chapters that explore the conceptual tensions within multiculturalism, calling critical attention to the problematic deployment of the concept of "culture" within multicultural discourses. In his chapter "Social Epistemology as a Critical Philosophy of Multiculturalism," Fuller argues that multiculturalism should be seen as a critical philosophy that goes beyond the universalist-relativist debate. After critically examining the history of such a debate, Fuller makes the case for a conception of multiculturalism as a form of cross-cultural interrogation. Coffey's chapter "What Puts the 'Culture' in 'Multiculturalism'? An Analysis of Culture, Government, and the Politics of Mexican Identity" explores the myriad uses of the word *culture* in various liberatory contexts (such as "critical culture"). Using Michel Foucault's concept of governmentality as a critical heuristic, Coffey looks at the Mexican government's production of cultural policy, particularly focusing on its incorporation and deployment of indigenous culture in the project of nation building and in the regulation of social conduct.

James Ladwig's chapter, as well as that of Cameron McCarthy and Greg Dimitriadis, examines the globalization of pedagogies. In his essay "World Institutions, World Dispositions: Curriculum in the World-Cultural Institution of Schooling," Ladwig argues for the need to strengthen the structural sociological analysis of education. Specifically, he points to the critical challenges posed by emerging patterns of migration and cultural hybridity that have deeply invaded the school, overwhelming curricular practices of homogenization. After outlining a global theory of schooling, Ladwig highlights the social epistemological concerns of contemporary education, calling attention to the kinds of inequalities that are produced in the practices of normalization and regulation of difference that are prosecuted in educational institutions. McCarthy's and Dimitriadis's chapter "Globalizing Pedagogies: Power, Resentment, and the Renarration of Difference" situates the subjects of diversity, knowledge, and power in a marginalized location that is outside the normal circuit of education. They argue that multiculturalist pedagogy should shift its attention from learning cultures to the broader issues of the cultural reproduction of difference and desire and the problem of social integration of modern subjects into contemporary institutions such as schools.

Michael Apple' chapter, as well as that of Peter McLaren, Zeus Leonardo, and Ricky Allen, deconstructs the link between the notion of whiteness and globalization. Each chapter approaches this from a different perspective: the former is neo-Marxist, while the latter is poststructuralist. Apple's chapter "Racing toward Educational Reform: The Politics of Markets and Standards" offers a relational political economy/cultural studies analysis of the politics of race and educational reform. Apple maintains that white privilege has serious consequences for education in Britain as well as in the United States. He contends that instead of dismissing out of hand the issues of whiteness that reside at the core of mainstream educational practices, the anxieties created by such constructions have to be countered and resisted. Ultimately, Apple argues for materialist analysis and intervention in the area of racial inequality in education, pointing to alliances across the boundaries of culture, class, and gender. In their chapter entitled "Epistemologies of Whiteness: Transgressing and Transforming Pedagogical Knowledge," McLaren, Leonardo, and Allen offer the outlines of a poststructuralist pedagogy grounded in George Bataille's theory of the gift. Their objective here is the very subversion of epistemologies of whiteness. In the capitalist mode of production, the resistance of whiteness to divestment of its excess results in a mandatory potlatch, as in the case of the Los Angeles riots. McLaren, Leonardo, and Allen propose a revolutionary multiculturalism derived from Bataille's vision of excess, which resonates with Karl Marx's imperative of class struggle, the gift of solidarity of the laboring class.

In the second section of the book, contributors critically examine the various tensions and contradictions in multicultural classroom practices. Ruth Vinz's chapter "Cautions against Canonizing (An)Other Literature" documents the tendency to canonize "other" literature(s) in three secondary-English teachers' classrooms. Her study illustrates the ways in which these three teachers transform minority literary texts into fetishized art objects. In her chapter "New Stories: Rethinking History and Lives" Nadine Dolby juxtaposes her ethnographic study of a history teacher, Mr. Connors, with a fictional history teacher (Mr. Crick, in the book and film *Waterland*). Her essay poses some critical questions about teaching perspectival history in a social constructivist classroom. Dolby asks the question, Whose ethnic purpose does such historical pedagogy serve? The chapter by Lalita Subrahmanyan, Steve Hornstein, and Dave Heine, "Multicultural

Discourse in Teaching Education: The Case of One Integrated Teaching Methods Block," discusses the success of a multicultural preservice unit in a predominantly white midwestern university. While the program has a positive impact on the preservice teachers' perceptions of the multicultural nature of the society, the findings suggest that the pedagogical task of getting students to critically examine stereotypes is a very difficult one indeed.

Section 2 closes with the critical pedagogical analyses of Ram Mahalingam and Rochelle Gutiérrez. These two chapters describe the pedagogical challenges that the implementation of multicultural mathematics curricula present to educators. In "Beyond Eurocentrism: Implications of Social Epistemology and Multicultural Mathematics Education" Ram Mahalingam addresses the paradoxical nature of the subaltern position in current discourses on multicultural mathematics education, arguing that the homogenization of cultures is conveniently extended to cultural products such as Indian mathematics. In the process, multiculturalism becomes a practice by which one elite system recognizes the highly selective cultural products of another. Mahalingam suggests that subaltern scholars should be more reflexive in response to the emerging historiography of marginalized groups such as that of Indian women's mathematics. Rochelle Gutiérrez's chapter "Is the Multiculturalism of Mathematics Doing Us More Harm than Good?" explores some of the pivotal pedagogical contradictions that are foregrounded in mainstream attempts at developing a multicultural curriculum for a privileged discipline such as mathematics. She argues that incorporating units on non-European mathematics (for instance ethnomathematics) in multicultural mathematics education, without an adequate history and sociology of how those knowledges have come into existence, would be counterproductive. Rather, a sociology and historiography of mathematics should be incorporated in multicultural mathematics education foregrounding the issues of the unequal power relations among various groups of knowledge producers.

The third section, "Policy," has four chapters. The first chapter, by Marc Chun, Susan Christopher, and Patricia Gumport, "Multiculturalism and the Academic Organization of Knowledge," analyzes the institutional arrangement of knowledge and the reorganization of higher education in the universities. Comparing the two new academic disciplines, technology and multiculturalism, the authors argue that the explicit recognition of the political nature of multicultural knowledge will forge alliances across the disciplines. Chun, Christopher, and Gumport maintain that this curricular development would help to subvert the impermeable nature of traditional boundaries of academic disciplines. Nancy Lesko and Leslie Rebecca Bloom, in their chapter "The Haunting of Multicultural Epistemology and Pedagogy," emphasize the need to be "disturbed" and "haunted" while teaching and developing a multicultural pedagogy. They discuss the transformative potential of "haunting," an experience that challenges the taken-for-granted realities of education and society and forces us to see the "unseen" in the process of developing a multicultural curriculum. George Kamberelis's "Hybrid Discourse Practices and the Production of Classroom (Multi)Cultures" describes an ethnographic study of the social construction of (multi)cultures through hybridity discourses. Using a Bakhtinian framework, the chapter discusses the curricular implications of hybrid discourse practices in fostering a (multi)cultural environment in the classroom and the school.

In the last chapter of the section and the final chapter of this book, Glenn Hudak ethically speaks back to the other contributors to the volume. In his chapter, "Reaping the Harvest of Shame: Racism and Teaching in a Time of Radical Economic Insecurity," Hudak provocatively places racism right back into the discourses of multiculturalism that too often seem to elide this thorny issue of American educational and social life. Hudak draws on his own ethnographic research to narrate the tensions over the legitimation of knowledge generated in the teaching of a mass media course. His chapter illustrates the intellectual and political negotiations that are conducted in the evolution of subject matter such as mass media studies, where the learner and the teacher have equal stakes in the recognition, appropriation, and legitimation of knowledge. All these pedagogical relations become fragile and attenuated in a context in which the social and economic futures beyond the school are rendered deeply unstable by the imperatives of capitalist globalization and the play of difference in the wider society and the world.

CONCLUSION

Ultimately, we contend that multiculturalism, as a set of epistemological and pedagogical practices, is in need of a paradigmatic shift in order to achieve its egalitarian goals. Although there is a growing volume of literature on the subject, multiculturalism as a concept is still too obvious, yet at the same time elusive. Instead of addressing the notion of "knowledge politics" in the appropriation of various forms of knowledge, the current trend in the multiculturalism discourse is often to relativize or romanticize the various cultural products that this discourse seeks to understand. By treating marginalized subaltern cultures in a historical vacuum, multiculturalism defeats its own purpose. Proponents too often uncritically place positive versions of group identities and cultures at the center of debates over the curricular fortunes of disadvantaged groups. They treat group characteristics in a primordial and an ahistorical manner, thereby undermining the rich potential of multiculturalism as a new discourse on knowledge politics and critical literacy about the human condition globally. As a result, multiculturalism is often criticized for its lack of a coherent framework to address the complex epistemological, ethical, and political issues in curriculum development, teacher development, and educational policy.

In this volume, we have tried to provide a critical framework for multiculturalism so that it might better address three present-day challenges to a postmulticultural world: (a) the hegemony of Eurocentrism; (b) essentialization of culture; and (c) globalization. Our book addresses knowledge politics in issues such as intracultural heterogeneity; positionality and the production and appropriation of various epistemic criteria about culture; and the location of the subject and social ontologies, power, and hybridity that are problematic in multicultural discourse. We hope that a paradigmatic shift in multiculturalism will elevate its status to a global intervention facilitating international scholars to reflexively participate in its discourse. Multiculturalism is not merely a recurrent theme in the West's struggle for self-understanding; rather, it is a paradigm for self-reflection for educators around the world.

Multiculturalism, as a phenomenon, is inherently paradoxical since it is sensitive to the multiple levels of social reality in which it is situated. For example, when textbook authors talk about the Indian contribution to mathematics, they invariably refer to elitist forms of Indian mathematics, not the contribution of the lower caste or the "untouchables." In this case, multiculturalism unwittingly appears to be affirming elitist forms of non-Western knowledge that are the most accessible to westerners. This poses a serious dilemma that is both epistemological and moral for educators, teachers, and policy makers.

As editors of and contributors to this volume, we have sought to elaborate a critical framework that analyzes the knowledge politics involved in the production of the multicultural "subject." We have also sought to critically reflect on the epistemic criteria for the inscription of egalitarian imperatives in the multicultural discourse. While problematizing the various tensions in the efforts of multicultural proponents to provide epistemic status and legitimation for the contributions (both personal and cultural) of the margins, contributors discuss ways to reconceptualize multiculturalism as a powerful praxis for educational reform around the world. By proposing a paradigmatic shift in multiculturalism, we intend to revitalize its egalitarian goals for the new millennium in which we anticipate that the problems of difference will proliferate rather than recede. Here, we have sought to rearticulate multiculturalism to critical theories such as cultural studies, postcolonialism, globalization theory, feminism, Marxist political economy, and poststructuralism. In so doing, we have tried to rearticulate the concept of culture to the logics of praxis, foregrounding powerful themes of negotiation, interdependence, hybridity, and reciprocity. These are radical themes that now stalk the world of ideas about race and identity in ways that render auratic notions of cultural "origins" obsolete. With global capitalism touted as the panacea for all "social(ist) evils," a revitalization of multiculturalism is critical and imperative. In *Multicultural Curriculum*, we have sought to demonstrate the complexities of such endeavor. We hope our discussion will open a critical space for a productive engagement with and a vital reinvestment in multiculturalism for the millennium that races into being.

REFERENCES

Anderson, B. R. 1983. *Imagined Communities: Reflections on the Origin and Spread of Nationalism.* London: Verso.

Appiah, K. A. 1992. *In My Father's House: Africa in the Philosophy of Culture.* New York: Oxford University Press.

Asante, M. K. 1987. *Afrocentric Idea.* Philadelphia: Temple University Press.

Bhabha, H. 1994. *The Location of Culture.* New York: Routledge.

Crenshaw, K. 1995. "The Intersection of Race and Gender." *Critical Race Theory: The Key Writings That Formed the Movement,* edited by K. Crenshaw et al., 357–82. New York: New Press.

Dirks, N. B., G. Eley, and S. B. Ortner. 1994. *Culture/Power/History: A Reader in Contemporary Social Theory.* Princeton, N.J: Princeton University Press.

Joseph, G. V. 1990. *The Crest of the Peacock: Non-European Roots of Mathematics.* New York: Penguin.

Hirsch, E. D. 1987. *Cultural Literacy: What Every American Needs to Know.* Boston: Houghton Mifflin.

Jameson, F. 1998. "Notes on Globalization as a Philosophical Issue." In *The Cultures of Globalization,* edited by F. Jameson and M. Miyoshi, 54–80. Durham, N.C.: Duke University Press. 1998.

Mahalingam, R., and C. McCarthy. 1999. *Multiculturalism for the Twenty-First Century: A Need of a Paradigm Shift.* Unpublished manuscript, University of Michigan.

Mignolo, W. M. 1998. "Globalization, Civilization Processes, and the Relocation of Languages and Cultures." In *The Cultures of Globalization,* edited by F. Jameson and M. Miyoshi, 32–53. Durham, N.C. : Duke University Press.

Ravitch, D. 1990. "Diversity and Democracy: Multicultural Education in America." *American Educator* 14, no. 1:16–48.

Rosaldo, R. 1993. *Culture and Truth: The Remaking of Sociological Analysis.* Boston: Beacon Press.

Spivak, G. C. 1996. *The Spivak Reader: Selected Works of Gayatri Chakravorty Spivak.* New York: Routledge.

West, C. 1993. *Prophetic Thought in Postmodern Times.* Monroe, Maine: Common Courage Press.

Part I

THEORY

1

SOCIAL EPISTEMOLOGY AS A CRITICAL PHILOSOPHY OF MULTICULTURALISM

Steve Fuller

University of Durham

1. INTRODUCTION: BEYOND HYPERCULTURALISM

Philosophical theories of knowledge have tended to stress normative approaches without considering their empirical realizability or political consequences. Sociological theories have suffered the reverse problem of capturing the empirical and ideological character of knowledge, but typically without offering guidance on how knowledge policy should be conducted. Social epistemology aims to consolidate the strengths and eliminate the weaknesses of these two approaches. Multiculturalism is of special interest to the social epistemologist because it escapes the usual philosophical and sociological ways of understanding knowledge. It will become evident in what follows that I mean *multiculturalism* in a rather specific sense that entails my unqualified support. Multiculturalism is more than simply the recognition that there are distinct cultures, which would amount to little more than a "separate but equal" doctrine for the human condition. It further implies that these cultures stand in certain relationships to each other that may change as those same relationships unfold in time and space. Perhaps the epitome of my sense of multiculturalism is the political and legal debates surrounding "affirmative action" (Cahn 1995; Fuller 1999b, chap. 4). I associate this perspective with the "critical multiculturalism" defended in Kincheloe and Steinberg 1997.

It follows that there are features of the current discourse surrounding multiculturalism from which I want to distance my own position. The following six tenets sum them up, together constituting what I call *hyperculturalism*, an exaggerated—perhaps even essentialized—sense of cultural difference that tends unwittingly to incapacitate the people on whose behalf its advocates speak.

1. Cultures correspond to geographical regions that only came into being with European colonial expansion. The result is a syncretistic conception of a region's cultural identity that "picks and mixes" a variety of practices, the combination of which has probably never been part of any single individual's life. As late as the 1960s, one spoke in Teutonic tones about the "ideal typical" character of such a culture, the subject of the "Hall of Man" exhibit in the average natural history museum. Now we would simply describe it as "post-modernism," without the irony. Talk of "Hindu nationalism" and "Afro-centrism" that presupposes the ontological integrity of "India" and "Africa," respectively, fall under this category.

2. Cultures have a strong sense of continuous identity over time. Indeed, a rough measure of a culture's "occidentality" is the degree to which historical change is constitutive of its identity: at the limit, the core Western cultures are defined as having exhibited a kind of directed change, called "progress," which leaves behind most elements of cultural identity altogether. This way of distinguishing "the West" from "the Rest" is a residue of the need to discriminate the civilized from the primitive, what Claude Lévi-Strauss (1964) canonized as the difference between "hot" (dynamic) and "cold" (static) cultures. The twist here is that the hyperculturalist reverses the values assigned to hot and cold: cold is now regarded positively.

3. There are clear criteria for distinguishing one culture from another, and especially who is and is not a member of a culture. Usually, these criteria presuppose that cultures—or at least cultural homelands—are geographically discrete entities and that one's cultural identity is determined by a combination of where oneself and one's parents (and their progenitors) were born, the balance depending on the culture in question. These criteria are a remnant of what Stephen Turner (1994) has called the "Mauss Problem," named for Marcel Mauss, the protégé of Emile Durkheim who recognized that the defining features of a culture's identity are those that strike external observers (i.e. anthropologists) as most different from their own culture.

4. Cultural differences are logically prior to differences in, say, class or gender. The result is a homogeneous sense of cultural identity that neglects the potentially skewed character of the culture's designated representatives, especially in forums outside that culture: for example, they may be among the few who have received formal training in writing, a skill that may be restricted to men of a certain class whose local power is then unwittingly reinforced in cross-cultural communicaton (Oruka 1990). (Taken together, points 3 and 4 above constitute the residue of the classical concept of race in the hyperculturalist's conception of culture.)

5. The historical authenticity of a cultural practice underwrites its relevance to the life circumstances of the current members of that culture. The adjective *indigenous* is often used in this context, especially in explanations of failed attempts to integrate Western technologies in non-Western contexts. At best, this talk reifies fairly concrete power relations between the West and non-

West into abstract epistemological distinctions between inherently Western and non-Western ways of knowing.

6. Only natives of a culture are authorized to speak on its behalf. Others' voices are regarded as suspect because they have not immersed themselves in the life of that culture. Max Weber is an important target of this argument, as he set the pace for Western understandings of the sociology of India and China without having visited either country or mastered its language. Yet if Weber is excluded on those grounds, then what do we say about Aijaz Ahmad (1992), who performed the reciprocal function of diagnosing the Western fetish for "third world" and "postcolonial" cultural studies from a strategically detached vantage point in New Delhi? Indeed, can the hyperculturalist in good faith condone the activities of Edward Said, a Palestinian Christian, whose academic training and practice has been in the United States but whose scholarship primarily concerns Europe's "orientalization" of Islam?

Hyperculturalism gains its initial plausibility as half of the dialectic that has dominated twentieth-century epistemology, neither side of which captures the phenomenon of multiculturalism especially well. On the one hand, many philosophically inspired approaches of knowledge attempt to show that the validity of certain claims to knowledge transcends any particular time and place. They are true or false everywhere and always. This position is usually called *universalism*. On the other hand, there are broadly sociological approaches that argue that the validity of a knowledge claim is specific to time and place. What passes as knowledge in one culture may not in another. This position is usually called *relativism*. The import of relativism is best understood if one thinks of cultures as well-defined spatiotemporal units, such as the history of a nation or the lore of a tribe. Without these clear boundaries, it is difficult to specify the extent of a knowledge claim's validity. In that sense, relativism loses its meaning if one cannot specify relative *to what*, exactly. But do claims to knowledge naturally carry such clearly marked jurisdictions (a.k.a. "validity conditions"), or must these be actively constructed and maintained? The hyperculturalist clearly believes the former, but I believe the latter. Indeed, a well-defined sense of culture—and the epistemological relativism it breeds—is itself relative to a certain period in the history of Western culture, one that roughly began in the late eighteenth century and has been unraveling throughout the second half of the twentieth. I have therefore dubbed my belief in the relativity of relativism *metarelativism* (Fuller 1993b, chap. 9; Fuller 1999c, chap. 7).

Metarelativism has the advantage of capturing some of the most historically salient features of human associations. Diverse groups of people have been thrown together in common places where none could claim a "natural" authority over the rest. Moreover, human beings have been perennially faced with the problem of determining who belongs to which group. No one has ever been entirely satisfied with using either parental lineage or personal appearance as principles for grouping people together. It was only with the rise of the modern nation-state—and its corresponding duplex of race/culture—that a concerted effort was made to force large numbers of roughly collocated people to abide by common laws, language, customs, and currency. Accompanying this effort was the systematic classification of people according to principles that made it easier both for the state to act upon them and for the people to feel they share a common stake in defending the state; hence, the intimate link between racial identity and patriotism. These groups were typically provided with an ancient history that was a gross, but expedient, simplification of a considerably more entangled past (Anderson 1983). The arts faculties of the modern European—and later, American—university played a major role in the construction and promulgation of these cultural identities (Bernal 1987). Yet this brief period of cultural stability is coming to an end with the resumption and escalation of nomadic living, as abetted by the scaled-up, quick, and cheap modes of communication and transportation that have emerged in the wake of transnational capitalism. "Melting pot" arguments that would have seemed eminently reasonable a generation ago for minorities assimilating to the dominant culture are now without purchase. If anything, the movement is now in the opposite direction of inserting non-Western knowledges in Western pedagogical settings. Thus, multiculturalism typically presupposes a much more mobile, even portable, conception of culture than either relativism or universalism allows.

In claiming that our main epistemological categories are inappropriate for understanding the multicultural world of knowledge production, I mean that we should not assume that the universalist-relativist distinction made perfect sense from the time of, say, the Greeks until the period when communication and migration patterns started to acquire their contemporary "postmodern" form. In short, the distinction is not itself universal. On the contrary, the universalist-relativist distinction has appeared vivid only for a limited period, from Britain's aggressive pursuit of a free-trade policy in the 1780s to the end of colonialism in the 1960s. The idea of culture as something attached to a particular people who are, in turn, attached to a particular place—the typical image of relativist knowledge production—is a late-eighteenth-century German innovation that emerged in reaction to the palpable disintegration of traditional forms of life by the spread of commercial values that were invariably traced to British thought, be it Adam Smith's or Jeremy Bentham's. During this period, utilitarianism was often demonized for reducing qualitative distinctions to a universal calculus of commensurable quantities. The reaction took the form of consolidating a unique cultural identity around the nation-state, mainly through uniform schooling and military service, two processes that did much to restrict people's spontaneous cognitive plasticity and physical mobility. By the end of this period, the second major round of nation-state building—this time in Africa and Asia—had occurred, during which similar arguments for cultural identity were made, this time in the face of the post–World War II Euro-American hegemony. Hyperculturalism is the residue of this development.

In the rest of this chapter, I pursue that history in more detail, as part considering multiculturalism as cross-cultural interrogation. Section 2 looks at some recent attempts to mobilize the history of multicultural encounters for purposes of evaluating the dominant and subalternated cultures involved. Section 3 deals with the process by which universalism and relativism came to be seen as opposites in the Western philosophical tradition. Resistance to the emerging capitalist world-system turns out to play an operative role, one that is masked by the abstract level at which the universalist-relativist debate is normally pitched. Finally, section 4 provides an opportunity to observe a clash of Western and non-Western sensibilities toward multiculturalism. Here I present some results of a cyberconference I organized to sample worldwide opinion on the meaning of "public understanding of science." In light of the argument pursued in this chapter, the most striking finding is that non-Westerners seem to have a much more permeable sense of cultural identity than Western relativism would allow. Consequently, they do not automatically equate the adoption of technologies underwritten by Western science with an implicit act of subalternation.

2. MULTICULTURALISM AS CROSS-CULTURAL INTERROGATION

The relativist conception of culture remains lodged in the minds of both friends and foes of multiculturalism. Symptomatically, problems bred by this conception occur when some multiculturalists are faced with the challenge of having their knowledge claims tested by the empirical methods dominant in Western culture. In other words, uncritical multiculturalists are prone to embrace hyperculturalism's tenet (6), whereby the testing process is preempted so that only accredited members of the relevant culture can pass judgment on the validity of one of its knowledge claims. A good recent example is the controversy surrounding melanin as the "scientific" ground for Afrocentrism. Melanin is the chemical responsible for skin pigmentation, the high concentration of which was supposedly the source of special psychic powers in precolonial blacks. Yet, physical anthropologists have been told that the melanin hypothesis is untestable by the usual experimental and clinical procedures (Ortiz de Montellano 1997). Some defenders of the melanin theory have gone so far as to maintain that such knowledge is accessible only to Africans. While superficially radical, this response retreats from the original mandate of multiculturalism to challenge Western forms of knowledge, since it simply asserts the autonomy of melanin-based knowledge from anything Westerners can know: "You have your knowledge, we have ours" seems to be the bottom line. While such assertions of autonomy play an important role in constructing a voice for traditionally suppressed groups, to tie one's academic politics exclusively to the maintenance of this voice is to court two undesirable prospects. In a liberal culture, it invites the familiar pattern of academic co-optation: namely, a "Center for Melanin Studies" that coexists peacefully with all the other departments, which themselves remain unchanged. In a more reactionary culture, it reinforces prejudices that blacks are beyond redemption by Western ways of knowing and should therefore be cut off entirely. Here one is reminded that the Ku Klux Klan supported Marcus Garvey's campaign in the 1920s to repatriate black Americans to Africa.

To avoid being boxed into this rhetorical corner, multiculturalists must realize that any "test" of their claims need not be one-sided. If "non-Western" forms of knowledge do not appear valid by "Western" methods, then that could just as easily reflect poorly on the testing methods as on the knowledge claims being tested. My version of social epistemology aims to replace the obsolescent relativist picture of culture with a more "interpenetrative" one that allows for this kind of mutual critique and a subsequent reconstruction of testing as a form of social interaction (Fuller 1993b, chap. 2). Thus, multiculturalists should not insist that they possess radically autonomous forms of knowledge. Rather, they should push the *standpoint* line that the West's neglect of their unique epistemic perspective reflects a substantial flaw in the West's own mode of knowledge production. This is not a trivial shift in argument. In educational circles, multiculturalism is typically defended as enabling cultural minorities to develop their own voices in the classroom. What has not been sufficiently stressed is the role that multiculturalism can play in reeducating cultural *majorities*, causing them to change their fundamental beliefs, even about a form of knowledge as seemingly universal as natural science.

It follows that the relationship between the Western inquirer and the non-Western inquired becomes more ethical than strictly epistemological; that is, inquiry is no longer an asymmetrical relation between an active knower and a passive known. Rather, each is rendered accountable to the other, as knower and known are recognized as roles performed by both parties simultaneously (Fuller 1997b, 1998). Even multiculturalists have tended to underplay this implication. A good case in point is the debate surrounding Charles Taylor's essay "The Politics of Recognition." Taylor (1992) argues that outrage at the repression of a native culture should not be equated with an endorsement of that cultural's universal value. Of course, the promotion of multiculturalism will make it easier for people outside that culture to become familiar with its distinctive ideas, artifacts, and character. But in the end, according to Taylor, one must remain open to the possibility that the repressed culture's contribution to "world culture" is rather limited. Taylor's argument assumes that, left unchecked, political conscience can obscure philosphical judgment. To be sure, Taylor is correct to criticize those who would see subalternation as an automatic mark of value. However, he fails to acknowledge that subalternation is a two-sided relation: that is, the prima facie diminished status of the subaltern party is integrally connected to the enhanced status of the dominant one—not least because "common standards" of cultural value are usually constructed as part of the process of subalternation, with an eye to the right cases falling on either side of the standard.

From his vantage point in Delhi, the father of Indian cultural studies, Ashis Nandy, has remarked on how even westerners have tried to play both sides of the dialectic of subalternation. Nandy (1987, 1988) has witnessed this ambivalence in the rhetoric surrounding the transfer of scientific knowledge as part of developmental aid. On the one hand, applications of science that delegitimate indigenous knowledges and generally cause the immiserization of the natives are blamed on the agents of application—profit-driven technologists, unscrupulous local politicians, and insensitive global policymakers. If science itself shares any responsibility, it is only by virtue of its perversion, with the implication that, were it not subalternated in this fashion, science would develop as a universally beneficial force. Given the five-hundred-year history of this alleged subalternation (i.e. from the start of European colonial expansion), Nandy reasonably wonders when science's subalternated state simply becomes its authentic form. On the other hand, reflecting on the very same history, Westerners have also argued that scientific knowledge travels so much better cross-culturally than other forms of knowledge because it has access to truths of universal scope. Clearly, this reading of the history of science presupposes that science's development has *not* been perverted. Specifically, this account fails to countenance that science's generalizability—especially when regarded as a performance standard for all forms of knowledge—may merely express imperialist imperatives at a higher level of abstraction, in terms of which local sources of epistemic authority are unsurprisingly found wanting.

That the history of Western science can be told in such radically different ways is not itself a problem. History does not arrive in a neat ontological package, with some parts labeled *necessary, universal,* or *true,* and others labeled *accidental, particular,* or *false.* Events happen in bundles, and only after some time has passed are they unraveled and labeled. This is the stuff of which historical narratives are made. Such retellings of the past, in turn, fortify our intuitions of what the world obliges, forbids, and simply permits. These are the first lessons of a constructivist social epistemology. They help explain the great difficulty that philosophers and scientists have had in pinpointing the so-called realist core of science, because that core has been nothing more (and nothing less) than those aspects of science that have held up well in cross-cultural translation. The advent of multiculturalist critiques of science has threatened yet again to upset the balance of intellectual trade. What nonwhite, nonmale, nonwesterners end up including of current science in their hybridized research practices will strongly influence what counts as the realist core of tomorrow's science. The dialectic of subalternation observed by Nandy opens the space for this selective appropriation of the Western heritage (see Fuller 1997, chap. 6, for the precedents set by Islam and Japan).

Of course, certain deadly diseases have been virtually eliminated, astronauts have flown in space, and atomic bombs have caused untold damage. However, the bone of contention is over the *explanation* given for these achievements, which, in turn, may affect the ultimate value assigned them. It is little more than secular superstition to suppose that Western science has some special explanatory purchase on widely used technologies, simply because its theories were the ones that first provided legitimacy for such technologies. Natural scientific theories generally played a relatively minor role in technological design until the late nineteenth century. Only then, technology started to be the product of large-scale industrial processes, the planning of which was predicated on scientific principles. Yet the superstition of an undifferentiated "technoscience" lives on in the imaginations of those who would claim that a technological innovation "implicitly instantiates" scientific principles that may not have been discovered until years later. Thus, an important charge of multiculturalism is to show how these technologies—insofar as they deserve global diffusion—can be explained and appropriated outside of the dominant cultural environments. Among the real heroes of multiculturalism, then, are the women and ethnic minorities who can appropriate, say, cyberspace for their own purposes—*not* those who refuse to engage with the new information technologies because they are seen as irrevocably tied to white male forms of knowledge. To make such a tight connection between science and technology, and between the combination of these and a particular culture, is to betray multiculturalism's potential for providing an emancipatory epistemological standpoint that transcends stale philosophical debates between universalism and relativism. Readers skeptical of purely philosophical arguments should consider the evidence presented from the first global cyberconference on public understanding of science, the results of which are analyzed in section 4.

3. The Prehistory of Multiculturalism: How Universalism and Relativism Came to Be Opposites

The historical specificity of the relativist-universalist distinction is lost in introductory philosophy courses that portray the debates between the Sophists and Socrates in Plato's *Dialogues* as the prototype of the zero-sum dialectical game nowadays defined by universalism and relativism. Thus, philosophers ask: Is man [*sic*] the measure of all things, or are there ideal forms in terms of which all knowledge must measure up? This forced choice turns out to be very misleading because the ancient statements of relativism were not usually formulated as negations of universalism. Take St Ambrose's seasoned advice to the young Saint Augustine, "When in Rome, do as the Romans do." He did not mean that what Romans do applies *only* in the city of Rome. After all, in Ambrose's day (the fourth century A.D.), Roman customs were prevalent in many precincts throughout Europe, Asia, and Africa. All that the slogan prohibits is a disregard for the customs already in place—but it leaves open just how extensive the "place" happens to be and, more important, the extent to which different customs may coexist in the same place. For example, after a relatively brief period of persecution, Christians coexisted with pagans in Rome and its foreign spheres of influence.

Indeed, before the aggressive campaigns to spread Christianity and Islam as "world religions," there were few, if any, instances of culture clash that could be reasonably cast in terms of universalism versus relativism. Most such clashes were more or less tolerated in an eclectic environment of *cosmopolitanism*. This applied even in cases of imperial domination, where one would most suspect universalist tendencies at work. Because it was in an imperial power's own interest to economize on the use of force, local customs were usually left in place as long as the locals regularly paid their taxes. Thus, the Romans would have been hard pressed to disavow Jesus' original instruction to his disciples to "Give Caesar what is Caesar's, but give God what is God's." In this respect, the tributarian character of imperial rule in the ancient world contrasts sharply with the culturally disruptive, capital-driven forms of imperialism in the modern world, as epitomized by the need to reorganize the local workforce in order to render it an efficient source of surplus value (Amin 1991).

That the recognition of local customs might come into conflict with forms of life that aspired to universality was first broached as a topic in international law, under the rubric of *the standard of civilization*, during the sixteenth-century European colonial expansion into the Americas (Gong 1984). Much of the early discussion was concerned with reconciling the avowed universality of Christian ethics with the fact that Christian colonists often slaughtered vast portions of native populations before establishing permanent settlements. The legal solution was to define a "civilized" country as one that allows Europeans to do business peacefully. Moreover, this definition was reintroduced to Europeans in the eighteenth century as the concept of "civility." By that time, Enlightenment intellectuals had come to believe that another form of life had to replace the role that Christendom had traditionally played in disciplining the passions, as sectarian struggles among Christians were seen as the source of two centuries of almost uninterrupted warfare within Europe itself. That new form of life was *commercialism*, or the pursuit of wealth.

The equation of civility with commerce—and the associated image of the humble merchant seeking recognition from others by catering to their needs—seemed to epitomize the essence of tolerance. But in fact, it opened a Pandora's box of problems, especially outside of Europe. Expatriate European merchants were keen on setting up as many exchanges as possible with the natives. These exchanges rendered native goods commensurable with—and hence potentially replaceable by—European ones. Taken to the limit, everything would eventually have its price. To open the door to Europeans de jure was de facto to Europeanize one's own culture. It seemed, then, that the only salient differences between the aggressive campaigns mounted by Christian and Islamic proselytizers and such "open door" trade policies were that the latter enabled the natives to lose their cultural identity in a less violent, more piecemeal fashion. Moreover, it did not require historical hindsight to appreciate this point. The decline of India after the influx of European trade in the sixteenth century kept China and Japan from opening their doors until they were effectively forced open in the mid-nineteenth century.

Thus, by returning to the early attempts to set international norms of civility in an increasingly interpenetrative world, we find crucial political ambiguities on both sides of the universalist-relativist divide. In the case of universalism, is universality a common or an elite feature of civilized societies? The "common" approach is illustrated by the enforcement of basic human rights that serve to level out local class and status differences, whereas the "elite" approach is reflected in the toleration of foreign spheres of influence that effectively privilege cosmopolitan over native practices. In the case of relativism, does relativity imply the resolution or the unresolvability of political differences? While the "unresolvability" approach reflects the mutual tolerance of equally powerful parties, the "resolution" approach often stems from the noblesse oblige attitude that a stronger party has toward a weaker one: the one breeds respect, the other condescension.

The worldwide diffusion of the commercial ethic revealed that the historical longevity of a set of social practices did not stop people from exchanging them for other practices that they perceived to be better. Of course, arguments arose over the proper settings for making such judgments. For example, can trade be truly "free" if a foreign navy is overseeing the proceedings? But more subtle forms of coercion were possible as well. In a world of free exchange where the items up for sale include armaments, who can afford not to always be purchasing state-of-the-art equipment, even if it means placing more genuinely native economic concerns on the back burner? Nevertheless, international lawyers were persuaded that there was at least one clear case of "free" appropriation, namely the Westernization of Russia under Peter the Great in the early eighteenth century. Czar Peter went so far as to provide tax breaks for leading Europeans willing to settle in Russia. The prospect of people peacefully exchanging their own past for a future manufactured elsewhere posed profound questions about the kind of hold that "tradition" can have over what people do in the long term. By the mid-eighteenth century, David Hume raised the matter in its most abstract and lasting form as *the problem of induction*: Why should we think that the future will be like the past?

Not surprisingly, Hume was a British subject. Britain took the lead in overcoming the principal obstacle to the spread of commercialism, which, expressed most abstractly, is the presumption of the past. At the level of domestic legislation, it entailed the levying of taxes on inherited wealth, unused land, and rents received on productive land. At the level of foreign policy, it meant that no traditional livelihood was to be treated as sacrosanct. A father imbued with the commercial ethic would not teach his son his trade unless he had reason to believe that there would be a market for the products of his trade in the long term. David Ricardo crystallized this mentality as *the principle of comparative advantage*, which illustrates just how alien commercialism is to relativism. The principle states that in a fully rationalized economy, people would not produce what they have traditionally produced, nor even what they produce best, but rather what they can produce better than other producers, *even if that turns out to be their second or third best product*. The result is universalism by what might be called "reverse relativism," since a producer's sense of identity emerges from learning what she can do that others cannot. It is easy to see how this scheme would generate global interdependency. But whether that would be to the equal benefit of all parties is another matter.

Ricardo anticipated that Britain would gradually come not to rely on domestic sources of farming, fishing, and mining once other countries were able to provide the same products of those practices more cheaply. These other countries would typically be overseas colonies that had not yet depleted their natural resources. However, colonialism was also motivated by the prospect that an overproductive Britain would not be able to sell all its goods unless it expanded its markets overseas. Thus, the cultivation of European tastes in non-European peoples became an essential part of Europe's strategy for preventing economic depression at home. By the end of the nineteenth century, one could find numbered among the leading British theorists of imperialism Joseph Chamberlain, a radical liberal who argued that an empire was little more than a protected space within which free trade could occur (Pieterse 1989).

What was immediately apparent to anyone *not* committed to this "free trade" ideology was that once the subsistence of a country's inhabitants is met, the value of its natural resources would then be entirely determined by what foreigners are willing to pay for them. The first appeals to "culture" in the spirit of an identity politics developed in continental Europe in reaction to this sensibility. Not surprisingly, the first modern science of society, political economy (later "economics"), emerged and remained dominant in Britain, dwarfing subsequent challenges to its claims to universality from sociology, anthropology, political science, and psychology. To be sure, by 1920, a suitably relativist anthropology had come to complement the universalism of economics at British universities, reproducing many of the binary oppositions—such as *qualitative versus quantitative* and *idiographic versus nomothetic*—that have come to dominate debates over social science methodology in the twentieth century. Nevertheless, in Alfred Marshall's memorable words, economics reigned supreme in its coverage of the entire "business of life."

The situation was quite different in continental Europe, where the other social sciences flourished in response to the need to legitimate the nation-state in light of the commercialist ideology formalized by the universalist brand of economics emanating from Britain (Wagner 1991; Wallerstein 1991b). Thus, value was held to reside not merely in the number of goods brought to market but in the distinctive institutions and patterns of social life that make those goods possible. Here it is worth recalling the difference between Ricardo's idea of comparative advantage and what is now called the "competitive advantage of nations" (Porter 1990). The latter repositions this original anti-Ricardist sentiment in the global arena by arguing that individual nations can restructure the terms of international trade so as to optimize the use of their native resources. In football parlance, the best defense may be a good offense. Thus, the countries most directly challenged by Britain in the world arena, France and Prussia, pursued state protectionist policies that stressed the distinctiveness of their goods, even where Britain seemed to have the upper hand. They seemed to be selling not only the use value of the goods themselves but also the quality of the labor and materials that went into their production. When first proposed, this policy drew on the classical idea that the land is the natural source of economic value; hence, the etymological kinship between *culture* and *agriculture*.

When *Kultur* first made its way into the German language in the 1780s through the work of Johann Gottfried von Herder, it referred to the handcrafts cultivated by rural folk. As might be expected, English turned out to be the last major European language in which "culture" appeared in ordinary usage, following the publication of Matthew Arnold's 1869 essay "Culture and Anarchy" (Kroeber and Kluckhohn 1963, 54). Nevertheless, his usage follows the pattern of other major European languages. By profession, Arnold was a schools inspector whose travels often took him to the European continent. Influenced by the emerging national educational systems there, Arnold regarded culture as the means by which the British state could civilize the "Philistines" (a.k.a. utilitarians), whose often progressive scientific and political views were informed by a commercial ethic that ran roughshod over Britain's long-standing values and traditions.

At the start of the nineteenth century, only in the realm of language (philology) had a systematic study of the past begun to enable the identification of distinct traditions and cultures with any degree of reliability. Before then, whenever legal entitlements to inheritance were contested, the claimants and their documents would be judged on criteria of face validity that varied substantially over time with changing views of what it would be "reasonable" for someone in a given position to have done. Thus, whatever continuity had been maintained in the social order over the centuries could not be attributed to the reliable transmission of a rich body of cultural lore, but rather to explicit lines of succession—say, in the monarchy or the papacy—that were themselves periodically disrupted and, in any case, did not exert much control over the organization of local life. In that sense, the modern nation-state, as the official guardian of something called "culture," constituted a sense of social order that previously had not existed.

The seminal figure in presenting the nation-state as a coherent locale possessing its own *Kultur* was Friedrich List. Having witnessed firsthand America's early successful efforts at protecting its economy from British free trade policies, List developed a general theory of national economies as incubating organisms grounded in irreducible ties between "blood" and "soil" (i.e., race and environment). Evidencing such ties was easier then than now because, prior to the acceptance of Darwinism, a population's culture was generally defined as the set of historically entrenched adaptations to the environment that were somehow transmitted to each successive generation. The lack of an adequate theory of genetics occluded politically sensitive issues about the biological limits on a population's ability to improve its culture over time. However, once Darwinism brought these issues into the open, a debate raged in Germany (home to some of Darwin's fiercest popularizers) over whether sociology should be given an explicitly racial foundation. The first president of the German Sociological Association, Ferdinand Tönnies, linked "organic solidarity" in communities to just such a strong sense of blood ties, thereby enabling the treatment of fundamental social entities as natural kinds. In contrast, Max Weber opposed this move in favor of a more plastic view of social life, which reflected his general tendency to treat a legal fiction like a state or a corporation as the paradigm case of a social entity (Proctor 1991, chap. 10).

In its biologically ambiguous form, List's theoretical orientation became the basis of the historical school of economics, which in turn helped to institutionalize sociology as an academic discipline in Germany (Pearson 1997, chap. 1). Under List's influence, both Tönnies and the French founder of sociology, Emile Durkheim, translated classical economic concepts like "division of labor" from the context of factory production to that of social stratification. "Rationality" underwent a similar fate. Classical political economy presupposed a relatively sharp distinction between naturally occurring passions and their transformation into rational self-interest (Hirschman 1977). Sociology then introduced forms of rationality that mediated—as well as blurred—this distinction. An example of such a hybrid conception of rationality is Weber's famous attempt to distinguish an action that is done according to a general principle *(Wertrationalität)* from one done for a specific end *(Zweckrationalität)*. The historically relevant distinction was between religious and economic practices during the Protestant Reformation. But in Weber's Wilhelmine Germany, general principles were ultimately embodied in the state. Rationalization, in this sense, meant nationalization. The paradigm cases of this process were mandatory public education and military conscription, which became two sides of the same coin of what Alvin Gouldner (1970) called the "welfare-warfare state," especially once the Franco-Prussian War of 1870 convinced the newly united Germany that it was in a state of "permanent emergency."

However, because the state's constitutive regions thrived prior to the imposition of the "philosophically designed order" of a national constitution, many social theorists held that, alongside a universal rationality consisting of explicitly formulated rules, there existed many implicit rationalities, access to which required living the life of someone from a given region. Yet the main evidence for the existence of these regionally based cultures was indirect—namely, their resistance to state- or market-led processes of "modernization" and "rationalization." These negative facts were then reified as attributable to a common origin, namely, deep-seated traditions or habits, sometimes interpreted in racial terms (Turner 1994). Nevertheless, just because the rationalization of society was largely an explicit, goal-driven process, it did not follow that resistance to this process had to be (tacit) versions of the same thing. Thus, Ferdinand Tönnies may have committed a category mistake when he entitled his 1883 classic *Gemeinschaft und Gesellschaft (Community and Society)*, as if the former were a sociological tendency in the same sense as the latter. On the contrary, *gemeinschaftlich* tendencies may be no more than those aspects of life that have not easily submitted to *gesellschaftlich* treatment. Invoking a famous spurious "negative entity" from the history of science, I have coined the term *phlogistemology* to capture the residual character of such explanatory appeals to the "social" (Fuller, 1996). Starting with the Chicago school of symbolic interactionism in the early twentieth century, this phlogistemic sensibility has crystallized into the qualitative methods associated with microsociology. Not surprisingly, these methods were typically developed in the context of studying ethnic minorities who resisted assimilation to a national identity, especially as reflected in the failure of official statistics to capture anything other than their deviant status.

In the end, it was the historically artificial character of the nation-state that ultimately posed the deepest conceptual and political problems for the universalist conceptions of social rationality. This was the problematic with which Weber struggled throughout his career. On its face, the obligation to enroll in school or the army is simply imposed by the state. At that level, the citizenry seems to be subordinated to mere means for satisfying national ends. However, for such an obligation to have the ennobling character it is supposed to have, citizens must appear to have undertaken it freely, however much it may seem to be against their interests as individuals. This requires that they be conceptualized as spontaneously forming associations (based on, say, "sympathy") that foster a collective identity, which national obligations then raise to self-consciousness. Immanuel Kant was only the first of a long line of thinkers who have insisted that a truly rational agent does not merely conform to reason but acts on the basis of it. Only a strong state can convert this conceptual distinction into an empirical reality by instilling in people the desire for enrollment. The problem is that a term like *Wertrationalität* is little more than a label for a particular kind of sociological tension. On the one hand, if these spontaneous forms of social life are reducible to explicit formulas, then they can be refined and replaced as the state or some other superagent sees fit, and people are once again reduced to means for another's ends. On the other hand, if these forms of social life are not so easily reducible, because of their "instinctive" or "racial" basis, then it is no longer clear how they can be said to embody a form of rationality, "natural" or otherwise.

The preceding worry afflicts social practitioners just as much as social theorists. No social practice can be reproduced in its entirety over large expanses of time and space. In fact, no society has ever really aspired to reproduce the entirety of its practices but only certain parts, to which the rest of society has then had to adapt. It may well be that most of what we identify as "social change" can be explained as unintended consequences of processes of social reproduction. Here, extending some of my own earlier work on translation practices, we can usefully distinguish between attempts to reproduce the (syntactic) *substance* and the (pragmatic) *function* of a social practice (Fuller 1988, 128–38; cf. Fuller 1993a, 96–106), depending on how the reproductive process is conceptualized. Sometimes cultural continuity is identified with the reproduction of specific artifacts and rituals that are seen as susceptible to decay unless they are conserved for each successive generation. Such substantive reproduction involves insulating the artifact or ritual from changes in the ambient environment, which typically means dissociating it from its original social functions. Seen in a positive light, this process testifies to the "intrinsic value" of whatever is reproduced, something that may only be seen in the fullness of time; in a negative light, the process reflects a collectively manifested form of compulsive behavior.

As culture comes to be the business of the nation-state, the processes of social reproduction become more functionally oriented. In other words, the main interest shifts toward maintaining the production of certain effects under certain conditions. As older practices diminish in their ability to fulfill their original functions, they are replaced by newer ones. Standing armies and social security systems replace mutual aid societies; professional training and industrial technology replace craft guilds. In most cases, there are lexical remnants of the older practices in the language used for talking about the newer ones, which convey the impression that the latter are "functionally equivalent" to the former (in their day). Once again, either a positive or a negative spin can be given to this process. Positively, it reflects the injection of efficiency into traditional forms of life; negatively, it signals the devaluation, deskilling, and otherwise "disenchantment" of the world.

A more neutral characterization of this process is *detraditionalization,* which brings out the transcontextual persistence of the thing that is reproduced without passing judgment on its normative desirability (Beck, Giddens, and Lash). Detraditionalization draws attention to the fact that most claims to cultural identity are based on a history that predates current national boundaries and commercial interests (Wallerstein 1991a). A good example of detraditionalization is the promotion of African names without teaching the source languages or, more important, providing a social context for instantiating the social practices associated with those languages. Here it is worth remarking that the detraditionalist approaches history rather differently from the classic Marxist demystifier. Whereas the demystifier sees history as offering critical leverage on the future by revealing the contingency of the past, the detraditionalist regards the past as a resource that can be multiply repackaged to serve contemporary purposes: the former focuses on the conditions of the past's production, the latter on the possibilities for its future consumption.

In summary, figure 1 encapsulates the parallel developments in nineteenth-century thought that constitute the prehistory of multiculturalism. The dialectical movement of thesis to antithesis to synthesis captures the stages by which Europe came to treat its indigenous commercial ethic as a world-historic mission, otherwise known as capitalism. As demanded by such a G. W. F. Hegel–inspired process, the "synthesis" must reveal the underlying idea attaining self-consciousness. Thus, vague Enlightenment invocations of universalism eventually yielded to more specifically European instantiations of "science," as the division of academic labor crystallized in Western universities came to be the leading edge of global colonial expansion. Still more concretely, differences between Britain and continental Europe were eventually sublimated as imperialist competition on the world stage. In this context, the difference between epistemology and ideology turns on whether this process is regarded in a positive or negative light.

	Worldview	Economics	Epistemology	Ideology
Thesis	Enlightenment	Commercialism	Universalism	Materialism
Antithesis	Romanticism	Protectionism	Relativism	Racism
Synthesis	Positivism	Imperialism	Scientism	Eurocentrism

Fig. 1. A Multiculturalist's Guide to Nineteenth-Century European Thought

4. The PCI Gestalt—"Postcolonial Inquiry" or "Politically Correct Imperialism"?

That the distinction between universalism and relativism is a peculiarly Western preoccupation was revealed in the first global cyberconference on the public understanding of science (PUS), which I convened from February 25 to March 11, 1998. (The complete set of exchanges from the conference are archived at http://www.dur.ac.uk/~dss0www1/.) The conference was the first phase of a pilot program by the U.K.'s main state funding agency for social science research, Economic and Social Research Council. It demonstrated, among other things, that participants who identify themselves as "non-Western" conceptualized the challenge that "multiculturalism" poses to science rather differently from their supposedly "politically correct" colleagues in the West. This was noticeable in at least a quarter of the exchanges.

Under the influence of the last twenty-five years of science and technology studies (STS) research, the distinctions among scientific research, social policy, and technology have become increasingly blurred. This blurriness has enabled researchers to trace the entanglement of actions and interests necessary for the maintenance and extension of a complex social order. The paradigm case for this approach is Latour 1987. Clearly, the foil of this blurred vision of "technoscience" is a value-free science that stands apart from its causes and effects in the larger world. However, because the ideology of value-free science has a specific Western provenance (largely, though not exclusively, tied to the nature of the university; see Proctor 1991), it does not automatically resonate with the PUS-related interests of researchers in other parts of the world. This point becomes especially clear when the interpenetrability of science, policy, and technology is then coupled with a relatively hard sense of the boundaries between "cultures," which make possible easy claims about whether or not a form of knowledge is "appropriate" to the culture in question.

On the contrary, it would appear that several of the more articulate voices for a multicultural approach to PUS believe that what has become the standard STS picture needs to be turned on its head. They want to retain relatively hard boundaries between science, policy, and technology as societal functions, while treating cultures in a porous or patchwork fashion that encourages a more "pick-and-mix" attitude toward their offerings. This sentiment is expressed in the following excerpts, taken from three different discussions. I have arranged them according to the extent to which they would separate scientific inquiry from political inquiry. The strongest sense of separability appears below:

Diego Camelo [Ibero-American mathematician at McGill University, Montreal]: Yes, local and appropriate techniques could help the situation, but I don't see how "resisting" western science, say genetics, could help defending us from criminal patent treaties or criminal genetic resources dealings. For this we have to both cultivate those disciplines as they are in the first world and popularize them to be able to gain political and legal support for the corresponding battles. Trying to fool ourselves with "third world" genetics or physics would be a formula for disaster. Intellectuals are going to have to stop hiding their heads under the sand and face the fact that the problem is not science, but ideology, not science but powerful techniques in the hands of abusive politicians and businessmen.

Some remarks could be made here, in the spirit of a famous theory of economic development, about the "dependency" of Latin America on Western conceptions of science. Next we have a comment that suggests that while the natural sciences may work for all societies, the social sciences cannot because of their implicit value commitments:

Ahmed Bouzid [Algerian Ph.D. student in STS, and systems analyst for Unisys in Philadelphia]: To be sure, reservations are frequently voiced when controversial issues such as artificial insemination, genetic engineering, and cloning are broached. But interestingly, the reaction to these ethical challenges is not necessarily expressed by rejecting the epistemological validity of the "scientific method," and even much less by challenging science's long-standing claim of universality, but rather by pointing an accusing finger at Islamic activism's favorite foil of science: social-scientific driven socioeconomic policy. It is the social sciences—or, rather, a reliance on them to tackle social, economic, ethical and moral problems—that are responsible for the dilemmas that are gripping the world (Islamic or not) at this advanced stage in the scientific and technological era.

Finally, we have the interesting case of the distinction between science and technology being drawn—but contrary to Western expectations, technology is endorsed as *not* requiring the ideological baggage of science associated with it in the West:

Soraj Hongladoram [Thai philosopher of science at Chulalongkorn University]: In my country people do not typically see a necessary conflict between Thai cultural tradition and science, whereas they see a lot of conflict between their culture and Western philosophy. There is no separate study of "Western" and "Eastern" biology, for example. . . . [Yet] Thai people had some kind of "science" as their explanation of the phenomena and indigenous technologies; however, when Western science was adopted in full force this indigenous knowledge was overlooked and now "Western" science is a redundant term here too. However, the case of philosophy is different. There is always the consciousness that it is a Western product, something foreign from the local culture, which has a philosophy all its own. Now if science is part and parcel of the thinking that constitutes "Western" philosophy, then how can it, and it alone, be singled out for adoption? It seems that this is only possible through viewing science as a finished product, something readily exportable. . . . Instead there are attempts to put together science and the traditional Asian thinking, and Buddhism is now being redescribed so that it can go along with science. (No wonder Fritjof Capra enjoys a great popularity here.)

In contrast, a westerner who persisted unfashionably in upholding the separability of science and technology would more likely reject technology as a perverse application of science.

The above excerpts underscore that one clear advantage for a multicultural approach to the public understanding of science as a set of discrete products, rather than an undifferentiated process, is that it sets limits on what exactly is appropriated from Western culture. Moreover, the stakes are lowered, so that appropriation is no longer an "all or nothing" matter. It is possible to selectively borrow from the West's scientific legacy without accepting the history of Europe as a societal blueprint, or even a philosophical or political template. One can adapt a technology or even the technical part of a scientific discipline to local needs by aligning them with theories and interests quite alien to their original contexts. This is the lesson that Europe learned from its encounters with Islam and Japan in the nineteenth century (Fuller 1997, chap. 6). Today we regard any belief in the interdependency of material progress and Western values as symptomatic of a distinctly "modernist" hubris, the imperialist's mortal sin. Yet, if our PUS interlocutors are to be taken seriously, a parallel character flaw accompanies STS's distinctly postmodernist inclination to regard science, policy, and technology as an undifferentiated "technoscience" that renders ascriptions of credit, responsibility, and especially choice virtually impossible to make. In both the modernist and postmodernist scenarios, the history of Western science is beyond critique and reproach because it could not have been other than it was without westerners being other than they are. The only difference is that the modernist takes this as an argument for the assimilation of other cultures to the West, whereas the postmodernist takes it as an argument for the distinctness of other cultures from the West.

It is equally clear that Western interlocutors have subtle ways of subverting whatever parallels might be made between the old imperialist arguments and the supposedly postcolonial ones of today. A good example was a response to Suraj Hongladoram that came from Colin Baron, a British citizen who has taught English throughout Asia and Africa, currently at the English Centre of Hong Kong University. Baron eloquently argued for reinterpreting East Asia's seemingly instrumentalist approach to Western science as a form of passive resistance through compartmentalization. A precedent here is the familiar account of

Indian civil servants under British rule as utilitarians by day but Hindus by night. Such an account begs the question in favor of seeing the "natives" as opting to immunize themselves against a complete cultural takeover rather than making a calculated exchange of allegiances for their own benefit: in hedonistic terms, an avoidance of pain over an extension of pleasure. But how would one demonstrate the difference empirically?

Without attempting to resolve this thorny problem of cross-cultural rationality, I can point to one moment when a non-Western attempt to resituate the multicultural character of PUS was rhetorically rejigged to match the currently dominant technoscience model. The interlocutors were Hideto Nakajima, a historian of science at Tokyo University who, a week after the cyberconference had ended, convened the first international STS conference in Japan, and Chris Stokes, an STS lecturer at Lancaster University, U.K.:

Nakajima: Should we promote public understanding of science (PUS), or public understanding of technology (PUT)? If the linear model (that science leads to technology) is not correct, public understanding of only science won't automatically boost science-based technology. Isn't there a confusion of science and technology in much talk of PUS? Actually, science literacy in Japan is far beyond the level of major western countries. Do we really need the project "public understanding of science" in Japan now? If we are to develop information technology, direct investment to information industry seems far better. And I would like to insist that what we really need is not PUS, but PUT. It will also serve to identify problems concerning technology like those relating to the Internet. [*The predominance of English in electronic communications puts off the average Japanese from logging on.*]

Stokes: Using "science" as an abbreviation for technology or for technoscience or whatever other entity that overflows the narrowest definition of science is not, to my mind, merely a device for saving paper and ink or retaining prosaic elegance. It helps to perpetuate the science-technology, scientist-engineer, knowledge-application dichotomies. And as STS scholars (even those who dabble in PUS) have been problematizing these dichotomies for years now, isn't it about time we banned the word "science" and the term PUS and accepted as a first step out of this hole SET [science, engineering, technology] and PUSET? Personally I'd prefer SETetc. and PUSETetc., just to drive home the extent of the impurity of technoscientific entities, processes . . .

Note how Stokes transforms Nakajima's "either/or" approach, symbolized by the choice of PUS versus PUT, into the "both/and" approach of PUSET. When Nakajima argues that the Japanese public's reception of the Internet is hampered by talk of PUS, because it suggests that scientific training is essential for an appropriate use of the technology, Stokes takes him to mean that the science and technology of the Internet need to be understood as inextricably bound together, the exact opposite point from Nakajima's. Clearly two PUS-related agendas are working at cross-purposes here. Like most STSers, Stokes is a technoscientific "lumper" who wants to display the culturally rooted character of science's allegedly universal claims to authority, whereas Nakajima is a "splitter" who wants to display the detachability of certain parts of the West's technoscientific legacy from its entire cultural package. It would seem, then, that while the playing field of political economy may have become somewhat leveled over the past century, the old cultural asymmetries between Western and non-Western understandings of science remain relatively intact—at least in the minds of westerners. In that sense, the distinction between universalism and relativism remains imperialism's last conceptual outpost in the West, the ultimate barrier to a genuinely critical multiculturalism.

5. CONCLUSION

If multiculturalism is to retain its critical edge in confronting knowledge practices that are taken for granted in the West, it must avoid what I have called "hyperculturalism," the reification of cultural differences into racelike essences. Social epistemology can assist in this task by specifying the sociohistorical conditions that have informed a seemingly time-honored distinction—universalism versus relativism—that provides philosophical ballast for hyperculturalist interpretations of multiculturalism. From a strictly historical standpoint, humanity has had little trouble tolerating the coexistence of diverse practices in one place, as well as the movement of people between places. Yet, our taken-for-granted notions of "culture" presuppose that such fluidity in the human condition is aberrant, if not pathological. Rootedness is presumed to be the norm. In this chapter, I have provided reasons for thinking that this is to get matters exactly backward. It is only by heightening levels of societal scrutiny and accountability—via capitalist expansion, on the one hand, and nationalist reaction, on the other—that the demand was created for people to behave uniformly over space in one time (universalism) and over time in one space (relativism). Double-entry bookkeeping and mandatory grammar classes symbolize this dual intensification. Such complementary demands were salient during the period of European global hegemony, roughly, from 1760 to 1960—but are no longer.

The sociohistorical relativity of our conception of culture—its "metarelativist" status, in my terms—has been overlooked, largely because we misinterpret the sociological character of philosophical distinctions like universalism versus relativism. They do not represent spontaneously recurring divisions in human thought, but rather the verbal residues of major attempts to arrest the flow of human activity. However, my recent cyberconference on public understanding of science suggests that this may be a peculiarly Western malaise. In the final section, I showed that non-Western participants had little difficulty divesting useful technologies of the scientific interpretations given to them, even though this amounted to removing the cultural value that Westerners attached to those technologies.

Yet before too much epistemological significance is attached to this result, we must not lose sight of the fact that we continue to inhabit a world where the West more often speaks for the non-West than vice versa. Nevertheless, it should be clear to the reader that I do not associate epistemic credibility with cultural origin. On the contrary, I place great store on the value of cultural detachment as a means of adopting a critical perspective. However, such detachment is far from generally available. Indeed, until global power asymmetries are redressed, we shall continue to witness the spectacle of a well-intentioned westerner like Manuel Castells, who travels around the world, writing voluminously about the social impact of information technology on societies whose members do not have the resources to respond to his analyses, let alone reciprocate with their own investigations of Castells's privileged San Francisco Bay community (Fuller 1999a). It is a sober reminder of the task that lies ahead for a comprehensively critical multiculturalism.

ACKNOWLEDGMENTS

The research in section 4 was conducted as part of the Public Understanding of Science initiative sponsored by the U.K.'s Economic and Social Research Council: grant L485274001. My thanks to Ram Mahalingam for inviting me to participate in the 1995 American Educational Research Association meetings in San Francisco, where an early version of this chapter was delivered.

REFERENCES

Ahmad, A. 1992. *In Theory: Classes, Nations, Literatures.* London: Verso.
Amin, S. 1991. "Ancient World-Systems versus the Capitalist World-System." *Monthly Review* 14:349–86.
Anderson, B. 1983. *Imagined Communities.* London: Verso.
Bernal, M. 1987. *Black Athena.* New Brunswick, N.J.: Rutgers University Press.
Cahn, S., ed. 1995. *The Affirmative Action Debate.* London: Routledge.
Fuller, S. 1988. *Social Epistemology.* Bloomington: Indiana University Press.
———. 1993a. *Philosophy of Science and Its Discontents.* 2nd ed. New York: Guilford Press.
———. 1993b. *Philosophy, Rhetoric, and the End of Knowledge: The Coming of Science and Technology Studies.* Madison: University of Wisconsin Press.
———. 1996. "Recent Work in Social Epistemology." *American Philosophical Quarterly* 33: 149–66.
———. 1997. *Science.* Milton Keynes, U.K.: Open University Press and Minneapolis: University of Minnesota Press.
———. 1998. "Making Science an Experimenting Society." In *The Experimenting Society: Essays in Honor of Donald T. Campbell,* Policy Studies Annual, vol. 11, edited by W. Dunn, 69–102. New Brunswick, N.J.: Transaction Books.
———. 1999a. "Review of Manuel Castells, *The Information Age,* 3 vols." *Science, Technology and Human Values* 24:159–66.
———. 1999b. *The Governance of Science: Ideology and the Future of the Open Society.* Milton Keynes, U.K.: Open University Press.
———. 1999c. *Thomas Kuhn: A Philosophical History for Our Times.* Chicago: University of Chicago Press.

Gong, G. 1984. *The Standard of Civilization in International Society.* Oxford: Oxford University Press.

Gouldner, A. 1970. *The Coming Crisis in Western Sociology.* New York: Free Press.

Harding, S., ed. 1994. *The Racial Economy of Science.* Bloomington: Indiana University Press.

Hirschman, A. 1977. *The Passions and the Interests: Political Arguments for Capitalism before Its Triumph.* Princeton, N.J.: Princeton University Press.

Kincheloe, J., and S. Steinberg. 1997. *Changing Multiculturalism.* Milton Keynes, U.K.: Open University Press.

Kroeber, A,. and C. Kluckhohn. 1963. *Culture: A Critical Review of Concepts and Definitions.* New York: Random House.

Kuhn, T. S. 1970/1962. *The Structure of Scientific Revolutions.* Chicago: University of Chicago Press, 2nd ed.

Latour, B. 1987. *Science in Action.* Milton Keynes, U.K.: Open University Press.

Lévi-Strauss, C. 1964. *The Savage Mind.* Chicago: University of Chicago Press.

Nandy, A. 1987. *Tradition, Tyranny, and Utopias.* New Delhi: Oxford University Press.

———, ed. 1988. *Science, Hegemony, and Violence: A Requiem for Modernity.* New Delhi: Oxford University Press.

Ortiz de Montellano, B. 1997. "Afrocentric Pseudoscience: The Miseducation of African Americans." In *The Flight from Science and Reason,* edited by P. Gross, N. Levitt, and M. Lewis, 561–72. Baltimore: Johns Hopkins University Press, 561–72.

Oruka, H. 1990. *Sage Philosophy: Indigenous Thinkers and Modern Debate in African Philosophy.* Leiden, Netherlands: E. J. Brill.

Pearson, H. 1997. *Origins of Law and Economics.* Cambridge: Cambridge University Press.

Pieterse, J. N. 1989. *Empire and Emancipation.* London: Pluto Press.

Porter, M. 1990. *The Competitive Advantage of Nations.* London: Macmillan.

Proctor, R. 1991. *Value-Free Science?* Cambridge, Mass.: Harvard University Press.

Taylor, C. 1992. *Multiculturalism and the Politics of Recognition.* Princeton, N.J.: Princeton University Press.

Turner, S. 1994. *The Social Theory of Practice: Tradition, Tacit Knowledge, and Presuppositions.* Chicago: University of Chicago Press.

Wagner, P. 1991. "Science of Society Lost: On the Failure to Establish Sociology in Europe during the 'Classical Period.'" In *Discourses on Society: The Shaping of the Social Science Disciplines,* edited by P. Wagner, B. Wittrock, and R. Whitley, 229–46. Dordrecht, Netherlands: Reidel.

Wallerstein, I. 1991a. *Geopolitics and Geoculture.* Cambridge: Cambridge University Press.

———. 1991b. *Unthinking Social Science.* Oxford: Blackwell.

2

WHAT PUTS THE "CULTURE" IN "MULTICULTURALISM"?

An Analysis of Culture, Government, and the Politics of Mexican Identity

Mary Coffey

Pomona College

The word *culture* suffuses the discourse on multiculturalism. Much multicultural pedagogy and theory uncritically fetishizes the field of culture, thus partaking in what Steve Fuller has characterized as *hyperculturism*. Yet even within the multiculturalism literature that eschews these facile positions, culture, a critical category itself, often remains uninterrogated. The "dominant culture," "hegemonic culture," "subalternated cultures," "critical culture," these are just a few of the terms invoked within this literature to examine the historical construction of privilege and difference, the maintenance of power and prejudice, or the quest for resistance and critique. As a crucial term embedded within the rubric under analysis in this volume, *culture* begs a similar rigorous consideration. Perhaps this lack of attention is due to the seeming self-evidence of culture; we all think we know what we are talking about when we use or read the word. However, culture is not simply an empirical phenomenon, and the commonsense approach to it as though it were obscures its relation to value, epistemological pursuits, and subject formation, all significant concerns for multiculturalism. The implications of this misapprehension of the very term at stake within multiculturalism is my concern in this essay.

The examination of culture and government that follows resonates in many ways with Henry Giroux's critique of academic multiculturalism and his call for an understanding of culture as a "public discourse." Through an analysis of the imbrication of culture and government drawn from my work on postrevolutionary Mexican nationalism, I will elaborate a theory of culture and power that takes into consideration the relationships among the production of knowledge, subject-formation, and social regulation. Furthermore, by approaching culture through an analysis of its relationship to government in the Mexican context, I want to move away from an emphasis within academia to treat culture as a reflection of truth, or conversely as an obstacle to truth, in order to understand its constitutive role in the production of truth.

WHAT IS CULTURE?

Two common definitions of the term *culture* circulate within and without academia. The first gives us culture as an aesthetic phenomenon, restricting it to the intellectual and creative activity of the so-called best and brightest of any given society. The second definition emanates from anthropology and describes—in the words of Raymond Williams (1976)—a "particular way of life, whether of a people, a period, or a group." (80). The latter is tacit within the discourse on multiculturalism, yet most discussions employ both intermittently. There is, however, a third definition of culture coming into currency that has yet to be explicitly addressed in these discussions.

Introduced by Tony Bennett in his landmark work on the museum (1995), this third definition is informed by Michel Foucault's late work on "governmentality." Accordingly, it conceptualizes the interstices of knowledge and power as they impact upon the subject through a concern with individual conduct as a problematic of rule. Bennett writes (1992) that culture "is more cogently conceived ... when thought of as a historically specific set of institutionally embedded relations of government in which the forms of thought and conduct of extended populations are targeted for transformation—in part via the extension through the social body of the forms, techniques, and regimens of aesthetic and intellectual culture" (26).

Culture, thus defined, is voided of an a priori empiricism as its constitutive relation to power is made manifest. Through the processes of social management, culture is crafted as both the object and instrument of government. This is not to say, however, that the objects and practices designated as "culture" don't exist (the linguistic determinism argument), but rather it signals a shift in analysis that emphasizes the ways that they are taken up by the apparatuses of knowledge and power. It is through this process that specialized and everyday practices are coded as "culture," and thereby designated as a category of value and made *useful* to a host of governing projects.

WHAT IS GOVERNMENT?

In his essay on governmentality, Michel Foucault traces the historical shift from autarchy to the modern state and argues that the weakening of divine rule occasioned the rise of doctrines on *how* to rule (see Foucault 1991; Gordon 1991). This signified a change in government from the accumulation of power and the rule of territory to the investment of the population with power and a concern with governing things and the relations between them. Rather than seeking to legitimate rule (as the divine sovereign did), modern forms of social and political organization are concerned with techniques of government, that is, *how* to rule.

This concern with "things and the relations between them" is manifested in a deep concern for the population now conceived through the discourses of economics and social science as productive potential. On this point Foucault writes that "the population now represents more the end of government than the power of the sovereign; the population is the subject of needs, of aspirations, but it is also the object in the hands of government, aware, *vis-à-vis* the government, of what it wants, but ignorant of what is being done to it" (1991, 100). Governing, then, is concerned with "conducting conduct" and it is carried out through diverse institutions and agencies. Despite the tendency to associate government with the state, the logic of governmentality is manifested in both state and private initiatives, and it calls into question the absolute sovereignty of the state. As Andrew Barry, Thomas Osborne, and Nikolas Rose have argued in the introduction to their *Foucault and Political Reason* (1996), the very category of the state may be a consequence of the rise of liberalism and the attempts to theorize the possibilities of freedom. Given this genealogy of government, they suggest (along with Foucault) that we turn our attention from the state as the center of government, to the multiple sites of government within what has traditionally been conceived as civil society (1–17).

Foucault's term *governmental* refers, in part, to the problematics of rule. Yet it also refers to the dimension of experience, the ways in which humans have reflected on the conduct of themselves and others and realized that reflection through governing practices (Rose 1996, 41). Governmentality is therefore a political rationality that has a moral concern for what is proper, an epistemological character in that it is concerned with conceptions of objects to be governed, and a style or reasoning such as intellectual techniques that render reality thinkable (Rose 1996, 42). Government in this sense refers to the myriad "authorities of truth" that impact the way in which we establish true and false accounts of who we are and what we should become (Dean 1996, 211). Most important to this concept of government is the way in which questions of being, personal conduct, and identity come to be linked to questions of politics, authority, and government (210).

We return, then, to Bennett's assertion that culture be understood as both the object and instrument of government. "Culture," he argues, is government's object "insofar as the term refers to the morals, manners and ways of life of subordinate social strata" (26). In other words, when government is conceived as a concern for conduct, the anthropological definition of culture is employed as the target of social initiatives and regulation. Similarly, culture is configured as an instrument of government, "insofar as it is culture in its more restricted sense— the domain of artistic and intellectual activities—that is to supply the means of a governmental intervention into the regulation of culture as the domain of morals, manners, codes of conduct, etc." When examined this way, culture, as a category of population or production, is produced rather than given. Furthermore, the attendant values that accrue to either sense are also mobilized by their function within a particular set of social relations. In Bennett's work the public museum provides an example of these social processes, for it is in the museum, as a space of rational recreation, that material objects and practices are codified as representative culture while they are employed as instruments of enlightenment. My point here is to call attention to the relations of power that generate these designations and to suggest that we think of the discourses and policies of multiculturalism through this rubric.

WHAT IS POWER?

The invocation of power begs further qualification and discussion about the relations between culture and power. At its most uncritical moments, the discourse on culture operates according to a "reflection" theory in which culture merely mirrors, for better or worse, the broader society. Questions of power are thereby rendered moot because representation is understood as a closed circle of correspondence between the object or practice and the "real world." Conversely, a more critical camp theorizes this relationship through the trope of "deception." Here culture provides a false representation that obscures the true workings of power in the social body. Karl Marx's ideology and Antonio Gramsci's hegemony are the two most sophisticated and deep-seated formulations of deception. Within the former, power is seated within a ruling class that seeks to subjugate the working class through an "ideological apparatus" that employs culture to mask the "real" operations of class privilege (see Althusser 1971). Gramsci provides a more nuanced view of the relationship between culture and power, modifying the rigidity of Marx's paradigm with the notion of a "hegemonic process." In this formulation, subjugation is not the product of a false consciousness constructed and maintained through the ideological deployment of culture; rather, it is a process that attempts to "transform society" through the creation of a consensus of values and goals, with culture as its primary agent (see Gramsci 1971; Laclau and Mouffe 1985).

While the former account of power attributes a purely negative value to culture, as a thing to be manipulated, the latter allows for the possibility of negotiation between different power sectors for consent, and as such culture assumes a positive potential as a site for the struggle over meaning. This latter understanding has been most useful within an academic multiculturalism that limits its analysis to representation and reading resistance within particular texts (Bennett 1992). Nonetheless, both variants treat power as property that can be seized or appropriated, as an attribute of only those who seek to dominate and ultimately as localized predominantly in the state and its institutions. As such, power shows itself through the violence of repression and the coercion of propaganda or ideology. In opposition to this model, I am arguing that power is a relation between forces, whether dominant or dominated, that it is exercised through techniques rather than possessed, and that it is productive first and foremost (see Foucault 1995, 1985, 1984, 1972). As Gilles Deleuze states, following Foucault, "power produces reality before it represses [and] it produces 'truth' before it ideologizes or masks" (Deleuze 1988, 28–29).

In the following discussion of the evolution of national culture in postrevolutionary Mexico, I am not concerned with either the processes of hegemony nor with locating culture within the realm of ideology. Rather than analyzing this history through what Foucault has called an "economy of untruth," I trace the production of certain "truths" about the nation and its origins. Eschewing ideology and hegemony is not, however, an attempt to ignore power. Rather, it is a way of understanding power as part of the production of truth, not merely its repression. Rather than trying to resuscitate what certain cultural products meant prior to their distortion at the hands of one dominating power or another, I explore the epistemological character of culture in order to examine how it functions within governmental apparatuses, like educational projects and public museums. This, as we will see, has implications for multiculturalism, both as a deconstruction of origins and national identity (two of the privileged terms operating within the hyperculturalist camp), and as an illustration of how to use governmentality to think the relation between culture and power. Furthermore, the Mexican example offers an interesting parallel to corporatist multiculturalism currently evident in the "managing of difference" within universities and other institutional sites. Like this contemporary phenomenon, the Mexican national culture project instrumentalized hybridity in an array of assimilationist projects aimed at social management. That hybridity and assimilation can be seen to work hand in hand in Mexico may not be an aberration, specific to this particular case, but rather a fundamental problem facing multiculturalism at the governmental level.

POSTREVOLUTIONARY MEXICO: A CASE STUDY IN GOVERNMENTAL CULTURE

Public culture is one "authority of truth," and in this paper, I focus on two of its sites: Diego Rivera's murals at Mexico's Ministry of Public Education, in which he inaugurated a nationalized visual vocabulary that asserted native "types" and geographic elements as the essential icons of the Mexican nation;[1] and the Museo Nacional de Antropología (National Anthropology Museum) in which the creative production and practices of indigenous populations have been crafted into a national cultural trust, a legacy that is employed to discipline the population into a functional and cohesive citizenry. This embrace of native culture is referred to as to "official *Indigenismo*," which David Bradding describes as the contradictory "insistence on the native roots of the Mexican people" and a simultaneous "affirmation of the necessity of modernity" evident in Mexico's cultural projects (Bradding 1988, 89). However, I argue that the employment of folkloric expression for the assimilation of Indian communities into the urban Hispanicized population is not contradictory but rather part of the disciplinary logic of modernizing nationalism.

DIAGNOSING THE NATIONAL BODY

At the close of the Mexican Revolution (circa 1917), national discourse focused on the problem of a historically contentious population comprised of "degenerate" indigenes, a large strata of mestizos (people of mixed racial heritage), and a minority of those of pure Spanish descent known as creoles. As a discourse framed by the psychological and historical conditions of postcolonialism, Mexican nationalism seized upon the mestizo as the actual and metaphorical "Mexican." In *La raza cósmica*, a pseudoscientific treatise on the future promise of "his people," José Vasconcelos elevates racial miscegenation to a transcendent eugenic principle. Arguing that a "mixture of races accomplished through the laws of social well-being, sympathy, and beauty" will lead to a *cosmic race*, "infinitely superior to all that have previously existed," Vasconcelos converted racial impurity from a sign of shame into one of pride (1979, 31). "We in America," he concludes, "shall arrive, before any other part of the world, at the creation of a new race fashioned out of the treasures of the previous ones" (40).

Yet despite his celebration of *mestizaje*, Vasconcelos laments the "race problem," stating, "whether we like it or not the mestizo is the dominant element of the Latin American continent" (1926b, 92). He continues, explaining, "From our local point of view in Mexico, I have started to preach the gospel of the mestizo by trying to impress on the minds of the new race a consciousness of their mission as builders of entirely new concepts of life. But if the mixed race is going to be able to do anything at all, it is first necessary to give it moral strength and faith in its own ability" (95). Vasconcelos reasons that the lack of "moral strength" and "faith" he detected in the mestizo was a result of his Indian blood. The Indian, he argues, is a "lower breed" without hope, who "reproduces madly" and languishes in a state of degradation (100). This is not merely a problem for the disenfranchised native, but more significantly a problem for the nation. Conceived as a mestizo nation, the intransigence of one part of the body politic is a detriment to the progress of the whole.

As the native "element" emerged as the sign of difference around which a new mestizo identity could be elaborated, the perceived "backwardness" of the living and breathing native persisted, a reminder of the repercussions of colonialism and a perennial sign of Mexico's lack. Consequently, postrevolutionary national discourse is obsessed with the "Indian Question."[2] In 1917, Mexican anthropologist Manuel Gamio founded the department of anthropology specifically to address this question. Its program, he explained, was to study the racial characteristics, material and intellectual culture, language and dialects, economic situation, and environmental and biological conditions of the regional populations of present and past Mexico. Through this, Gamio insisted that his program would then be able to establish "official institutions" to "stimulate physical, intellectual, moral and economic development of the people" with the ultimate goal of "cultural fusion, linguistic unification and economic equilibrium" (1926, 173). Concluding a lecture entitled "Incorporating the Indian into the National Population," Gamio stated emphatically, "It is unquestionably urgent, most urgent, to investigate the indigenous population of Mexico scientifically, for until this is done thoroughly, social contacts cannot be normalized and oriented authoritatively, a thing by all means desirable since it requires convergent racial, cultural, and spiritual fusion to secure unification of tongue and equilibrium of economic interests. This, and only this, can place the Mexican nation as a nation, upon a solid, logical, consistent, and permanent base" (127).

In accordance with this sentiment, the Secretaría de Educación Pública (Ministry of Public Education), or SEP, was founded in 1921, immediately after the military struggles of the revolution subsided (1910–20). José Vasconcelos was appointed its director and it was his messianic vision that shaped its activities. In his biography, he states explicitly that the purpose of the SEP was "five-fold," with the promotion and development of schools, libraries, and the fine arts as its essential parts and "bringing the Indian into the current of Spanish culture" and "literacy to the masses" its "auxiliary activities" (Vasconcelos 1963, 157). For him, "ignorance" was a "plague" that afflicted the modern native population, and education was the "redemptive" agent of their inclusion within the Mexican nation. This desire to redeem Mexico's native populations undergirded his interest in developing a national culture. This project was merely one front of a broad educative mission, and Vasconcelos often compared his role as minister of education with that of the Spanish priests who converted the inhabitants of New Spain. As such, the national culture project needs to be understood as a disciplinary initiative that employed education and the arts as techniques of government to reorganize the conduct of targeted populations.

Under Vasconcelos's leadership, the SEP commissioned Mexican artists to paint large murals on public buildings, thus inaugurating the "Mexican mural renaissance" as a new category of culture. By employing Mexican artists to beautify the walls of the city, Vasconcelos sought to aggrandize the nation and enhance the lives of its citizens; for him, culture was an instrument of enlightenment, and his aesthetic theories are quite explicit on this point. In 1923 Diego Rivera convinced Vasconcelos to make available the courtyard walls of the SEP's administration building so that he and a number of other important contemporaries could create murals. While working on them from 1923 to 1928, Rivera evolved the visual vocabulary, style, and themes that would come to be recognized as the iconography of Mexican nationalism. During this period, Mexican artists were catalyzed by the Communist Party, a marriage of art and politics that produced a new aesthetic commitment to the "values of the Mexican Revolution."

SITE NUMBER 1: DIEGO RIVERA'S SEP MURALS

Rivera's murals explicitly display a political conviction to a militant socialism inflected by the values of Zapatismo. He writes in his autobiography that in these murals he wanted to "reflect the social life of Mexico as I saw it, and through my vision of the truth to show the masses the outline of the future" (Rivera and March 1960, 79). His desire to reveal the "truth" to the "masses" in order to benefit the "future" recalls the disciplinary rhetoric of Vasconcelos and Gamio, and it finds its first visual articulation in these paintings. Rivera asserts the native as the essence of the body politic but reverses the moral hierarchy attributed to race in most of the diagnostic literature discussed earlier. However, by narrating a progressive movement from rural and agrarian idyll to an urban and proletarian future, Rivera's murals invoke the native largely in the name of socialism.

Recognizing the different ways the "native" was conceived of and positioned within the social projects of public education, artistic representation, and anthropological study is important because it discourages the tendency to find a conspiracy between power sectors to "repress" the native. Each of these projects manifested a deep (albeit paternal) concern for Mexico's indigenous populations, and through their expertise sought to affect their conduct and include them in national citizenship. By emphasizing the reiteration of certain statements across the fields of social knowledge, I want to call attention to the diffuse nature of government and demonstrate that sites often located outside or in opposition to the state do in fact participate in the processes of rule.

The subject matter of Rivera's artistic cycle is divided into two categories, the courts of labor and fiestas, which correspond to the two three-story courtyards of the SEP. The three stories of the Court of Labor are decorated with murals dedicated to the industrial and agricultural labors of the Mexican people, intellectual labor, and portraits of revolutionary heroes. The first-floor murals reflect the values of Zapatismo through images of natives and *campesinos* (farm workers) working the land under dangerous conditions of labor. They foreground the exploitation of the indigenous poor by corrupt *hacendados* (landowners). Panels such as *The Liberation of the Peon* (1923) depict the rescue of a mistreated native by revolutionary soldiers, who are again visible in *The New School* (1923) overseeing the education of peasants. Each of these images is set in a vast landscape that references the rich and diverse topography of the country, and calls to mind the revolutionary slogan of Emiliano Zapata, *"Tierra y Libertad"* ("Land and Liberty"). Furthermore, paintings of volcanoes, magueys, and cacti, as well as identifiable architectural landscapes such as the hillsides of stacked housing typical of Guanajuato, begin to elaborate an allegorical topography infused with political values. Likewise, panels dealing with industrial labor symbolically reinforce the theme of exploitation. For example, in *Entry into the Mines* (1923) the mine shaft has been rendered in the guise of a skull, effectively equating this dangerous work with death.[3] These images of cruel labor are contrasted with idyllic portraits of Tehuanas dying cloth and natives making and decorating pottery, clearly a contrast between pre-Hispanic communitarian modes of production and colonial and postcolonial forms of class exploitation and labor for the purposes of wealth and export.

The Court of Fiestas illustrates popular religious and political festivals and illustrated revolutionary *corridos* (songs). On the first floor, amid panels describing native and popular festivals, Rivera has placed three large murals representing agrarian reform, May Day, and the popular market, which is represented as a modern equivalent to the ancient Aztec market—the *tianguis*—for which it is titled. The physical disbursement of these three panels produces an equation of events. These murals are the central focus and therefore the visual anchors of the three painted courtyard walls. Thus an equation between native traditions, the revolution, and socialism is reinforced visually as well as through the literal procession of the viewer through the space. Rivera's ideological disposition is clear in these panels, where masses of soldiers, agrarians, and factory workers are depicted as culturally unified by local traditions and politically unified by the promise of socialism. Throughout the SEP cycle, the spatial distribution of individual mural paintings builds a progressive narrative that is elaborated and communicated as much through representation as it is through the physical movement of the visitor through the building's courtyard. The movement from the revolution and its values toward a proletarian society is conveyed throughout, but it is best illustrated through the narrative convention of *corridos* on the third floor and the physical climb up the stairwell corridor. In both of these spaces, representations of indigenous peoples help to legitimize Rivera's visions of past and future Mexico.

The equation between the values of the Mexican Revolution and socialism is even more evident in the third-floor panels, which are connected by a painted red ribbon upon which agrarian and proletarian songs are printed. These panels contrast bourgeois values with socialist ones, by lampooning figures like J. D. Rockefeller and lionizing the communist worker and the revolutionary soldier. For example, *Wall Street Banquet* (1928) depicts wealthy Manhattanites dining on champagne and ticker tape. *Our Bread* (1928), on the other hand, portrays a humble table presided over by a worker in blue overalls, wearing the red star of communism, and breaking bread while a Tehuana proffers a basket of indigenous fruits. At the table, individuals gathered from across Mexico's racial and social classes sit, while a soldier and farmer stand nearby. The entire scene is set in front of a "factory-scape," a motif that references the (vulgar) Marxist belief that technology would hasten the destruction of capitalist society and thereby social inequality.

The third-floor images are introduced by *The Distribution of Arms* (1928), a painting that prophesies the proletarian revolution in its imagery as well as through the proletarian song that frames it and whose slogans structure the vignettes that follow. The opening lines, "Así será la Revolución Proletaria" ("And so it will be, the Proletarian Revolution") place the event in the future, as each subsequent image describes how this will proceed. At the culmination of this song, a revolutionary *corrido* begins, rendered in the same red ribbon. The similarity in iconography between the text and images of each illustrated song articulates the Mexican revolution to a prophesied proletarian revolution and asserts that one follows logically from the other. Here the "spontaneous" eruption born out of a subjugated people's collective sense of injustice is equated with the political organization of the international communist movement. Conversely, the authenticity of the local event naturalizes an imported political agenda by asserting that both are structured by the same values.[4]

The dynamic between space and representation is best captured in the stairway at the SEP, which is painted from the ground up with a symbolic landscape of social evolution that is conveyed through geological change and the sociocultural development of "peoples" from "pre-modern society" to proletarian social order

(Wolfe 1939, 181–96). These panels make explicit the structure of the SEP murals as a whole. There is a general progression throughout, as one moves from ground floor to the upper balconies, with the native symbolizing an essential yet primitive past and the communist worker representing a unified future. The staircase images are both topographic and ethnographic as they depict a progression from "subterranean waters" through tropical lands, high plateau, and finally, snow-capped mountains. Inhabiting these Mexican landscapes are native peoples from Mexico's past and present. The mixing together of past and contemporary indigenous populations suggests a continuity between Mexico's pre-Columbian past and postrevolutionary present. Nonetheless, there is a subtle chronological progression that commutes this cycle to a history lesson as well. The early panels are mythologized marine-scapes that, while inhabited by modern technologies, give no indication of an abusive relationship between man, machine, or land. However, as one moves up from sea level into the tropics of Tehuantepec, the image of a sugar hacienda emerges, complete with lazy boss and exploited labor. The locals are gradually clothed, which suggests the encroachment of "civilization" along with conquest and colonization. The revolution is clearly alluded to in a burial image that recalls Gustave Courbet's famous painting *A Burial at Ornans* (1849), as well as Rivera's depictions of slain heroes in his Chapingo murals. Finally, with the passing of the revolution, Rivera represents the overcoming of exploitation with an image of cowering figures depicting the church, capital, and the corrupt military being struck down by a red thunderbolt, a symbol of the proletariat. In the upper right-hand corner, a new, socialist society is presented through the united trinity of soldier, worker, and farmer. The final image, at the top of this historical narrative, depicts Rivera the artist, represented as a technical worker along with the stone cutter and architect.

Rivera's SEP murals equate the people and the land literally and figuratively, and thereby establish one of the most recurrent strategies for naturalizing the psychic sense of community propounded by national rhetoric. These murals, dedicated to the Mexican people, their labors, and their celebrations, assert that the nation is founded in the native soil and its native populations. However, both soil and people ultimately undergo changes, as industrialization and Marxist social organization assimilate the disparate populace into a collective, proletarian working force and exploit the natural values of the land toward that end. By advocating this change in his imagery, Rivera issues the same tacit mandate to the Mexican masses that Gamio endeavored to do in *Forjando Patria* (*Forging a Fatherland*—his multivolume study of the Valley of Teotihuacán) and that Vasconcelos promoted through his educational policies. Native peoples and their practices are addressed as the essential "Mexicans" as all the while they are asked to express their citizenship within the new nation by assimilating socially and adapting to new collective values.

DISCIPLINING A NATIONAL CITIZENRY

By representing the Mexican nation through an equation between racial types and landscapes, Rivera's SEP murals present a visual counterpart to the literature on Mexican nationalism at the time. For example, in an essay entitled "Similarity and Contrast," José Vasconcelos details at length the topographical variety of Mexico and then equates this "land of contrasts" with its various peoples and their characteristics (1926a, 3–43). The equation between natives and their natural environment was also a component of Gamio's massive research into Teotihuacán. As part of this discursive context, Rivera's murals illustrate the prevailing logic of early-twentieth-century nationalism, both in his reliance upon essentialist traits such as "race" and "climate" as well as in his enthusiasm about the potential for social control through harnessing these "physical" determinants toward a greater social good, future development, and "proper citizenship." Vasconcelos argues that Mexico is a "nation of contrast" with a history that is "a series of layers composed of materials that do not mix," a "social condition" that is characterized by a "compound of races that have not yet become thoroughly combined," and where a mere "glance at our physical structure will only add to the puzzle of the Mexican problem" (5–7). He speculates that "perhaps the reason of the social contrast lies in the varied physical, temperamental, and historical factors that intervene in the making of our soul" (7).

The crafting of the "Mexican soul" was the explicit project of postrevolutionary cultural nationalism. The "will to nation" expressed in this literature came to fruition with the concept of *mestizaje*, simultaneously producing and circumscribing the sphere of the "indigenous" as an object of study, regulation, and representation. The emergent school of Mexican anthropology sought to know the native while governmental programs endeavored to inculcate this disenfranchised population into the newly "imagined community" of mestizo nationhood. Furthermore, national culture seized upon the Indian as an object of representation and a producer of "authentic" Mexican art. The institutional relationship between these fields of practice functioned together to produce powerful popular truths about the nation, its heritage, and the conditions of citizenship.

Rivera's SEP murals offer a "folkloric" appreciation of native life in the name of an advancing modernization. While he asserts that the social organization of proletarian culture is based upon the communitarian social organization of pre-Hispanic Mexico, his depiction of modern Mexico is as a mestizo nation in which racial and social distinctions no longer matter. In short, his is a vision of assimilation in the name of social development, and as such a visual corollary of the disciplinary rhetoric of nationalism. They are lessons in citizenship that rely upon the "natural" racial and territorial markers of a "nation of contrasts." While Rivera's vision of *mestizaje* is cultural rather than racial (as Vasconcelos's was), the underlying principle of achieving a proper balance between the desirable traits of different racial and social sectors was based upon a discriminate and selective criteria in the service of a modernizing national project.[5]

PROBLEMATIZING THE NATION

Michel Foucault's notion of "problematization" helps to bring together the discourse on nationalism, governmental initiatives in the fields of education and anthropology, and the artistic project of mural creation. In a 1984 interview with

François Ewald, Foucault (1990) discusses the relationship between "problematization" and truth, saying, "Problematization doesn't mean representation of a pre-existing object, nor the creation by discourse of an object that doesn't exist. It is the totality of discursive or non-discursive practices that introduces something into the play of true and false and constitutes it as an object for thought (whether in the form of moral reflection, scientific knowledge, political analysis, etc.)" (257). In postrevolutionary Mexico, the "truth" of the nation is problematized and a new set of objects is offered up to thought. Within the discursive and nondiscursive practices discussed thus far, the native centers questions regarding appropriate being or conduct and political reason or rule. The contemporary native is an object of study and therefore knowledge, an object of moral reflection, an object of representation, and an object of government. The problematization of Mexico-as-nation produced statements of truth about the native: that in the contemporary period the native existed in a degraded state that mandated intervention; that their culture was essential to the nation and the only proper expression of difference; that they were in need of welfare; that they were the historical agents of national becoming; that they had to assimilate to some new form of collective or community. The personal conduct of the native became essential to the question of rule and representation, and these truths structured the ways in which the native and nation could subsequently be thought. The struggle over the nation, was therefore a struggle over the native. The allegiance of indigenous peoples was sought while they were simultaneously subjectified as "the indigenous" through governing practices that ranged from anthropological scrutiny to institutional representation.

What is significant here is that the problematization and production of Mexico's indigenous population occurred across a variety of discursive sites, and that culture needs to be understood as one of these. More important, these different sites were not all organized from a single perspective; rather, each was pursuing this problem from a different vantage point and with differing agendas. The socialist politics and anticlericalism of Rivera was in direct opposition to the elitism and Catholicism of Vasconcelos, so much so that the latter rescinded his support upon his resignation from the SEP in 1924. Gamio and his team of anthropologists were interested in preserving and studying indigenous culture under the sign of "pure science." The articulation of these many projects through the national culture project over a number of years and across many institutional sites is important to understand lest we fall into too simplistic an understanding of either culture or the processes of government. While regularities occurred across these discourses, it was the resonance between them that established the aforementioned truths about Mexico's indigenous populations.

Site Number 2: The Museo Nacional de Antropologia

In the early decades of the twentieth century, indigenous populations were conceived as a "problem population." The national culture project delimited a range of practices as distinctive culture and employed them in governing projects. Through the museum, these populations were objectified as the targets of government even while their daily practices were instrumentalized within the institutions dedicated to the nation's pre-Hispanic origins.

I want to turn briefly from the early national culture project to the newer Museo Nacional de Antropología, inaugurated in 1964, in order to examine the museum as a technique of government in which the subjectification of the Mexican through the deployment of indigenous culture is most evident and powerful. Here the museum is understood as a complex social space of representation and regulation, an instrument of modern government whose raison d'être lies in its civilizing capacity, its ability to improve the morals, and, more important, to shape the conduct of its public.

As the most visited museum in the country, the Museo Nacional de Antropología has come to embody "Mexicanness." Its success has been attributed to its sophisticated spatial organization and displays that assert that national culture has its origins in the indigenous sectors of the Mexican population. However, as Néstor García Canclini (1995) has argued, it does this by marking the limits of the ethnic through a separation of ancient and contemporary cultures. This separation is enacted by a distinction between anthropology (housed on the first floor) and ethnography (located on the second); within the museum, the former is given much greater emphasis.

The museum's collections are distributed across the two floors of galleries, which form a rectangle around an open patio. While patrons are free to enter each gallery from this patio, there is a clearly marked place at which to begin their experience—an introductory hall that explicates the museum's mission and articulates its objects to and through the science of anthropology, or the study of "man." In his statement (1968) about the "origins, aims and achievements" of this museum, Ignacio Bernal, director of the Instituto Nacional de Antropología e Historia (National Institute of Anthropology and History) in the 1960s, makes explicit the significance of the science of anthropology to the Mexican nation. He writes, "The diverse indigenous cultures of Mexico, both those which flourished in prehistoric times and those which have persisted until the present day, present anthropology with a vast field for study while providing museums with rich and valuable materials for display.... Keeping this in mind, those who planned the new National Museum of Anthropology decided to include an initiatory hall that would justify the Museum's name and at the same time present a universal framework into which the Mexican cultures could be fitted in space and time, as well as allowing visitors to compare their cultural contributions with those of other peoples" (14). This introductory hall, designed to pay homage to the science that organizes and explains "man's origins"—along with the final hall of the ethnographic section, entitled "Modern Autochthonous Mexico"—was intended to frame the viewers' experience of the museum. While the introductory hall devoted to anthropology prepared the viewer to understand the objects in subsequent galleries as both national in content and universal in significance, the final hall punctuated their experience with an invitation to utilize their new knowledge by becoming proper modern citizens.

This last hall presented, in the words of Bernal, a "synthesis of the process of social and cultural change taking place in Mexico today" (193). The synthesizing processes of modern Mexico were represented through a photomosaic in which photographs of various ethnic groups were montaged into a progressively unified and modernized image of the national populace. Bernal explains that this image calls for the "participation of the native peoples, through which the National Indigenist Institute is trying to integrate the various ethnic groups into Mexican national life" (193).[6]

Functioning as bookends to the museum experience, these halls convert the viewer's progress through the exhibitions into an evolutionary performance that begins in a glorified past and looks to the future. This "ritual of citizenship" implies that the synthetic vision of the nation's future is the fulfillment of a promise embodied in the culture of the past. At once historicized and patriotic, it places the viewer in an evolutionary relationship to the cultures and peoples on display. Finally, it asks them to recognize themselves in the indigenous past, but to participate in a synthetic future.

The museum was thus planned to glorify and educate; as such, each room was organized to present easily understood lessons. A report published in 1961 outlines the museum's overt mission, its organization, and the scientific means by which its efficacy should be tested and ensured. Arguing that museum exhibitions "from the didactic point of view only have value with respect to the educative function they perform in relation to the public," the authors of the report suggest a preliminary study of the "general characteristics" of the public in order to fashion viewer surveys aimed at quantifying the "educative influence" of its exhibitions (Sánchez Bueno and Salgado 1961, 1). So at the planning stage this museum was organized with a political pedagogy in mind. As one of the only public museums in the country to receive its own building designed specifically to facilitate its didactic message, the Museo Nacional de Antropología is a unique but paradigmatic public museum in postrevolutionary Mexico. More than a mere representation of the nation, its ritualized space deploys cultural objects in order to produce an identification between its indigenous visitors and the Mexican nation. As Néstor García Canclini eloquently explains, "the watchword that governs this ritual is 'become what you are'" (1995, 135).

CULTURE AND SUBJECTIFICATION

The use of culture in postrevolutionary Mexico is a "pursuit of the popular"—a desire to name, know, and create the "people" as well as to proscribe the modes of their conduct. In this sense the people are a "representational effect" of cultural texts as well as a "knowledge effect" of investigations and regulations of the population (Miller 1998, 250). The pursuit of this "fictional" entity on the part of multiple agencies is part of the cultural revolution that established artistic practice as a ritual of citizenship and part of the governmental program concerned with popular conduct. As Toby Miller argues, through government, "living and breathing subjects who act in the everyday become objects of contemplation and intervention" (251). The museum is an important site for establishing a relationship between the national collective and the individual citizen; as Miller argues, it "seeks to attract newcomers and to draw reactions that will be taken into the exterior world through a temporary, voluntary enclosure of the visitors that combines information and entertainment, instruction and diversion" (235).

Miller's attention to the relationships among institution, knowledge, and subject formation brings out the disciplinary component of subjectivity and identity that Foucault began to delimit in his late work. According to this definition, subjectivity does not designate an autonomous self-knowledge nor a socially constructed automation; rather, it indexes a relationship to the self brought into being by processes of subjectification "through which individuals are able, are obliged, to recognize themselves as subjects" (Foucault 1985, 4). In "The Subject and Power," Foucault reminds us that there are two meanings to the word *subject:* "subject to someone else by control and dependence; and tied to [one's] own identity by a conscience or self-knowledge" (1984, 420). In both senses, an individual does not escape the forces of power and knowledge; rather, the truth of one's individuality is produced at the interstices of both. Culture, as we have seen, is a technique of government and consequently one of the instruments of subjectification by which one is called upon or obliged to recognize oneself through particular formations of identity. *Identity* must be understood as a category produced through disciplinary and governmental initiatives that impinge upon the individual, and not as a naturalized category of being. This formulation of the subject helps to highlight the subjugation and regulation that proceeds through the production and naturalization of racial, ethnic, national, and sexual identities. Furthermore, by analyzing the role culture plays in these formations, we can attend to the deleterious effects of identity politics as they emerge within the emancipatory projects of multicultural education.

In Mexico's national culture project, "culture" was produced and disseminated across the axes of regulatory bodies, patrimony legislation, and institutions. Neither murals nor pre-Hispanic artifacts are unproblematically "culture." Their production as such is inextricably linked to the governmental project of public education and the epistemological pursuits of anthropology, philosophy, and the diagnostic literature on the "Mexican problem." Furthermore, the instrumentalization of this culture of difference within spaces devoted to national consolidation demonstrates the extent to which we must look at how culture functions within broader contexts. Rather than treating culture as a self-evident product to be reviled as ideology or resuscitated through critical reading practices, an analysis of the very constitution of "culture," its uses within governmental spaces, whether state supported or not, and its articulations to other discursive fields will reveal the complexities of this phenomenon.

By calling attention to the intricacies of culture within governmental and disciplinary processes, I endeavor to demonstrate that power is a constitutive component of culture, not merely an impositional force that arrives after the fact. Ultimately it behooves us not to try to determine what culture is, in its essence, but rather how it is produced as a category (whether aesthetic or "life world") and how it functions in particular institutional or policy contexts. This attention to culture and government can only augment the "insurgent multiculturalism" that Henry Giroux describes as a "pedagogical terrain in which relations of power and racialized identities become paramount as part of the language of critique and possibility" (1997, 235). Continuing, he writes, "This suggests challenging the narratives of national identity, culture, and ethnicity as part of a pedagogical effort to provide dominant groups with the knowledge and histories to examine, acknowledge, and unlearn their own privilege" (236). In Giroux's formulation, multiculturalism is not merely the celebration of marginalized identities and their essentialized cultural production; it is instead a strategy for understanding the emergence of privilege and its conditions of production.

In conclusion, I want to suggest that to understand privilege, we need to understand government as a set of diffuse techniques exercised in and through myriad locations, practices, and authorities. With that in mind, we need to ask what the relations are between multiculturalism as a critical pedagogy, and the processes of government implicit in the educational context. How are the concepts of culture employed in multicultural discourse linked up with other forms of expertise, and what are the effects of these articulations? Finally, I argue that understanding culture as a technique of government helps to make intelligible the strategies by which we are governed, and this consequently provides the possibility for the contestation of those strategies. My analysis of national culture in Mexico is a description of how "culture" is produced, but it also points to a theory of subjectification that takes into account the production of knowledge and its relation to governmental power. This in turn provides a perspective on the mechanics of privilege, but it also demonstrates the need to retheorize resistance through governmentality.

NOTES

I would like to thank the Tinker Foundation and the Center for Latin American and Caribbean Studies at the University of Illinois for sponsoring two research trips to Mexico. This research enabled and informed my arguments regarding the Mexican national culture project in what follows.

1. Throughout my discussion of Mexico's national culture project, I use the word *native* repeatedly. While this term reflects the terrible legacy of European colonialism and the extent to which this legacy still structures much of academic discourse through language, I have chosen to maintain this term for two reasons. The first is that it is a part of the discourse I am trying to reconstruct, and as such it reflects and captures a certain flavor that is pertinent to my larger point, that this literature was disciplinary and paternalistic as well as elitist. Purging the term from quotations or my discussion of this literature would obscure this. The second reason I have maintained this vocabulary is that the term *native* signifies very different things in different historical and social contexts. So while its use in a discussion of Africans is wholly repugnant, it has been maintained to some extent in the Americas in phrases such as "Native Americans" or "native peoples." The newer term *first nations* has not really been taken up in the discourse on Mexico's indigenous populations. And while I opt for *indigenous* whenever I am wholly in my own "voice" or to signify a shift in institu-

tional language, it too is a product of the disciplinary project I am describing, as will become clear.

2. While I have emphasized Vasconcelos and Gamio here, the "diagnostic quality" evident in these examples pervades the intellectual discourse of this period regardless of genre or subject-matter. For other prominent examples see A. Caso, *La existencia como económia y caridad* (Mexico City: Porrua, 1916) for a philosophical argument; A. J. Pani, *Hygiene in Mexico* (New York: G. P. Putnam's Sons, The Knickerbocker Press, 1917) for a discussion of social policy and problems; P. Henriquez Ureña, *Plenitud de América, ensayos escogidos* (Buenos Aires: Peña, del Giudice, 1952) for essays on Mexico's "new culture." These are just three examples of many that reflect the variety of this discourse.

3. For this iconographic detail I am indebted to an anonymous guard who was working at the SEP in 1997 when I first saw and photographed these murals. He asked why I was taking pictures and upon learning that I studied Mexican murals engaged me in a very nuanced discussion of the iconography of this particular panel. I have to admit that before our talk I had never noticed the skull; furthermore, it has not been a standard iconographic identification within the literature on this mural. To my knowledge, Leonard Folgarait is the first to have written about it in his 1998 publication *Mural Painting and Social Revolution in Mexico, 1920–1940* (Cambridge: Cambridge University Press). This anecdote, while it can't be held up as representative of the whole Mexican population, makes clear that for some Mexicans this art speaks volumes.

4. This strategy is not exclusive to Rivera; in fact, the belief that the communitarian values of Mexico's pre-Hispanic and contemporary indigenous cultures were evidence of proto-socialist organization was common in postrevolutionary intellectual circles. In particular, the Zapotecs from the isthmus of Tehuantepec were discussed in this way. See for example, M. Covarrubias, *Mexico South: The Isthmus of Tehuantepec* (New York: Alfred A. Knopf, 1967).

5. Rivera's "cultural *mestizaje*" is made all the more explicit in *Portrait of Mexico,* a book written by his biographer and friend, the socialist Bertram Wolfe, and illustrated by the artist. In this collaborative text, the two present a history of Mexico from pre-Hispanic times to the present, but preface this with their own diagnostic take on the "Mexican problem." Establishing a homology between the "land of many tierras" and its diverse populations, they too lament the difficulty of unifying a population that in its cultural variety mirrors the incomensurability of Mexico's many regions. While they value this diversity, they insist that it is rapidly becoming a thing of the past due to Mexico's transition into a nation-state and its incorporation into the global economy. They argue that the inevitability of this transition necessitates that the process be guided by the appropriate interests, namely their socialist agenda. To this end, they make recommendations throughout about how to help Mexico's native populations preserve what is "worthwhile" in their traditions while simultaneously incorporating them "into a free union of peoples on the basis of a common national, and ultimately international economy." It is clear throughout this book that, as usual, it is the preindustrial native that needs to brought into modernity, through governmental support, and that those aspects of communal life that hinder modernization must be eliminated. Bertram D. Wolfe, *Portrait of Mexico* (New York: Covici, Friede Publishers, 1937).

6. It is important to note that like many museums, the Museo Nacional de Antropología has undergone renovations since it opened in 1964. Increasingly the museum's displays are changing in response to criticism from Mexican intellectuals and international initiatives within museology. The ethnographic installations are currently being reorganized to more accurately reflect the hybridity of contemporary indigenous life. This is being accomplished through the inclusion of modern appliances and technologies, such as computers, in displays of domestic life. Furthermore, the struggle for self-definition, most fervently asserted by present-day Mayans, is acknowledged in text panels and photographs that undermine the vision of unified nationalism presented throughout the institution. Most significant, perhaps, has been the removal of the final hall. It has been replaced by a

temporary exhibition space. Nonetheless, while some of the most egregious offenses have been eliminated, the progressive and developmental narrative of the installations as a whole remains intact.

REFERENCES

Alvarez, S. E., E. Dagnino, and A. Escobar, eds. 1998. *Cultures of Politics/Politics of Cultures: Re-visioning Latin American Social Movements.* Boulder, Colo.: Westview Press.

Althusser, L. 1971. "Ideology and Ideological State Apparatuses." In *Lenin and Philosophy and Other Essays*, translated by B. Brewster, 121–73. New York: Monthly Review.

Barry, A., T. Osborne, and N. Rose, eds. 1996. *Foucault and Political Reason: Liberalism, Neo-Liberalism and Rationalities of Government.* Chicago: University of Chicago Press.

Bernal, I. 1968. *The Mexican National Museum of Anthropology.* London: Thames and Hudson.

Bennett, T. 1992. "Putting Policy into Cultural Studies." In *Cultural Studies*, edited by L. Grossbert, C. Nelson, and P. Treichler, 23–27. London: Routledge.

———. 1995. *The Birth of the Museum: History, Theory, Politics.* London: Routledge.

Brading, D. A. 1988. "Manuel Gamio and Official Indigenismo in Mexico." *Bulletin of Latin American Research* 7, no. 1:75–90.

Dean, M. 1996. "Foucault, Government and the Enfolding of Authority." In *Foucault and Political Reason: Liberalism, Neo-Liberalism and Rationalities of Government*, edited by A. Barry, T. Osborne, and N. Rosen, 209–29. Chicago: University of Chicago Press.

Deleuze, G. 1988. *Foucault*, translated by S. Hand. Minneapolis: University of Minnesota Press.

Foucault, M. 1995. *Discipline and Punish: The Birth of the Prison*, translated by A. Sheridan. New York: Vintage.

———. 1991. "Governmentality." In *The Foucault Effect: Studies in Governmentality*, edited by G. Burchell, C. Gordon, and P. Miller, 87–104. Chicago: University of Chicago Press.

———. 1990. "The Concern for Truth." In *Politics, Philosophy, Culture: Interviews and Other Writings, 1977–1984*, edited by L. D. Kritzman, 255–67. New York: Routledge.

———. 1984. "The Subject and Power." In *Art after Modernism: Rethinking Representation*, edited by B. Wallis, 417–32. New York: The New Museum of Contemporary Art and Boston: David R. Godine.

———. 1985. *The Use of Pleasure*, translated by R. Hurley. New York: Random House.

———. 1972. "Truth and Power." In *Power/Knowledge: Selected Interviews and Other Writings, 1972–1977*, edited by C. Gordon, 109–33. New York: Pantheon Books.

Gamio, M. 1926. "Incorporating the Indian into Mexican Society." In *Aspects of Mexican Civilization: Lectures on the Harris Foundation*, edited by M. Gamio and J. Vasconcelos, 105–29. Chicago: University of Chicago.

García-Canclini, N. 1995. *Hybrid Cultures: Strategies for Entering and Leaving Modernity*, translated by C. L. Chiappari and S. L. López. Minneapolis: University of Minnesota Press.

Giroux, H. A. 1997. *Pedagogy and the Politics of Hope: Theory, Culture, and Schooling.* Boulder, Colo.: Westview Press.

Gordon, C. 1991. "Governmental Rationality: An Introduction." In *The Foucault Effect: Studies in Governmentality*, edited by G. Burchell, C. Gordon, and P. Miller, 1–52. Chicago: University of Chicago Press.

Gramsci, A. 1971. *Selections from the Prison Notebooks*, translated and edited by Q. Hoare and G. N. Smith. London: Lawrence and Wishart.

Laclau, E., and C. Mouffe. 1985. *Hegemony and Socialist Strategy: Towards a Radical Democratic Politics.* London: Verso.

Miller, T. 1998. *Technologies of Truth.* Minneapolis: University of Minnesota Press.

Rivera, D., with G. March. 1960. *My Art, My Life.* New York: Dover.

Rose, N. 1996. "Governing 'Advanced' Liberal Democracies." In *Foucault and Political Reason: Liberalism, Neo-Liberalism and Rationalities of Government*, edited by A. Barry, T. Osborne, and N. Rose, 37–64. Chicago: University of Chicago Press.

Salgado, I. M., and M. C. Sánchez Bueno. 1962. "Estudio preliminar de las características generales del público." In *Consejo de Planeación e Instalación del Museo Nacional de Antropología. Informe general de las labores desarrollades durante, del 1° de enero al 31 de diciembre de 1961*, edited by L. Aveleyra and I. Marquina, 2–20. Mexico City: INAH, CAPFLE, SEP.

Vasconcelos, J. 1963. *A Mexican Ulysses: An Autobiography*, translated by W. R. Crawford. Bloomington: Indiana University Press.

———. 1926a. "Similarity and Contrast." In *Aspects of Mexican Civilization: Lectures on the Harris Foundation*, edited by M. Gamio and J. Vasconcelos, 105–29. Chicago: University of Chicago.

———. 1979. *The Cosmic Race: A Bilingual Edition*, translated by D. T. Jaén. Baltimore: Johns Hopkins University Press.

———. 1926b. "The Race Problem in Latin America." In *Aspects of Mexican Civilization: Lectures on the Harris Foundation*, edited by M. Gamio and J. Vasconcelos, 75–104. Chicago: University of Chicago.

Williams, R. 1976. *Keywords*. London: Fontana.

Wolfe, B. D. 1939. *Diego Rivera: His Life and Times*. New York: Alfred A. Knopf.

———. 1937. *Portrait of Mexico*. New York: Covici, Friede.

3

WORLD INSTITUTIONS, WORLD DISPOSITIONS

Curriculum in the World-Cultural Institution of Schooling

James G. Ladwig

The University of Newcastle, Newcastle, Australia, and
the University of Queensland, St Lucia, Australia

> Segregated and separated on earth, the locals meet the globals through the regular televised broadcasts of heaven. The echoes of the encounter reverberate globally, stifling all local sounds yet reflected by local walls, whose prison-like impenetrable solidity is thereby revealed and reinforced.
>
> —Zygmunt Bauman, *Globalization: The Human Consequences*

By now, questions of globalization and cultural hybridization, if not already passé, would be familiar to socially minded theorists of education. Clearly, many scholars and practitioners are attempting to understand how the recent rapidly changing social fabric of human existence impacts on, or carries implications for, our understanding of education and schooling. While much of this work is of great value and important, this essay comes at issues of globalization from a different starting point. That is, in this essay I attempt to demonstrate that a world theory of schooling and curriculum serves well as an explanation of some of the processes of globalization that have captured the attention of so many "globals."

Social commentators such as Bauman (1998) are quite correct to point out the new ways in which global societies are unjustly and starkly stratified by structures that segregate and separate "locals" and "globals." But, unlike many of my colleagues, I do not think that these global dynamics in themselves require a new theory of schooling. It seems to me that this stance has put the proverbial cart before the horse. What the processes of globalization have made clear is that our social-theoretical understandings of schooling never were all that powerful (Ladwig, in press). Rather than assume that a firm understanding of the processes of globalization will provide a better explanation of schooling, I would argue that a sound theory of the world institution of schooling serves as an important (though partial) explanation of the world order. For while the regulated cadences of schooling have indeed reverberated globally, through mind and body, it seems clear to me that if we are to better understand the nature and dynamics of the fault lines identified by globalization theorists, such as those between Bauman's locals and globals, at this historical juncture we need a theory that builds from the recognition that world institutions such as schools have been the building blocks of globalization all along. Toward this end, the essay below develops the insights of theorists of schooling as a world-cultural institution (Meyer et al. 1997) in relation to curriculum and the nature of the human subjects being produced, globally, by schools.

WHERE DOES THIS WORK FIT?

To begin, I would like to analytically position this work in relation to issues of globalization and cultural hybridity. There are some other positional relations that should become evident, but I make this positioning explicit for two reasons. The first of those is that I believe it would not be readily seen by many readers. The works I draw on have often been placed in opposition to each other, and this opposition itself is something I find unfortunate and unnecessary. My sense of this opposition relates to my second reason for what is admittedly a too brief excursion into extant globalization literature. That is, part of the reason I find existing theoretical oppositions unfortunate is that there remain, to my knowledge, huge theoretical gaps between competing theories, especially so within what I know of globalization analyses. To the extent I might lace rhizomatic threads within this space, I take this work to offer an as-yet-unarticulated theoretical strategy.

Throughout the English-speaking academic world, so-called globalization has become a central concern, especially over the past two decades or so. Indeed, across a wide range of disciplines—including sociology, psychology, philosophy, anthropology, history, literature, economics, and education—the academic literature currently dedicated to understanding social relations on a global scale is now vast. Following a long and protracted period of unresolved theoretical debate, the current centrality of the problem of globalization has been seen by some social theorists as a step beyond previous debates between structural and modernist theories, on the one hand, and so-called poststructural and postmodern theoretical transgressions on the other (Featherstone and Lash 1995). In such reinscriptions of past theories, analyses of globalization are said to offer new analytical languages based in metaphors of space, geography, and networks (Latour 1995).

Outside the field of educational research, very little is said about the functions of schooling in the larger networks of globalization studied. The major exception to this is that body of globalization literature that raises issues of national identity and citizenship. Yet within the noneducational literature on citizenship and its implications for education, most of the argumentation either (1) carries assumptions of a unified rational subject or (2) addresses issues of multiculturalism with a commodified conception of culture and identity. Strangely, this is often the case even within analyses of hybrid identities (Nederveen Pieterse 1995).

Within the field of education a large body of literature has begun to address questions of globalization, building on nearly every line of analysis found outside the educational literature. Commodified conceptions of culture are as common in educational research as they are outside of education. For example, many analyses of multicultural education are based on understandings of culture in which cultural identity is presumed to be represented by static, celebratory icons of so-called cultural difference. In fact, much of the popular research in multicultural education and most of the well-known multicultural curriculum reforms are based on constructions of culture embodied in objectified cultural artifacts, be it new canons of so-called Afrocentric knowledge, tokenistic celebratory "days," or cuisine (see McCarthy 1993 for commentary on such assumptions). The view of culture operating in such research and development is commodified in the sense that culture is seen to be identifiable in objects—either physical objects or objectified notions of time (a day) or objectified constructions of knowledge (a canon). As objects, such forms of cultural presentation become the commodity in the economics of political compromises.

As Homi K. Bhabha (1994) tells us, "Hybridity is the sign of the productivity of colonial power, its shifting forces and fixities; it is the name for the strategic reversal of the process of domination through disavowal. . . . For the colonial hybrid is the articulation of the ambivalent space where the rite of power is enacted on the site of desire, making its objects at once disciplinary and disseminatory" (112).

This is, of course, not the only body of educational research working within the problematic of globalization. In what can be seen as a distinct body of postcolonial analyses, many educational theorists have drawn from literary studies, for example, to redefined understandings of race and culture. In these analyses, a main emphasis has been on the historically contingent construction of race and the mutable role education has played within larger sociopolitical struggles over race. As an example, one path of this research highlights the ways in which even blatantly colonial forms of curriculum can, in certain historical constellations, work toward a counterhegemonic construction of race (McCarthy 1998). Another clear path of postcolonial analyses in education is in the articulation of cultural hybridity and its implication for feminist pedagogies (Singh 1995).

In this postcolonial educational research, I would argue that there is a very different and important understanding of culture operating. That is, while the political, macro-level, public representations of hybrid identities clearly form an axis of this research, it is built from a "deep" concept of culture in which the basic dispositions of subjectivities are at issue. As many authors within the social space of postcolonial analysis have pointed out, the notion of hybridity can only make any sense in relation to hegemony; it is this observation that reminds us that these constructions of postcolonial analysis are often set in opposition to analyses of educational inequality in which theories of cultural reproduction are said to carry presumptions about schooling smoothly functioning in a totalizing fashion (and, supposedly, lack sufficient notice of "human agency").

What I hope this framing of globalization literature and studies in cultural hybridity makes clear is that each current path of research that attempts to link schooling into larger studies of globalization carries its own theoretical limitations, and these limitations are often the basis for perceived oppositions. From this framing, the elements I seek to draw together from this work should be relatively clear. First, I work from a conception of culture that focuses on the "deep" dispositions that are often unconscious. This conception recognizes that culture is time-space sensitive, and is based on an understanding of practice. While not always the case, I find that this notion of culture (besides being more empirically accurate) is closely linked with sociopsychological studies of multiple subjectivities, and the basis on which I would claim that an analytical congruence exists between theories of hybrid micro-identities (as opposed to group political representations of hybridity) and poststructural analyses of multiple subjectivities (see Henriques et al. 1984).

At a deep cultural level, this link between hybridity and multiple subjectivity is, I think, not a contentious claim. Yet making this link explicit is an important step for my analysis; that is, where postcolonial studies of race, culture, and identity have been immensely helpful in articulating and describing the "realities" of life in contemporary societies, they have been weak in their structural sociological moments. Where Stuart Hall looks to link hybridity into a structural analysis, for example, he does so by reference to hegemony (Hall and du Gay 1996). Hall's specific history and connection with cultural Marxism make this link understandable, but that history does not make up for the limitations that concepts constructed for literary analysis bring into a postmodern, empirically based sociology. Simply put, the concept of hegemony remains potentially totalizing and/or highly reliant on modes of analysis that remain (at least for now) rhetorically unreliably within the state. Publicly justifying curriculum because it might be counterhegemonic is at best a politically risky proposition in many contexts.

Since the question of cultural hybridity can rely on a deep and dynamic concept of culture, and since that hybridity can be understood in terms of the cultural dispositions that are incorporated in multiple subjectivities (in singular bodies), it is possible to understand contemporary subjects (individuals) within the theoretical framework of cultural dispositions outlined in Pierre Bourdieu's sociologies of education, science, and the state (1996, 1998). Linked with an understanding of power, habitus, and social fields, this makes it possible then to understand cultural hybrids as individuals simultaneously operating within multiple social dynamics (legitimating principles in social fields) that are themselves interrelated and ultimately connected into a larger and dynamic societal (and global) structure of power. Whatever else we might think of this notion of a societal structure of power, it is clear that it is not singular and not static:

> The sociodicies through which dominant groups aim to produce "a theodicy of their own privilege," to quote Weber, do not come to us in the form of a unique and fully unified discourse, as the phrase "dominant ideology" would suggest.... While the structure of the field of power has undoubtedly included constants throughout the most varied historical configurations, such as, for instance, the fundamental opposition in the division of labor of domination between temporal and spiritual or cultural power holders—warriors and priests, *bellatores* and *oratores*, businessmen (sometimes called industrial knights) and intellectuals—it depends at any given time on the forms of capital implemented in the struggles for domination and on their relative weight in the structure. (Bourdieu 1996, 266)

Schooling, in this framing, is understood as an institution fundamental to the processes of the production and social distribution of capital (forms of power). The history of sociological analyses of education bears this out, but a further link needs articulation. As an institution intimately formed in the historical processes of modernity, schooling as a whole relies on biotechnical regimes of power (compare Foucault 1977 with Bourdieu 1998) that are themselves implicated in the processes of legitimation. Examples from the educational debates about intelligence and race are well known and illustrate how schooling forms bodies according to presumed structures of knowledge and power. The explicit link between moral codings of intelligence and racism are also abundantly clear when the historical uses of the concept of race are examined (see, e.g., Augstein 1996, and the well-known Gould 1981). Overall, then, one axis of the thesis I seek to construct would be positioned in the relations opened to examination in studies of cultural hybridity, in the interconnections between *a historically dynamic conception of multiple subjectivities* and conceptions of the *biotechnical regimes of our global networks*.

A Skeleton of a World Theory of Schooling

If there is a basic ground point from which this theory is being constructed, it is on the basis of an observation about the way in which schooling as a world-cultural institution operates in the production of educational inequalities. This observation is, of course, constructed within historically specific space-time parameters and is developed from a more detailed set of propositions about schooling. In past articulations, I have set out this observation in seven distinct propositions:

1. That the inhabitable planet has been divided into entities called nation-states, and this fact, in itself, represents the development of a world-cultural system.

2. That within most of the planet's nation-states, formal educational systems have been constructed.
3. That these educational systems are demonstrably quite similar and thereby mark a further advance of a world-culture.
4. That these modern educational systems, in every instance, are demonstrably associated with social inequality.
5. That schooling is demonstrably intertwined in the processes of producing each nation-state's societal inequality.
6. That a basic medium by which schools produce social inequality is knowledge, most obviously embodied in official and hidden curriculum.
7. That underlying the educational production of social inequality is the relationship between power and curriculum. (Ladwig 1996, 10–11.)

This articulation of a starting point for a theory of schooling itself builds from a wide array of educational theory and research, some of which is quite well known (Ladwig 1996). What is perhaps not clear about this starting point is the degree to which schooling is seen here as but one of those biotechnical regimes of our *global* networks.

Pace Ian Hunter (1994), I would argue that world development of schooling and its specific technologies has not been entirely accidental. While I might nearly agree that the modus operandi of school is strongly based in a biotechnical moral coding (a "pastoral duty," as Hunter calls it), it is also clear that alternative technologies of schooling have been available but not adopted. In addition to the research specifically questioning the role of schooling as a world-cultural institution (Boli and Ramirez 1986; Meyer, Kamens, and Benavot 1992), one can easily point to a large number of examples in which transnational organizations have directly influenced the development of specific forms of schooling, building educational systems of particular kinds around the globe. The most obvious agencies that have been involved in such developments include the United Nations Educational, Scientific, and Cultural Organization (UNESCO) and the World Bank (see Jones 1992). For the purposes of this essay, however, the task is to show how this very stark skeleton of a framework might be fleshed out in a broad theory of schooling, and to tease out some of the implications this view has for our understanding of curriculum and pedagogical reforms.

WHAT ARE THE TISSUES OF THIS THEORY?

Without going over old ground too much, recall that explanations of educational inequality have come to rely almost exclusively (there are some stalwart materialist Marxists still around) on notions of cultural difference to explain the degree to which students from dominated social groups fail. In this view, students who come to schooling from various cultural backgrounds that are not incorporated in school practices are globally excluded from formal school systems around the planet. As just two examples, whether we try to build this explanation from the work of Bourdieu and his notion of habitus, or from the work of Basil Bernstein and his notion of code (or, for that matter, from the work of some feminists and notions of masculine knowledges), our explanations for why social groups of students fail in schooling have come to rely on some notion of background or underlying cultural dispositions. While I have argued, and will continue to argue, that we do not adequately understand the patterns of exclusion and success linked to these dispositional differences, some general insights seem sensible and empirically defensible.

Following along the lines of what Bernstein and his colleagues call realization and recognition rules, it has been repeatedly demonstrated that specific forms of curricular knowledge are associated with the relative success of specific social groups (see Morias et al. 1992). While the specific social groups excluded from schooling vary from place to place around the globe, one main hypothesis here is that the forms and structures of knowledge typically sanctioned in schooling are made up from a relatively limited set and are relatively stable around the globe. This may not seem a particularly contentious claim, but it is one made with little systematic empirical verification and is in need of much further study.

The global overflow of "constructivist" pedagogies and Vygotskian psychological models (I have personally seen these models held up as the next wave of wondrous education on four continents) may well mark a shift in the emphasis that is called for in schools—that is, if schools manage to deliver what is now being asked of them. "More important," explains Reich, "these fortunate children learn how to conceptualise problems and solutions. The formal education of an incipient symbolic analyst thus entails refining four basic skills: abstraction, system thinking, experimentation, and collaboration" (229). Indeed, the research of James Gee and his colleagues raises very important questions about just whose interests are being served by the current educational restructuring moves to emphasize collaborative, information-dense pedagogies. Effectively what Gee, Hull, and Lankshear (1996) document is that the current collaboratively based school restructuring pedagogies ride in tandem with the demands of the newer forms of capitalism based on quality-control technologies and information technologies. The irony made clear is that these forms of pedagogy were once those held up as benchmarks of progressive pedagogy. (I should note that they also fit well into Bernstein's early-1970s criticisms of new-middle-class school reforms.)

The current message about these "newer" forms of pedagogy is rather mixed, indeed. While Reich (1992) and many others point out that these forms of pedagogy are accessible only to a very small minority in the information-based contexts of the planet, research into "successful school restructuring" in the United States has demonstrated that when students from a variety of traditionally educationally unsuccessful social backgrounds do face "authentic" pedagogy, the production of educational inequality is slowed (Lee and Smith 1995, 1997; Newmann and Associates 1996). This level of theoretical analysis is clearly a "next step" in building the broader theory of schooling, a step I would simply label a question of understanding the dynamics of institutionalized pedagogy.

I know of no one who is particularly optimistic about the chances of schooling universally shifting its pedagogical practices, particularly within the industrialized countries. This is especially clear when so-called alternative pedagogies are examined from a Foucauldian institutional view in which the relative stability of techniques of power within modern institutions becomes evident (Gore 1998). So it is when examining most school restructuring success stories that we are left with a rather more stark example of "the rich getting richer and the poor getting poorer." In this case, however, the basic capital is culture, and the rich may well look something like the crew of the starship *Enterprise*—every human speaking some variety of American English, and following the Federation code of ethics. This observation opens the steps from the institutional level to whatever forms of regional association the twenty-first century may bring, what we now call nation-states. I name this vaguely because I have in mind *whatever forms of organization sponsor schooling*. At the moment this is, by and large, a function of the state in most countries, but the current privatization of schooling taking place around the planet may well, in the very near future, change this in the so-called centers of the world systems.

By now, I would expect the reader to be wondering what this mapping of institutionalized, regulated schooling has to do with postcolonial conditions and cultural hybridity. In effect, a global theory of schooling needs to juxtapose the simultaneous ebbs and flows of social incorporation found in world institutions and the descriptive realities documented in studies of globalized hybridity. Central to this recognition of the dynamic nature of history, however, is also the realization that schooling as an institution has become a cultural pivot point for most people on this planet. Where I see striking similarities among various forms of "new" pedagogy around the globe, I also see striking similarity in the conditions in which cultural hybrids live, and a number of other well-documented forms of subjectivity typically associated with marginalized groups. That is, where cultural hybrids trespass across colonial boundaries—working-class youth, for example, who "make it" into middle- and upper-class professions—they experience similar dispositional incongruences. Another example of partially equivalent forms of multiple subjectivities has been discussed by Bill Green and Chris Bigum (1993), in this case built from questions about the effects of information technologies, which have also been discussed in relation to the "newer" subjectivities of "youth culture." Green and Bigum polemically point out that forms of adolescent subjectivity developed in relation to new forms of technology are partial, multiple, and possibly qualitatively new in historical terms. From this last example, one might well ask if the "aliens" in our classrooms are those humans who still cling to the hope of a unified subjectivity and spiritual wholeness.

When placed in relation to world institutional analyses, the way in which occidental, bureaucratic dispositions have become a world-cultural phenomenon becomes clear. John Meyer and his colleagues have articulated a much more specified notion of just what constitutes this ostensibly growing world culture. Not surprisingly, the culture Meyer and his colleagues see as related to the institution of schooling is decidedly bureaucratic:

> Cultural forces defining the nature of the rationalized universe and the agency of human actors operating under rationalized natural laws play a major causal role in social dynamics, interacting with systems of economic and political stratification and exchange to produce a highly expansionist culture.... In this cultural complex, a demystified, lawful, universalistic nature forms the common frame within which social life is embedded, and unitary moral laws and spiritual purposes are clearly differentiated from nature. Spiritual obligations and rights originally devolving from an active and interventionist god are now located in humans and their communities, making individuals the ultimate carriers of responsible purposive action. As legitimated actors having agency for themselves and others, individuals orient their action above all toward the pursuit of rationalized progress. (Meyer et al. 1997, 168)

Clearly, this image of the developing world culture is drawn from a keen understanding of pseudorational bureaucratic behavior and Weberian analyses of *zweckrational*, or means-ends rationality.

The Weberian quality of this analysis is of outmost importance because, although Meyer and colleagues claim that a world culture develops alongside of, or as part of, the globalization of the institution of schooling, it is not the case that such a global development leads to cultural homogeneity on a societal level. As they put it,

> Faithful and energetic enactment of this cultural framework yields collective authority: Proper actors reciprocally legitimate each other.... [Yet the] distinctive structure of actorhood that characterizes world society pushes the limits in this regard, for several reasons. First, no universal actor (world state) has central control or repressive capacity to limit lower-level action. Second, the universally legitimated actors of world society are defined as having similar goals, so competition for resources is enhanced. Third, legitimated actorhood operates at several levels (national, organizational or group, and individual) that partially compete with one another. Fourth, internal contradictions and inconsistences in world-cultural models make certain forms of struggle inevitable in world society. Taken together, these factors generate widespread conflict, mobilization, and change. (Meyer et al. 1997, 168–69)

Even if a monocultural human existence were a rationalized ideal of the world-cultural institution, the decoupling within that world-cultural institutional system makes cultural homogeneity not only implausible, but virtually impossible.

The place of schooling within the construction of these dispositional incongruences cannot be overstated, nor can they be written off as some historical accident. As Bourdieu (1998) says in his understandings of the state, "The monopolization of the universal is the result of a work of universalization which is accomplished within the bureaucratic field itself" (59). As part of the now global bureaucratic state mechanisms, any attempt to address multiple cultures will face the amazingly stable institutionalized dispositions of schooling.

WHY IS SUCH A THEORY NEEDED?

I noted at the outset of this essay that I am concerned with developing a theory that is strategically viable in two senses. First, I am wary of developing conceptual apparatuses that cannot in some way or another translate into politically intelligible and tactically useful understandings of schooling. I am under no illusion that discussions of multiple subjectivities, world-cultural institutions, or even cultural hybridity would be politically viable in most state politics I know. I would argue, however, that the conceptual framework outlined above could be readily translated into more conventional discussions of school reform, school restructuring, and equity, and could intervene in the current wave of effective schooling policy narratives (see Lingard, Ladwig, and Luke 1998). This attempt at a theoretical framework is intended to directly provide a way of radically rethinking conventional notions of school reform. The technical regimes of power spoken of earlier are, after all, the very organizational and pedagogical practices currently under keen inspection in the more radical experimentations of school restructuring. The redesigning of the central practices of schooling documented in some of the U.S. school restructuring literature, for example, can be seen as but one example of how the world's schools and teachers are attempting to find ways to help hybrid students break the code of occidental dispositions of power.

Many past attempts to understand these questions have at very least been caught in the antinomies of structural and poststructural paradigmatic ruptures, and soundly criticized for the degree to which new orthodoxies arise from old. Constructed in dual oppositional sets of relations, the conceptual framework here is, I think, a bit different. The central concepts adopted here are themselves deconstructive (hybrids do not reproduce, networks have a limited life span, states and fields of power are here conceived in relational and historically specific terms). Without the construction of a new, predefined utopia, but with some notion that there is more human justice to be had on this planet, the question of how schooling produces and distributes power is set in relation to relational and procedural understandings of the distribution of social goods. While I would hope these thoughts offer some alternative insights, I am under no illusion that they represent a completed theory—nor would I want to suggest that a world theory of schooling could ever be completed in an ahistorical sense.

As one who continually questions claims that we need yet another theory, I would like to close by way of a justification for this work. To set up this justification consider an observation about something I consider an educational paradox of postmodernity.

Adult literacy projects around the globe, as many scholars have shown, have been highly influenced by the works of people concerned with offering emancipatory literacy projects to a host of indigenous populations. Aside from the theoretical debates that might question the telos of such emancipatory projects, consider some basic realities in which these projects function.

It is not uncommon to find such emancipatory projects constructed within the political struggles of indigenous populations that face, still today, colonialized forms of education in which literacy is based in the language and institutional practices of the colonizers. Arguing for literacy programs based in indigenous languages, many critical literacy scholars will point out that underlying such struggles is much more than an issue of language per se; there is also, from the point of view of "center theorizing," an issue of cultural imperialism. (How the very notion of cultural imperialism enacts geocentric symbolic violence is another matter (see Luke and Luke, in press).

Given that within these struggles each project attempts to build organically from the unique cultures of the people facing such cultural imperialism, one might expect a great diversity in the dynamics of these struggles. But if we look at the details of what constitutes this cultural imperialism, we discover oppositions to those forms of bureaucratic, institutionalized culture found in most forms of schooling around the globe. In opposition to the individualization of modern schooling, many indigenous struggles maintain a defense of group "subjective" identity. In opposition to the linear demarcation of time and space found in the architecture and regimes of schooling, we find indigenous struggles maintaining a defense of more fluid understandings of geography, the land, and our place in the time and space we inhabit. In opposition to hierarchical forms of knowledge and classification systems, we find indigenous knowledges defying the simple syllogisms of Western logic. In sum, we find a relatively common rejection of occidental "bioregimes" of schooling (which includes unified and regimented subjects, space and time, and knowledge).

There is, however, a huge tension here. At one and the same time emancipatory educational projects seek to work outside of occidental bioregimes, and seek to help indigenous peoples construct or maintain their own identities and culture, other transnational networks are working very hard to exploit the land and resources on which these indigenous peoples live. And the legal/juridical power games that control the degree to which that land will be taken are not conducted in the culture of indigenous peoples; they are conducted in the same juridical/bureaucratic culture that has been rejected as irrelevant or at least seen to be related to the educational exclusion of dominated groups. That is, the basis of many of these political struggles will be ownership (of land and other resources) based on individual claims (or group representatives embodied by individuals), set out in juridical contracts based in linear understandings of time and space.

The paradox here should be fairly obvious. If these emancipatory projects were entirely successful in producing unified subjects whose culture was wholly based in the so-called traditional culture of indigenous peoples, these peoples would be entirely without resources and capital, thereby having no way of surviving to maintain any culture at all. Of course, the realities of such situations are much more complex than I just outlined; but the structure of the outline is meant to highlight the tensions, catch-22s, and paradoxes faced by virtually any social group that survives outside of the dominant occidental culture of world institutions, especially so when the exemplar context is placed in the peripheries of the world system. In this case, I presume we can be thankful that no regime is entirely totalizing and no subjectivity is entirely unified (i.e., translators and cultural defectors exist aplenty).

In answer to the question "Why do we need a global theory of schooling?" I would simply build on this brief description of one of the many paradoxes facing the world's cultures and point out that the role and functioning of schooling might best be understood in broad world terms. We can now safely predict that some form of inequality will be constructed and produced alongside the development of school systems; and we can reasonably assert that wherever these mechanisms of marginalization are put in place they, by themselves, will not be entirely successful in producing a totalized polity, nor totally unified subjects. In a manner consistent with much radical educational theorizing, the question of whether or not schools do produce inequalities could better be formulated, once again, as a question of which forms of inequality schools are currently producing (thereby opening more normative debates). The question of whether or not schools produce monocultural subjects could better be formulated as a question of which forms of hybridity are recognized and valued in schooling. And the question of whether or not schooling can be organized in a socially just manner could be better formulated as a question of how to produce more equitable and just distributions of educational capitals (a question that is only answerable in relation to how educational capitals convert into other capitals, of course).

In a sense, then, the intent of this theoretical framework is to provide a way to formulate traditional research concerns about equity in a manner that neither presumes a utopian and authoritarian ideal nor gives up on the possibility of developing transportable, systemic strategies of school reform. While questions of the production and reproduction of social inequalities have attracted substantial attention from radical educational theory and research, the role of the institution of schooling primarily has served as an object of critique. Historically, this critique has developed at the very moment when that institution has gone global. The fact that schooling is now a world-cultural institution serves as a reminder that there is little known about ways in which the technical and bureaucratic mechanisms of institutionalized schooling could be deployed in more equitable and just manner.

We are, then, a long way from making any practical and systemic assertions about how to build schooling differently. Since we know that the practices of schooling track along global transnational networks, and that many nation-states are facing attempts to build schooling more or less equitably from nation-state to nation-state, it seems advisable for those of us concerned about the marginalizing effects of school to begin a rather collective attempt to more systematically understand the relations between our historically dynamic multiple subjectivities and the biotechnical regimes of schooling. It seems clear that whatever plausible alternative normative positions may be developed, they will be simultaneously context-specific and globally partially equivalent. To the small extent a world theory of schooling might assist the endeavor to find partially transportable alternative and just pedagogies, its purpose would be served.

REFERENCES

Augstein, H. F., ed. 1996. *Race: The Origins of an Idea, 1760–1850.* Bristol, U.K.: Thoemmes Press.
Bauman, Z. 1998. *Globalization: The Human Consequences.* Cambridge: Polity Press.
Bhabha, H. K. 1994. *The Location of Culture.* London: Routledge.
Boli, J., and F. O. Ramirez. 1986. "World Culture and the Institutional Development of Mass Education." In *Handbook of Theory and Research for the Sociology of Education,* edited by J. G. Richardson, 65–90. New York: Greenwood Press.
Bourdieu, P. 1996. *The State Nobility,* translated by L. C. Clough. Oxford: Polity Press.
———. 1998. *Practical Reason.* Oxford: Polity Press.
Deleuze, G., and F. Guatarri. 1983. *Anti-Oedipus,* translated by R. Hurley, M. Seem, and H. R. Lane. Minneapolis: University of Minnesota Press.
Featherstone, M., and S. Lash. 1995. "Globalization, Modernity and the Spatialization of Social Theory: An Introduction." In *Global Modernities,* edited by M. Featherstone, S. Lash, and R. Robertson, 1–24. London: Sage.
Foucault, M. 1977. *Discipline and Punish,* translated by Alan Sheridan. New York: Pantheon Books.
Gee, J., G. Hull, and C. Lankshear. 1996. *The New Work Order: Behind the Language of the New Capitalism.* Sydney: Allen and Unwin.
Gore, J. 1993. *The Struggle for Pedagogies: Critical and Feminist Discourses as Regimes of Truth.* London: Routledge.
———. 1998. "On the Limits to Empowerment through Critical and Feminist Pedagogies." In *Power/Knowledge/Pedagogy: The Meaning of Democratic Education in Unsettling Times,* edited by D. Carlson and M. W. Apple. Boulder, Colo.: Westview Press.
Gould, S. J. 1981. *The Mismeasure of Man.* New York: W. W. Norton.
Green, B. and C. Bigum. 1993. "Aliens in the Classroom." *Australian Journal of Education* 37, no. 2:119–41.
Hall, S., and P. du Gay, eds. 1996. *Questions of Cultural Identity.* London: Sage.
Henriques, J., W. Holloway, C. Urwin, C. Venn, and V. Walkerdine. 1984. *Changing the Subject: Psychology, Social Regulation, and Subjectivity.* London: Methuen.
Hunter, I. 1994. *Rethinking the School.* Sydney: Allen and Unwin.
Jones, P. W. 1992. *World Bank Financing of Education: Lending, Learning and Development.* London: Routledge.
Ladwig, J. G. 1994. "For Whom This Reform: Outlining Educational Policy as a Social Field." *British Journal of Sociology of Education* 15, no. 3:341–63.
———. 1996. *Academic Distinctions: Theory and Methodology in the Sociology of School Knowledge.* London: Routledge.
———. 1999. "Where Are We?: An Essay on the Limits of Contemporary Social Analyses of Educational Governance." *Discourse: Studies in the Cultural Politics of Education* 20, no. 2: 295–303.
Latour, B. 1993. *We Have Never Been Modern.* Cambridge, Mass.: Harvard University Press.
Lee, V. E., and J. B. Smith. 1995. "Effects of High School Restructuring and Size Gains in the Achievement and Engagement for Early Secondary Students." *Sociology of Education* 68, no. 4:241–70.

————. 1997. "How High School Organization Influences the Equitable Distribution of Learning in Mathematics and Science." *Sociology of Education* 70, no. 2:128–50.

Lingard, B., J. Ladwig, and A. Luke. 1998. "School Effects in Postmodern Conditions." In *Effective for Whom? School Effectiveness and the School Improvement Movement*, edited by R. Slee, S. Tomlinson, and G. Wenier, 84–100. London: Falmer Press.

Luke, A., and C. Luke. In press. "The Complexity of Cultural Globalization: Implications for Educational Policy." In *Globalization and Educational Policy*, edited by N. Burbules and B. Torres. New York: Routledge.

McCarthy, C. 1993. "After the Canon: Knowledge and Ideological Representations in the Multicultural Discourse of Curriculum Reform." In *Race, Identity and Representation in Education*, edited by C. McCarthy and W. Crichlow, 289–305. London: Routledge.

————. 1998. *The Uses of Culture*. New York: Routledge.

Meyer, J. W., D. H. Kamens, and A. Benavot. 1992. *School Knowledge for the Masses: World Models and National Primary Curricular Categories in the Twentieth Century*. London: Falmer Press.

Meyer, J. W., et al. 1997. "World Society and the Nation-State." *American Journal of Sociology* 103, no. 1:144–81.

Morais, A., F. Fontinhas, and I. Neves. 1992. "Recognition and Realisation Rules in Acquiring School Science—The Contribution of Pedagogy and Social Background of Students." *British Journal of Sociology of Education* 13: 247–70.

Nederveen Pieterse, J. P. 1995. "Globalization as Hybridization." In *Global Modernities*, edited by M. Featherstone, S. Lash, and R. Robertson, 45–68. London: Sage.

Newmann, F., and Associates. 1996. *Authentic Achievement*. San Francisco: Jossey-Bass.

Reich, R. B. 1992. *The Work of Nations*. New York: Vintage Books.

Singh, P. 1995. "Voicing the 'Other', Speaking for the 'Self': Disrupting the MetaNarratives of Educational Theorizing with Poststructural Feminisms." In *After-Postmodernism: Education, Politics and Identity*, edited by R. Smith and P. Wexler, 182–206. London: Falmer Press.

4

GLOBALIZING PEDAGOGIES

Power, Resentment, and the Renarration of Difference

Cameron McCarthy

University of Illinois, Urbana-Champaign

Greg Dimitriadis

State University of New York, Buffalo

INTRODUCTION

Over the years, we have come to see multiculturalism—as a set of propositions about identity, knowledge, power, and change in education—as a kind of normal science, a form of disciplinarity of difference in which the matter of alterity has been effectively displaced as a supplement. On the terms of its present trajectory, multiculturalism can be properly diagnosed as a discourse of power that attempts to manage the extraordinary tensions and contradictions existing in modern life that have invaded social institutions, including the university and the school. At the heart of its achievement, multiculturalism has succeeded in freezing to the point of petrification its central object: "culture." Within the managerial language of the university, *culture* has become a useful discourse of containment, a narrow discourse of ascriptive property in which particular groups are granted their nationalist histories, their knowledges, and alas, their experts. Cultural competence then becomes powerfully deployed to blunt the pain of resource scarcity and to inoculate the hegemonic knowledge paradigms in the university from the daylight of subjugated knowledges and practices.

It is a wish fulfillment on the part of university bureaucrats, however, to attempt to hold at bay the extraordinary social currents unleashed in popular life now bearing down upon the modern subjects that inhabit contemporary industrial societies. These currents can be located, in part, in the destabilizing political

70

economy and cultural imperatives unleashed in the push and pull of globalization and localization. On the one hand, the tensions and contradictions of economic reorganization, downsizing, and instability in the labor market have spawned paranoia and uncertainty among the working and professional classes. On the other hand, culture and ideology ignite the false clarity of essential place—essential home—and the attendant practices of moral and social exclusionism. These dynamic forces have taken hold in the "body politic," so to speak. They reveal themselves at the level of the subject in terms of excess of desires, unfulfilled appetites, incompleteness and general insecurity, anger and violent passions, frustrations and resentment. At the level of social institutions these tensions of unfulfillment must be understood as a problem of social integration of difference in a time of scarcity. The educational project then becomes a site of unbridled consumerism—shopping for futures in the context of what C. L. R. James calls "the struggle for happiness" (1993, 166).

For cultural critics like ourselves, a key place to read these dynamics is at the level of the popular. We therefore want to take the subjects of diversity, knowledge, and power to a place that is normally considered outside the circuit of the education field itself, to the end point and margin of education, to the terrain of popular culture and its pedagogies of wish fulfillment and desire. *Desire* is understood here as a productive agency of lack, the excess rising below and above needs, the latent wish for totality and completeness in a context of containment, limits, and constraints—power, disguised and raw.

In so doing, we want to shift attention from the multiculturalist complaint over current modes of teaching and curriculum per se to the broader issue of the cultural reproduction of difference and the coordination of racial identities—what Larry Grossberg (1992) calls the "organization of affect." We want to look at the problem of diversity and difference in our time as a problem of social integration of modern individuals and groups into an increasingly bureaucratic, commodified, and deeply colonized and stratified life world. All of this raises the stakes for the practices of cultural reproduction and their role in identity formation, foregrounding the connections between the production and reproduction of popular cultural form and the operation of power in daily life. *Power* is understood here as a modern force in the Foucauldian sense, inciting and producing certain possibilities, subject positions, relations, limits, and constraints. Power in this sense does not simply prohibit or repress. It is a force that is dispersed. It circulates. It is not outside relations; it *produces* relations. It is not simply a question of who or what exercises power, but how power is exercised in the concrete (Hall 1980).

Power is above all discursive—technologies and practices of "truth" that deeply inform how social individuals conduct themselves in relation to each other in the domain of the popular. This is the whole area that Michel Foucault calls "governmentality": the site at which state, industry/economy, and education meet the massive technologies of textual production and meaning construction associated with media and the popular arts. The locus of power struggles in the modern society is not now to be found pure and simple in the classic sites of state politics, labor-capital arm wrestling, or bulldozing actions of civil rights and union-based political actors and their detractors. Modern power struggles are quintessentially located in the deeply contested arena of the popular, the domain of struggles over social conduct, popular commitments, anxieties and desires, and ultimately, the disciplining of populations (Miller 1998).

The cultural Marxist C. L. R. James similarly maintained that understanding popular culture was critical to understanding the play of power in modern life. In critical ways, as James asserts in such books as *American Civilization* (1993), one can get a better insight into the tensions and contradictions of contemporary society by observing and interpreting popular culture than by analyzing canonical educational texts. James makes this argument in a radical way, in his essay "The Popular Arts and Modern Society." As he explains, "It is in the serious study of, above all, Charles Chaplin, Dick Tracy, Gasoline Alley, James Cagney, Edward G. Robinson, Rita Hayworth, Humphrey Bogart, genuinely popular novels like those of Frank Yerby (*Foxes of Harrow, The Golden Hawk, The Vixen, Pride's Castle*) . . . that you find the clearest ideological expression of the sentiments and deepest feelings of the American people and a great window into the future of America and the modern world. This insight is *not* to be found in the works of T. S. Eliot, of Hemingway, of Joyce, of famous directors like John Ford or Rene Clair" (119). What James is pointing toward through this revisionary strategy is the fact that what we call popular culture is our modern art, a modern art deeply informed by and informative of the crises and tensions of cultural integration and reproduction in our time.

The tensions indexed in popular art forms have been inextricably complicated by global pressures working on and through popular media industries today. Multinational companies are consolidating at the point of distribution while proliferating at the point of production. Hence, consumers around the globe have a seemingly increasing array of "choices" about which products they will consume today, products that are picked up and used in a variety of ways by many and differently situated audiences. However, these products are also forged in the service of increasingly few, vertically integrated multinationals, thus exerting a key counterpressure to the above. The result, as Morley and Robins (1995) tell us, is a constant contest between homogeneity and heterogeneity in cultural texts and the kinds of identities they enable. Social integration and reproduction have become, in turn, much more complex phenomena that need to be explored and interrogated in multiple sites.

One of the principal crises of social integration in modern life is the crisis of race relations. We are defining racial antagonism, in this essay, as an effect of the competition for scarce material and symbolic resources in which strategies of group affiliation and group exclusion play a critical role. This crisis of racial antagonism must be seen within the historical context of the contradictions of modern society and the rapid changes taking place in the material reality and fortunes of people, their environments, the institutional apparatuses that govern and affect their lives, their relations with each other, and their sense of location in the present and in the future. Rapid changes of this kind have meant rapid movement and collision of peoples and media images across the globe, disrupting the traditional isomorphism between self, place, and culture. Above all, as Arjun Appadurai (1996) has argued, these processes have necessitated a diremption of the central site of the work of the imagination from the ecclesiastic arena of high art and aesthetics to the banality of everyday practices and the wish fulfillment of the great masses of the people across the globe, from the United States to the Caribbean and beyond.

These tensions, as one of us has argued elsewhere, must be foregrounded in any discussion of the resurgence of racial antagonism and the accompanying restlessness among the working and professional white middle classes (McCarthy 1998). In what follows, we try to understand these developments by reading patterns of recoding and renarration in public life as foregrounded in popular culture and policy discourses. Though we focus, by and large, on the United States, these issues are entirely imbricated in complex and disjunctive global processes. We direct attention in this area to the twin processes of racial simulation or the constant fabrication of racial identity through the production of the pure space of racial origins and resentment (the process of defining one's identity through the negation of the other). We look at the operation of these two processes in popular culture and education. We argue that these two processes operate in tandem in the prosecution of the politics of racial exclusion in our times, informing key policy debates.

The Public Court of Racial Simulation

Highlighting the centrality of simulation and resentment foregrounds the fact that American middle-class youth and suburban adults "know" more about innercity black and Latino youth through electronic mediation—particularly film and television (e.g., the show *Cops*)—than through personal or classroom interaction, or even textbooks. Yet these processes are coconstitutive, as school textbooks, like academic books, generally have become part of a prurient culture industry with their high-definition illustrations, their eclectic treatment of subject matter, and their touristic, normalizing discourses of surveillance of marginalized groups. In this sense, education (and multicultural education in particular) is articulated to popular culture in ways that implicate broader cultural imperatives.

The logics here are multiple and complex. Hence, critical pedagogues like Steinberg and Kincheloe (1997) are correct to note the ways in which popular texts and their complex pleasures and pedagogies are elided from dominant classroom culture today, an insight underscored by an important body of work in cultural studies and education (see, e.g., Giroux 1996). In this sense, school life is largely divorced from the realities of the popular. However, in another and equally important sense, schools are, in fact, entirely imbricated in the kinds of market logics and imperatives so intrinsic to popular culture. As Andy Green (1997) notes, for example, movements for "school choice" index the ways schools are accommodating, not contesting, dominant discourses of consumer capitalism. These discourses are implicated at all levels of the educational process—from decisions about policy and administration to the situated realities of the classroom. As such, Ruth Vinz calls attention to the "shopping mall" approach to multicultural education so prevalent today, giving a most compelling (hypothetical) example:

> On Monday of a given week, students begin their unit on Native Americans. They learn that Native Americans lived in teepees, used tomahawks to scalp white folks, wore headdresses, and danced together around a fire before eating their meal of blue corn and buffalo meat. By Wednesday of the same week, literature is added as an important cultural artifact; therefore, one or two poems (sometimes including Longfellow's "Hiawatha") represent tribal life of the past and present. By Friday, students take a trip to The Museum of the American Indian with its unsurpassed collection of artifacts and carry home their own renditions of teepees, tomahawks, or headdresses that they made during their art period. (Vinz, in press)

The following week, she notes, students might continue their virtual tour of the globe, moving to, for example, Latin American cultures. As Vinz makes clear, dominant approaches to multicultural education evidence a kind of market logic, putting multiple and fabricated cultural products at the fingertips of students, so that they may consume these products in very superficial ways. This "we are the world" approach to education elides the complexity and tension of the emerging global reality, making it one more product for consumers to consume in simple, and simply unproductive, ways.

In this sense, educational institutions are always in sync with popular culture in terms of strategies of incorporation and mobilization of racial identities. Indeed, we live in a time when "pseudoevents" fomented in media-driven representations have usurped any relic of reality beyond that which is staged or performed—driving, it is crucial to note, incredibly deep and perhaps permanent wedges of difference between the world of the suburban dweller and her inner-city counterpart. Daniel Boorstin (1975) writes that "we have used our wealth, our literacy, our technology, and our progress to create a thicket of unreality which stands between us and the facts of life" (3). These Durkheimian "facts of life"—notions of what, for example, black people and Latinos are like—are invented and reinvented in the media, in popular magazines, in newspaper and in television, music, and popular film. As critics such as Len Masterman (1990) point out, by the end of his teenage years, the average student will have spent more time watching television than he would have spent in school. In the United States, it is increasingly television and film that educate American youth about race. Here again, popular culture and dominant educational imperatives are mutually articulated in complex ways.

RESENTMENT, IDENTITY-FORMATION, AND POPULAR CULTURE

In his *On the Genealogy of Morals* (1967), Friedrich Nietzsche conceptualized resentment as the specific practice of identity displacement in which the social actor consolidates his identity by a complete disavowal of the merits and existence of his social other. A sense of self, thus, is only possible through an annihilation or emptying out of the other, whether discursively or materially. Understanding Nietzsche's notion of resentment is crucial, for, as Robert Soloman (1990) argues, contemporary politics are "virtually defined by resentment" (278). Practices of ethnocentric consolidation and cultural exceptionalism are evident on a global scale and now characterize much of the tug-of-war over educational reform and multiculturalism—and the stakes could not be any higher for all parties involved.

Resentment in late-twentieth-century society is the project of the disoriented, white, working and professional classes, confronted with the panoply of difference that marks the institutional and social environment in which modern subjects live in industrialized societies. Indeed, resentment has become perhaps *the* preeminent trope in which (and through which) "whiteness" is lived in the United States today. Whiteness is an unspoken norm, made pure and real only in relation to that which it is not. "Its fullness," as Michelle Fine and Lois Weis (1998) note, "inscribes, at one and the same time, its emptiness and presumed innocence" (156–57). Offering a key example, Fine and Weis explore, in telling ethnographic detail, the saliency of resentment for the white, working-class men of Jersey City, New Jersey, and Buffalo, New York, two cities ravaged by de-industrialization. As they note, these men who have lost the economic and cultural stability of the past blame "ethnic others" for their condition. While the marginalized black men Fine and Weis interview (as part of the same research project) are more apt to offer critiques of "the system," white men ignore such considerations. Personal resentment reigns supreme. Larger structures, the structures that have traditionally supported and served them, are left uninterrogated and naturalized. "Assuming deserved dominance," they write, "[white working-class men] sense that their 'rightful place' is being unraveled, by an economy which they argue privileges people of color over white men in the form of affirmative action, and by pressure from blacks and Latinos in their neighborhoods wherein they feel that their physical place is being compromised" (133). Hence, resentment has become a key way to buck a growing and, for these men, painful tide of difference. This sense of resentment is reinforced and undergirded by several key discourses made available in popular culture and academic circles today—discourses that seek to manage the extraordinary complexities so marking contemporary cultural life. These discourses have become most salient for white men, but they cannot be and have not been so contained. Rather, they proliferate in complex and contradictory ways, offering and enabling multiple effects for differently situated groups and individuals, both in the United States and beyond. These discourses now dominate the public sphere and involve the critical process of the renarration of social identities in a time of ever-widening economic and cultural anxiety. We will limit our discussion to four such discourses. First, we would like to call attention to *the discourse of origins* as revealed, for example, in the Eurocentric/Afrocentric debate over curriculum reform. Discourses of racial origins rely on the simulation of a pastoral sense of the past in which Europe and Africa are available to American racial combatants without the noise of their modern tensions, contradictions, and conflicts. For Eurocentric combatants such as William Bennett (1994) or George Will (1989), Europe and America are a self-evident and transcendent cultural unity. For Afrocentric combatants, Africa and the diaspora are one "solid identity," to use the language of Molefi Asante (1993). Proponents of Eurocentrism and Afrocentrism are themselves proxies for larger impulses and desires for stability among the middle classes in American society in a time of constantly changing demographic and economic realities. The immigrants are coming! Jobs are slipping overseas into the third world! Discourses of Eurocentrism and Afrocentrism travel in a time warp to an age when the gods stalked the earth.

These discourses of racial origins provide imaginary solutions to groups and individuals who refuse the radical hybridity that is the historically evolved reality of the United States and other major Western metropolitan societies. The dreaded line of difference is drawn around glittering objects of heritage and secured with the knot of ideological closure. The university itself has become a playground of the war of simulation. Contending paradigms of knowledge are embattled as combatants release the levers of atavism, holding their faces in their hands as the latest volley of absolutism circles in the air.

For example, Michael Steinberg (1996) tells the story of his first job (he was hired during the 1980s) as "the new European intellectual and cultural historian at a semi-small, semi-elite, semi-liberal arts college" in the Northeast. As Steinberg notes, during a departmental meeting, he unwittingly contradicted the hegemonic hiring practices of his new institution by "voting for the appointment to the history department of an African Americanist whose teaching load would include the standard course on the Civil War and Reconstruction." Several minutes after the meeting, one of the white academic elders of this northeastern college informed Steinberg that (a) his function as a European intellectual was "to serve as the guardian of the intellectual and curricular tradition"; (b) that he should "resist at all costs the insidious slide from the party of scholarship to the party of ideology"; and (c) that if he "persisted in tipping the scales of the department from tradition to experimentation and from scholarship to ideology" he would be digging his own grave insofar as his own "traditionally defined academic position would be the most likely to face elimination by a newly politicized institution" (105). Unwittingly, Steinberg had been thrown pell-mell into the war of position over origins in which the resources of the history department he had just entered were under the strain of the imperatives of difference.

A second resentment discourse at work in contemporary life and popular culture is *the discourse of nation.* This discourse is foregrounded in a spate of recent ads by multinational corporations such as IBM, United and American airlines, MCI, and General Electric (GE). These ads both feed on and provide fictive solutions to the racial anxieties of the age. They effectively appropriate multicultural symbols and redeploy them in a broad project of coordination and consolidation of corporate citizenship and consumer affiliation.

The marriage of art and economy, as Stuart Ewen (1988) defines advertising, is now commingled with the exigencies of ethnic identity and nation. One moment, the semiotic subject of advertising is a free American citizen in the open seas, sailing up and down the Atlantic or the translucent aquamarine waters of the Caribbean sea. In another, the free American citizen is transported to the pastoral life of the unspoiled, undulating landscape of medieval Europe. Both implicate a burgeoning consumer culture undergirded by the triumph of consumer capitalism on a global scale.

Hence, the recent GE "We Bring Good Things to Life" ad (which plays quite regularly on the CNN and ABC television networks) in which GE is portrayed as a latter-day Joan of Arc fighting the good fight of American entrepreneurship overseas, bringing electricity to one Japanese town. In the ad, GE breaks through the cabalism of foreign language, bureaucracy, and unethical rules in Japan to procure the goal of the big sell. The American nation can rest in peace as the Japanese nation succumbs to superior U.S. technology.

Third, there is *the discourse of popular memory and popular history*. This discourse suffuses the nostalgic films of the last decade or so. Films such as *Dances with Wolves* (1990), *Bonfire of the Vanities* (1990), *Grand Canyon* (1993), *Falling Down* (1993), *Forrest Gump* (1994), *A Time to Kill* (1996), *The Fan* (1997), *Armageddon* (1998), and *Saving Private Ryan* (1998) foreground a white middle-class protagonist who appropriates the subject position of the persecuted social victim at the mercy of myriad forces—from "wild" black youth in Los Angeles (in *Grand Canyon*), to Asian store owners who do not speak English well (in *Falling Down*), to a black baseball player, living the too-good life in a moment of corporate downsizing (in *The Fan*). All hark back to the "good old days" when the rules were few and exceedingly simple for now-persecuted white men.

Joel Schumaker's *A Time to Kill* is a particularly good example here, offering key pedagogical insight about social problems concerning difference from the perspective of the embattled white suburban dweller. The problem with difference is, in Schumaker's world, symptomatic of a crisis of feeling for white suburban middle classes—a crisis of feeling represented in blocked opportunity and wish fulfillment, overcrowding, loss of jobs, general insecurity, crime, and so forth. The contemporary world has spun out of order, and violence and resentment are the coping strategies of such actors.

In *A Time to Kill*, Schumaker presents us with the world of the "New South," Canton, Mississippi, in which social divides are extreme and blacks and whites live such different lives that they might as well be on separate planets. But this backwater of the South serves as a social laboratory in which to explore a burning concern of suburban America: retributive justice. When individuals break the law and commit acts of violent antisocial behavior, the upstanding folks in civil society, the film argues, are then justified in seeking their expulsion or elimination. The film thus poses the rather provocative question: When is it respectable society's "time to kill"? Are there circumstances in which retribution, revenge, and resentment are warranted? The makers of *A Time to Kill* resoundingly say "Yes!" This answer is impervious to class or race or gender. As a technology of truth, the film works to piece together a plurality of publics.

In order to make the case for retributive justice, Schumaker puts a black man at the epicenter of this white normative discourse—what Charles Murray (1984) calls "white popular wisdom." What would you do if your ten-year-old daughter was brutally raped and battered, pissed on, and left for dead? You would want revenge. This is a role play that has been naturalized to mean white victim, black assailant—the Willy Horton shuffle. In *A Time to Kill*, however, the discourse is inverted: The righteously angry are a black worker and his family, as two redneck assailants brutally rape and nearly kill his daughter. Carl Lee, the black lumberyard worker, gets back at these two callous criminals by shooting them down on the day of their arraignment; one brutal act is answered by another. One is a crime, the other, righteous justice. Crime will not pay. In this revenge drama, the message of retributive justice is intended to override race and class lines. We are living in the time of an eye for an eye. The racial enemy is in our private garden. In the face of bureaucratic incompetence we have to take the law into our own hands.

These films are steeped in nostalgia, enmeshed in the project of rewriting history from the perspective of bourgeois anxieties and the feelings of resentment that often drive them. This project is realized perhaps most forcefully in the wildly successful *Forrest Gump*. A special-effects masterwork, this film literally interpolates actor Tom Hanks into actual and re-created historical footage of key events in U.S. history, renarrating the latter part of the twentieth century in ways that blur the line between fact and fiction. Here, the peripatetic Gump steals the spotlight from the civil rights movement, Vietnam War protesters, the feminist movement, and so forth. Public history is overwhelmed by personal consumerism and wish fulfillment. "Life," after all, "is like a box of chocolates. You never know what you're gonna get." You might get Newt Gingrich. But who cares? History will absolve the American consumer.

Finally, we wish to call attention to *the conversationalizing discourses of the media culture.* From the television talk shows of Oprah Winfrey and Jenny Jones to the rap music of Tupac Shakur, to pseudoacademic books like *The Bell Curve, The Hot Zone,* and *The Coming Plague;* to self-improvement texts like *Don't Sweat the Small Stuff . . . and It's All Small Stuff,* these examples from popular culture all psychologize and seemingly internalize complex social problems, managing the intense feelings of anxiety that are so much a part of contemporary cultural life. Television talk shows, for example, reduce complex social phenomena to mere personality conflicts between guests, encouraging them to air their differences before encouraging some kind of denouement or resolution. Histories of oppression are thus put aside as guests argue in and through the details of their private lives while mediated, as they often are, by so-called experts. Racial harmony becomes a relative's acceptance of a "biracial" child. Sexual parity is reduced to a spouse publicly rejecting an adulterous partner. Psychologistic explanations for social phenomena reign supreme, and are supported by a burgeoning literature of self-improvement texts that posit poor self-esteem as the preeminent societal ill today. These popular texts and media programs are pivotal in what Deborah Tannen (1998) calls the "Argument Culture," in which the private is the political, and politics is war by other means.

Identities are thus being formed and re-formed—"produced," following Edward Said—in this complex social moment, where the *global* "tide of difference" is being met by profound renarrations of history. It is precisely this kind of rearticulation and recoding that one of us has called "nonsynchrony" (McCarthy 1998). Here we have tried to draw attention to how these complicated dynamics operate in debates over identity and curriculum reform, hegemonic cultural assertions in advertising, popular film, and in the conversationalizing discourses of contemporary popular culture. Further, as we have shown, these discourses are imbricated in an emergent popular culture industry, one that has radically appropriated the new to consolidate the past. This is the triumph of a nostalgia of the present as "difference" comes under the normalizing logics and disciplinary imperatives of hegemonic power. Diversity, as such, can sell visits to theme parks as well as it can sell textbooks. Diversity can sell AT&T and MCI long-distance calling cards as well as the new ethnic stalls in the ethereal hearts of the shopping mall. And sometimes, in the most earnest of ways, diversity lights up the whole world and makes it available to capitalism.

Educational Policy and the Pedagogy of Resentment

What is important and most disturbing, we wish to note, is that this kind of diversity is also increasingly informing—indeed *producing*, in the Foucauldian sense—educational policy on both the right and left, as evidenced by several key debates now circulating in the public sphere. These debates have had very real material effects on the dispossessed, those quickly losing the (albeit meager) benefits of affirmative action (e.g., California's Proposition 209), bilingual education (through California's Proposition 227—the so-called English for the Children initiative), and need-based financial aid. The idea of high-quality (public) education as the great potential equalizer—a good in and of itself—is now being lost to the bitter resentments at the heart of contemporary culture, lost to petty market logics and the free-standing subject-positions so enabled by them. The pressures of globalization—for example, new patterns of immigration, the proliferation of media images, or the ravages of deindustrialization—have been met here and elsewhere by calls for the weakest kinds of self-serving "diversity." This diversity, as noted, is encouraged by a consumer capitalism that is entirely linked to the imperatives of resentment explored throughout. In a particularly stark example of this process, Martin Luther King Jr.'s revolutionary dream of the day when his "four little children will . . . live in a nation where they will not be judged by the color of their skin, but by the content of their character," has been appropriated by right-wing commentators like Shelby Steele (1990) to contest the advances of affirmative action.

How the discourse of resentment has (explicitly) propelled the conservative agenda here is fairly obvious. A new and seemingly beleaguered middle class is looking to recapture its once unquestioned privilege by advocating "color-blind" hiring and acceptance policies (in the case of affirmative action) while forging a seemingly unified—and, of course, white Anglo—cultural identity through restrictive language policies (in the case of bilingual education). Indeed, the consolidation of seamless and coherent subjects so at the heart of contemporary cultural media flows (as explored above) has enabled and encouraged the overwhelming public support and passage of such bills as California's Propositions 209 and 227 (in the case of the latter, by a two-to-one margin). These evidence the popular feelings of resentment that Fine and Weis so powerfully document among white working-class men in *The Unknown City*.

Yet these resentments run deep and operate on numerous levels here—hence, the tensions now erupting between African Americans and Latinos vis-à-vis such legislation. A recent *Time* magazine article entitled "The Next Big Divide?" explores burgeoning conflicts between African Americans and Latinos in Palo Alto, California, over bilingual education, noting that these disputes "arise in part from frustration over how to spend the dwindling pot of cash in low-income districts. But they also reflect a jostling for power, as blacks who labored hard to earn a place in central offices, on school boards and in classrooms confront a Latino population eager to grab a share of these positions" (Ratnesar 1997, 1).

It has been suggested, in fact, that efforts to institute black "ebonics" as a second language in Oakland was prompted by competition for shrinking funds traditionally allotted to bilingual (Spanish) programs. Resentment, spawned by increasing competition for decreasing resources, is key to unraveling the complexities of these struggles, for, as Joel Schumaker tells us, its power transcends both race and class lines.

Perhaps more important, however, is that the discourse of resentment at the same time informs more seemingly liberal responses to these issues and bills. The importance of public education in equalizing the profound injustices of contemporary American society is increasingly downplayed in favor of discourses about self-interest and the rigid feelings of resentment that undergird them. Affirmative action, thus, is a good because education will keep "dangerous minorities" off "our streets" by subjecting them to a lifetime of "civilizing" education, crafting them into good subjects for global cultural capitalism. Further, the story goes, affirmative action really helps middle-class women more than blacks or Latinos, so it should—quite naturally—remain in place.

These discourses inform the debate on bilingual education as well, a debate that has similarly collapsed liberal and conservative voices and opinions. Indeed, bilingual education, many argue, should be supported (only) because it will prepare young people for an increasingly polyglot global cultural economy, hence keeping immigrants and minorities off public assistance, allowing them to compete in an increasingly diverse (in the sense developed above) global community. Cultural arguments are also elided from within these positions, for, as many so eagerly stress, bilingual education really helps immigrants learn English and become assimilated faster—a bottom line supported by an ever-present spate of quantitative studies.

Market logics are all-pervasive here and are deeply informed by self-interest and resentment. These forces have shown themselves most clearly in recent decisions to provide less need-based financial aid for higher education to the poor, apportioning the savings to attract more so-called qualified middle-class students (Bronner 1998). Competition for the "best" students—seemingly without regard for race, class, and gender—has become a mantra for those wishing to further destroy educational access for the dispossessed. Indeed, many argue, why should poor minorities take precious spots away from the more qualified wealthy? The resentment of the elite has now come full circle, especially and most ironically, in this moment of unmatched economic wealth. As Jerome Karabel, professor of sociology at the University of California, Berkeley (the site of key rollbacks in affirmative action), comments, "College endowments are at historically unprecedented heights, so the number of need-blind institutions should be increasing rather than decreasing" (Karabel quoted in Bronner 1998, 16). As we all know, these are not lean, mean times for everybody. We also live in an era of unbridled wealth, won in large measure for the elite through, in part, divide-and-conquer strategies and the triumph of resentment and its ability to dictate public policy.

CONCLUSION

Resentment, in sum, is produced at the level of the popular, at the level of the textual. Yet its implications run deep, across myriad contexts, including that of public policy, which is increasingly defined by the logics of resentment. Thus, those of us on the left, those wishing to help keep the promise of public education a real one, must question the terms on which we fight these battles. We must question if our responses will further reproduce a discourse with such devastating and wholly regressive implications. As Foucault reminds us, we must choose what discourses we want to engage in, the "games of truth" we want to play. Indeed, what will be our responses to the burgeoning trend of eliminating need-based financial aid policies? What game will we play? And toward what end?

Such questions are crucial, as this moment is replete with both possibility and danger. This period of intense globalization and multinational capital is witness to the ushering in of the multicultural age—an age in which the empire has struck back, and first world exploitation of the third world has so depressed these areas that there has been a steady stream of immigrants from the periphery seeking brighter futures in the metropolitan centers. With the rapid growth of the indigenous minority population in the United States, there is now a formidable cultural presence of diversity in every sphere of cultural life. Clearly, as Appadurai

(1996) reminds us, social reproduction and integration have been inextricably complicated by globalization and the new and unpredictable flows of peoples as well as the money, technology, media images, and ideologies it has enabled. All, he stresses, must be interpreted individually *and* in tandem if we are to understand the emerging cultural landscape and its imbrication in a multifaceted global reality.

Indeed, if this is an era of the post, it is also an era of difference—and the challenge of this era of difference is the challenge of living in a world of incompleteness, discontinuity, and multiplicity. It requires generating a mythology of social interaction that goes beyond the model of resentment that seems so securely in place in these times. It means that we must take seriously the implications of the best intuition in the Nietzschean critique of resentment as the process of identity formation that thrives on the negation of the other—the dominant response from those facing a new and complex global and local reality. The challenge is to embrace a politics that calls on the moral resources of all who are opposed to the power block and its emerging global contours.

This age of difference thus poses new, though difficult, tactical and strategic challenges to critical and subaltern intellectuals as well as activists. A strategy that seeks to address these new challenges and openings must involve as a first condition a recognition that our differences of race, gender, and nation are merely the starting points for new solidarities and new alliances, not the terminal stations for depositing our agency and identities or the extinguishing of hope and possibility. Such a strategy might help us to better understand the issue of diversity in schooling and its links to the problems of social integration and public policy in modern life. Such a strategy might allow us to "produce" new discourses as well, especially—and most importantly—in this highly fraught and exceedingly fragile moment of historical complexity.

REFERENCES

Appadurai, A. 1996. *Modernity at Large: Cultural Dimensions of Globalization.* Minneapolis: University of Minnesota Press.
Asante, M. 1993. *Malcolm X as Cultural Hero, and Other Afrocentric Essays.* Trenton, N.J.: Africa World Press.
Bennett, W. 1994. *The Book of Virtues.* New York: Simon and Schuster.
Boorstin, D. 1975. *The Image: A Guide to Pseudo-Events in America.* New York: Atheneum.
Bronner, E. 1998. "Universities Giving Less Financial Aid on Basis of Need." *New York Times,* 21 June, A1.
Ewen, S. 1988. *All Consuming Images: The Politics of Style in Contemporary Culture.* New York: Basic Books.
Fine, M., and L. Weis. 1998. *The Unknown City: Lives of Poor and Working-Class Young Adults.* Boston: Beacon Press.
Giroux, H. 1996. *Fugitive Cultures: Race, Violence, and Youth.* London: Routledge.
Green, A. 1997. *Education, Globalization and the Nation State.* London: Macmillan.
Grossberg, L. 1992. *We Gotta Get Out of This Place: Popular Conservatism and Postmodern Culture.* New York: Routledge.
Hall, S. 1980. "Cultural Studies: Two Paradigms." *Media, Culture, and Society* 2:57–72.

James, C. L. R. 1993. *American Civilization*. Oxford: Blackwell.

McCarthy, C. 1998. *The Uses of Culture: Education and the Limits of Ethnic Affiliation*. New York: Routledge.

Masterman, L. 1990. *Teaching the Media*. New York: Routledge.

Miller, T. 1998. *Technologies of Truth: Cultural Citizenship and the Popular Media*. Minneapolis: University of Minnesota Press.

Morley, D., and K. Robins. 1995. *Spaces of Identity: Global Media, Electronic Landscapes and Cultural Boundaries*. London: Routledge.

Murray, C. 1984. *Losing Ground: American Social Policy, 1950–1980*. New York: Basic Books.

Nietzsche, F. 1967. *On the Genealogy of Morals*, translated by W. Kaufman. New York: Vintage.

Ratnesar, R. 1997. "The Next Big Divide?" *Time*, 1 December, 52.

Soloman, R. 1990. "Nietzsche, Postmodernism, and Resentment: A Genealogical Hypothesis." In *Nietzsche as Postmodernist: Essays Pro and Con*, edited by C. Koelb, 267–94. Albany: SUNY Press.

Steele, S. 1990. *Content of Our Character: A New Vision of Race in America*. New York: St. Martin's Press.

Steinberg, M. 1996. "Cultural History and Cultural Studies." In *Disciplinarity and Dissent in Cultural Studies*, edited by C. Nelson and D. P. Gaonkar, 103–29. New York: Routledge.

Steinberg, S., and J. Kincheloe, eds. 1997. *Kinderculture: The Corporate Construction of Youth*. Boulder, Colo.: Westview Press.

Tannen, D. 1998. *The Argument Culture: Moving from Debate to Dialogue*. New York: Random House.

Vinz, R. In press. "Learning from the Blues: Beyond Essentialist Readings of Cultural Texts." In *Sound Identities*, edited by C. McCarthy et al. New York: Peter Lang.

Will, G. 1989. "Eurocentricity and the School Curriculum." *Baton Rouge Morning Advocate*, 18 December, 3.

5

RACING TOWARD
EDUCATIONAL REFORM

The Politics of Markets and Standards

Michael W. Apple

University of Wisconsin, Madison

RIGHT TURN

In his influential history of curriculum debates, Herbert Kliebard has documented that educational issues have consistently involved major conflicts and
compromises among groups with competing visions of "legitimate" knowledge,
what counts as "good" teaching and learning, and what is a "just" society (Kliebard
1986). That such conflicts have deep roots in conflicting views of racial, class, and
gender justice in education and the larger society is ratified in even more critical
recent work as well (see, e.g., Rury and Mirel 1996; Teitelbaum 1996; Selden 1999).

Today is no different than in the past. A "new" set of compromises—a new
alliance and new power bloc—has been formed that has increasing influence in
education and all things social. This power bloc combines multiple fractions of
capital who are committed to neoliberal marketized solutions to educational
problems; neoconservative intellectuals who want a "return" to higher standards
and a "common culture"; authoritarian populist religious fundamentalists who
are deeply worried about secularity and the preservation of their own traditions;
and particular factions of the professionally oriented new middle class that are
committed to the ideology and techniques of accountability, measurement, and
"management." While there are clear tensions and conflicts within this alliance, in
general its overall aims are in providing the educational conditions believed necessary both for increasing international competitiveness, profit, and discipline
and for returning us to a romanticized past of the "ideal" home, family, and
school (Apple 1993, 1996).

In essence, the new alliance has integrated education into a wider set of ideological commitments. The objectives in education are the same as those that

84

guide its economic and social welfare goals. They include the dramatic expansion of that eloquent fiction, the free market; the drastic reduction of government responsibility for social needs; the reinforcement of intensely competitive structures of mobility both inside and outside the school; the lowering of people's expectations for economic security; the "disciplining" of culture and the body; and the popularization of what is clearly a form of social Darwinist thinking, as the recent popularity of *The Bell Curve* (Herrnstein and Murray 1994; see also Kincheloe and Steinberg 1996) so obviously and distressingly indicates.

The seemingly contradictory discourse of competition, markets, and choice on the one hand and accountability, performance objectives, standards, national testing, and national curriculum on the other have created such a din that it is hard to hear anything else. These tendencies actually oddly reinforce each other and help cement conservative educational positions into our daily lives (Apple 1996). In this chapter I want to show some of the complex and "overdetermined" race, class, and gender dynamics at work here and illuminate the differential effects that are produced. At the end, I shall suggest that—even though racial dynamics have both their own histories and autonomy and sometimes act through and contradict other dynamics of power—even when "race" is invisible in the overt policies and practices of such "reforms," much of this effort at "reform" *is* articulated with racializing discourses and practices. Behind many of these tendencies, as Cameron McCarthy has so clearly recognized, is the fact that schooling has become an especially contested site for defining one's identity through the negation of "the other." Such ressentiment results from the unsettling of racially hegemonic groups, as "communities of minorities and postcolonial immigrants now populate metropolitan schools and suburban towns" (McCarthy 1998, xi). In analyzing this situation, I shall speak not only about the United States, but internationally as well—especially about the emerging situation in Britain, since many of the educational reforms being proposed in the United States originated there.

NEW MARKETS, OLD TRADITIONS

Underpinning a good deal of the New Right's emerging discursive ensemble is a position that emphasizes "a culturalist construction of the nation as a (threatened) haven for white (Christian) traditions and values" (Gillborn 1997a, 2). This involved the construction of an imagined national past that is at least partly mythologized, and then the employment of it in order to castigate the present. Gary McCulloch argues that the nature of the historical images of schooling has changed. Dominant imagery of education as being "safe, domesticated, and progressive" (that is, as leading toward progress and social/personal improvement) has shifted, so education has become "threatening, estranged, and regressive" (McCulloch 1997, 80). The past is no longer the source of stability, but a mark of failure, disappointment, and loss. This is seen most vividly in the attacks on the "progressive orthodoxy" that supposedly now reigns supreme in classrooms in many nations (Hirsch 1996).

For example, in England—though much the same is echoed in the United States, Australia, and elsewhere—Michael Jones, the political editor of the *Sunday Times*, recalls the primary school of his day, saying, "Primary school was a happy time for me. About 40 of us sat at fixed wooden desks with ink wells and moved from them only with grudging permission. Teacher sat in a higher desk in front of us and moved only to the blackboard. She smelled of scent and inspired awe" (quoted in McCulloch 1997, 78). The mix of metaphors invoking discipline, scent (visceral and almost "natural"), and awe is fascinating. But he goes on, lamenting the past thirty years of "reform" that transformed primary schools. Speaking of his own children's experience, Jones says, "My children spent their primary years in a showplace school where they were allowed to wander around at will, develop their real individuality and dodge the 3Rs. It was all for the best, we were assured. But it was not" (quoted in McCulloch 1997, 78).

For Jones, the "dogmatic orthodoxy" of progressive education had "led directly to educational and social decline." Only the rightist reforms instituted in the 1980s and 1990s could halt and then reverse this decline (McCulloch 1997, 78). Only then could the imagined past return.

Much the same is being said on this side of the Atlantic. These sentiments are echoed in the public pronouncements of such figures as William Bennett, E. D. Hirsch Jr., and others, all of whom seem to believe that progressivism is now in the dominant position in educational policy and practice and has destroyed a valued past. All of them believe that only by tightening control over curriculum and teaching (and students, of course), restoring "our" lost traditions, making education more disciplined and competitive (as they are certain it was in the past), can we have effective schools. These figures are joined by others who have similar criticisms, but who instead turn to a different past for a different future. Their past is less that of scent, awe, and authority, but one of market "freedom." For them, nothing can be accomplished—not even the restoration of awe and authority—without setting the market loose on schools so as to ensure that only "good" ones survive.

We should understand that these policies are radical transformations. If they had come from the other side of the political spectrum, they would have been ridiculed in many ways, given the ideological tendencies in our nations. Further, not only are these policies based both on a romanticized pastoral past and on hidden unstated racialized identities and understandings, but they have also not been notable for their grounding in research findings. Indeed, when research has been used, it has often either served as a rhetoric of justification for preconceived beliefs about the supposed efficacy of markets or regimes of tight accountability. Such preconceived beliefs have been based, as in the illustrated case of John Chubb and Terry Moe's (1990) much publicized work on marketization, on quite flawed research (see, e.g., Whitty 1997).

Yet no matter how radical some of these proposed "reforms" are and no matter how weak the empirical basis of their support, they have now redefined the terrain of debate of all things educational. After years of conservative attacks and mobilizations, it has become clear that "ideas that were once deemed fanciful, unworkable—or just plain extreme" are now increasingly being seen as common sense (Gillborn 1997b, 357).

Tactically, the reconstruction of common sense that has been accomplished has proven extremely effective. For example, there are clear discursive strategies being employed here, ones that are characterized by "plain speaking" and speaking in a language that "everyone can understand." (I do not wish to be wholly negative about this. The importance of these things is something many "progressive" educators, including many writers on critical pedagogy, have yet to understand [Apple 1988].) These strategies also involve not only presenting one's own position as "common sense," but also usually tacitly implying that there is something of a conspiracy among one's opponents to deny the truth or to say only that which is "fashionable." As David Gillborn (1997b) notes, "This is a powerful technique. First, it assumes that there are no *genuine* arguments against the chosen position; any opposing views are thereby positioned as false, insincere or self-serving. Second, the technique presents the speaker as someone brave or honest enough to speak the (previously) unspeakable. Hence, the moral high ground is assumed and opponents are further denigrated" (353). It is hard to miss these characteristics in some of the conservative literature such as Richard Herrnstein and Charles Murray's (1994) publicizing of the unthinkable "truth" about genetics and intelligence or Hirsch's (1996) latest "tough" discussion of the destruction of "serious" schooling by progressive educators.

MARKETS AND PERFORMANCE

Let us take as an example of the ways in which all this operates one element of the conservative restoration—the neoliberal claim that the invisible hand of the market will inexorably lead to better schools. As Roger Dale reminds us, "the market" acts as a metaphor rather than an explicit guide for action. It is not denotative, but connotative. Thus, it must itself be marketed to those who will exist in it and live with its effects (Dale, quoted in Menter et al. 1997, 27). Markets are marketed, are made legitimate, by a depoliticizing strategy. They are said to be natural and neutral, and governed by effort and merit. And those opposed to them are by definition, hence, also opposed to effort and merit. Markets, as well, are supposedly less subject to political interference and the weight of bureaucratic procedures; they are, in addition, grounded in the rational choices of individual actors (Menter et al. 1997, 27). Thus, markets and the guarantee of rewards for effort and merit are to be coupled to produce "neutral," yet positive, results. Mechanisms, hence, must be put into place that give evidence of entrepreneurial efficiency and effectiveness. This coupling of markets and mechanisms for the generation of evidence of performance is exactly what has occurred. Whether it works is open to question.

In what is perhaps the most comprehensive critical review of all of the evidence on marketization, Geoff Whitty cautions us not to mistake rhetoric for reality. After examining research from a number of countries, Whitty argues that while advocates of marketized "choice" plans assume that competition will enhance the efficiency and responsiveness of schools, as well as give "disadvantaged" children opportunities that they currently do not have, this may be a false hope. These hopes are not now being realized and are unlikely to be realized in the future "in the context of broader policies that do nothing to challenge deeper social and cultural inequalities" (1997, 58). Whitty goes on to say, "Atomized decision-making in a highly stratified society may appear to give everyone equal opportunities, but transforming responsibility for decision-making from the public to the private sphere can actually reduce the scope of collective action to improve the quality of education for all" (58). When this is connected to the fact that, as I shall show shortly, in practice neoliberal policies involving market "solutions" may actually serve to reproduce—not subvert—traditional hierarchies of class and race, this should give us reason to pause (Whitty 1997; Whitty, Edwards, and Gewirtz 1993; Apple 1996).

Thus, rather than taking neoliberal claims at face value, we might want to ask about their effects, too often invisible in the rhetoric and metaphors of their proponents. Given the limitations of what one can say in a chapter of this length, I shall select a few issues that have been given less attention than they deserve, but on which there is now significant research.

The English experience is apposite here, especially since proponents of the market such as Chubb and Moe (1990) rely so heavily on it and because that is where the tendencies I analyze are most advanced. In England, the 1993 Education Act documents the state's commitment to marketization. Governing bodies of local educational authorities (LEAs) are now mandated to formally consider "going GM" (Grant Maintained, that is, opting out of the local school system's control and entering into the competitive market) every year (Power, Halpin, and Fitz 1994, 27). Thus, the weight of the state stands behind the press toward neoliberal reforms there.[1] Yet, rather than leading to curriculum responsiveness and diversification, the competitive market has not created much that is different from the traditional models so firmly entrenched in schools today (Power, Halpin, and Fitz 1994, 39); nor has it radically altered the relations of inequality that characterize schooling.

In their own extensive analyses of the effects of marketized reforms "on the ground," Stephen Ball and his colleagues point to some of the reasons why we need to be quite cautious here. As they document, in these situations educational principles and values are often compromised such that commercial issues become more important in curriculum design and resource allocation (Ball, Bowe, and Gewirtz 1994, 19). For instance, the coupling of markets with the demand for and publication of performance indicators such as "examination league tables" in England has meant that schools are increasingly looking for ways to attract "motivated" parents with "able" children. In this way, schools are able to enhance their relative position in local systems of competition. This represents a subtle but crucial shift in emphasis—one that is not openly discussed as often as it should be—from student needs to student performance and from what the school does for the student to what the student does for the school. This is also accompanied uncomfortably often by a shift of resources away from students who are labeled as having special needs or learning difficulties, with some of these needed resources now being shifted to marketing and public relations. "Special needs" students are not only expensive, but deflate test scores on those all-important league tables.

The entire enterprise establishes a new metric and a new set of goals based on a constant striving to win the market game. What this means is of considerable import not only in terms of its effects on daily school life but in the ways all of this signifies a transformation of what counts as a good society and a responsible citizen. Let me say something about this generally.

I noted earlier that behind all educational proposals are visions of a just society and a good student. The neoliberal reforms I have been discussing construct this in a particular way. While the defining characteristic of neoliberalism is largely based on the central tenets of classical liberalism, in particular classic economic liberalism, there are crucial differences between classical liberalism and neoliberalism. These differences are absolutely essential in understanding the politics of education and the transformations education is currently undergoing. Mark Olssen clearly details these differences in the following passage, which is worth quoting in its entirety:

> Whereas classical liberalism represents a negative conception of state power in that the individual was to be taken as an object to be freed from the interventions of the state, neo-liberalism has come to represent a positive conception of the state's role in creating the appropriate market by providing the conditions, laws and institutions necessary for its operation. In classical liberalism, the individual is characterized as having an autonomous human nature and can practice freedom. In neo-liberalism the state seeks to create an individual who is an enterprising and competitive entrepreneur. In the classical model the theoretical aim of the state as to limit and minimize its role based on postulates which included universal egoism (the self-interested individual); invisible hand theory which dictated that the interests of the individual were also the interests of the society as a whole; and the political maxim of laissez-faire. In the shift from classical liberalism to neo-liberalism, then, there is a further element added, for such a shift involves a change in subject position from "homo economicus," who naturally behaves out of self-interest and is relatively detached from the state, to "manipulatable man," who is created by the state and who is continually encouraged to be "perpetually responsive." It is not that the conception of the self-interested subject is replaced or done away with by the new ideals of "neo-liberalism," but that in an age of universal welfare, the perceived possibilities of slothful indolence create necessities for new forms of vigilance, surveillance, "performance appraisal" and of forms of control generally. In this model the state has taken it upon itself to keep us all up to the mark. The state will see to it that each one makes a "continual enterprise of ourselves" ... in what seems to be a process of "governing without governing." (1996, 340)

The results of Ball's and his colleagues' research document how the state does indeed do this, enhancing that odd combination of marketized individualism and control through constant and comparative public assessment. Widely publicized league tables determine one's relative value in the educational marketplace. Only those schools with rising performance indicators are worthy. And only those students who can "make a continual enterprise of themselves" can keep such schools going in the "correct" direction. Yet, while these issues are important, they fail to fully illuminate some of the other mechanisms through which *differential* effects are produced by neoliberal reforms. Here, class and race issues come to the fore in ways that Ball, Bowe, and Gewirtz (1994) make clear.

Middle-class parents are clearly the most advantaged in this kind of cultural assemblage, and not only as we saw because schools seek them out. Middle-class parents have become quite skilled, in general, in exploiting market mechanisms in education and in bringing their social, economic, and cultural capital to bear on them. Middle-class parents, Ball and his colleagues assert, "are more likely to have the knowledge, skills and contacts to decode and manipulate what are increasingly complex and deregulated systems of choice and recruitment. The more deregulation, the more possibility of informal procedures being employed. The middle class also, on the whole, are more able to move their children around the system" (1994, 19). That class and race intersect and interact in complex ways means that—even though we need to be clear that marketized systems in education often *expressly* have their conscious and unconscious raison d'être in a fear of "the other" and often are hidden expressions of a racialization of educational policy—the differential results will "naturally" be decidedly raced as well as classed.[2]

Economic and social capital can be converted into cultural capital in various ways. In marketized plans, more affluent parents often have more flexible hours and can visit multiple schools. They have cars—often more than one—and can *afford* driving their children across town to attend a "better" school. They can as well provide the hidden cultural resources such as camps and after school programs (dance, music, computer classes, etc.) that give their children an "ease," a "style," that seems "natural" and acts as a set of cultural resources. Their previous stock of social and cultural capital—who they know, their "comfort" in social encounters with educational officials—is an unseen but powerful storehouse of resources. Thus, more affluent parents are more likely to have the informal knowledge and skill—what Pierre Bourdieu would call the habitus (Bourdieu 1984)—to be able to decode and use marketized forms to their own benefit. This sense of what might be called "confidence"—which is itself the result of past choices that tacitly but no less powerfully depend on economic resources to actually have had the ability to make economic choices—is the unseen capital that underpins their ability to negotiate marketized forms and "work the system" through sets of informal cultural rules (Ball, Bowe, and Gewirtz 1994, 20–22).

Of course, it needs to be said that working-class, poor, and/or immigrant parents are not without skill in this regard, by any means. (After all, it requires an immense amount of skill, courage, and social and cultural resources to survive under exploitative and depressing material conditions. Thus, collective bonds, informal networks and contacts, and an ability to work the system are developed in quite nuanced, intelligent, and often impressive ways here.) However, the match between the historically grounded habitus expected in schools, and in its actors, and in those of more affluent parents, combined with the material resources available to the more affluent, usually leads to a successful conversion of economic and social capital into cultural capital (see Bourdieu 1996; Swartz 1997). And this is exactly what is happening in England.

These claims, both about what is happening inside schools and about larger sets of power relations, are supported by even more recent synthetic analyses of the overall results of marketized models. This research on the effects of the tense but still effective combination of neoliberal and neoconservative policies examines the tendencies internationally by comparing what has happened in a number of nations—for example, the United States, England and Wales, Australia, and New Zealand—where this combination has become increasingly powerful. The results confirm the arguments I have made here. Let me enumerate some of the most significant and disturbing findings of such research.

It is unfortunately all too usual that the most widely used measures of the "success" of school reforms are the results of standardized achievement tests. This simply will not do. We need to constantly ask what it is that reforms do to schools as a whole and to each of their participants—including teachers, students, administrators, community members, local activists, and so on. To take one set of examples, as marketized "self-managing" schools grow in many nations, the role of the school principal is radically transformed. More, not less, power is actually consolidated within an administrative structure. More time and energy is spent on maintaining or enhancing a public image of a "good school" and less time and energy is spent on pedagogic and curricular substance. At the same time, teachers seem to be experiencing not increased autonomy and professionalism, but intensification (Apple 1988, 1993). And oddly, as noted before, schools themselves become more *similar*, and more committed to standard, traditional, whole-class methods of teaching and a standard and traditional (and often monocultural) curriculum (Whitty, Power, and Halpin 1998, 12–13). To only direct our attention to test scores would cause us to miss some truly profound transformations, many of which we may find disquieting.

One of the reasons these broader effects are so often produced is that in all too many countries, neoliberal visions of quasi markets are usually accompanied by neoconservative pressure to regulate content and behavior through such things as national curricula, standards, and systems of assessment. The combination is historically contingent; that is, it is not absolutely necessary that the two emphases be combined. But there are characteristics of neoliberalism that make it more likely that an emphasis on the weak state and a faith in markets will cohere with an emphasis on the strong state and a commitment to regulating knowledge, values, and the body.

This is partly the case because of the increasing power of the "evaluative state." This signifies what initially may seem to be contradictory tendencies. At the same time as the state appears to be devolving in power to individuals and autonomous institutions that are themselves increasingly competing in a market, the state remains strong in key areas (Whitty, Power, and Halpin 1998, 36). As I claimed earlier, one of the key differences between classical liberalism and its faith in "enterprising individuals" in a market and current forms of neoliberalism is the latter's commitment to a regulatory state. Neoliberalism does indeed demand the constant production of evidence that one is in fact "making an enterprise of oneself" (Olssen 1996). Thus, under these conditions not only does education become a marketable commodity (like a loaf of bread or a car) in which the values, procedures, and metaphors of business dominate, but its results must be reducible to standardized "performance indicators" (Whitty, Power, and Halpin 1998, 37–38; see also Clarke and Newman 1997). This is ideally suited to the task of providing a mechanism for the neoconservative attempts to specify what knowledge, values, and behaviors should be standardized and officially defined as "legitimate," a point I shall expand upon in the next section of this chapter.

In essence, we are witnessing a process in which the state shifts the blame for the very evident inequalities in access and outcome that it has promised to reduce—from itself onto individual schools, parents, and children. This is, of course, also part of a larger process in which dominant economic groups shift the blame for the massive and unequal effects of their own misguided decisions from themselves onto the state. The state is then faced with a very real crisis in legitimacy. Given this, we should not be at all surprised that the state will then seek to export this crisis outside itself (Apple 1995; Whitty, Power, and Halpin 1998).[3]

The problems go further than this, however. In nearly all of the countries studied, the market did *not* encourage diversity in curriculum, pedagogy, organization, clientele, or even image. It instead consistently devalued alternatives and increased the power of dominant models. Of equal significance, it also consistently exacerbated differences in access and outcome based on race, ethnicity, and class (Whitty, Power, and Halpin 1998, 119–20).

The return to "traditionalism" led to a number of things. It *delegitimated* more critical models of teaching and learning. It both reintroduced restratification within the school and lessened the possibility that detracking would occur. More emphasis was given to "gifted" children and "fast-track" classes, while students who were seen as less academically able were therefore "less attractive." In England, the extent of this was nowhere more visible than in the alarming rate of students of color being excluded from schools. Much of this was caused by the intense pressure to constantly demonstrate higher achievement rates. This was especially powerful in marketized contexts in which the "main driving force appeared to be *commercial* rather than *educational*" (Whitty, Power, and Halpin 1998, 90).

In their own analysis of these worrisome and more hidden results, Whitty and colleagues demonstrate that among the dangerous effects of quasi markets are the ways in which schools that wish to maintain or enhance their market position engage in "cream skimming," ensuring that certain students with particular characteristics are accepted, while certain other students are found wanting. For some schools, stereotypes were reproduced in that girls were seen as more valuable, as were students from some Asian communities. Afro-Caribbean children were often clear losers in this situation.

Some of these data come largely from schools outside the United States, although they should stop us dead in our tracks and give some very serious thought as to whether we want to proceed with similar policies here. Yet the United States still sits at the center of much of the discussion in this literature. For example, charter schools and their equivalents in the United States and England are also put under critical scrutiny. In both places, they tend to attract parents who live and work in relatively privileged communities. Here too, "it would appear that any new opportunities are being colonized by the already advantaged, rather than the 'losers' identified by Chubb and Moe" (Whitty, Power, and Halpin 1998, 98).

The overall conclusions are clear: "[In] current circumstances choice is as likely to reinforce hierarchies as to improve educational opportunities and the overall quality of schooling" (14). As Whitty and colleagues have put it in their arguments against those who believe that what we are witnessing in the emergence of "choice" programs is the postmodern celebration of difference, "There is a growing body of empirical evidence that, rather than benefitting the disadvantaged, the emphasis on parental choice and school autonomy is further disadvantaging those least able to compete in the market.... For most disadvantaged groups, as opposed to the few individuals who escape from schools at the bottom of the status hierarchy, the new arrangements seem to be just a more sophisticated way of reproducing traditional distinctions between different types of school and the people who attend them" (42).

All of this gives us ample reason to agree with Henig's insightful argument (1994) that "the sad irony of the current education-reform movement is that, through over-identification with school-choice proposals rooted in market-based ideas, the healthy impulse to consider radical reforms to address social problems may be channeled into initiatives that further erode the potential for collective deliberation and collective response" (222).

This is not to dismiss either the possibility or the necessity of school reform. We do, however, need to take seriously the probability that only by focusing on the exogenous socioeconomic features, not simply the organizational features, of "successful" schools can all schools succeed. Only by simultaneously eliminating poverty through greater income parity; establishing effective and much more equal health and housing programs; and positively refusing to continue the hidden and not-so-hidden politics of racial exclusion and degradation that so clearly still characterize daily life in many nations (and in which marketized plans need to be seen as partly a structure to avoid the body and culture of "the other")— can substantive progress be made.

These empirical findings are made more understandable in terms of Pierre

Bourdieu's (1996) analysis of the relative weight given to cultural capital as part of mobility strategies today. The rise in importance of cultural capital infiltrates all institutions in such a way that there is a relative movement away from the *direct* reproduction of class privilege (where power is transmitted largely within families through economic property) to *school-mediated* forms of class privilege. Here, "the bequeathal of privilege is simultaneously effectuated and transfigured by the intercession of educational institutions" (Wacquant 1996, xiii). This is *not* a conspiracy; it is not "conscious" in the ways we normally use that concept. Rather, it is the result of a long chain of relatively autonomous connections among differentially accumulated economic, social, and cultural capital operating at the level of daily events as we make our respective ways in the world, including, as we saw, in the world of school choice.

Thus, while not taking an unyieldingly determinist position, Bourdieu (1996) argues that a class habitus tends to reproduce the conditions of its own reproduction "unconsciously." It does this by producing a relatively coherent and systematically *characteristic* set of seemingly natural and unconscious strategies—in essence, ways of understanding and acting on the world that act as forms of cultural capital that can be and are employed to protect and enhance one's status in a social field of power. He aptly compares this similarity of habitus across class actors to handwriting, saying,

> Just as the acquired disposition we call "handwriting," that is a particular way of forming letters, always produces the same "writing"—that is, graphic lines that despite differences in size, matter, and color related to writing surface (sheet of paper or blackboard) and implement (pencil, pen, or chalk), that is despite differences in vehicles for the action, have an immediately recognizable affinity of style or a family resemblance—the practices of a single agent, or, more broadly, the practices of all agents endowed with similar habitus, owe the affinity of style that makes each a metaphor for the others to the fact that they are the products of the implementation in different fields of the same schemata of perception, thought, and action. (273)

This very connection of habitus across fields of power—the ease of bringing one's economic, social, and cultural resources to bear on "markets"—enables a comfort between markets and self that characterizes the middle-class actor here. This constantly *produces* differential effects. These effects are not neutral, no matter what the advocates of neoliberalism suggest. Rather, they are themselves the results of a particular kind of morality. Unlike the conditions of what might best be called "thick morality," wherein principles of the common good are the ethical basis for adjudicating policies and practices, markets are grounded in aggregative principles. They are constituted out of the sum of individual goods and choices. "Founded on individual and property rights that enable citizens to address problems of interdependence via exchange," they offer a prime example of "thin morality" by generating both hierarchy and division based on competitive individualism (Ball, Bowe, and Gewirtz 1994, 24). And in this competition, the general outline of the winners and losers *has* been identified empirically.

National Curriculum and National Testing

I showed in the previous section that there are connections between at least two dynamics operating in neoliberal reforms—"free" markets and increased surveillance. This can be seen in the fact that in many contexts, marketization has been accompanied by a set of particular policies for "producers," for those professionals working within education. These policies have been strongly regulatory, quite instrumental in reconstituting common sense. As in the case of the linkage between national tests and performance indicators published as league tables, they have been organized around a concern for external supervision, regulation, and external judgment of performance (Menter et al. 1997, 8) and have increasingly been colonized by largely white and more affluent parents who possess what is seen as "appropriate" economic, social, and cultural capital. This concern for external supervision and regulation is not only connected to a strong mistrust of "producers" (e.g., teachers) and to the need for ensuring that people continually make enterprises out of themselves. It is also clearly linked both to the neoconservative sense of a need to "return" to a lost past of high standards, discipline, awe, and "real" knowledge and to the professional middle class's own ability to carve out a sphere of authority within the state for its own commitment to management techniques and efficiency. The focus on efficient management plays a prime role here, one that many neoliberals and neoconservatives alike find useful.

There is no necessary contradiction between a general set of marketizing and deregulating interests and processes, such as voucher and choice plans, and a set of enhanced regulatory processes, such as plans for national curricula and national testing. "The regulatory form permits the state to maintain 'steerage' over the aims and processes of education from within the market mechanism" (Menter et al. 1997, 24). Such steerage has often been vested in such things as national standards, curricula, and testing. Forms of all of these are being pushed for in the United States currently and are the subject of considerable controversy, some of which cuts across ideological lines and shows some of the tensions within the different elements contained under the umbrella of the conservative restoration.

I have argued that, paradoxically, a national curriculum and especially a national testing program are the first and most essential steps toward increased marketization. They actually provide the mechanisms for comparative data that "consumers" need in order to make markets work as markets (Apple 1996). Without these mechanisms there is no comparative base of information for "choice." Yet we do not have to argue about these regulatory forms in a vacuum. Like the neoliberal markets I discussed in the previous section, they too have been instituted in England; and, once again, there is important research available that can and must make us duly cautious in going down this path.

One might want to claim that a set of national standards, curricula, and tests would provide the conditions for "thick morality." After all, such regulatory reforms are supposedly based on shared values and common sentiments that also create social spaces in which common issues of concern can be debated and made subject to moral interrogation (Ball, Bowe, and Gewirtz 1994, 23). Yet, what counts as the "common," and how and by whom it is actually determined, is rather more thin than thick.

In general, it is nearly a truism that there is no simplistic linear model of policy formation, distribution, and implementation. There are always complex mediations at each level of the process. There is a complex politics that goes on within each group and between these groups and external forces in the formulation of policy, in its being written up as a legislative mandate, in its distribution, and in its reception at the level of practice (Ransom 1995, 436). Thus, the state may legislate changes in curriculum, evaluation, or policy (which is itself produced through conflict, compromise, and political maneuvering), but policy writers and curriculum writers may be unable to control the meanings and implementations of their texts. All texts are "leaky" documents. They are subject to "recontextualization" at every stage of the process (Ransom 1995, 436; see also Bernstein 1990).

However, this general principle may be just a bit too romantic. None of this occurs on a level playing field. As with market plans, there are very real differences in power in one's ability to influence, mediate, transform, or reject a policy or a regulatory process. Granted, it is important to recognize that a "state control model"—with its assumption of top-down linearity—is much too simplistic and that the possibility of human agency and influence is always there. However, having said this, this should not imply that such agency and influence will be powerful (Ransom 1995, 437).

The case of national curriculum and national testing in England and Wales documents the tensions in these two accounts. It was the case that the national curriculum that was first legislated and then imposed there was indeed struggled over for some time. It was originally too detailed and too specific, and hence was subject to major transformations at the national, community, school, and then classroom levels. However, even though the national curriculum was subject to conflict, mediation, and some transformation of its content, organization, and invasive and immensely time-consuming forms of evaluation, its utter power is demonstrated in its radical reconfiguration of the very process of knowledge selection, organization, and assessment. It changed the entire terrain of education radically. Its subject divisions "provide more constraint than scope for discretion." The "standard attainment targets" that have been mandated cement these constraints in place. The imposition of national testing "locks the national curriculum in place as the dominant framework of teachers' work whatever opportunities teachers may take to evade or reshape it" (Richard Hatcher and Barry Troyna, quoted in Ransom 1995, 438).

Thus, it is not sufficient to state that the world of education is complex and has multiple influences. The purpose of any serious analysis is to go beyond such overly broad conclusions. Rather, we need to "discriminate degrees of influence in the world," to weigh the relative efficacy of the factors involved. Hence, although it is clear that while the national curriculum and national tests that now exist in England and Wales have come about because of a complex interplay of forces and influences, it is equally clear that "state control has the upper hand" (Ransom 1995, 438).

The national curricula and national tests did generate conflict about issues. They did partly lead to the creation of social spaces for moral questions to get asked. (Of course, these moral questions had been asked all along by dispossessed groups.) Thus, it was clear to many people that the creation of mandatory and reductive tests that emphasized memory and decontextualized abstraction pulled the national curriculum in a particular direction—that of encouraging a selective educational market in which elite students and elite schools with a wide range of resources would be well (if narrowly) served (O'Hear 1994, 66). Diverse groups of people argued that such reductive, detailed, and simplistic paper-and-pencil tests "had the potential to do enormous damage," a situation that was made even worse because the tests were so onerous in terms of time and record keeping (55–56). Teachers had a good deal of support when as a group they decided to boycott the administration of the test in a remarkable act of public protest. This also led to serious questioning of the arbitrary, inflexible, and overly prescriptive national curriculum. While the curriculum is still inherently problematic and the assessment system does still contain numerous dangerous and onerous elements within it, organized activity against these elements did have an impact (56–57).

Yet unfortunately, the story does not end there. By the mid-1990s, even with the government's partial retreat on such regulatory forms as its program of constant and reductive testing, it had become clearer by the year that the development of testing and the specification of content had been "hijacked" by those who were ideologically committed to traditional pedagogies and to the idea of more rigorous selection (O'Hear 1994, 68). The residual effects are both material and ideological. They include a continuing emphasis on trying to provide the "rigor [that is] missing in the practice of most teachers, . . . judging progress solely by what is testable in tests of this kind" and the development of a "very hostile view of the accountability of teachers" that was seen as "part of a wider thrust of policy to take away professional control of public services and establish so called consumer control through a market structure" (65–66).

The authors of an extremely thorough review of recent assessment programs instituted in England and Wales provide a summary of what has happened. Caroline Gipps and Patricia Murphy argue that it has become increasingly obvious that the national assessment program attached to the national curriculum is more and more dominated by traditional models of testing and the assumptions about teaching and learning that lie behind them. At the same time, equity issues are becoming much less visible (Gipps and Murphy 1994, 209). In the calculus of values now in place in the regulatory state, efficiency, speed, and cost control replace more substantive concerns about social and educational justice. The pressure to get tests in place rapidly has meant that "the speed of test development is so great, and the curriculum and assessment changes so regular, that [there is] little time to carry out detailed analyses and trialing to ensure that the tests are as fair as possible to all groups." The conditions for "thin morality"—in which the competitive individual of the market dominates and social justice will somehow take care of itself—are reproduced here. The combination of the neoliberal market and the regulatory state, then, does indeed work; however, it works in that the metaphors of free market, merit, and effort hide the differential reality that is produced. While on the one hand this makes a socially and culturally critical (and specifically antiracist) pedagogy even more essential, it also makes it much more difficult to actually accomplish.

The Absent Presence of Race in Educational Reform

I have told a complex story here, one in which an overdetermined set of contradictory dynamics creates the conditions for the production of differentiated processes and outcomes. Yet a focus on complexity in power relations, while highlighting specificity and conjunctures, can lead us to downplay the importance of race. In this last section, I want to return to connections I have hinted at throughout my discussion—the nexus that ties state educational policies about markets and standards to issues of culture, identity, and racialized and racializing structures, discourses, and practices.

In their exceptional analysis of the way the discourses of race have operated in the United States, Omi and Winant (1994) argue that race is not an "add-on," but is truly constitutive of many of our most taken-for-granted daily experiences:

> In the U.S., race is present in every institution, every relationship, every individual. This is the case not only for the way society is organized—spatially, culturally, in terms of stratification, etc.—but also for our perceptions and understandings of personal experience. Thus as we watch the videotape of Rodney King being beaten, compare real estate prices in different neighborhoods, size up a potential client, neighbor, or teacher, stand in line at the unemployment office, or carry out a thousand other normal tasks, we are compelled to think racially, to use racial categories and meaning systems in which we have been socialized. Despite exhortations both sincere and hypocritical, it is not possible or even desirable to be "color-blind." (158–59)

Not only is it not possible to be color-blind, as they go on to say, but "opposing race requires that we notice race, not ignore it." Only by noticing race can we challenge it, "with its ever-more-absurd reduction of human experience to an essence attributed to all without regard for historical or social context." By placing race squarely in front of us, "we can challenge the state, the institutions of civil society, and ourselves as individuals to combat the legacy of inequality and injustice inherited from the past" and continually reproduced in the present (159).

While Omi and Winant are analyzing racial dynamics in the United States, I would hope that by now it is equally clear that their claims extend well beyond these geographical borders to include the United Kingdom and many other nations. It would not be possible to understand the history, current status, and multiple effects of educational policy in the United Kingdom or the United States without placing race as a core element of one's analysis.

Placing race at the center is less easy than one might expect, for one must do this with due recognition of its complexity. Race is not a stable category. What it means, how it is used and by whom, how it is mobilized in public discourse, and its role in educational and more general social policy—all of this is contingent and historical. Indeed, it would be misleading to talk of race as an "it." "It" is not a thing, a reified object that can be measured as if it were a simple biological entity. Race is a *construction*, a set of fully social *relationships*. This unfortunately does not stop people from talking about race in simplistic ways that ignore the realities of differential power and histories.[4] Yet complexity needs to be recognized here as well. Racial dynamics have their own histories and are relatively autonomous. But, as I have shown in the previous sections on neoliberal and neoconservative policies, they also participate in, form, and are formed by other relatively autonomous dynamics involving, say, class, colonial and postcolonial realities, state power, cultural struggles of many kinds, and so on—all of which are implicated in and related to the social construction both of race and of racialized results in education. Further, racial dynamics can operate in subtle and powerful ways even when they are not overtly on the minds of the actors involved.

We can make a distinction between intentional and functional explanations here. Intentional explanations are those self-conscious aims that guide our policies and practices. Functional explanations, on the other hand, are concerned with the latent effects of policies and practices (see, e.g., Liston 1988). In my mind, at times the latter are more powerful than the former.

In essence, this rightly turns what is called the "genetic fallacy" in logic on its head, so to speak. Let me be specific here. We are apt to think of the genetic fallacy in particular ways. We tend to castigate authors who assume that the import and meaning of any position is totally determined by its original grounding. Thus, for example, it is clear that E. L. Thorndike—one of the founders of educational psychology—was a confirmed eugenicist and was deeply committed to the project of "race betterment" and had a vision of education that was inherently undemocratic. Yet one is on shaky ground if one concluded that every aspect of his work is totally "polluted" by his (repugnant) social beliefs. Thorndike's research program may have been epistemologically and empirically problematic, but a different kind of evidence and a more complex analysis is required to debunk all of it than to simply claim (correctly) that he was often racist, sexist, and elitist (see Gould 1981 and Haraway 1989 for how this more complex program might be undertaken). Indeed, it is not difficult to find progressive educators drawing on Thorndike's work for support of what were then seen to be radical positions.

When we are talking about racism and reform in current policies, we need to turn the genetic fallacy around. The overt motivations of the sponsors of, say, the British Labour Party's policies in the United Kingdom or of the Clinton proposals for education such as the establishment of national testing in the United States may not have been about race or may have assumed that such proposals would "level the playing field" for everyone. Their intentions may have been self-consciously "meritorious." (I mean very much this play on words.) Yet, as I showed in my discussion of how markets work in class and race terms, conscious originating motives do not guarantee at all how arguments and policies will be employed, what their multiple and determinate functions and effects will be, whose interests they will ultimately serve, and what identifiable patterns of differential benefits will emerge, given existing and unequal relations of economic, cultural, and social capital and given unequal strategies of converting one form of capital to another in our societies (Bourdieu 1984).

Such differential functions and outcomes are again clear in some very recent analyses of race and education in England in ways that confirm my earlier arguments. For example, in David Gillborn's and Deborah Youdell's (1998) report of the results of their investigation of the effects of national benchmarks and similar "reforms" in schools with significant populations of children of color, they state that the available data suggest that "beneath the superficial gains indicated by a year-on-year improvement against the benchmark criterion ... in some areas there has been a widening of inequality; between students, schools and in some cases, ethnic groups" and that this is especially the case for white and Afro-Caribbean students (7).

It should not be surprising at all that Gillborn and Youdell find what they call an "educational triage" system at work in the school. Indeed, it would be surprising if they didn't, given what we know about the effects in other institutions of specific racialized patterns of income inequality, of employment and unemployment, of health care and housing, of nutrition, of incarceration, and of school achievement in nations like the United States (see, e.g., Apple 1996, 68–90). These patterns and effects make a mockery of any claim to a level playing field, and one should not be surprised that in times of fiscal and ideological crises multiple forms of triage will be found in multiple institutions.

Yet Gillborn's and Youdell's cautionary tale should make us extremely skeptical that the constant search for "higher standards" and for ever-increasing achievement scores can do much more than put in place seemingly neutral devices for restratification. As they demonstrate (though considerably more empirical research would be required to fully substantiate the more general claim), in situations such as these there is a narrowing of the curriculum. Increasing a school's test scores means focusing both on those subjects and those students who can contribute to higher school performance. As they go on to show, class, race, and gender interact in complex ways here. White boys' achievement, especially for

those who are on the "borderline" of passing (and, hence, whose better performance can raise a school's overall scores on tests), is all too often seen as mutable.
For black male students, their supposedly "lesser ability" is tacitly assumed.
"Valuable" students, then, are not usually black, seemingly by a set of natural acci-
dents (Gillborn and Youdell 1998). All of this is not necessarily intended; it is due
to a set of overdetermined historical relations and to the complex micropolitics
over resources and power within the school and between the school and the local
and national state, as well of course to the dynamics of power in the larger society.

However, even as I say this, I do not want to suggest that this makes race less
powerful. Indeed, my claim is exactly the opposite. It gets a good deal of its power
through its very hiddenness. Nowhere is this more true than in the discourse of
markets and standards.

While some commentators may be correct that "the competitive schools market in the UK as envisioned by neo-liberals was created without reference to
implications for ethnic minorities" (Tomlinson 1998), this may be true only at the
level of conscious intentions. While race talk may be overtly absent in the discourse of markets, it remains an absent presence that I believe is fully implicated
in the goals and concerns surrounding support for the marketization of education. The sense of economic and educational decline, the belief that private is
good and public is bad, and so on is coupled with an often unarticulated sense of
loss, a feeling that things are out of control, an anomic feeling that is connected to
a sense of loss of one's "rightful place" in the world (an "empire" now in decline,
an economic power made mortal by international competition), and a fear of the
culture and body of "the other." The "private" is the sphere of smooth running
and efficient organizations, of autonomy and individual choice. The "public" is
out of control, messy, heterogenous. "We" must protect "our" individual choice
from those who are the controllers or the "polluters" (whose cultures and very
bodies are either exoticized or dangerous). Thus, I believe that there are very close
connections between support for neoliberal visions of markets and free individuals and the concerns of neoconservatives with their clear worries about standards,
"excellence," and decline.

For these very reasons, I believe that it is the case that under current conditions
marketization and national curricula all too often actually represent a step backward in antiracist education (although we should never romanticize the previous
situation; not all that much antiracist education was actually going on, I fear).
Isn't it odd that just as gains were being made in decentering dominant narratives, dominance returns in the form of national curricula (and national testing)
that specify—often in distressing detail—what "we" are all like? Of course, in
many nations the attempts at building national curricula and/or national standards were and are forced to compromise, to go beyond the mere mentioning of
the culture and histories of "the other." (Certainly, this was and is the case in the
United States.) And it is in such compromises that we see hegemonic discourse at
its most creative (Apple 1993, 1996).

Take as one example the new national history standards in the United States and the attempt in textbooks to respond to the standards' creation of a multicultural narrative that binds "us" all together, to create that elusive "we." Such a discourse, while having a number of progressive-sounding elements, demonstrates how hegemonic narratives creatively erase historic memory and the specificities of difference and oppression. All too many textbooks in our schools construct the history of the United States as a story of "immigrants" (Cornbleth and Waugh 1995). "We" are a nation of immigrants. We are *all* immigrants, from the original Native American people who supposedly trekked across the Bering Strait to more recent people from Europe, Asia, Africa, and Latin America. Well, sure we are! But such a story totally misconstrues the different conditions that existed. Some "immigrants" came in chains, were enslaved, and faced centuries of repression and state-mandated apartheid. Others were subjected to death and forced enclosure as official policies. And there is a world of difference here between the creation of (an artificial) "we" and the destruction of historical experience and memory (Apple 1996).

This destruction and how it is accomplished is again related to how race functions as an absent (at least for some people) presence in our societies. This can be made clearer by directing our attention to the invisibility of whiteness. Indeed, along with many others, I want to suggest that those who are deeply committed to antiracist curricula and teaching need to place much more of their focus on white identity (see Kincheloe and Steinberg 1998).

It may be unfortunate, but it is still true that many whites believe that there is a social cost, not to being a person of color, but to being *white*. Whites are the "new losers" in a playing field that they believe has been leveled now that the United States is a supposedly egalitarian, color-blind society. Since "times are tough for everybody," policies to assist underrepresented groups—such as affirmative action—are "unfairly" supporting nonwhites. Thus, whites can now claim the status of victims (Gallagher 1995, 194). These feelings are of considerable importance in the politics of education in the United States, but also in many other nations. As it is being shaped by the conservative restoration, whiteness as an explicit cultural product is taking on a life of its own. In the arguments of the conservative discourses now so powerfully circulating, the barriers to social equality and equal opportunity have been removed. Merit is now the arbiter, an arbiter that works fairly through market choice, common curricula, and "objective" standardized testing. Whites, hence, have no privilege. Much of this is untrue, of course. Although undercut by other dynamics of power, there is still considerable advantage to being white in this society. However, it is not the truth or falsity of these claims that is at issue here; rather, it is the production of retrogressive white identities.

The implications of all this are profound, politically and culturally. For, given the right's rather cynical use of racial anxieties, given the economic fears and realities many citizens experience, and given the historic power of race on the U.S. psyche and on the formation of identities in so many other nations, many members of these societies may develop forms of solidarity based on their "whiteness." To say the least, this is not inconsequential in terms of struggles over meaning, identity, and the characteristics and control of our major institutions.

How do we interrupt these ideological formations? How do we develop anti-racist pedagogic practices that recognize white identities and yet do not lead to retrogressive formations? These are complex ideological and pedagogical questions. Yet these issues cannot be dealt with unless we focus directly on the differential power relations that have created (and been created by) the educational terrain on which we operate. This requires an insistent focus on the role of the state, on state policies, on the shift to the right by the Labour Party in the United Kingdom and by the Democratic Party in the United States, and on the reconstruction of common sense in which the right has successfully engaged.

If we were to be true to the historical record, whiteness is certainly not something we have just discovered. The politics of whiteness has been enormously, and often terrifyingly, effective in the formation of coalitions that unite people across cultural differences, across class and gender relations, and against their best interests (Dyer 1997, 19). It would not be possible to write the history of "our" economic, political, legal, health, and educational institutions—indeed, *all* of our institutions—without centering the politics of whiteness either consciously or unconsciously as a core dynamic. Of course, I am saying little that is new here. As critical race theorists and postcolonial writers have documented, racial forms and identities have been and are constitutive building blocks of the structures of our daily lives, imagined and real communities, and cultural processes and products.[5]

Let us look at this situation a bit more closely. Race as a category is usually applied to "nonwhite" peoples. White people are usually not seen and named. They are centered as the human norm. "Others" are raced; "we" are just people, as Richard Dyer explains in his telling book, *White* (1997). "There is no more powerful position than that of being 'just' human," he says. "The claim to power is the claim to speak for the commonality of humanity. Raced people can't do that—they can only speak for their race. But, non-raced people can, for they do not represent the interests of a race. The point of seeing the racing of whites is to dislodge them/us from the position of power, with all of the inequities, oppression, privileges, and sufferings in its train, dislodging them/us by undercutting the authority with which they/we speak and act in and on the world" (2)

"Our" very language speaks to the invisibility of power relations in our ordinary talk about whiteness. "We" speak of a sheet of white paper as "blank." A room painted all white is seen as perhaps "needing a bit of color." Multiple other examples could be cited. But the idea of whiteness as neutrality, as a *there* that is *not there*, is ideally suited for designating that social group that is to be taken as the "human ordinary" (Dyer 1997, 47).

In the face of this, in the face of something that might best be called an absent presence, a crucial political, cultural, and ultimately pedagogic project then is *making whiteness strange* (Dyer 1997, 4). Thus, part of our task in terms of pedagogy and political awareness and mobilization is to tell ourselves and to teach our students that identities are historically conferred. We need to recognize that "subjects are produced through multiple identifications." We should see our project as not reifying identity, but both understanding its production as an ongoing process of differentiation, *and*, most important, as subject to redefinition, resistance, and change (Scott 1995, 11).

Of course, focusing on whiteness can simply generate white guilt, hostility, or feelings of powerlessness. It can actually prevent the creation of those "decentered unities" that speak across differences and that can lead to broad coalitions that challenge dominant cultural, political, and economic relations. Thus, doing this requires an immense sensitivity, a clear sense of multiple power dynamics in any situation, and a nuanced and (at times risky) pedagogy.

Issues of whiteness may seem overly theoretical to some readers, or like one more "trendy" topic that has found its way to the surface of the critical educational agenda. This would be a grave mistake. As I have argued here, what counts as "official knowledge" consistently bears the imprint of tensions, struggles, and compromises in which race—even when hidden—plays a substantial role (Apple 1993). Further, as Steven Selden has so clearly shown in his recent history of the close connections between eugenics and educational policy and practice, almost every current dominant practice in education—standards, testing, systematized models of curriculum planning, gifted education, and so much more—has its roots in such concerns as "race betterment," fear of the other, and so on (Selden 1999). And these concerns were themselves grounded in the gaze of whiteness as the unacknowledged norm. Thus, issues of whiteness lie at the very core of educational policy and practice. We ignore them at our risk.

Of course, this is partly an issue of the politics of identity, and there has been increasing attention paid over the past decade to questions of identity in education and cultural studies. One of the major failures of research on identity, however, is its failure to adequately address the hegemonic politics of the right, identities and politics that often provide support for neoliberal and neoconservative policies. The conservative restoration has been more than a little successful in creating active subject positions that incorporate varied groups under the umbrella of a new hegemonic alliance. It has been able to engage in a politics inside and outside of education in which a fear of the racialized other is connected to fears of nation, culture, control, and decline—and to intensely personal fears about the future of one's children in an economy in crisis. All of these are sutured together in tense, but creative and complex, ways (Apple 1993, 1996; Carlson and Apple 1998). Given this, those of us who are committed to antiracist and critical educational policies and practices and who are engaged in bearing witness to the actual functioning of existing and newly proposed educational "reforms" would be wise to direct our attention not only to the racial effects of markets and standards, but just as much to the creative ways neoliberal and neoconservative (and in the United States, authoritarian populist religious fundamentalist) movements work to convince so many people (including many of the leaders of the Labour Party in the United Kingdom and in the Democratic Party here in the United States) that these policies are merely neutral technologies. They're not. And the differential race and class ways that they are not gives some social bite to the term "racing" toward educational reform.

Notes

Parts of this chapter will appear in a forthcoming essay, "The Absent Presence of Race in Educational Reform," *Race, Ethnicity, and Education* 2, no. 1:9–16; and in *Revolutionary Pedagogies*, edited by P. Trifonas (New York: Routledge, in press).

1. Whether there will be significant changes in this regard given the victory by the "New Labour" party over the conservatives in the last election remains to be seen. Certain aspects of neoliberal and neoconservative policies have already been accepted by Labour, such as the acceptance of stringent cost controls on spending put in place by the previous conservative government and an aggressive focus on "raising standards" in association with strict performance indicators.
2. See the discussion of the racial state in Omi and Winant 1994 and the analyses of race and representation in McCarthy and Crichlow 1994 and McCarthy 1998.
3. Of course, the state is not only classed but inherently sex/gendered and raced as well. See Whitty, Power, and Halpin 1998 for an argument about the gendered nature of the ways in which the management of schools is thought through. This coheres with the work of others who claim that our very definitions of public and private, of what knowledge is of most worth, and how institutions should be thought about and run are fully implicated in the gendered nature of this society. See, for example, Fraser 1989, 1997.
4. I am thinking of *The Bell Curve* here; see Herrnstein and Murray 1994 and my analysis of why such widely discredited positions are accepted in Apple (in press).
5. There is a vast amount of literature here. See, for example, Omi and Winant 1994; McCarthy and Crichlow 1994; Tate 1997; Fine et al. 1997; and McCarthy 1998.

References

Apple, M. W. 1988. *Teachers and Texts.* New York: Routledge.
———. 1993. *Official Knowledge.* New York: Routledge.
———. 1995. *Education and Power,* 2nd. ed. New York: Routledge.
———. 1996. *Cultural Politics and Education.* New York: Teachers College Press.
———. In press. *Power, Meaning, and Identity.* New York: Peter Lang.
Apple, M. W., and J. A. Beane, eds. 1995. *Democratic Schools.* Washington, D.C.: Association for Supervision and Curriculum Development.
Ball, S., R. Bowe, and S. Gewirtz. 1994. "Market Forces and Parental Choice." In *Educational Reform and Its Consequences,* edited by S. Tomlinson, 13–25. London: IPPR/Rivers Oram Press.
Bernstein, B. 1990. *The Structuring of Pedagogic Discourse.* New York: Routledge.
Bourdieu, P. 1994. *Distinction.* Cambridge, Mass.: Harvard University Press.
———. 1996. *The State Nobility.* Stanford, Calif.: Stanford University Press.
Carlson, D., and M. W. Apple, eds. 1998. *Power/Knowledge/Pedagogy.* Boulder, Colo.: Westview Press.
Chubb, J., and T. Moe. 1990. *Politics, Markets, and America's Schools.* Washington, D.C.: Brookings Institution.

Clarke, J., and J. Newman. 1997. *The Managerial State.* London: Sage.

Cornbleth, C., and D. Waugh. 1995. *The Great Speckled Bird.* New York: St. Martin's Press.

Dyer, R. 1997. *White.* New York: Routledge.

Evans, J., and D. Penney. 1995. "The Politics of Pedagogy." *Journal of Education Policy* 10:27–44.

Fine, M., L. Weis, L. Powell, and W. Mun, eds. 1997. *Off White.* New York: Routledge.

Fraser, N. 1989. *Unruly Practices.* Minneapolis: University of Minnesota Press.

———. 1997. *Justice Interruptus.* New York: Routledge.

Gallagher, C. 1995. "White Reconstruction in the University." *Socialist Review* 94:165–87.

Gillborn, D. 1997a. "Race, Nation, and Education." Unpublished paper, Institute of Education, University of London.

———. 1997b. "Racism and Reform." *British Educational Research Journal* 23:345–60.

Gillborn, D., and D. Youdell. 1998. "School League Tables and Selection in Multiethnic Secondary Schools." Paper presented at the symposium Racism and Reform in the United Kingdom, American Educational Research Association, San Diego.

Gipps, C., and P. Murphy. 1994. *A Fair Test?* Philadelphia: Open University Press.

Gould, S. J. 1981. *The Mismeasure of Man.* New York: W. W. Norton.

Haraway, D. 1989. *Primate Visions.* New York: Routledge.

Henig, J. 1994. *Rethinking School Choice.* Princeton, N.J.: Princeton University Press.

Herrnstein, R., and C. Murray. 1994. *The Bell Curve.* New York: The Free Press.

Hirsch, E. D., Jr. 1996. *The Schools We Want and Why We Don't Have Them.* New York: Doubleday.

Kincheloe, J., and S. Steinberg, eds. 1996 *Measured Lies.* New York: St. Martin's Press.

———, eds. 1998. *White Reign.* New York: Peter Lang.

Kliebard, H. 1986. *The Struggle for the American Curriculum.* New York: Routledge.

Liston, D. 1988. *Capitalist Schools.* New York: Routledge.

McCarthy, C. 1998. *The Uses of Culture.* New York: Routledge.

McCarthy, C., and W. Crichlow, eds. 1994. *Race, Identity, and Representation in Education.* New York: Routledge.

McCulloch, G. 1997. "Privatizing the Past?" *British Journal of Educational Studies* 45:69–82.

Menter, I., P. Muschamp, P. Nicholls, J. Ozga, with A. Pollard. 1997. *Work and Identity in the Primary School.* Philadelphia: Open University Press.

O'Hear, P. 1994. "An Alternative National Curriculum." In *Educational Reform and Its Consequences,* edited by S. Tomlinson, 55–72. London: IPPR/Rivers Oram Press.

Olssen, M. 1996. "In Defence of the Welfare State and Publicly Provided Education." *Journal of Education Policy* 11:337–62.

Omi, M., and H. Winant. 1994. *Racial Formation in the United States.* New York: Routledge.

Power, S., D. Halpin, and J. Fitz. 1994. "Underpinning Choice and Diversity?" In *Educational Reform and Its Consequences,* edited by S. Tomlinson, 26–40. London: IPPR/Rivers Oram Press.

Ransom, S. 1995. "Theorizing Educational Policy." *Journal of Education Policy* 10: 427–48.

Rury, J., and J. Mirel. 1997. "The Political Economy of Urban Education." In *Review of Research in Education,* vol. 22, edited by M. W. Apple, 49–110. Washington: American Educational Research Association.

Scott, J. 1995 "Multiculturalism and the Politics of Identity." In *The Identity in Question,* edited by J. Rajchman, 3–12. New York: Routledge.

Selden, S. 1999. *Inheriting Shame.* New York: Teachers College Press.

Swartz, D. 1997. *Culture and Power.* Chicago: University of Chicago Press.

Tate, W. 1997. "Critical Race Theory and Education." In *Review of Research in Education,* vol. 22, edited by M. W. Apple, 195–247. Washington: American Educational Research Association.

Teitelbaum, K. 1996. *Schooling for Good Rebels.* New York: Teachers College Press.

Tomlinson, S. 1998. "Markets, Reform, and Disadvantage." Paper presented at the symposium Racism and Reform in the United Kingdom, American Educational Research Association, San Diego.

Wacquant, L. 1996. Foreword. In P. Bourdieu, *The State Nobility*. Stanford, Calif.: Stanford University Press.

Whitty, G. 1997. "Creating Quasi-markets in Education." In *Review of Research in Education*, vol. 22, edited by M. W. Apple, 3–47. Washington: American Educational Research Association.

Whitty, G., T. Edwards, and S. Gewirtz. 1993. *Specialization and Choice in Urban Education*. New York: Routledge.

Whitty, G., S. Power, and D. Halpin. 1998. *Devolution and Choice in Education*. Buckingham: Open University Press.

6

EPISTEMOLOGIES OF
WHITENESS

Transgressing and Transforming
Pedagogical Knowledge

Peter McLaren, Zeus Leonardo,
and Ricky Lee Allen

University of California, Los Angeles

In California, the white empire is striking back. Neo-Nazis, skinhead surfers, the Ku Klux Klan and their acolytes, and the White Aryan Resistance are just a few of the racist groups whose memberships are on the rise, a trend that is disturbing but not altogether surprising. Yet these groups are on the fringes of a significantly more coherent, broad-based, and influential whiteness movement that threatens to sever many of the lifelines that people of color have created throughout the years. The recent passage of California's Propositions 187, 209, and 227 represents more than a mere round of mean-spirited political victories for the radical right, but is alarmingly suggestive of the political coalescence of white identity formation that has been fomenting in the swamps of racial intolerance at least since the civil rights movement. These California propositions succeeded not because they were an example of *bien trouvé* legislation, but because they were able to effectively invest in a white subjectivity whose *point d'appui* hinges on the desperate fear of losing control of moral, economic, and cultural space. These propositions reflect the secret teeth of racist formations and are expressive of the "angry white male" narrative that views whites as being summarily "imposed upon" by people of color. For example, the visual images used to cultivate support for Proposition 187, the "anti–illegal alien" legislation (i.e., the attack on undocumented immigrants), were selections from a security camera videotape of Mexicans dashing through an opening in the fence at the highly militarized U.S.-Mexico border. Pro-187 television ads expressly avoided representations of the many whites from countries such as Canada who work without documents throughout the southwestern United States. Imagine trying to muster white support for Proposition 187 by televising Air Canada flights unloading more Anglo Canadians at Los Angeles International Airport! The new California politics of whiteness, with its public spectacles of white power, even places former Klansman David Duke in the mainstream of political discourse. During a debate on Proposition 209, a referendum on affirmative action, Duke expressed his moral concern that California was beginning to "look like Mexico" (Bernstein 1996; McLaren 1997). Many white Californians were enthusiastic about the new admissions policies at the University of California that ended decades of affirmative action. In abolishing affirmative action, the University of California regents effectively mandated that "minority taxpayers subsidize the educations of those who successfully discriminate against them" (Lipsitz 1998).

In what follows, we trace much of the present insecurity among whites to that *fons et origo malorum* known as global capitalism, a condition that has encompassed a judicious slice of history, one that predates the transatlantic slave trade and encompasses today's "capitalist globalization, neoliberalism, unregulated speculative financial markets, monstrous indebtedness and impoverishment of the Third World, environmental degradation, [and the] gravely menacing ecological crisis" (Löwy 1998).

Recent public displays of white nationalism, as instanced in these racially inflamed California propositions, weaken what little institutional credibility multiculturalism has managed to create over the years, particularly among white teachers. A long-standing concern of the multiculturalist movement has been the fact that white teachers, who comprise approximately 86.5 percent of the nation's teachers (Acuña 1997), exercise overwhelming control over the environment of most urban schools. Historically, most multicultural curricula in teacher education programs have focused on educating white teachers about the cultural histories and knowledge of students of color as an indirect way of battling white racism. More radical versions of multiculturalism move beyond simple "colorblind" and "nonracial" thinking. Radical multiculturalists argue that the ethical fate of the United States hinges on the success of the decolonization of the white population as well as the fulfillment of the aspirations of the oppressed to embody history (Sleeter and McLaren 1995; McLaren 1995, 1997; McCarthy 1990). As the white nation continues its agenda of recolonizing its lost historical horizons, it would be judicious and circumspect for multicultural scholars to pay increased attention to the critical study of whiteness.

This chapter seeks to examine the emerging social context of whiteness through its intersections with production and expenditure. The production of whiteness is discussed in terms of a Marxist geography of white racial identity. It also examines the significance of Georges Bataille in the critical study of whiteness and outlines how whiteness even colonizes those features of social life that are distinct from processes of production and consumption.

Producing Whiteness

In the *Communist Manifesto* (1848/1964), Karl Marx and Friedrich Engels state that the bourgeoisie "creates a world in its own image" (64–65). That is to say, the bourgeoisie seeks to manufacture and regulate a hospitable environment for its own plans for humanity. One of the modalities of place-making for the bourgeoisie has been the racialization of material, discursive, and social spaces associated with the human body. To a significant extent, the image that the bourgeoisie has created for itself is an image of whiteness. After all, the bourgeoisie was not and is not without material bodies, and for much of the world the bodies of the bourgeoisie are imagined and experienced as white. In essence, global capital is white capital in that the bodies of most capitalists are seen as white—or something close to white.

As capitalism has deepened around the globe, the racial signifier of "white" has grown exponentially in value, and, like any other overly valued product, it is closely inspected for quality control during the production process to ensure its purity to the consumers of whiteness. The capitalist technology of racial production and consumption, particularly in the Western world, is "whiteness," an ideological system of racialization and power that constructs racial identities as it simultaneously bestows privilege to those identified as "white"(McLaren 1997; Lipsitz 1998; Kincheloe et al. 1998). As an oppressive, socially constructed system, its processes and consequences must be named and elaborated in order to transform the spaces it manufactures.

The key to producing whiteness, of course, is not to refer to it explicitly, but to make it an all-encompassing field of communication, to have it so visible that it is not noticed. For critical multiculturalists, the methodological apprenticeship needed for dismantling whiteness is to learn to see what is visible and to denaturalize it. Whiteness produces itself with built-in elevation so that it is always more than it signifies. It signifies its own preexistence to the other. It knots together a popular reciprocity: If you aren't recognized here, you don't really count! Its message is its milieu. It is a constant transmission around which social life is both organized and hierarchized. But whiteness as backdrop is simultaneously a protective screen—it "screens out" as well as colonizes meaning. We forget that the world of whiteness has a materiality, a history, and proceeds apace only by virtue of its ability to erase itself, its history of genocide or horror.

What is a white racial identity, or any identity, without a space to which it refers? The survival of whiteness in global capitalism requires the continual production and reproduction of spaces in which its order and existence is organized. One of the primary organizers of capitalism is the idea that social spaces are interpreted or planned as "markets" based on their perceived value or potential value for economic exploitation. The production of markets in capitalism has been dominated by whites, and this domination has situated the bodies of most people of color as a market of cheap labor.

The social spaces of whiteness are those of power, territories that confer privilege and domination for whites. As such, the actual social and spatial rituals that form white racial identity in global capitalism might best be revealed through the politically and spatially focused lens of human territoriality. According to Robert Sack (1986), territoriality is a spatial matter "of transmitting energy and information in order to affect, influence, and control the ideas and actions of others and their access to resources" (26). Territoriality is essential to understanding the construction of any type of domination at the level of human interactions since it is the spatial practice of attempting to control the materials and discourses of others. Territoriality is the spatial manifestation of what Michel Foucault describes as "governmentality." Governmentality is a territorial strategy for the control and disciplining of bodies and thoughts on a microgeopolitical scale. For Foucault, most theorizations of power underconceptualize the impact of activities and interactions of social agents in constructing social compliance on microgeopolitical scales (Hesse 1997). In order for power to be structured across time and space in the modern nation-state, it must be surveilled through the disciplined rationales of individual agents (Foucault 1978). Whiteness exists through the territoriality of white agents whose consciousnesses are informed and infected by the rubric of white governmentality, a social and psychological condition that scripts the behavior of whites. The territoriality of whiteness draws breath from the processes of white governmentality that turn the spaces of the human body into a readily identifiable signpost of differential social value and location. These signposts guide the surveillance of white domination in white territories.

To be a person of color in white territory is to be monitored, marked, and excluded. To be white in white territory is to be able to pass the gaze of its bourgeois sentries and traverse its social space as an included, or at least properly subjugated, member. Beverly Daniel Tatum (1997) uses Rosabeth Moss Kanter's (1980) social psychology model of the experience of differentness in an organization to outline the spatial practice of surveilling whiteness. As Tatum explains, "In a Tale of O, psychologist Rosabeth Moss Kanter ... highlights what happens to the O, the token, in a world of Xs. In corporate America, Black people are still in the O position. One consequence of being an O ... is heightened visibility. When an O walks in the room, the Xs [white people] notice. Whatever the O does, positive or negative, stands out because of this increased visibility. It is hard for an O to blend in. When several Os are together, the attention of the Xs is really captured" (89).

Membership in the white community can be revoked, at least in the eyes of other whites, if the warning sensors are triggered under the watch of white governmentality, as white territoriality is essentially a geography of racial selectivity. White governmentality operates in a regulatory mode where as long as people and property are fulfilling their idealized roles in the logic of white capitalism they will be allowed to move about within the given constraints. Among whites, there are codes that determine whether another white person is in line with white governmentality and keeping territorial order. Like some sort of secret handshake, these codes form racial bonds that are difficult for some dissenting whites to see until they themselves experience being surveilled. For example, a group of white girls in the farm town of Morocco, Indiana, went to their mostly white school dressed in the hip-hop style of baggy jeans, dreadlocks, and combat boots (Ignatiev and Garvey 1996). They were physically harassed and threatened at school by other whites for "acting black." In the following months, the school received bomb threats and a visit from the Ku Klux Klan. White territoriality in this case was quite visibly enacted in a public space for all to see.

Yet the maintenance of white territoriality is typically more subtle than this. One of its subtleties has to do with the connectivity among whites or the white community that forges the governmentality for making whiteness. Many times, the testing of bonds in the white community is hidden away in the private spaces of whiteness. Multicultural educator Christine Sleeter (1996) describes a feature of whiteness called "white racial bonding" that acts to "affirm a common stance on race-related issues, legitimating particular interpretations of oppressed groups, and drawing we-they boundaries" (216). As evidence, she tells the story of a conversation she had with a white neighbor whom she barely knew. Almost immediately after exchanging their greetings, the neighbor commented on how pleased she was that the federal government was sending welfare mothers back to work. Sleeter says that racial bonding among whites often works through this type of discursive engagement—a tactic that we call "baiting"—around social issues. Discursive baiting is a common interaction among whites who are acquaintances. It begins with a simple exchange of pleasantries and quickly moves into a test of white solidarity. One of the consequences for giving the wrong answer to discursive bait is to have an extended, oddly antagonistic debate whereby the instigator, or "white sentry," attempts to discipline the logic of the resistor, or "white infidel," and bring her back into the order of whiteness. Of course, another possible consequence for a white infidel is to be socially shunned altogether and made an outsider to whiteness.

Produced through time and space at the nexus of racial oppression and white territoriality, the logic of white governmentality is coded by whites as a means of minimizing the material effects of what is perceived to be a multicultural invasion of the United States—that is, of the white nation. Though whites often do not wish to discuss their own privilege, their recognition of and responses to broad social issues are replete with racial rhetoric and representative of a definite group identity, or "white community." In an important empirical study of white college students, Gallagher (1997) found that the white students in his study feel that people of color are or will be responsible for lowered standards of living for whites. Their fear of material deprivation is also located in a white victimization narrative whereby they believe that whites are unfairly attacked by equity programs, such as those of affirmative action. Contradicting the typical notion in whiteness research that whites do not think of themselves as white, Gallagher's research suggests a different trend. As he explains, "The majority of whites in this study have come to understand themselves and their interests as white. Many of my respondents now think about themselves as whites, not as ethnics; they see themselves as individuals who are members of a racial category with its own particular set of interests" (7).

The students expressed an interest in making a new white identity that is non-demonized. One antidemonization strategy currently used by white students to territorialize their white identities in discursive space is to strip away all sense of historical and material reality while representing the white race as simply "equal" to all other races. In spite of the current realities of real oppression, whites argue that society is a utopia of equality, with one exception: whites are now an oppressed class. They contend that true equality can be achieved by eliminating affirmative action, being blind to race, and wiping out "reverse racism" against whites. Within this strategy of white governmentality, whites readily adopt "color blindness" because they see it as a way of promoting their agenda of white victimization, dismissing further criticisms of whiteness, and presenting an image that they are humane for not wanting to refer to others in racial terms.

White racial identity sees the material lives of people of color, and thus, of themselves through the smoke of a historical illusion. In particular, urban spaces such as the inner city, ghetto, barrio, and suburbia are racial signifiers in that their material conditions are inscribed in the logic of white governmentality as readily understood or "plain to see." To most whites, the inner city is a place of dirt, filth, chaos, incivility, and laziness whereas the suburbs are envisioned as orderly, productive, civil, comfortable, and secure. In the logic of white capitalism, the Manichean distinctions between the inner city and suburbia are supposed evidence that a pure and just meritocracy governs social life. Whites morally rationalize the unevenness of urban space through a puritanical work-ethic narrative: those who work hard get to live in the comfort of suburbia while those who are lazy and inept are exiled and then quarantined in the inner city. Douglas Massey and Nancy Denton (1993) describe in great detail how the federal government, banking institutions, and real estate agencies constructed whiteness in its urban form. At the turn of the century, blacks and whites were more likely to live in integrated neighborhoods than they are today. Starting in the 1930s, the federal government initiated mortgage insurance policies so that banks would accept a lower down payment for purchasing a home, in order to spur the housing market. These programs, however, served to support white racism by institutionalizing a system called "redlining" that identified the neighborhoods that were considered suitable or unsuitable locations for investment. As part of its institutional policy, the Federal Housing Administration (FHA), Veterans Administration (VA), and commercial banks seldom gave federally insured mortgage loans to buyers, who were almost exclusively people of color, in redlined neighborhoods. Additionally, the FHA considered racial segregation as a necessary tactic to maintain stable housing values, at least in white areas. For example, a 1933 FHA report written in conjunction with realtors concluded that the English, Germans, Scottish, Irish, and Scandinavians were good for neighborhood stability while Mexicans and blacks were not. Five years later, the FHA warned bank-loan officers in its underwriting manual that they should beware of "incompatible" racial groups that might invade and devalue a neighborhood. Meanwhile, whites were receiving federal backing for a historically unprecedented residential construction project—

the building of American suburbia. Today, most of these homes are still owned by whites and continue to increase in value; and unfair banking practices persist. Current studies of banking practices reveal that banks across the country create surplus capital by taking more in deposits *from* black communities than they invest *in* them. Banks then shift the surplus toward investment in white ventures (Lipsitz 1995). Many whites remain oblivious to the very real institutional processes that continue to help make their privileged place in the world.

To this day, government institutions are responsible for placing landfills, hazardous waste sites, and chemical manufacturers close to abandoned low-income minority communities. Government institutions single out minority communities for toxic waste sites, as Robin D. Kelley (1997) points out, since it is estimated that "three out of five African-Americans live dangerously close to abandoned toxic waste sites and commercial hazardous landfills" (148). Women of color often take the lead in community-based organizing. For instance, South Central Los Angeles in the 1960s witnessed the growth of the Watts Women's Association, the Avalon-Carver Community Center, the Mothers of Watts Community Action Council, Mothers Anonymous, the Welfare Recipients Union, the Central City Community Mental Health Center, the Neighborhood Organization of Watts, and the South Central Bureau of Los Angeles as precursors for such contemporary groups as Mothers Reclaiming Our Children, and the Mothers of East Los Angeles. In 1984 the Mothers of East Los Angeles won a protracted battle against the prison-industrial complex that wanted to build a prison in East Los Angeles; they also defeated attempts at constructing an oil pipeline and hazardous waste incinerator in the heart of their community. Still, the largest hazardous waste landfill in the country is located in Emelle, Alabama, whose population is nearly 80 percent black. Kelley also notes other disturbing facts: that the greatest concentration of hazardous waste sites is in the mostly black and Latino south side of Chicago; federally sponsored toxic cleanup programs take longer and are less thorough in minority neighborhoods; and polluters based in minority areas are treated less severely by government agencies than those in largely white communities. White capitalism as a practice of oppression resides in its ability to spatialize race as well as racialize space.

Ironically, most whites do not see themselves as privileged and, as previously mentioned, have even come to see themselves as social victims. Whites have a problematic construction of privilege primarily because they come to know the world within the boundaries of white territoriality. Peggy McIntosh (1997) argues that privilege is relational and not absolute. One group can only become unprivileged through the privileging of another group. She summarizes the essence of white privilege when she says, "Being white, I am given considerable power to escape many kinds of danger or penalty as well as to choose which risks I want to take" (297).

For people of color, their stories about the organization of privilege in white capitalism are certainly not the same as those of whites. As people of color encounter alienation in the territories of whiteness, survival depends on the ability to construct counterterritorialities that are resistant to white governmentality and provide a spatially productive experience for the recovery and assemblage of nonwhite racial identities. Stephen Nathan Haymes (1995) makes the argument that black identity coincides with the (re)production of black public spaces that challenge the moral order of whiteness in urban space. Rather than reading the inner city as a site of black passivity and victimization, Haymes situates it as a home place for the black counterpublic.

In particular, if power is linked to the production of urban meaning, then those public spaces located at the center of city life dominate its meaning, and in so doing, define the cultural and political terrain in which marginalized public spaces—in this case black public spaces—resist, form alternative identities, and make culture in the city (Haymes 1995, 113).

The culturally specific institutions of black public spaces are being disassembled through white territorial practices like gentrification and the production of desaturated spaces of whiteness known as "urban renewal." The gaze of white governmentality situated in the mind of whites perceives black urban spaces as places of decay, ineptitude, and dysfunction. Whites fantasize about ritualistically purifying black urban space through the ceremony of urban renewal. White capitalistic desires are satiated when defiled black spaces are morally laundered by the invisible hand of the market. All of this transpires while black communities in the inner city have been forced to live in steadily more concentrated quarters. We agree with Haymes when he argues that educators must have a critical understanding of the place-making practices of white institutions that continually attempt to turn the city into a safe space for whiteness under the guise of "reform."

White teachers must also develop an understanding of how students of color experience the territoriality of whiteness at school in ways that form their racial identities. William Cross (1991) has put forth a model that codifies the structure of the psychological process of becoming black in a white-dominated context. According to Cross, black people begin with the belief that they are part of the dominant culture until their experiences with racism raise their consciousness about their social status and location. Black children who have reached this stage of "encounter" typically seek out other black children who share a similar racialized experience. As black children form friendships with those that they perceive to be similar to themselves, informal groups crystallize and serve as a space for black racial identity formation. Around the age of adolescence, black children immerse themselves in differentiated and particular public spaces that act to organize their new identities as representations of their lived struggles with white culture, or as we would argue, with and against white territoriality. On a similar note, John Ogbu (1992) casts this resistance aspect of the encounter stage as a "cultural inversion" of whiteness. Black students that assimilate to white models of educational success run the risk of being tagged as "acting white" by other black students. Regardless of the strategies employed by students of color, the bottom line is that whiteness affects, influences, and controls the identity formation of people of color through the territorial manipulation of the discursive and material spaces of schooling.

A critique of epistemologies of whiteness necessitates interrogating the ways regimes of white knowledge produce white privilege and reproduce the social conditions that exploit racialized "others." The production of whiteness is simultaneously the creation of racial hierarchies by institutionalizing white-centric norms. But this only works through the control of institutions and social formations, without which white culture becomes one signifier among many. As an institution concerned with producing knowledge, education becomes a prosthesis—the long arm of whiteness—in its quest to reterritorialize social life. Transforming pedagogical knowledge becomes that much more urgent.

WHITENESS AND THE THEORY OF EXPENDITURE

Transforming labor, and consequently student work, requires a revolutionary disposition toward relations of production. In particular, it is imperative that educators link the transformation of the economy with a critique of whiteness. However, theories of whiteness must be linked to the idea that capitalism is not only the exploitation of knowledge for profits, but the simultaneous repression of expenditure, or what Georges Bataille (1997, 1991, 1988, 1985) describes as the human proclivity to expend energy and not to accumulate it. Transformation of labor produces social relations that flourish in conditions free of alienation and exploitation. A discourse on production must also consider alternative theoretical frameworks to explain students' inner experiences and the knowledge they gain from them. Transforming relations of production allows students, as concrete subjects, to experience schooling in new ways, but Bataille's theory of expenditure provides a general framework that explains how we come to know these inner experiences *themselves*, a theory that functions not within the logic of production, but within that of waste. As Bataille (1988) explains,

> On the surface of the globe, for *living matter in general*, energy is always in excess; the question is always posed in terms of extravagance. The choice is limited to how the wealth is to be squandered. . . . The general movement of exudation (of waste) of living matter implies him [*sic*], and he cannot stop it; . . . it destines him, in a privileged way, to that glorious operation, to useless consumption. The latter cannot accumulate limitlessly in the productive forces; eventually, like a river into the sea, it is bound to escape us and be lost to us. (23; emphasis in the original)

Schools accumulate useful knowledge to the point where they cannot hold it. Students memorize, tabulate, and synthesize knowledge for future-oriented purposes. Eventually, unproductive student behavior erupts and then spreads as students resist and rebel against work as a *guiding principle*. The conventional explanation for disruptive student behavior is "unproductivity." Resistant students are either alienated or lazy, and they willfully opt out of work. Bataillean pedagogy understands this to be a state of wasteful activity that cannot be fully explained by a productivist logic. It represents the "blind spot" of the discourse on work. Bataille's pedagogy attempts to transgress the utility of current school knowledge. Educators isolate unproductive students from their peers to ensure that they "do their work" or detain them after school to give them extra work. Meanwhile, what escapes our understanding is the principle of expenditure, or how students squander schoolwork for no apparently useful or productive reason.

The theory of expenditure does not deny the presence of work, let alone the importance of liberated labor. It acknowledges the production of life for purposes of subsistence, survival, and improvement of the species. Furthermore, the modified theory of expenditure we are presenting recognizes the importance of revolutionizing student work as part of an overall transformation of social life. In fact, Bataille (1997) clarifies, "Class struggle ... becomes the grandest form of social expenditure when it is taken up again and developed, this time on the part of the workers, and on such a scale that it threatens the very existence of the masters" (178).

It is at this intersection between work and nonwork that we locate a revolution both of student work and waste. Injected in this dialectic is the indictment of whiteness as an ideology that alienates students from real knowledge as well as preventing them from rejoicing in the event of knowing, unfettered from utilitarian concerns.

School knowledge has become not only a commodity in the Marxian sense, but has taken on the quality of a thing that exists for other things. And as things go, school knowledge is deemed useful for something outside of itself, to fulfill a destiny that has been predetermined, such as grades or higher education. Bataille's perspective decries this utilitarian condition wherein students are subjected to schoolwork that apparently has no intrinsic worth but an exchange value in the markets of white capitalism.

A radical education understands that combating capitalism is the call for unalienated student work, but it also recognizes that liberated work then affords students the opportunity for leisure, or luxurious work. As Herbert Kliebard (1986) notes, the etymological root of *school* finds itself in the word *leisure*. This is to say that as much as capitalism exploits labor, it also reduces our capacity to celebrate nonwork life. This mode of celebration is not to be found in white societies but expresses itself in what Jean Baudrillard (1975) calls "primitive" societies. As Bataille (1997) describes it, one finds the "festival" or "potlatch" in social arrangements that function under the sign of the gift exchange. Euro-white societies, which function under the sign of classical economics, find the gift exchange rather foreign and irrational. In his endorsement of the gift principle imported by Marcel Mauss, Bataille (1997) writes,

> The "merchants" of Mexico practised the paradoxical system of exchange I have described as a regular sequence of gifts; these customs, not barter, in fact constituted the archaic organization of exchange. Potlatch, still practised by the Indians of the north-west coast of America, is its typical form. Ethnographers now employ this term to designate institutions functioning on a similar principle; they find traces of it in all societies. Among the Tlingit, the Haida, the Tsimshian, the Kwakiutl, potlatch is of prime importance in social life. . . .

Potlatch is, like commerce, a means of circulating wealth, but it excludes bargaining. More often than not it is the solemn giving of considerable riches, offered by a chief to his rival for the purpose of humiliation, challenging and obligating him. The recipient has to erase the humiliation and take up the challenge; he must satisfy the obligation that was contracted by accepting. He can only reply, a short time later, by means of a new potlatch, more generous than the first: he must pay back with interest. (202)

Expenditure is a form of social obligation between subjects who exchange "gifts" and then transcend their limits. A "countergift" raises the stakes. Seen this way, expenditure is inherently intersubjective and anti-individualistic. It binds, for example, teachers and students with one another as each benefits from the other's challenge. The gift is an alternative form of exchange opposed to classical economic transactions. The gift is ruled by the principle of loss, not profit or accumulation. Accumulating gifts without offering countergifts violates the exchange and institutes power in favor of the giver over the receiver. To maintain the equilibrium, it is necessary to perpetuate the exchange, and more important, to raise the stakes with more extravagant gifts. Indeed, in some cases the gift object is produced, but it is produced only to be squandered.

In schools, the moment of learning is subjugated to the utilitarian economic principle of saving the concrete knowledge gained, for an abstract, future purpose. This is the pathological consequence of autocapitalism, which becomes obsessed with "growth for growth's sake" (Ashley 1997), a process with no end in sight. Student curiosity and spontaneity are forsaken, and the excitement—the Aha!—of learning is deferred. What results is the alienation of student subjectivity for utilitarian goals. In short, the gift of knowledge is violated.

Bataillean pedagogy reinstitutes the challenge involved in transgressing the current regimes of school knowledge surveilled by white governmentality through considering schooling as a gift to be returned. Furthermore, this intersubjective process is guided by the principle of expenditure rather than accumulation for utilitarian purposes.

A critical perspective on epistemologies of whiteness considers the general terrorism of the Protestant ethic to negate nonwork life in schools. Within our framework, we suggest that Max Weber's immanent insight neglects the evolution of the spirit of whiteness along with the coevolution of capitalism and Protestantism. In its search to procure salvation through work and accumulation of things, the parallel evolution of Protestantism, whiteness, and capitalism suppresses students' capacity to enjoy the fruits of their work. Students' immediate gratification from work is always either denied or deferred. Salvation through work becomes the only good, against which all other endeavors are measured (Richardson 1994). A student quickly learns that one's worth becomes coextensive with one's work. Human identity becomes the kind of work one takes up: *I am* an attorney! *I am* a doctor! Take note of the dejection a person feels when he loses his job. Over and beyond the feeling of improvidence, he feels worthless. Extending Weber's thesis, we argue that capitalism is also linked with the *Prot-*

estant ethic, or the hyperutilitarianism found in white patriarchal capitalism. That is, Weber's findings neglect the *construction of whiteness* with respect to work and utilitarianism, or the making of a *Protestant ethnic*. We suggest that any discourse that negates white capitalism as the exploitation of labor for profit must also critique the way it exploits *all* facets of learning as determined by utilitarian labor.

Homogeneous societies, or social formations determined by utility, are characterized by limits because their imagination is bound by a foreseeable end that turns any form of waste into what Bataille calls the "accursed share," or the cursed portion of society. On the other hand, heterogeneous societies, or social formations determined by expenditure, know no bounds since they are driven by transgression of the sacred. The accursed share, those denigrated discursive and material spaces of people of color in white territories, is jettisoned by the mechanisms of white capitalism since it is seen as unproductive by white governmentalities. The high unemployment of people of color is considered a natural residue of competition and ameliorating homelessness an inefficient endeavor. In Donnie Brasco's words, "Forget about it." Learning-disabled students, gang members, physically handicapped children, and high school dropouts represent the cursed parts of schooling and are grouped under the sign "unproductive." Yet their heterogeneous existence points to their alternative way of being, an experience that can be explained through its contrast with utilitarian work. This does not suggest that these subjects do not want to work, or work hard for that matter. Often, as Paul Willis (1977), Peter McLaren (1999), and Jay MacLeod (1987) have shown, some of the most alienated students are the ones who valorize work. But it goes without saying that their perceived incompatibility with production is responsible for labeling them as part of the accursed share of white capitalism. Bataillean pedagogy speaks up for the oppressed segments of our schools, the heterogeneous other of the workaday world (Pefanis 1991).

Much has been said about white fascism (see, e.g., McLaren 1995, 1997). For Georges Bataille (1997), fascism's renegade morality represents something of the order of the heterogeneous and warrants critical attention from the perspective of expenditure. In his studies of German and Italian fascism, Bataille writes,

> Opposed to democratic politicians, who represent in different countries the platitude inherent to homogeneous [i.e., productive] society, Mussolini and Hitler immediately stand out as something other. Whatever emotions their actual existence as political agents of evolution provokes, it is impossible to ignore the force that situates them above men, parties and even laws: a force that disrupts the regular course of things, the peaceful but fastidious homogeneity powerless to maintain itself (the fact that laws are broken is only the most obvious sign of the transcendent, heterogeneous nature of fascist action). (128)

Bataille does not promote fascists and their human atrocities. This is unequivocal, and his unrelenting critique of fascism is well documented (Richardson 1994). What captures his interest is fascism's utmost heterogeneity and extreme authority, which exists for itself before it exists for any useful or productive reasons. To Bataille, the psychological structure of fascism exceeds any conventional ideas about morality involving good and bad. There seems to be no boundary to fascist atrocities. "Evil" just does not seem to suffice as a descriptor. What can we call Adolf Hitler's disgusting campaign of death? What signifier fits the image, the punishment for the crime? Fascism is driven to extreme social hypnosis as a way of concentrating the people's effective flows before it is linked with any productive ends. It is wasteful in all its manifestation, and fascism—etymologically tied to "uniting" or "concentrating" (Bataille 1997, 135)—becomes the hoarding of human energy for the fascist leader. In short, what was originally explorable in terms of expenditure becomes a convenient story about accumulation of power, of energy, and ultimately of homogeneous purpose.

White fascism is not only the enforcement of white territorial control of the means of production. It is also the simultaneous policing of excess, of curbing expenditure and revelry (not to mention ribaldry) where these may threaten the puritanical code of white governmentality. How many examples do we have of the carnivalesque activity, outlawry, and social brigandage of student behavior quelled by the repressive power of state or local police? Celebration is confused for lawlessness as the antiriot unit marches into the potlatch to subdue its energy. School classrooms function under this sign of general repression where quietude is valued over movement and vitality. Yet shift the scene to a crowded hallway or students on their way to their lockers and the noise deafens even the hard of hearing. White fascism is as much about the control of expenditure as it is the control of the means of production. As an apparatus of whiteness, schools become places of the saving of energy rather than the spending of it.

It should be plain to see that white capitalism has encoded the colored body as a site of excess. To the white fascist, black students (especially males) have become the site of supersexuality and the Latina body a site of superreproduction. On the other hand, the white body has been constructed as the site of rationality and savings. The white body is almost nonsexualized. This erotic economy of "excess" is linked to a genocidal tendency in the history and geography of whiteness to the extent that white ideology has been involved in consistent crimes against the eroticized other. The oppression of the sexual other is evidence of a certain repression of the expenditure that whiteness represses in itself. That is, whiteness recognizes an excess beyond productivity but fails to squander it, fearing the ecstatic consequences of such a waste.

It is a vicarious living of sorts that robs whiteness of any life of its own. It is a mitigated, *surreptitious* experience that partitions the erotic—that is, the irreducible experience—into fantasies rather than participating in its flows. It is a projection of what whiteness fears about itself and fails to understand: a certain excessive drive. This may sound like the eroticization of the racialized subject represented in the white imaginary. For it seems a standard white discourse to portray the other as a site of excess. However, remaining consistent with Bataille's theory, expenditure is a general economy that inheres in all humans. It is not an economic drive particular to non-Western societies, but one that finds its expression in them, and its repression in whiteness.

Simple life forms excrete waste, factories spew smoke, and stars explode as supernova only to give birth to new star formations from leftover stellar material. Inasmuch as capitalism commodifies any and all social spaces for profit, whiteness refuses to divest itself of excess but saves it for further growth, forestalling its inevitable and disastrous expression. Wars, riots, and civil unrest are today's social potlatch.

CONCLUSION

The theory of expenditure proposed here is a modified Bataillean pedagogy. It represents an alternative theory to production that nevertheless depends on the transformation of labor to realize its luxurious goals. A modified theory of expenditure recognizes the value in school experiences promoting knowledge that serves no master. But it also realizes that a master currently exists and must be deposed strategically. The double helix of whiteness and capitalism is the conspiratorial first cause. Pushing the contradictions of white capitalism to their extreme exposes the weak joints of the economy. Only then can we approach what Bataille calls "unknowing," or knowledge divorced from utilitarian ends, because it reconciles student interests in work as these evolve in their liberated and not as they (re)produce certain outcomes. Bataillean pedagogy, as Jürgen Habermas (1987) suggests, appears like a form of fantastic anarchism because it lacks a rational basis for valuing one form of student work over another (since this is beyond linguistic representation). Moreover, Bataille is involved in a performative contradiction that uses reasoned arguments to reject the metanarrative of rational knowledge (Jay 1993). However, it is also possible to construct Bataille's suggestions not as anarchistic, but as an opening up of knowledge to all possibilities. Transforming student labor and transgressing utilitarian experience represents the double move out of alienated school knowledge.

A revolutionary multicultural education entails teaching students and teachers about the productive basis of schools and social life. It calls for white teachers to pay attention to how they manifest their whiteness through their territorial control over production and expenditure. Revolutionary multiculturalists assist students in constructing a concrete education by exposing the contradictions found in their encounters with the normative spatial orders of whiteness. Revolutionary multiculturalism encourages young minds to link their critique of school knowledge with the white exploitation of racialized labor. However, revolutionary multiculturalism also recognizes the importance of a theory of expenditure in order to guard against the uncritical valorization of utilitarian labor coextensive with whiteness. Squandering knowledge without return or profit is not the opposite of production but rather its completion. Revolutionary multiculturalism is involved in planning the counterterritorial construction of spaces for forging liberating relationships between expenditure and production. But we should problematize those relationships between expenditure and production that serve the interests of white capitalism. For example, a certain factory in Los Angeles employs mostly Mexicans for the production of audio speakers. On Cinco de Mayo, the mostly white administration of this factory hires mariachi bands to perform for the workers during their lunch break. In this scenario, expenditure has been folded into capitalist production. The mariachis are hired not to promote the resistance of labor, but to make the laborers more productive and loyal to the company. This is not the kind of relationship between production and expenditure that is counterhegemonic. A revolutionary multiculturalism calls for whites to be allies with people of color in authoring spatialities that intervene in the normative functioning of white privilege in white capitalism.

A revolutionary multiculturalism sharpens on the whetstone of liberation. Bataille's vision of excess and Marx's imperative of class struggle can help us to formulate such a revolutionary project in order to sever both the economic thralldom through which the oppressed are imprisoned by the capitalist class as well as the systems of classification and intelligibility that are used to justify the current social and spatial division of labor. We need not wait to be given the gift of solidarity from the gods of progress nor expect it to be produced by the inevitability of revolution. Rather, we must take that first step toward revolutionary praxis. That is one gift we can bestow on ourselves.

REFERENCES

Acuña, R. 1997. *Anything but Mexican: Chicanos in Contemporary Los Angeles.* London: Verso.
Ashley, D. 1997. *History without a Subject.* Boulder, Colo.: Westview Press.
Banks, J. 1989. "Multicultural Education: Characteristics and Goals." In *Multicultural Education: Issues and Perspective,* edited by J. Banks and C. M. Banks, 2–26. Needham Heights, Mass.: Allyn Bacon.
Bataille, G. 1985. *Visions of Excess: Selected Writings 1927–1939,* translated by A. Stoekl. Manchester: Manchester University Press.
———. 1988. *The Accursed Share.* Vol. 1, translated by R. Hurley. New York: Zone Books.
———. 1991. *The Accursed Share.* Vols. 2 and 3, translated by R. Hurley. New York: Zone Books.
———. 1997. *The Bataille Reader,* edited by F. Botting and S. Wilson. Cornwall: Blackwell.
Baudrillard, J. 1975. *The Mirror of Production.* St. Louis: Telos Press.
Bernstein, S. 1996. "The Storm Rises Over Ex-Klansman in Debate." *Los Angeles Times,* 11 September, A3, A14.
Cross, W. E. 1991. *Shades of Black: Diversity in African-American Identity.* Philadelphia: Temple University Press.
Foucault, M. 1978. *Discipline and Punish: The Birth of the Prison,* translated by A. Sheridan. New York: Pantheon Books.
Gallagher, C. 1997. "White Racial Formation: Into the Twenty-First Century." In *Critical White Studies: Looking behind the Mirror,* edited by R. Delgado and J. Stefanic, 6–11. Philadelphia: Temple University Press.
Habermas, J. 1987. *The Philosophical Discourse of Modernity,* translated by F. G. Lawrence. Cambridge, Mass.: MIT Press.
Haymes, S. N. 1995. *Race, Culture, and the City: A Pedagogy for Black Urban Struggle.* Albany: State University of New York Press.
Hesse, B. 1997. "White Governmentality." In *Imagining Cities: Scripts, Signs, Memory,* edited by S. Westwood and J. Williams, 86–103. London: Routledge.

Ignatiev, N., and J. Garvey. 1996. "Free to Be Me." In *Race Traitor*, edited by N. Ignatiev and J. Garvey, 1. New York: Routledge.

Jay, M. 1993. *Downcast Eyes*. Berkeley and Los Angeles: University of California Press.

Kanter, R. M. 1980. *A Tale of "O": On Being Different in an Organization*. New York: Harper and Row.

Kelley, R. D. G. 1997. *Yo' Mama's Disfunktional! Fighting the Cultural Wars in Urban America*. Boston: Beacon Press.

Kincheloe, J., S. Steinberg, N. Rodriguez, and R. Chennault, eds. 1998. *White Reign: Deploying Whiteness in America*. New York: St. Martin's Press.

Lipsitz, G. 1995. "The Possessive Investment in Whiteness: Racialized Social Democracy and the 'White' Problem in American Studies." *American Quarterly* 47, no. 3:369–87.

Lott, E. 1993. "White Like Me: Racial Cross-Dressing and the Construction of American Whiteness." In *Cultures of United States Imperialism*, edited by A. Kaplan and D. E. Pease, 474–98. Durham, N.C.: Duke University Press.

Löwy, M. 1998. "Globalization and Internationalism: How Up-to-Date Is the *Communist Manifesto?*" *Monthly Review* 50, no. 6:16–27.

MacLeod, J. 1987. *Ain't No Makin' It*. Boulder, Colo.: Westview Press.

McIntosh, P. 1997. "White Privilege and Male Privilege: A Personal Account of Coming to See Correspondences through Work in Women's Studies." In *Critical White Studies: Looking Behind the Mirror*, edited by R. Delgado and J. Stefanic, 291–99. Philadelphia: Temple University Press.

McCarthy, C. 1990. *Race and Curriculum*. London: Falmer Press.

McIntyre, A. 1997. "Constructing an Image of a White Teacher." *Teachers College Record* 98, no. 4:653–81.

McLaren, P. 1999. *Schooling as a Ritual Performance*, 3rd ed. Boulder, Colo.: Rowman and Littlefield.

———. 1995. *Critical Pedagogy and Predatory Culture*. London: Routledge.

———. 1997. *Revolutionary Multiculturalism*. Boulder, Colo.: Westview Press.

Marx, K., and F. Engels. 1964. *The Communist Manifesto*, translated by S. Moore. New York: Simon and Schuster.

Massey, D., and N. Denton. 1993. *American Apartheid: Segregation and the Making of the Underclass*. Cambridge, Mass.: Harvard University Press.

Ogbu, J. 1992. "Understanding Cultural Diversity and Learning." *Educational Researcher* 21, no. 8:5–14.

Pefanis, J. 1991. *Heterology and the Postmodern*. Durham, N.C.: Duke University Press.

Sack, R. 1986. *Human Territoriality: Its Theory and History*. Cambridge: Cambridge University Press.

Sleeter, C. 1996. "White Silence, White Solidarity." In *Race Traitor*, edited by N. Ignatiev and J. Williams, 257–65. New York: Routledge.

Sleeter, C., and P. McLaren, eds. *Multicultural Education, Critical Pedagogy, and the Politics of Difference*. Albany: State University of New York Press.

Tatum, B. D. 1997. *"Why Are all the Black Kids Sitting Together in the Cafeteria?" and Other Conversations about Race*. New York: Basic Books.

Willis, P. 1977. *Learning to Labor*. New York: Columbia University Press.

Part II

PRACTICE

7

CAUTIONS AGAINST CANONIZING (AN)OTHER LITERATURE

Ruth Vinz

Columbia University

> Little Elihue learned everything he needed to know well, particularly the fine art of self-deception. He read greedily but understood selectively, choosing the bits and pieces of other men's ideas that supported whatever predilection he had at the moment. Thus he chose to remember Hamlet's abuse of Ophelia, but not Christ's love of Mary Magdalene; Hamlet's frivolous politics, but not Christ's serious anarchy.... For all his exposure to the best minds of the Western world, he allowed only the narrowest interpretation to touch him.
>
> —Toni Morrison, *The Bluest Eye*

Little Elihue, alias Soaphead Church, advertises himself as "Reader, Adviser, and Interpreter of Dreams" (Morrison 1970, 130). He embodies a warning about the characteristics of a reader and adviser whose interpretive distortions result from using bits and pieces selectively to support predilection. Elihue cannot conjure either language or practices that allow him to do more than create a crazy quilt of others' meanings. Possibly we suffer from the Elihue factor in both the rhetoric that advocates a multicultural literature education and its implementation in classrooms because we fail to conceive a sufficiently complex explanation of purposes and practices.

Advocates of multicultural literature education in secondary classrooms focus their rationale on making underrepresented groups visible. Exposure to the heritage, values, rituals, and experiences of nondominant groups, it is assumed, will acquaint students with a nonambiguous "other." In keeping with the overused strategy of "add-ons" in curriculum, many proponents assume that multicultural literature should be added to canonical texts, structuring these into "inter-units" that resemble intermissions. Typically, units rely on thematic, authorial, racial, or ethnic groupings.

Curriculum committees and English teachers deem literature "multicultural" if the text brings minority experiences to majority students or represents the classroom's minority students with literature meant to "mirror" their experiences. Textbook companies have responded to the need, inundating the market with new anthologies divided into African American, Native American, Asian American, and Latino/a, or compiling collections of women, contemporary continental, or postcolonial writers. Most anthologies provide three or four selections clustered into representative groupings. Thematic categories provide the organizing structure of some anthologies, classifying minority authors into thematic presentations of love, death, finding home, or living as outsiders. Whatever the approach, the multicultural texts or units are often embedded into a canon-as-usual curriculum or offered as an elective course for honors students. Many of the approaches remind me of crazy quilts: "new" literary texts stitched together with "old" practices.

These practices result in the literary text itself becoming a fetishized art object, intended to bring (multi) culture to the student reader and fulfill what some advocates of a multicultural education see as major purposes of such an education—to mirror, expose, or validate difference. Such practices have the potential for the "representative" texts to essentialize writers and their fictions into racial, cultural, or other identity categories if the discussion around these texts defines culture, race, or difference in comparison to self and other. A caution: Like all such generalizations, the ones I've just made have exceptions.

As a longtime secondary teacher, I know first hand the urge to (re)member my literary education into practices that led my students to read as I had learned to read. On the other hand, there was always the yearning for inspiration or information to teach differently. The practices that I learned and subsequently taught—new criticism (focus on text) and reader response (focus on readers' construction of meaning)—encouraged students to interpret texts and move inward to discover self-connecting meanings. Both pedagogies leave little space for students to question, redefine, or reshape prior understandings or to enter uncharted realms where they come together with unknown others.

Simply naming a literature education "multicultural" does not disrupt the traditional Western ideological confines and normative inscriptions that canonize literary texts as well as the honored practices of literary interpretation. If old purposes and practices are canonized with (an)other literature, we will profit from interrogating how it might be otherwise. What habits of mind, what interpretive strategies, what knowledges of authorial and reader intentions have we relied on previously? Do these practices foreground instabilities of singular concepts of identity, culture, race, gender, sexual orientation, or other intersections of difference? If not, how might we move beyond present strategies?

In what follows, I describe some of the issues that surfaced as three secondary English teachers implemented multicultural literature in their curricula in 1997–98. I spent a school year in their urban classrooms to better understand the purposes, curriculum and instruction, and student and teacher learning that went on there.[1]

It's overwhelming to attempt representation of the richness, puzzlements, disappointments, and exhilarations. By focusing on some of the classroom events, scenes, and teacher reflections that surrounded the implementation of texts and practices, I hope to illustrate how they began to conceptualize a multicultural literature curriculum, as well as to introduce some of the cautionary notes that surfaced as we reflected on their work.

INTENTION AND DETERMINACY

In mid-September in a classroom filled with seventh graders, Marilyn Ferrell nods toward Reynold, whispers how he seems resistant to the novel she has assigned. Ms. Ferrell says she doesn't know why she mentions Reynold to me. "Maybe I just want to prepare you or to rationalize that *he* isn't my fault. Of course, I know I need to find ways to get through to him, but I just want you to know that I don't know how right now. Suggestions are always welcome," she laughs as she picks up a copy of *Annie John* and gazes over the emptying room after the last bell of the day sounds.

Ms. Ferrell states her intentions for reading Jamaica Kincaid's *Annie John*. "We have this requirement to include minority authors as a way to bring new perspectives to show students how similar they are to other people. The novel deals with many themes the kids confront in their own lives. It's just that Annie grows up in Antigua. What's so different? But Reynold's comment was, 'It's a girl's book with these girls in some kinda love fest.' I don't know how to help him see that Annie connects with his life." (From interview after class observation, 9/19)

Just what will it mean for teachers to do more than meet a requirement with literature that "affirms" others' perspectives? Just what will it take for Reynold to explore the intersections of race, gender, sexual orientation, place, and culture "performed" in narrative fictions? As Marilyn Ferrell and I began to study both the sources and outcomes of her beliefs, I came to see how difficult it is to move to a discourse of possibility as long as pervasive intentions (purposes for teaching) and the need for determinacy (a known path for proceeding) continue to commodify and invade the possibilities for new conceptions of a multicultural literature curriculum. Essentially, old habits die hard.

MEETING INTENTIONS

Intentions often drive curriculum in literature education: the desire to teach the notion that literature has the power to transform; the need to teach that characters portray universal desires, identities, and aspirations; the impulse to create *particularisms* of characters, plots, and themes that serve as models for minorities, thus making them inclusive subjects.

Marilyn Ferrell expressed what she hoped her seventh graders would take from their reading of the novel *Annie John*. "I want to help them find themselves in others, and others in them." Yet, how productive is it to frame meaning of literature in this way—to meet old and well-established intentions—especially if we

hope to educate readers to interrogate and to talk back to multiple constructions of cultural, social, and political differences rather than universalist or par-
ticularist ones?

Secondary teachers did not invent these intentions that define purposes for
reading and studying literature. Strains of universalizing and particularizing are
embedded in their literature education—in literary criticism, curriculum guides
provided to them by departments or districts, and literature anthologies used by
their students. As Ms. Ferrell explained, "I've always thought my purpose was to
help kids recognize that different ways of living and believing are surface differences. We all need family, food, shelter, and love to grow and flourish. How we fill
our needs may vary, but we're all human. Is that naive?" Naive, maybe; certainly
pervasive. Keep in mind that a teacher whose stance emphasizes universals in literature is likely to focus on expressions of shared values, morals, habits, or rituals
as central to interpreting characters' motives or actions through the reader's own.

The universalist intention goes largely unchallenged. For example, in his 1982
Modern Language Association Presidential Address, Wayne Booth asked the rhetorical question: "Whatever our terms for it, whatever our theories about how it
happens or why it fails to happen more often, can we reasonably doubt the importance of the moment, at any level of study, when any of us—you, me, Malcolm
X, my great-grandfather—succeeds in entering other minds, or 'taking them in,'
as nourishment for our own?" (318). Booth assumes that entering the minds of
characters, "'taking them in,' as nourishment" is at the heart of reading literature.
Booth locates an authentic, intrinsic outcome that valorizes "cojoining" the
minds of reader, author, or characters.[2] The concepts of "entering," or "taking in"
give no hint of the passions or conflicts that result from readers' encounters with
competing, contradictory, or other dissonance-producing perspectives.

I nodded when Booth asked the question in 1982 (I was then a sixteen-year
veteran of high school English teaching, wanting to believe that literature's existential project was to show universals). Since that time, I have come to understand
how literature is the product of *locations* rather than connections—geographic,
gendered, racial, cultural, bodily, and temporal locations that manifest themselves
in the invention of characters, settings (historical and cultural), and events in literary fictions. Literature as a production of subjectivity—for both writer and
reader—foregrounds its improvised, hybrid, and multidimensional expressions
rather than universal or cojoining ones. The day-to-day practices of universalizing or particularizing have the paradoxical effect of moving students toward pre-
configured identities rather than destabilizing their generalizations. Looking at
particular teaching practices in Ms. Ferrell's classroom illustrates the strong influences this intention has on framing her students' readings, and how her consciousness of this fact leads her to think about alternative ways.

ERASING DIFFERENCE

Ms. Ferrell decided that she would teach *Annie John* to her two seventh-grade
classes at different times during the year so her first experience might inform the
second. Jamaica Kincaid's novel tells the story of Annie, the main character and

narrator, coming of age in Antigua. Her ambivalent bonds with friends and family, awareness of her sexuality, and recognition of the effects of colonization bring to Annie's story a range of complex, often competing and contradictory portrayals of her emotions and beliefs.

Ms. Ferrell framed the students' reading of Kincaid's novel in this way:

> "We're going to read a novel that I think you'll like," Ms. Ferrell says, holding up a copy of *Annie John*. "The main character is a young girl about your age or a little younger and she goes through all the typical problems with friends, and especially difficulties with her mother. She lives in Antigua. We'll look it up on a map. But, I won't say more. I don't want to ruin the story for you. Here's a question I want you to write about so that you can have a record later to see what you were thinking when you began reading the novel. If you don't write it down, you'll probably forget." Ms. Ferrell writes the question on the board: What are the main causes of tensions between you and your friends? With your family members? Teachers? "Now, take about ten minutes to write in your journals. . . ." (From class observation, 9/15)

Ms. Ferrell framed the students' reading of events and characters in the novel with "causes of tension" in their personal lives—tensions she believed would connect to Annie John's. Ms. Ferrell hoped to connect students' experience at home, with peers, and in school to Annie's. Although the assumption behind drawing such connections is to help student readers value a character's experience, it might be said that drawing such connections encourages students to believe that Annie's situation is important only in so far as they, as readers, can validate her experiences through their own. Paradoxically, what starts out as a gesture toward connectedness might end up erasing difference.

Ms. Ferrell chose these young readers' interpretive path for them. One class discussion illustrates her strategy. Jamal read the following passage from chapter 5, "Columbus in Chains," aloud to the entire class:

> Pointing a finger at Ruth, Miss Edward asked a question the answer to which was "On the third of November 1493, a Sunday morning, Christopher Columbus discovered Dominica." Ruth, of course, did not know the answer, as she did not know the answer to many questions about the West Indies. I could hardly blame her. Ruth had come all the way from England. Perhaps she did not want to be in England, where no one would remind her constantly of the terrible things her ancestors had done; perhaps she had felt even worse when her father was a missionary in Africa. I could see how Ruth felt from her face. Her ancestors had been the masters, while ours had been the slaves. She had such a lot to be ashamed of, and by being with us every day she was always being reminded. We could look everybody in the eye, for our ancestors had done nothing wrong except just sit somewhere, defenseless. Of course, sometimes, what with our teachers and our books, it was hard for us to tell on which side we really now belonged—with the masters or the slaves—for it was all history, it was all in the past, and everybody behaved differently now; all of us

celebrated Queen Victoria's birthday, even though she had been dead a long time. (Kincaid 1985, 75–76)

The following class discussion ensued:

Ms. Ferrell: So, what does this section help you learn about Annie?

Julian: She's hyper-critical of Ruth. It's like girls I know who want their sistas (to get into trouble.)

Trina: (Pleazzzz! You just) shootin your mouth. Annie's not Ruth's friend. It's more like she's seeing how different they are and Annie starts thinkin about that and wonderin why.

Ms. Ferrell: Well, you two don't agree but what could you say about how Annie reminds you of some of your own attitudes?

Julian: We like to see other kids get in trouble?

Ms. Ferrell: Yes. But why is that? Do you learn from Annie something that might explain why you feel that way sometimes?

Carole: I think Annie blames Ruth for past history. She's making Ruth all of the (English people.)

Audre: (Well, it's) true! Annie's just honest about (what happened.)

June: (Who says) honest? It's just one little kid's opinion. She's brainwashed.

Ms. Ferrell: But you're moving away from the question: What does Annie teach you about your own attitudes or about how people explain the world as they want to see it?

Audre: We all have opinions?

Julian: Mine's better than (yours!)

Ms. Ferrell: (Julian, come) on. Help us here. You say what Annie teaches you about yourself.

Julian: Okay. You want it that way. Annie teaches me that I'm glad I'm no girl who even thinks about the (dead ago past).

Ms. Ferrell: (I'm serious) now. Who else can help me here?

Emily: Annie just reminds me how my mind goes wandering off when I'm bored.

Trina: Annie teaches us about life. She explains who she is because of her history.

Jamal: She teaches us about her life. You can't say everybody get the same breaks.

Ms. Ferrell: Do we all have histories we want to share? What would each of you choose to say about your history if you could? Think about that for a minute and write about it in your reading journal tonight. It's almost time—uh, write about that and finish the chapter for tomorrow. Okay, clear for tomorrow. (From audiotaped transcription 9/25; parentheses indicate overlap in speaking)

The authority of Ms. Ferrell to refocus students' attention vies for power with Annie's authority and knowledge. Ms. Ferrell pulls the students back from ideas that interest them: "seeing how different they are"; "She's making Ruth all the English people"; "She's brainwashed"; " "She wants to explain who she is because of her history." Through her questions, Ms. Ferrell seeks the students' compliance with "response as universalizing." "Okay," says Julian, "You want it that way." Trina says, echoing Ms. Ferrell, "Annie teaches us about life." When the interpretive path is set for students, they will not be encouraged to seek out and follow the more complex landscapes of Annie's world.

When Ms. Ferrell read the transcript of this session, she noted: "I keep them back from important discussions. . . . I'm looking at this in one way. I don't know why kids should see only themselves. I need to think how literature can help us, well, imagine what difference means." Tearing open old paradigms and exposing the entrails of intentions within, tolerating the unpredictable and surprising, insinuating ourselves into the unknown, sharing responsibility for the future— these are roles for teachers to take seriously. But, at that moment for Ms. Ferrell, the concern was how to move forward with what was not yet.

THE SECOND TIME AROUND

In mid-October, Marilyn Ferrell and I reviewed the transcribed tapes of class discussions, her planning notes, and the students' reading journals from the first class that read *Annie John*. This is part of what she had to say afterward:

> The kids were trying to get there and I held them back—really kept them distant from Annie and her concerns. I'm not comfortable with controversy or things out of control and if I'm honest, I didn't want issues of sexuality to take off. But, I want to do this better. I have to think about what both the students and I can learn from multicultural literature. It's easier if I just don't think about it. Maybe I really just want to put my head in the sand. . . . I need to help kids explore their issues and questions. Now I see what's in *Annie John*—so much about identity. But I didn't see that the first time around. (From interview on 10/16)

Maybe teachers are personifications of paradox, disavowing the need for definitiveness but searching out certainty—the need to know and to figure out ahead of time. Ms. Ferrell's competing intentions leave her in a quandary. She must account for the dilemma of not feeling comfortable with controversy (particularly sexuality, because those discussions just "take off") and her desire that students need to bring their "issues and questions" to the learning.

As I've learned through past research (Vinz 1995, 1996), teachers often reproduce in their classrooms the traditional center/periphery relations where power, agency, and responsibility emanate from the center (teacher and planned curriculum) outward to students who receive rather than participate in the construction of meaning. Controlling the center means controlling, for teachers of literature, subjects they do and don't feel comfortable discussing. Power exercised in this way takes many forms, but the consequences of center/periphery relations are exaggerated into fuller contradiction if multicultural literature education is viewed as an opportunity to provide space for exploration of difference—recognizing multiplicity, confronting complexity, and tracing variabilities in values and meaning.

Ms. Ferrell began to challenge her control over classroom events and topics by creating more venues for the second group of seventh graders to share their responses and raise issues important to them. Three major structural changes were implemented: First, *reading journals* (shared only with Ms. Ferrell and me in the first iteration) became *dialogue journals*. Students chose a dialogue partner and the pair wrote reactions to each other for the duration of the novel study. Second, small groups were assigned. These groups met every other day to initiate discussion of self-sponsored topics from the assigned reading. Each small group led a segment of class discussion on alternate days. Third, Ms. Ferrell's role was to review the audiotaped small group discussions, notes from class discussions led by students, and random samplings of dialogue journals in order to prepare a plenary session on days when small groups didn't meet.

To introduce *Annie John*, Ms. Ferrell asked four discussion groups to begin reading aloud, taking turns and stopping every few paragraphs to talk. One group stopped for their first discussion after the following paragraph:

> At school, I told all my friends about the death. I would take them aside individually, so I could repeat the details over and over. They would listen to me with their mouths open. In turn, they would tell me of someone they had known or heard of who had died. I would listen with my mouth open. One person had known very well a neighbor who had gone swimming after eating a big lunch at a picnic and drowned. Someone had a cousin who in the middle of something one day just fell down dead. Someone knew a boy who had died after eating some poisonous berries. "Fancy that," we said to each other. (Kincaid 1985, 6–7)

The discussion began:

Gerald: Stop, stop. There, let's talk now. I saw a dead body of a (baby).
Rosie: (Me), I saw my Nana in the coffin.
Wade: Coffin, man, that's something I don't (want).
Gerald: (Yeah), some people gets buried alive.
Wade: Think a wakin up and you can't see anything and you feel (around).
Mannie: (Feeling) that shiny stuff. (What's it?)
Lettie: (Satin). It's satin in a coffin. Like wedding dresses.
Rosie: Oh, G-r-oss! Stop! I don't wanna think about dyin. My brother, he died last
    year and when this guy closed the box I got the shakes.
Gerald: Now who's talkin ('bout dying?)
Lettie: (No, like a) wedding. Do ya hear me? It's the same thing for marryin and
    buryin.
[Laughter. Ms. Ferrell stops at the table to listen]
Wade: You got it right. My mom tells my dad she'd rather be dead than see him
    every time he comes around.
Gerald: Think of them in a coffin together.
[Laughter]
Wade: Yeah, they'd hafta get on top of each other.
Gerald: They might get after (each other).

Ms. Ferrell: (Now, you're) too far away. What does Annie John notice about how
    people react when she tells the story of seeing a dead person for the first time?
Rosie: They all tell about someone dying. They listen to her story and tell their own.
Ms. Ferrell: And, anything else you notice?
Wade: Well, we thought about dead people.
Lettie: Until you two [directed at Wade and Gerald] turn everything to S-(E-X.)
Wade: (What's that?) You makin it up and readin your ideas in. All right. All right. I
    knows what's on your (mind).
Lettie: (You do) the same tired-ass routine. Wade, don't say nothin to me forever.
    Don't say nothin' to me for-ever.
Rosie: You know what I'm thinkin? What does Annie need? She's tellin a trauma
    for her and everybody's thinkin' about themselves? What's Annie need? Not us
    to tell our story. It's for us to listen and feel hers. Maybe it's not about any-
    (body else's).
Gerald: (Yeah. You) know. Wasn't she scared? Wasn't she tryin to get her friends to
    notice? They's thinkin' about (theirselves).
Rosie: (Not caring.)
Lettie: What? Why? No, wait.
Gerald: (Yeah.)
Lettie: (Stop). You (said).
Wade: (Why) is it . . . ?
Lettie: Wait. Wait. This is to Rosie and not you, Wade. How you know they don't?
Gerald: Don't (what)?
Lettie: (Let) Rosie talk. I'm asking Rosie.
Rosie: They says "Fancy that." Who'd say it?
Gerald: Some faggot or some(thin').
Wade: (Hey.) Anybody coulda said it—like "cool." I don't know no faggots, but it
    could be anybody, just a saying, like if I was shocked I could say it if I lived—
    where (is it)?
Lettie: (Antig)ua, lead head, Antigua.
Gerald: So Antigua's full of fags. That's all I have to say.
Rosie: It's just not wanting to get too close to death. It's like trying to pretend these
    are just stories—oh, fancy that—not real life and death. (Transcript created from
    audiotaped discussion, 10/20)

I can read into this a remarkably rich array of turns, recants, and displace-
ments—moves that make clear that interpretation is sometimes a gesture, at
other times posturing, bantering, and provoking—filled with disorganizing and
integrative energies that wrestle ideas, one around another and back in these seventh graders' discussion. Or, I might read the conversation for what it potentially
reveals about these students' fears, concerns, constructs of gender, sexuality, and
more. Was the conversation any more "productive" than the writing assignment
or class discussion from the first group? That, of course, is part of what Ms. Ferrell
needed to answer for herself.

BEYOND DETERMINACY

The need for determinacy competed with Ms. Ferrell's desire to let the students control the conversation. The most compelling concern for her was trying to figure out how to continue conversations begun in small groups. In only one of four groups, for example, many issues needed to be addressed, among them, (1) Rosie's need to be heard about the deaths in her family ("What does Annie need? She's tellin a trauma for her and everybody's thinkin about themselves"); (2) Wade's introduction of his parents' relationship; (3) Mannie's silence; (4) Lettie's concern about the discussion being directed to "S-E-X"; (5) Gerald's and Wade's posturing on sexual orientation, with Gerald's dismissal of any further discussion ("So Antigua's full of fags. That's all I have to say"). Later we learn in one entry in his dialogue journal (written to his partner) that Gerald read *Annie John* in his sixth-grade class: "Our teacher told us that Annie acts that way with girls. She loves girls! I just wonder if reading books can make you weird? What do you think?"

Ms. Ferrell is left with a challenge, and she feels uncomfortable when "students are all over the place. I'm not sure if their discussions are going anywhere." How might, would, or should she try to deal with the different agendas raised in small group conversations, journal entries, and the plenary sessions? With twenty-two students in this class, Ms. Ferrell suggests, "It's easier to take kids down a path. I mean, *easier.* I'm learning that I don't think it's a good idea, but easier. I'm at a loss about how to move forward when so much is going on. Like Gerald. His beliefs need to be challenged. And each of the kids is a Gerald in one way or another. My biggest problem now is not feeling like I know how to help kids, but I'm learning. I think it's hard to find ways to do all this differently." Ms. Ferrell continued throughout the year to structure various configurations for small and whole class discussions, letting students take the lead but continuing to feel that she had much to learn about how to help her students construct knowledge together.

It's easy to tell someone else about the importance of living with ambiguity and complexity, but when facing upward of 120 secondary students a day, the rhetoric is easier than the act. Ms. Ferrell was learning to create structures that would support her desires, but, as she noted, "I often slip back into the kinds of interpretation that encourage the kids to universalize. I don't think that's inappropriate. It's just that doing only that distorts kids' ideas about the purposes of reading. At least I'm getting better at balancing several approaches." Ms. Ferrell shows us one teacher's developing awareness, as Adrienne Rich (1979) has pointed out, of the responsibility "not to pass on a tradition but to break its hold over us" (35).

CHALLENGING READERS AND THEIR READINGS

Only through the writer's explorations could I have begun to discover the human dynamism of the place I was born to and the time in which it was to be enacted. Only in the prescient dimension of the imagination could I bring together what had

been deliberately broken and fragmented; fit together the shapes of living experience, my own and that of others, without which a whole consciousness is not attain-
able. I had to be part of the *transformation of my place* in order for it to know me.
                                    —Nadine Gordimer, "That Other World That Was the World"

Once we factor in consumption of the text (the reader) as a critical part of the
multicultural activity, a series of questions come to mind. What strategies might
challenge readers to do more than universalize characters and plots in fictions
into ethnic, racial, or cultural traits of actual groups? What strategies subvert
reading as a "mirroring of self"? How do differences—be they linguistic, cultural,
racial, or gendered (all of which have been included under an umbrella of "multicultural")—affect the process of reading literary texts? Is literature intended to
result in emancipatory readings? Hopefully this panoply of questions helps illustrate a central point: The examinations that researchers and teachers need to
undertake are complex and with many parenthetical complications.

In his eighteenth year of teaching high school, Robert Lloyd decided to focus
on challenging his student readers to deconstruct a text as a way of supporting a
more multicultural literature curriculum. "I need to challenge them as readers by
questioning how they read literary selections," he explained. "I'm not so concerned with selecting the literature as I am thinking about *how* to raise their
consciousness, if not their hackles." It's the how of reading from which Mr. Lloyd
believed he could construct a more multicultural literature education for his
combined eleventh- and twelfth-grade classes.

Mr. Lloyd hopes to challenge the dominant formulations of "reader" that conceptualize the internal, cognitive processes—a culture and ideology free-zone
where reader meets text without preconception. Despite a growing body of theory and research about social and cultural dimensions of reading, many teachers
emphasize practices based on the cognitive or psychological interactions between
reader and text. The production of readers in secondary schools is often based on
learning competencies—knowledge (elements of characterization, plot structure,
themes, experience) that has shaped the interpretive practices that are valued, and
on which readers are evaluated. Those who espouse undisturbed and placid theories of reader response continue to emphasize that the experience of the reader
makes the experience of the world.[3]

Doing What They Were Taught

Emily: Usually I try to get a good idea of what is going on by reading closely. That
    means looking for images or descriptions that tell what the author's really saying
    behind the words. I've been taught to read into the words to find a deeper mean-
    ing. It's in class discussions or essay tests that I tell what I think the story is about.
Edward: I like when a writer says what he means. I get tired of trying to read
    between the lines. In school I know I need to look for hidden meanings but that
    isn't the way I read. Why can't a writer just come out and say what's on his mind

instead of hiding behind all the words? I think teachers read too much in. When I write an essay the teacher always tells me I don't dig deep enough.

Dane: I learned to read for character development. I had one teacher who had us write zillions of character development papers—character, character, character. I can't get it out of my mind. I guess I focus on character mostly, yes, I'm sure of it. Now that I like to write stories myself I study characters to try and figure out how to create them.

Natasha: Well, I learned this man vs. man, man vs. nature, man vs. himself, and, well, some other versus isn't there? What is it? I still think of that when I read a story, like, which versus is it? But, then I wonder if everything in literature must be one thing versus another. Do you think? I always start with that when I write papers on a book. (From interviews with Mr. Lloyd's students, 9/16)

I conducted interviews with twenty-one of Mr. Lloyd's students during the first two weeks of the school year to get some ideas about the ways in which they read, why they read, and how their readings were used and heard. The excerpts above highlight that students have learned particular conventions—character, themes, symbol, setting, images—as a way of making sense of literature. They have learned to read closely and between the lines, examining language, authors' intentions, and hidden meanings. Most read because they are assigned literature in school and share their reactions through class discussion and written assignments. A few talk with others about what they read outside of school. Dane is the only student who suggested that literature teaches him about crafting his own writing. None expressed the opinion that literature offers problematic representations that challenge their constructs of the world. Of course, many of these students expressed beliefs based on how they had studied literature in previous years, or what they assumed Mr. Lloyd valued in student readers.

How was Mr. Lloyd, then, to challenge these young readers and their readings? In what follows, I use one class session at the beginning of the year to demonstrate Mr. Lloyd's approach. The class read Nadine Gordimer's (1992) short story "Comrades." The story opens:

As Mrs. Hattie Telford pressed the electronic gadget that deactivates the alarm device in her car a group of youngsters came up behind her. Black. But no need to be afraid; this was not a city street. This was a non-racial enclave of learning, a place where tended flowerbeds and trees bearing botanical identification plates civilized the wild reminder of campus guards and dogs. The youngsters, like her, were part of the crowd loosening into dispersion after a university conference on People's Education. They were the people to be educated; she was one of the committee of white and black activists. . . .

—Comrade . . . —She was settling in the driver's seat when one so slight and slim he seemed a figure in profile came up to her window. He drew courage from the friendly lift of the woman's eyebrows above blue eyes, the tilt of her freckled white face: —Comrade, are you going to town?— (91–92)

In the spirit of the conference, Hattie offers the young men a ride to their bus stop. She learns that the young men live in a distant province and arrived late to the conference. Thus, Hattie infers that they had missed the free lunch and offers to take them to her home for a snack before driving them back to town to catch their bus.

Throughout the story Gordimer makes us aware of the inner workings of Hattie's mind: "She trooped them in through the kitchen because that was the way she always entered her house, something she would not have done if they had been adult, her black friends whose sophistication might lead them to believe the choice of entrance was an unthinking historical slight" (93–94). They ate, exchanging names and little else because of language barriers. Hattie became upset at the inadequacy of the meal, realizing the boys were young and hungry. Talking with the spokesman, Dumile, Hattie asked him about school and learned that he no longer attended, that "youngsters their age have not been at school for several years, they are the children growing into young men and women for whom school is a battleground, a place of boycotts and demonstrations." (95).

With this realization, Hattie comes to understand that "they, suddenly here in her house, will carry the AK-47s they only sing about, now, miming death as they sing. They will have a career of wiring explosives to the undersides of vehicles." (96). At story's end, as they continue to sit at the table making small conversation, she thought: "In this room, the space, the expensive antique chandelier, the consciously simple choice of reed blinds, the carved lion: all are on the same level of impact, phenomena undifferentiated, indecipherable. Only the food that fed their hunger was real" (96).

I give this lengthy explication in order to provide context for the students' reading of "Comrades." This discussion took place during the third week of the school year:

1. Mr. Lloyd: Let's start discussing. I'm going to interrupt sometimes to get you thinking about how you talk to each other. I'll question ways you get the interpretation going, but you need to take the lead on what you want to talk about.

2. Emily: Hattie thinks she's rebelling against apartheid by giving these guys a ride. She thinks she isn't racist. But, she sees them. Look after the first sentence. Black. That stresses it's her priority. That's what she notices first.

3. Edward: I don't think she can attend a meeting and that makes everything better. She'd have to live in a racially mixed society on a daily basis like we do here. You only escape being racist if you are constantly together.

4. Mr. Lloyd: Edward, how is what you're saying connected to what Emily said? I want to stop you for a minute to think about that. Work out of each others' comments. You know, tell me what Emily said that made you think of your idea. What did you hear?

5. Edward: Emily said Hattie thinks she's kidding herself.

6. Mr. Lloyd: Okay, just keep in mind. Everybody, keep in mind to work out of what's been said.

7. Samantha: I want to add to what Edward said about her living isolated from blacks. Hattie needs to live like we do to really test herself. Giving somebody a ride and a little food isn't the same as actually living in the same neighborhood or sharing the same classrooms. She's not learned like we have because they live separate.

8. Mr. Lloyd: What did you hear Samantha say?

9. Lane: That Hattie believes in her little white neighborhood separated from blacks, that living together is the only way to know. You can't know from your little suburban house. I agree. I know partly what it is like to be black because, well, my best friend is and he's a lot more like me. And, me, as Asian. I've learned about racism because of my skin color. Hattie's experiment doesn't count.

10. Mr. Lloyd: Because Hattie doesn't live in the same condition as you then her actions don't count? Help me here—is that it?

11. Rashid: She isn't making sacrifices to go to this meeting or give them food.

12. Emily: What Rashid said. She doesn't have to live with them all the time.

13. Wes: I hear Rashid saying [Mr. Lloyd nods to class laughter] that she'd hafta make sacrifices for it to count. Who says? So if we live in a mixed place that means we sacrifice?

14. Sarah: Hattie is a representative of the white people in South Africa. She's trying to show some kindness. I agree with Wes. Who says you must sacrifice?

15. Jamal: She has the responsibility to help them out. It's a way for her to get rid of her guilt. There's somethin' about her. She does this for herself. But they all have to take it out on the street again.

16. Sue: It's like she's saying, Oh, I'm not racist. I'm against apartheid. Actually having the young guys in her house puts a racist taint on how she sees herself. Then she has to say, From a certain perspective I am guilty like every other white South African.

17. Jamal: Hattie feels a rush of excitement. She feels good about herself.

18. Mr. Lloyd: Okay. Stop a minute. Where do you read "she feels good"? Where'd you get that?

19. Jamal: Well, it's okay to feel good about yourself. Good may come from it and maybe it's okay to feel good. I didn't mean nothin' critical.

20. Mr. Lloyd: Critical's okay. But as readers we need to look where that's coming from when we attribute motivations to a character. It's a way of checking for yourself. Are you all with me? Know what I mean? Jamal?

21. Jamal: Yes . . . yeah, not overstep with our opinion.

22. Natasha: Hattie's thinking, What have I done? I got these black boys in my car and I'm white.

23. Edward: I hear what you're sayin', but I don't know where you reading it from. She's sort of along for the ride at first but she realizes what life's like for the boys.

24. Natasha: She got you Ed. She's just playin' a little game!

25. Edward: Natasha, where you gettin that. You makin' her up.

26. Mr. Lloyd: Okay. Time out. Just a minute. Natasha, how are you creating poor Hattie that way? [jokingly] How do you see her like that? Give us some lines.

27. Natasha: She's ridin' for me between the lines.
28. Mr. Lloyd: Okay, let's look at Hattie. I want each of you to write down three different statements on Hattie [audible groans] that explain her motivations. I want you to say three different ways. Mine might be (1) Hattie is playing a game. (2) Hattie is serious about wanting to take political action but doesn't know how. (3) Hattie is learning from the boys. You write three and then get together in groups and talk through each and get opinions from each other.
29. [Fifteen minute break]
30. Mr. Lloyd: Okay, okay. Let's stop talking. Listen. Now. Here's the thing. I don't want you to read the statements you wrote down, but I want some of you to say what you thought about or learned after you put all your statements together with the other people in your group.
31. Kim: Hattie learns by contrast. When she starts looking at all the status around her in contrast. It's been unjust. Emily pointed it out. That shocks her.
32. Eliah: Well, Mahinder thought Hattie was a symbol of the middle class who plays with the idea of revolution. Like Kim and Emily, we started thinking that the author keeps emphasizing that Hattie doesn't live the life the boys have. She takes education for granted. But she is most concerned how the boys will think about her.
33. Les: Someone in our group admired Hattie for at least giving it a shot.
34. Leigh: But that sort of erodes. She's sort of fascinated and, like—the feelings you have of the exotic. I'm not making sense. She sort of gets paralyzed.
35. Medina: Well, I think we meant it raises Hattie's racial consciousness. She represents racial consciousness and white supremacy. She sees it can't be a world without races and classes. She's trapped and they are trapped into the lives they were born into.
36. Dane: Another problem is the personal one. Hattie can't speak the dialect. The maid can speak to the young men and Hattie's communication is, well, very superficial with only one of the guys who can speak a little English. Some of my family speak Afrikaans, but choose not to. You know what I mean? When they get together—oh, it's beautiful to hear the language. But, around English speakers, they get quiet.
37. Medina: There's the "tsotsi-taal" too, isn't it? Street language. If you are outside it, well, you feel like you can't get in. I think that makes people suspicious. So we can do this better because we speak one language.
38. Emily: It's sort of ironic. Hattie thinks this congress will help but she has really mixed feelings. She is part of a system that is racist and yet she's challenging that system. So what are her choices now? But we have done that better in this country with civil rights. South Africans just don't know how to approach it and could learn a good lesson from us. We live together don't we?
39. Mr. Lloyd: Now, one more thing. What word comes to mind that describes what you are thinking about the story? Write the word down and then let's hear.
40. [Five minute break]
41. Sam: "Consoling" is the word. Hattie consoles herself by consoling the boys'

hunger and they are consoling themselves with thoughts of revolution. Then their presence consoles her and they are consoled with food. It's all a cycle of consoling.

42. Mahinder: Well, I don't see consoling.
43. Mr. Lloyd: Mahinder, say what you *heard* Sam say first. What did he say?
44. Mahinder: He said she is consoled—makes herself feel good feeding them.
45. Mr. Lloyd: Who is he?
46. Mahinder: Sam.
47. Mr. Lloyd: Only she is consoled?
48. Mahinder: Well, that's it. I heard Sam say that she consoles them with food.
49. Mr. Lloyd: Was that it?
50. Mahinder: Yes, as I heard it.
51. Mr. Lloyd: Sam, what else did you say?
52. Sam: I thought about it more as a cycle of consolation. She feels good, they feel good, but she consoles herself by thinking of them in different ways.
53. Mahinder: Do you think she empathizes with them?
54. Sam: I don't think so. I think they make *her* feel good.
55. Mahinder: My word was "empathy." I thought she understood something by the end of the story about their perpetual hunger—for a better life and everything. And, they empathized with her—seemed they were quiet and sort of felt her fear and uncertainty.
56. Leonard: "Violence." I kept thinking of the underlying violence—inflicted on the boys who can't even get an education and on her living in this place where you just never know what will break out. Seems there would be no protection.
57. Dane: "Irrelevance" was my word. Black resistance will build, no matter what. These guys are empowered—like the African National Congress.
58. Liz: "Repression" is my word for this new political game. Nobody realizing the full extent of the problem—the boys or Hattie. I don't think Hattie understands what the cause is about until the end: "Only the food that fed their hunger was real."
59. Rashid: Does anyone get the idea that the author wants us to side with Hattie or with the boys? Hattie does a favor but it isn't like it *cost* her anything and the boys are just getting some dinner and then go on their way. Nobody is really touched by this.
60. Wes: But this is fiction. Does fiction tell the truth about race or real events? Is Hattie like every other white in South Africa?
61. Mr. Lloyd: Now, there's a place to pick up tomorrow. We only have a couple of minutes so think about what Wes said. What does fiction tell us? Is Hattie like every other white? Can a character be that? We'll read some other stories and poems on South Africa—let different stories speak to each other. (Transcription of class discussion, 9/22)

Mr. Lloyd struggles with how to teach students to talk about literature consciously and strategically. He believes that students must move beyond discussions of plots, themes, and character development to more substantive issues involving cultural differences, conflicts, struggles, and "a sense of how they impose their views on others or produce new understandings." I hope to point out from the class discussion how literature is a site where many of the struggles involved in rethinking constructs such as culture, identity, race, and other complexities of human experience are manifest. Mr. Lloyd believes it is important to challenge how students interact with each other during discussion.

Resentment and Other Alienated Representations

Cameron McCarthy explains, "We are living in a time of an extraordinary ethnicization of culture. Much of this cultural balkanization is translated through processes of what I wish to call alienated representation of the other; that is, practices of defining one's identity through the negation of the other—practices that Friedreich Nietzsche (1967) called 'ressentiment'" (1998, xi). Schooling educates our young into forms of resentment. This is particularly true of literature education. By claiming a rhetoric of tolerance, acceptance, and universalism as purposes, interpretation depends on comparison with some version of readers' abstract values—a moral center to be detailed through motivations and desires, heroes and heroines, admirable deeds, hubris, sacrifice, and symbolic and material landscapes detailed in narrative fictions.

Mr. Lloyd recognizes that many students "read into the literature their own value systems and negate any ideas except their own, any values except theirs, any ways of living that don't meet their standards. This was particularly true in the discussion of Hattie." Note Edward's comment (3) "She'd have to live in a racially mixed society on a daily basis like we do here." Edward believes that his version of "racially mixed" provides him with a better understanding of racism than Hattie can experience in South Africa. Samantha (7) suggests that Hattie "needs to live like we do." These students nullify Hattie's experience. They state that they know more about race because they live in racially mixed neighborhoods. Lane's version (9) is even more extreme: Hattie "can't know . . . I know partly what it is like to be black because, well, my best friend is and he's a lot more like me. And, me, as Asian. Hattie's experiment doesn't count." Rashid (11) and Emily (12) seem to support the assumption that Hattie doesn't make sacrifices; the implicit message is that Rashid and Emily do. Where the assumptions come from isn't entirely clear, leading to Mr. Lloyd's challenge (see 4, 10), and Wes's (13) question, "So if we live in a mixed place that means we sacrifice?" Until this point, no other student has challenged the idea that Hattie, as a South African white, knows less about race relations than they do.

The proclivity to empower self through negation of others seems a common impulse. Note Medina's comments (37), "So we can do this better in this country because we've agreed to speak one language." Of course, we need to unpack from the words "better," "agreed," and "one" (among other assumptions ripe for deconstructing) as a place to begin the discussion. Emily adds, "But we have done that better in this country. . . . South Africans just don't know how to approach it" (38). These students' personal and community identities intertwine with the fictional portrayals in ways that allow them to assert superiority. Too often such readings go unchallenged in literature discussions. What better place to encourage explicit discussions of resentment than with students who have made these statements? I might be tempted to list all their conjectures on a sheet of paper and work with students on the implications of what they have come to understand.

COMPETING CLAIMS

Another way to look at the discussion is to focus on the competing claims students make. Several broad claims illustrate (22, 32, 35) a reader's acceptance of singular rather than multiple subject positions of race, gender, generational, or class (based on the content of this particular story). Mr. Lloyd takes it as his responsibility to help students think beyond these claims and initial categories. "I want students to think about what overlaps in identification—Hattie is a woman, and white, and older than these boys. All of those things count. The kids tend to see one factor at a time. I want to prod them. I try to push them to pose more questions that work against some simple claim about a character or situation." Yet, he knows this will take time and constant attention.

Mr. Lloyd's interventions could be described as *breach points*, breaks in the flow of discussion or activity where he challenges an interpretation or a student's misreading of another's response. At times, Mr. Lloyd asks a student to repeat what another has said. At other times, he breaks the discussion off temporarily to move students into writing (28, 39). Mr. Lloyd hopes to push for more complex understandings by asking students to make three hypotheses about Hattie and share them with others. Each aspect of the assignment is intended to complicate the portrayal of Hattie (30, restating another's interpretation) that many students seemed to be simplifying. The second writing activity (39) refocuses the students' attention on the overall story rather than on Hattie specifically. This shifts the discussion to the interactions among characters. Mr. Lloyd directly challenges students' claims (in 10, 18, 20, 26). Mr. Lloyd believes that students become literate in a multicultural world by learning how to read context, behavior, and beliefs without normalizing the reference group in the interpretation.

(IM)POSTURINGS

Many responses that are recorded from readers are, in themselves, fictions. At times students feel tremendous dissonance between what they want to talk about and what they do talk about publicly. As part of their formal schooling, students encounter the preferences of their teachers and others regarding the types of responses emphasized or valued. Those preferences have in turn been shaped by larger forces of school and its agents, and students have learned that revealing self is risky.

Mr. Lloyd and I began to see the tension between constructed responses and some students' attempts to mask or (im)posture themselves in discussion and/or writing. I saw this most clearly with Jamal and Wes. After-class interviews provided me with some details about how this worked. As Jamal, one of six African-American students in the class, wrote,

I worry about how to keep myself private. Mr. Lloyd pushed me to go further [15, 17–21]. Today I wanted to say Hattie was racist. She's doing all this to feel good about herself. But I went lightly 'cause everybody thinks I see everything as race. I keep what's on my mind to myself, so I don't get somebody else's mind. So, I just said what I thought Mr. Lloyd wanted to hear [19, 21]. I didn't say more after that. I just gave it up. (From interview, 9/22)

To shun self-revelation is reasonable—considering the structure and power patterns, assumed or imposed, in a literature discussion. Wes felt,

I asked a question when I really wanted to make a statement. Where do some people get off thinking that it is a sacrifice to live in a mixed place [13]? But the subject got changed and I didn't want to bring it up again. I waited until the end [60] and said, But this is fiction, like what is the problem here? But usually it's not worth the fight. (From interview, 9/22)

I talked with Beverly, who did not speak during the discussion, who said:

Well, I have a hard time with these discussions of race. I always end up feeling like I'm supposed to be the guilty one because I'm white and I either have to make a big deal and apologize, so I just act shy. I choose to go that way and most people end up thinking I'm shy but mostly I just don't feel I need to apologize. I couldn't disagree more with the idea that Hattie is racist and doing all this for herself—selfish, you know? But if I say that then somebody else will say, "Oh, sure, well you don't know how it is." (From interview, 9/22)

With all we can learn from students' interactions, we only learn as much as they want to tell us; more lurks beneath the surface. Thus, at the individual student level, whether deliberately or not, the process of silencing or choosing silence forms a basis for more careful focus and deliberation on the teacher's part.

BECOMING A READER

How might we begin to conceive frameworks for questioning our own and others' interpretations? Maybe literature is intended to "disturb." Critical fictions (Mariani 1991) shake us out of our sense of selves. Note that Mr. Lloyd ended discussion, following Wes's lead, by asking students to think about what fiction tells us (61). Understanding literary texts as disturbances rather than universalizing agents may help promote what Mr. Lloyd suggests—"let different stories speak to each other" (61). Leslie Marmon Silko describes the structure of Pueblo expressions as resembling "something like a spider's web—with many little threads radiating from a center, criss-crossing each other" (1979, 54). "One story is only the beginning of many stories," she explains (56), and what appears irrelevant or digressive to Euro-American eyes is meaningful and integral to the Pueblo sensibility. To avoid canonizing another literature, we might conceive literature curriculum as a spiderweb of stories in dialogue with other stories, as a reader's stories tangle as one of many in the web.

Mr. Lloyd's strategy for creating such a web is to (1) provide opportunities for students to wrestle with cultural conflicts that are raised by their immersion into the literature; (2) make clear that rhetorical practices are culturally constructed and subject to change; (3) teach the importance of listening to multiple perspectives (and narratives) that constitute evidences of complexity; (4) juxtapose belief systems that may be highly individual rather than representative; and (5) recognize the enhanced awareness of the function of language to name, to signify, or connote difference.

Whatever the purpose: to examine the contingency of values, recognize or legitimize heterogeneity, or trace "cultural force fields" as a way "to reconstellate the field" (Porter 1994, 468, 510), we will need to attend to practices that support such efforts. Arnold Krupat (1992) suggests multiculturalism is a "particular organization of cultural studies which engages otherness and difference in such a way as to provoke an interrogation of and a challenge to what we ordinarily take as familiar and our own" (3). Isaiah Smithson (1994) stresses that "culture studies is committed to understanding how texts acquire meaning, examining the relations among texts and the nation's several cultures, expressing dissent based on these investigations, and fostering social change" (9). In the scheme of grand theory, these sixteen- and seventeen-year-olds' discussions of "Comrades" may seem far removed from where Porter, Krupat, and Smithson are theorizing. It is important, however, to work at the classroom level in tandem with theorizing, or we run the risk of developing theory without adequate depth of understanding about the complexities of pedagogies capable of reconstituting a field of study.

Deconstructing the Teacher as Reader

I have argued that which literary texts are chosen for multicultural study is only part of the issue. The practices that a teacher formulates must focus attention on complicated understandings about how gender, race, and other identities influence the reader as a cultural being. In determining how teachers can better plan and provide effective multicultural literature education, we cannot forget how important is for teachers to reflect on their own beliefs, assumptions, and practices.

Hamilton Davis, in his seventh year of teaching high school, felt the need to turn inward before engaging his students in multicultural literature study. He needed to articulate who he was as a reader. Mr. Davis's first reading of Toni Morrison's *Song of Solomon,* and his rehearsal of plans for teaching the novel to his tenth graders, illustrate what he learned through the articulation of his beliefs and assumptions. Mr. Davis had not taught Morrison before, so this was a good opportunity to see what we could discover about the connection between his ways of reading and the initial and revised plans he made.

TEACHERLY READINGS

Sometimes I think I don't know how to read for myself any longer. I realize that I do these teacherly readings where I'm always looking for things to point out to kids or things I think they will connect with. I also look for all the things we teach—textual structures, symbolism, themes, plot, characterization. All of that. (From interview with Hamilton Davis, 9/29)

Mr. Davis notes that reading for teaching is different from reading for self. Mr. Davis breaks the story into manageable parts for student readers. He points out that his involvement is much less emotional and experiential when he reads for teaching.

One of Mr. Davis's goals is to help students interpret literary works. Preferred ways of interpreting include understanding theme, structure, characters, setting, and symbolic interpretation—specifically tropes and images as they relate to theme. These aims shape how he reads a novel that he intends to teach.

READING SONG OF SOLOMON

My first notices were how hard this story is. I couldn't get into it at first. The characters are distant and strange, mostly unfeeling. Then, Milkman's search for his past began to capture me and the fragments of the song. I had to reread the first chapter to figure out what was going on. I read the chapter about four times. In the second reading I could start to visualize the scenes. Then the community and the family members of Macon Dead took shape. It's almost like the first scenes place the reader into a haze and then out of this haze, well, it's like the setting and characters begin to rise up. Partly that comes from the symbolism in Milkman's song of flight. Morrison disrupts our normal sense of time in order to tell several stories at once.

I tracked Milkman's journey to find his identity and understand his past. I noticed that Milkman is named by everyone around him—that's where his identity comes from. He is Pilate's nephew, Macon's son, Lena's brother, Guitar's friend. And the name Milkman is symbolic because it results from his own mother's actions. Until Milkman begins his journey to discover himself, he is a combination of all those who have named him. Once I realized that, I understood Song of Solomon: "The fathers may soar / And the children may know their names." That's Milkman's whole journey. That realization gave me some satisfaction and I could relate more to what was going on in the story.

The journey isn't much different than that taken by Telemachus or the Invisible Man. Milkman's journey is multiple journeys. Milkman is caught in the dichotomies—the fanaticism of Guitar and his own generosity of spirit, between his parents, between Macon and Pilate. And what does he really search for? To find the gold, but he finds his grandfather's bones. And with the bones comes love. All the themes of love intersect then: his mother's smothering love, Hagar's irrational love, Macon's inability to love, and Pilate's abounding love.

I can't quite reconcile the journey and the idea of flight—Morrison uses the flight trope extensively throughout. Something like, "You can't just fly on off and leave a body." We start with Mr. Smith's flight and end with Milkman's. I'm still working on the meaning. Myths that get ripped open—the green bag, Pilate's navel, flight, and conjuring and black magic. Maybe Milkman ends by naming for himself. (From interview with Hamilton Davis, 10/1)

Mr. Davis's reading is text based. His comments illustrate how closely he stays with the story and its details through the analysis of events, characters, and tropes. He seldom expresses personal reactions; those, he indicated, "are too evaluative. I want to know what is there and take it in." When he shares opinions, he finds textual justifications. "Until Milkman begins his journey, . . . he is a combination of all those who have named him." Plot drives the story, the journey to find self, and most of his interpretation relates to this. Note how Mr. Davis offers analysis of parallel events—the naming of Milkman as related to a journey, themes of love, and flight. He works out of these to "broaden" his interpretation by considering a thematic strand—journey of self; discovery is naming for the self.

Mr. Davis hesitates to connect the literature to personal experience. Although he thinks it is important for students to make connections across a broad range of textual references and intertextual moves, he is not comfortable with them connecting the fictional narrative to their personal lives. "I don't think much is accomplished. Students get so far away from the story. We end up in this sort of free association where anything counts as a valid interpretation. In *Song of Solomon* kids would probably talk about how sorry they feel for Milkman and their parents don't understand them. The fictional story disappears in all their stories, and I'm never sure they get to live in the moment of the fiction. The job of the reader seems to me to be to analyze the story. When it says 'flight' so many times you know it is about 'flight' and not something else. Maybe there is a happy medium, finally. But, I've fallen into these patterns. Thematic generalizations are my biggie."

Textual Teaching of Morrison

"I'd probably start by asking kids to read the first chapter and see what themes are introduced in the separate stories. Have them separate out what I see as four stories that they can trace throughout the novel." Mr. Davis's reliance on textual responses is reflected in the type of literary instruction he proposes. "I'd ask them to trace these themes through their reading of the rest of the novel. They'd look for evidence of those themes in characters, metaphors, setting, and wherever else they find them. Themes are the heart of the novel and this seems the best way to help kids pay attention to how themes are forwarded." Mr. Davis identifies several themes he would examine with students: (1) the theme of drifting and disintegration (accompanying metaphors of increasingly disordered and fragmented families and communities); (2) a theme of flight (accompanying stories of flight, song, and the awakening of ghosts); (3) the journey toward self-discovery (*bildungsroman* introduced as a term, Milkman's physical and emotional journey); and (4) the importance of relationships (emphasized in family and community).

"Themes are a way to help kids find a place to land in the text. They have something to hang on to as they try to figure out what is going on." Mr. Davis explains practices that would support thematic study. Students would keep a reading log in which they would write down quotes and passages that move the themes through the text; trace imagery, language choices, and tropes; and put all this together to explain how each theme is significant. Students would bring textual evidence recorded in their logs to class discussions. "I want the kids to have something written down. Otherwise the conversation just goes everywhere. Another possibility is to have students chart character development and the relationships among characters. This will ultimately lead them to themes. They'll see what a master Morrison is at weaving stories into stories. I see my plan as weaving our way through the text by weaving the themes."

TEACHING MULTICULTURALLY

Mr. Davis tries to avoid controversial issues. "Stick to the text. That's my motto." He wonders what implications his use of multicultural literature will have on the interpretive practices he teaches. "More authorial perspective because that ties to the cultural identity of the writer." But, as he is quick to point out, that perspective alone can be misleading. Mr. Davis recognizes that if he is to help students develop a capacity to challenge deeply inscribed understandings of difference, instructional practices for interpretation will need to change.

Mr. Davis rehearsed how he might teach differently. It would be helpful to show how the first chapter introduces circularity and the layering of stories. He recognized that it would help his students if he worked them through some discussion of traditions in oral storytelling and the differences in aesthetic practices of storytelling across cultures. "I'd just always thought about some of this literature as difficult rather than seeing it as artistic practices that different cultures bring to bear. I have so much to learn, but it makes some sense to me as a way to begin a study of multicultural texts—different ways that people have envisioned presenting the human imagination and experience—in cycles, layers, magic realism, multiple tellings (like Momaday's *The Way To Rainy Mountain*), use of musical or film structures would help me help kids see this, especially blues and jazz with Morrison. That's exciting really. It gives me a place to start." This approach may still keep Mr. Davis focused on textual matters (where he feels most comfortable), yet this leads him to step beyond a previous boundary, tempting himself with thoughts of other possibilities.

"I keep thinking that, as a black man myself, I don't have the right to get too political or racial. I don't want to start something that gets out of hand." In some ways, Mr. Davis's reticence on this issue reminded me of Parini's (1995) admonition, "Knowing how much or how little emphasis to put on ideology in interpretation strikes me as the beginning of wisdom" (A52). Recognizing what constrained and what opened possibilities toward reconceptualizing practice helped Mr. Davis make choices. He knew it would be easier to teach new texts in old ways than to stretch himself to confront the dilemma of how he positions himself as a reader and subject of his own history. "I need to come to terms with myself before I can see how to use multicultural literature as a resource to help students understand how we position ourselves and each other. Ironic, isn't it?"

Ironies, yes. Defining self, constructing others, not defining for fear of defining, defining someone else, and continually placing ourselves and others in relation to our own developing definitions. Ironies and dilemmas and complexities. Once more, Mr. Davis rehearsed another possible way to teach the novel:

> I think I would start with some study of the social and political situation in America at the time of the story. I would introduce slave narratives and probably something on the white appropriation of those. I can present many sides of this without students feeling that I'm siding one place or another. I'm just not comfortable doing that. I think I'd want the kids to read Morrison's "The Site of Memory," where she explains her reason for writing this book and the relationship of this story to her father's death. I would be comfortable raising discussion on gender issues in the novel—they are so powerfully delineated that, again, I don't feel like I'd be controlling the agenda. And I sure have stories of my own about strong, black women in our family! If I took it that way at all, I'd need to figure a way to let my own and students' stories become part of the conversation with Morrison's stories of women. Otherwise, it's that "them and us" thing that happens, and, of course, we're [the students] always right and better. I'm not completely comfortable. I don't know how I'll deal with some aspects of the book: "There are no innocent white people because every one of them is a potential nigger-killer, if not an actual one.... The earth is soggy with black people's blood" [Morrison 1978, 155]. (From interview with Hamilton Davis, 10/3)

Mr. Davis recognizes that racism is a topic that can't be avoided: "It's so strong in the novel. To ignore it, as frankly I'd do with thematic study, just isn't possible if I'm trying to rethink this. We'll need to look at how racism and prejudice seem to exist in the environment of the novel. In some ways, talking this through makes me a little more comfortable, but I must admit, I have a roaring headache!"

DIS-POSITIONING OURSELVES

After working with Marilyn Ferrell, Robert Lloyd, and Hamilton Davis during one school year as they struggled with the meaning of a multicultural literature education, I was reminded of what Madeleine Grumet wrote in *Bitter Milk: Women and Teaching* (1978): "Curriculum is a moving form. That is why we have trouble capturing it, fixing it in language, lodging it in our matrix" (172). What we know thus far in the theorizing or pedagogy about a multicultural literature curriculum presents a partial knowing. I hope this chapter is one of many that will encourage all of us to continue imagining and questioning the forms that multicultural literature education might take. The forms of our knowing are moving, elusive of any curriculum or prophesying that gets written down, but ultimately captured, perhaps, in them as representations of what we value at given moments. Mostly, I suspect that the inherent meaning in what we do is found in the spaces (silences?) between the statements, among the artifacts of our teaching, or in the stories that we tell ourselves and each other about our work.

I am heartened by the willingness of the three to struggle with these issues as they continuously reconceive the language, stories, curriculum, practices, and theorizing that guide their work. The challenge these teachers faced when implementing multicultural approaches in their classroom complicated the easy rhetoric they had read in the professional literature or heard through staff development workshops. So many advocates of more multicultural approaches suggest a unitary spirit of purpose and practice. Multicultural education is good for everyone. Yet these teachers found their attempts disquieted their earlier assumptions of how easy that work would be. Complacency or self-satisfaction won't lead us to further wrangle through the complicated labyrinths of meaning. That said, there are dispositions of mind that can keep us accessible and receptive.

To begin, I think these three teachers show us how important it is to *disposition* through *un-knowing*, giving up present understandings (*positions*) of teaching to make spaces in which to *(re)member* themselves as they examine the principles behind their practices and articulate their beliefs into practice. To *unknow* is to scratch at the marrow of understanding for a multiplicity of meanings.

Not knowing is easier and harder. To *not know* is to acknowledge ambiguity and uncertainty—dis-positioning from the belief that teachers should know or construct unambiguous journeys toward knowledge through curriculum and practice. To *not-know* the classroom and the learning and teaching that will take place there is to admit vulnerability. The uncertainty may lead to a roaring headache, as Mr. Davis suggested, or to the loss of solid footing in a world we thought we had learned to read.

Here's how I think it works. I'm not advocating that we dis-position in order to reposition. Dispositions of *un-knowing* and *not knowing* may help us face discordant work. In the classroom we are constantly reading and rereading, acting and reacting, dancing a very complex dance with our students' intentions and desires and with our own understandings. Teachers continuously bend, pivot, and turn as various desires and agendas circulate and unfold in the classroom. As I think of Ferrell, Lloyd, and Davis, I am reminded again of how difficult it is to enter the slippery world of teaching where nothing remains stable except the instability. As anthropologist Loren Eiseley (1975) has suggested, "Then some fine day, the kaleidoscope through which we peer at life shifts suddenly and everything is reordered. A blink at the right moment may do it, an eye applied to a crevice, or the world seen through a tear." (77). Seen through a tear as in the eyes well up, or through a tear as in a rent in fabric?

Literature has the potential to engage readers in putting an eye to the kaleidoscope of life. Narrative fictions, inhabited by characters who are unruly when let loose with a writer's and a reader's imaginings, are performances of sometimes cacophonous, sometimes essentialized, but often idiosyncratic intersections of gender, race, sexual orientation, ethnicity, or culture. Far more than representing some one form of otherness (if indeed such can exist), literary texts guide receptive readers through metaphoric worlds of social and cultural heritages where characters articulate themselves. These literary texts are, as Cameron McCarthy (1998) suggests, "fictive maps in which power and communication are conceived as operating horizontally, not vertically; not top down as in encoding-decoding, but rhizomatically in the sense that cabalistic passageways link the mighty and the meek on shared and complex terrains" (24). Words written down rise up to take form on these shared and complex terrains only through the reader's willingness to bring them to see "through a tear." In classrooms, it is in the hands of teachers to work mindfully with young readers to encourage receptivity and a willingness to both look and listen. So the story goes.

NOTES

1. The three teachers—Marilyn Ferrell, Robert Lloyd, and Hamilton Davis (pseudonyms)—are teachers in the New York City area. At the time of this study, Ms. Ferrell was beginning her third year of teaching, Mr. Lloyd his eighteenth, and Hamilton Davis his seventh. All three expressed enthusiasm for implementing a curriculum that included multicultural literature, though each continued to assign canonical texts as well. Ms. Ferrell taught seventh and eighth graders the year of the study, Mr. Lloyd had classes of both eleventh and twelfth graders, and Mr. Davis taught tenth graders. Data were collected from multiple sources—teacher and student interviews, classroom observations, and artifacts (lesson plans, curriculum guides, tests, written assignments, and student journals).

2. Paul Jay helped me understand how deeply embedded in U.S. literary and cultural criticism is the tension between a transcendental/metaphysical idealism and a pragmatic/contingent approach to interpretation. In *Contingency Blues* (1997), Jay makes the case that Emerson inherits, from the Enlightenment, the challenge of responding to the transcendental/pragmatic tension. Emerson's ambivalence, Jay points out, is shown in "how Emerson's insistence that American art be rooted in the actual and the local is complicated by his further insistence that what is vital there has *its* roots in a higher, transcendental reality. The primacy of the specific and the local in Emerson is continually superseded by the primacy of Spirit, so that whatever begins as particularly 'American' in his essays ends up getting validated by its participation in a larger, transcendent, timeless, and ahistorical reality" (9–10).

   As Jay points out, the tension between these views stays with us into the twentieth century. Jay notes that John Dewey carries forward the tension in American cultural history thus: "[Dewey] invests art and aesthetic production with the very metaphysical properties he tried to banish from philosophical thought. This, coupled with a concept of "experience" that borrows heavily from Emerson's transcendentalism, leaves Dewey's approach to art and culture as divided as Emerson's. Moving back and forth between a pragmatic and an idealist approach, he dramatizes a surprisingly conservative response to modern experience in his own time . . . the transcendentalist bent that resurfaces in *Art as Experience* underscores how persistently the legitimation crisis continued to haunt modern American criticism" (80).

   Booth's question illustrates the tension in contemporary times: the ideal/universal has healthy sway over attitudes about the purposes and practices in literature education that grow out of literary theory and interpretation, which still struggles with its own contradictory positions toward community, self, literature, and culture. Although Booth has within his work strains of the pragmatic, the question he poses in his address is reminiscent of the ideal of "cojoining" and "commingling" as a desired outcome of a reading encounter. Carried into the discourse on multicultural literature education are unexamined counterstatements that lurch between idealizing and universalizing literature and/or using literature pragmatically or politically as a referential function in the larger work of social critique or action. Partly as a result of undermining the legitimacy of the canon, an unstable and arbitrary frenzy to searching out alternative literatures resulted without the substantive discussions, theorizing, and research to determine reading practices and interpretive/critical theories that might support a multicultural literature education.

3. It is important to consider how students have been taught to read literature in their educational experiences and whether their reading instruction changes with different texts, particularly multicultural texts that may exhibit very different aesthetic principles and practices from one to the next. What "reading" means in terms of literature study is a learned activity. We read "well" in school settings when we perform particular iterations on the text. For example, literature instruction often includes finding patterns, motifs, symbols, and metaphors or, more recently, interrogating silences. We carry these and other interpretive strategies with us and use them as tools for the analysis of particular types of texts we have been required to read in school. This raises issues for multicultural literature education not only about the texts chosen but about the development of reading strategies consonant with principles and practices of examining difference. We have much to learn about how the text and its author invoke and expose meaning as well as how readers create their own. Jonathan Culler, a reading theorist, encourages us to question the easy assumption about generic readers when he posits: "If the experience of literature depends upon the qualities of the reading self, one can ask what difference it would make to the experience of literature and thus to the meaning of literature if this self were, for example, female rather than male. If the meaning of a work is the experience of a reader, what difference does it make if the reader is a woman?" (1982, 42) Similarly, Code (1991) raises the question, "Is the sex of the knower epistemologically significant?" (7). Or race, sexual orientation, majority/minority, etc.? What difference does it make, and are we making light of these differences in the rhetoric that I have tried to point out is mostly about understanding, affirming, and embracing the worlds and lives of others through literary texts? The tranquillity represented in the tone describing purposes and practices in multicultural literature education testifies to how untested it is—in classrooms, with real teachers and kids.

REFERENCES

Booth, W. 1983. Presidential address, "Arts and Scandals." *PLMA* 98:313–18.

Code, L. 1991. *What Can She Know? Feminist Theory and the Constuction of Knowledge.* Ithaca, N.Y.: Cornell University Press.

Culler, J. 1982. *On Deconstruction: Theory and Criticism after Structuralism.* Ithaca, N.Y.: Cornell University Press

Gordimer, N. 1992. "Comrades." In *Jump and Other Stories,* 91–96. New York: Penguin.

———. 1995. "That Other World That Was the World." In *Writing and Being,* 114–34. Cambridge, Mass.: Harvard University Press.

Jay, P. 1997. *Contingency Blues: The Search for Foundations in American Criticism.* Madison: University of Wisconsin Press.

Kincaid, J. 1985. *Annie John.* New York: Plume.

Krupat, A. 1992. *Ethnocriticism: Ethnography, History, and Literature.* Berkeley and Los Angeles: University of California Press.

Mariani, P., ed. 1991. *Critical Fictions: The Politics of Imaginative Writing.* Seattle: Bay Press.

McCarthy, C. 1998. *The Uses of Culture.* New York: Routledge.

Momaday, S. 1973. *The Way to Rainy Mountain.* New York: Harper and Row.

Morrison, T. 1970. *The Bluest Eye.* New York: Pocket Books.

———. 1978. *Song of Solomon.* New York: Signet.

———. 1987. *Beloved.* New York: Alfred A. Knopf.

Parini, J. 1995. "Point of View." *Chronicle of Higher Education,* 17 November, A52.

Porter, C. 1994. "What We Know That We Don't Know: Remapping American Literary Studies." *American Literary History* 6:467–526.

Rich, A. 1979. "When We Dead Awaken: Writing as Revision." In *Lies, Secrets, and Silence.* New York: W. W. Norton.

Silko, L. M. 1979. "Language and Literature from a Pueblo Indian Perspective." In *English Literature: Opening up the Canon,* edited by L. A. Fiedler and J. A. Baker Jr., 54–72. Baltimore: Johns Hopkins University Press.

Smithson, I. 1994. "Introduction: Institutionalizing Cultural Studies." In *English Studies/Culture Studies: Institutionalizing Dissent,* edited by I. Smithson and N. Ruff, 1–22. Urbana: University of Illinois Press.

Vinz, R. 1996. *Composing a Teaching Life.* Portsmouth, N.H.: Heinemann, Boyton/Cook.

———. 1995. "Opening Moves: Reflections on the First Year of Teaching." *English Education* 27: 158–207.

8

NEW STORIES

Rethinking History and Lives

Nadine Dolby

University of Illinois, Urbana-Champaign

As I enter the classroom, Jim Connors walks briskly up and down the aisles, passing back homework to his class of high school sophomores at Lincoln High School. He is in his mid-forties, and dressed as usual in jeans, a solid flannel shirt, a wide leather belt with a brass buckle, and sneakers. I take my customary seat in the row of desks near the door, against a wall lined with posters illustrating the French Revolution. Within seconds, Mr. Connors begins to sketch a chart on the board, adding another link to the endless flow of modern European history.

Mr. Crick, like Connors a high school teacher in his mid-forties, also teaches modern European history; but he exists only in the realm of the imaginary, as the main character in the book (Swift 1983) and subsequent film *Waterland* (Gyllenhaal 1992). In this essay, I will probe how Mr. Connors and Mr. Crick approach the teaching of history. Despite surface similarities between the real Mr. Connors and the fictional Mr. Crick, their experiences and the way they have created meaning from those realities have led them to different perspectives of history, the stories of their lives, and their relations with students. Specifically, I will illustrate the divergent ways in which they access and present history, and their use of personal narrative in the classroom. Through drawing their lives, I focus attention on the dynamics of power and perspective. I illustrate two conflicting answers to a question raised by Henry Louis Gates Jr. (1992), "How does something get to count as knowledge?" which is a predominant concern of multicultural education (329).

After a brief discussion of the ethnographic site and the production of ethnographic texts in this essay, I juxtapose scenes from Mr. Connors's classroom and life with similar moments from Mr. Crick's life as portrayed in *Waterland*. In the conclusion I connect my portraits (Lightfoot 1983) of Mr. Connors and Mr. Crick with current discussions about the value of perspectival history (Levstik 1997) in the debates about the construction of knowledge and multiculturalism.

PRODUCING THE FIELD

Lincoln High School is a small (282 students and 25 full-time faculty) laboratory school connected to a major research university in the Midwest. Admission is selective, and many of the students are the children of university faculty and professionals in the small town in which Lincoln is located. In 1994, the student body was predominantly white (75.9 percent) and Asian (19.5 percent), with a small number of African American (3.2 percent) and Hispanic (1.4 percent) students. During the fall of 1994, I spent three months observing two of Mr. Connors's classes at Lincoln: a freshman class in ancient European history, and a sophomore class in modern European history. I also interviewed Mr. Connors, students from both classes, the chair of the history department, and the school principal. In addition to the time I spent in Mr. Connors's class, I spent several hours a week at the school observing and participating in students' extracurricular activities as a way of getting to know students outside of the formal atmosphere of the classroom. Nonetheless, the majority of my time at Lincoln was spent in Mr. Connors's classroom.

The method I use to present my data, that of juxtaposing "fiction" and "nonfiction," is unusual, and is meant to address postmodern concerns about the production of ethnographic texts. Instead of telling a single, unified story, I present two stories that weave, cut, and disrupt each other, creating spaces for interpretation and a multivocality that goes beyond arraying divergent voices. Mr. Crick's story reveals gaps in Mr. Connors's, and though I do not deliberately highlight it, Mr. Connors's story can also reveal gaps in Mr. Crick's.

Multiple fictions exist in this text: that of my writing, and the creation of Mr. Connors; my interpretation and deployment of the fictional Mr. Crick; and my decision to highlight certain facets of each of their lives, and then to juxtapose the two teachers to illuminate a particular facet of the debates around multicultural education, specifically how historical knowledge is produced and marked. My interpretations, the stories I tell from my engagement with Mr. Connors, Mr. Crick, and the texts I create, are both art and politics (Denzin 1994). While ethnographers influenced by postmodern theorists have generally accepted that "the field" does not exist in an objective form that can be simply captured and recorded, this essay underlines the created and interpreted nature of that reality through its imaginary construction of a field. The truths I create and the interpretations I put forward are necessarily and starkly partial.

HISTORY IN MR. CONNORS'S CLASS:
LET ME TELL YOU ONE STORY

Mr. Connors developed an interest in history in elementary school. He recalls, "I got into history because of those old movies like *Hercules* and *Hercules Unchained* that are set way back in time. There were guys knocking down temples and beating up armies: that was my view of history for a long time. Now I've got a broader view. I keep reinventing myself. You always have to be reinventing yourself."

When Mr. Connors arrived at Lincoln High School, he was given a text from which to teach ancient history. Eventually discarding the text as "hideous," he began a seven-year process of writing his own materials from which he teaches ancient and modern European history to freshmen and sophomores, respectively. These materials, which include readings and flow charts that explicate the process of history, provide the blueprint for a conception of history that in its selection and presentation highlights particular aspects of history while marginalizing others.

The Flow of History

In Mr. Connors's history class there is no textbook; there are no papers, no projects; rarely are there essays. Instead, there are short narrative descriptions of events and corresponding charts that represent these events. Mr. Connors usually lectures, creating the chart from the beginning and periodically asking students to fill in the necessary information. The flow-chart method of history endlessly emphasizes cause and effect, seeing historical events strung together in a continuous chain that stretches back to the beginning of history and forward to the end. Because the charts are event-driven, they lend themselves to military, political, and economic history. To supplement this, Mr. Connors occasionally gives the students "random notes" to fill in the gaps: these includes themes and ideas that don't fit under the flow chart (for example, an explanation of nationalism); developments in other arenas, such as art; and stories about famous characters in history. Generally students are only tested on the flow charts, not the random notes. Thus, for the students, flow charts are central.

To illustrate the design of a flow chart, I will give a brief example from a chart on the development of new military tactics during the French Revolution. The French Revolution leads to three events: (1) it frees men to create new symbols such as nationalism; (2) it creates turmoil and crisis; and (3) it frees men to think of innovative solutions to problems of war. In turn, each of these concepts leads to one or two more things, and so on, and in this flow chart, all ideas eventually flow together to lead to the spread of liberalism and nationalism.

The students are enthusiastic about the flow charts, saying that they help them to organize their thoughts, understand how events link together, and allow them to see relationships between history and today. Beth Hedges, the department head, was initially skeptical about the flow chart method but now sees that it "does encourage critical thinking in terms of cause and effect. . . . I think it definitely gets them away from memorization." The principal of Lincoln High, Dr. Miriam Clark, has only been at the school since the beginning of this academic year and thus cannot profess extensive knowledge of the flow charts; however, she agrees with the department head: "I think he [Mr. Connors] is not interested in the kids just memorizing facts, he wants to give them a real sense of history."

The flow charts do get the students away from memorizing names, dates, and battles and that is a move toward a more effective teaching of history. The flow charts, however, also tend to silence and erase the same history that is neglected in traditional methods. In that sense, the flow charts represent a new way of organizing content, but not a substantive change in philosophy as to what counts as history and knowledge, and whose realities are valued. In concentrating on military, political, and economic history, the flow charts necessarily reflect and represent the perspective of rulers, kings, and leaders: the voices of women or the common person rarely if ever are heard. The flow charts present one perspective on European history and do not leave room for conflicting views or interpretations. In this way, they tend to reproduce the myth that one coherent historical tale can be narrated, "presenting a unitary story that emphasizes origin myths over interpretation and consensus over controversy" (Levstik 1997, 48; see also Loewen 1995).

Beth Hedges reflects on the limitation of the flow charts and how the flow charts represent Mr. Connors's view of history:

> We have long talks about this. Ten years ago when we started these discussions, Jim was so convinced that what he was putting forth was the true history. I challenged him in many areas to say what about the common man experience, what about women? He's looking at it more, but down in his gut I don't think he sees it yet; he's coming closer and he's a lot closer than he was some years ago.

When I ask Mr. Connors about the place of women in his curriculum, he notes that he had developed a flow chart on women in the nineteenth century and is starting to bring women into the curriculum. But the method appears to be additive, giving women one flow chart during an entire year or semester, while center stage is continually occupied by powerful men. The lack of attention to, for example, women's role in history, has led at least two girls in Mr. Connors's class to believe that women did not have a much of a role in history. For example, Susan reflects,

> There weren't a lot of leading ladies, and I didn't like women's roles in the past. I don't know what he would teach us about women, but I'd like to know what they were doing. I think the girls would especially like to learn about women, I don't know why the guys would.

This quote reflects Susan's belief that while male history is universal and important knowledge for everyone, women's history is of minor value and only of interest to girls and women. Similarly Eve, another of Mr. Connors' students, comments,

> I realize women didn't really have much of a role, as they were viewed as subservient to men. It would be nice to know what they were doing along with the men and if anyone tried to break through the barriers. I don't want to ask at every single stage we get to, because then it might seem like I'm a strong feminist or something. I real-

ize that most of the time they really couldn't do anything; so though I would hope to have some romantic figure come and break down all the barriers—Yes, the triumph of the woman—I don't think that really happens in what we are studying.

Like Susan, Eve believes that women did not have much of a role in history, defining history as it has been presented to her, in terms of military, political, and economic actions, and decisions made by men. Furthermore, she is reluctant to ask for information about women, as she is afraid that she will be branded a feminist. Neither Susan nor Eve can conceptualize a different type of history in which women's roles are valued. Susan's and Eve's views on women and history have been formed progressively through the years, and certainly Mr. Connors's class is not the sole, or even major, source of their generation. However it is clear that his conception of history does nothing to break or disrupt their ideas about women in history.

Despite its innovative form, Mr. Connors's flow-chart approach to history is, as Sonia Nieto (1994) argues, monocultural education. What counts as historical knowledge, as historical "fact," is narrowly defined. In contrast, the fictional Mr. Crick steps away from Connors's conceptualization of history, and opens up new possibilities and new stories.

WATERLANDS, SCENE 1:
HISTORY IN MR. CRICK'S CLASSROOM

Both Mr. Connors's and Mr. Crick's views of history were shaped by their childhood experiences. For Mr. Connors, history was Hercules movies. For Mr. Crick, it was different: "My becoming a history teacher can be directly ascribed to the stories which my mother told me as a child, when, like most children, I was afraid of the dark." The Crick family is a family of storytellers, and Mr. Crick begins his search for the "Grand Narrative, the filler of vacuums, the dispeller of fears in the dark" (Swift 1983, 62).

For Mr. Crick the search for a true history is a search for meaning. Similarly, the flow charts used in Mr. Connors's classroom represent such a search: to order history in a way that makes sense, that tells one story that will give meaning to the world and that will create laws and rules that are universally followed. Mr. Crick, however, can no longer accept this view of history. "So I began to demand of history an Explanation," he tells us. "Only to uncover in this dedicated search more mysteries, more fantasticalities, more wonders and grounds for astonishment than I started with; only to conclude forty years later ... that history is a yarn" (62).

Rupture: Mr. Crick's View of History [1]

It is 1974 in Pittsburgh, a gray, overcast winter day. Tom Crick, a man in his mid-forties, is teaching his European history class about the French Revolution. "The mob supports this party, then that," he says, "but once its particular grievances are met, once it is no longer hungry, it will follow a Napoleon as readily as a Danton.

There can be no revolution, perhaps, without a mob, but the mob are not the revolutionaries.... So where does it lie, this revolution.... It's a curious thing, but the more you try to dissect events, the more you lose hold of them—the more they see to have occurred largely in people's imagination."

Price, a student in the class, interrupts him, "Should we be writing this down, sir? The French Revolution never really happened, it only happened in the imagination." Mr. Crick replies, "Don't be literal, Price. I'm speculating. But we're all free to interpret." Price answers, "You mean, we can find whatever meaning we like in history?"

Crick's exchange with Price forces an abrupt shift in the ways in which Price engages with history. While Mr. Crick would not necessarily define himself as an "emancipatory" educator, his approach parallels Warren Crichlow's and his colleagues' (1990) description of emancipatory education as a practice that is "concerned with the effect and meaning of representation, and seeks to open up an appropriate space for teachers and students to engage in additional ways of knowing, thinking, and (more importantly) being" (102). For Mr. Connors, history is the search for meaning, structure, and explanation that will order the world, and promulgate universal truths by which students can both understand and construct their lives. Mr. Crick, however, can no longer sustain the mythical grand narrative of history: this rupture has consequences for his teaching, and for the philosophical reorientation of the meaning and transmission of history.

Teach the Children: Lessons from My Life

Connors's teaching of history goes beyond the enactment of the formal curriculum, which in his classroom is exemplified by the flow charts. In addition, he often uses stories from his personal life to teach moral lessons: to demonstrate that particular lessons and values can be learned from life experiences.

It is the beginning of class and students are settling down for the ritual Deep Thought before they begin the day's lesson.[2] But today's Deep Thought will not be plucked from a collected book of quotes; it will arise instead from Mr. Connors's life. Sitting on the edge of his desk, he tells the students that his father, who is almost eighty, was admitted to the hospital with pneumonia, and is now undergoing tests for cancer. Mr. Connors tells his class, "He might die, but he's eighty years old, and death is a part of life. That is the one thing I am trying to teach you about in here, to teach you about life. Last night, what's happening with my father got me thinking about my life, and about what's important to me. I don't think anyone on their deathbed says, 'Gee, I wish I had made more money,' that's not what's important in life. What I want to do, what I've always wanted to do, is to teach history. That's what's important to me."

Mr. Connors's decision to share this personal story with his class is illustrative of the value he puts on family. Beth Hedges reiterates that family values are important to Mr. Connors. "This is a theme with him. I think it emerged as his kids have gotten older. He has said how important it is for his kids to be here [as students at Lincoln] to see their dad doing what he does." His subsequent and spo-radic absences over the next few weeks because of his father's illness and eventual death are a further lesson to his students as Mr. Connors is wholly dedicated to his teaching, having never missed a day. Nevertheless his prolonged absence because of family obligations tangibly demonstrates to students that family is first.

For Mr. Connors, family values are not simply a choice that he is making: they are the key to social stability and social order. During an interview, he repeats a favorite quote of his which he attributes to Confucius: "If there's harmony in the home, there's order in the nation; if there's order in the nation, there's peace in the world." He continues,

> Today you really need both parents working together, there's so much out there that can lead kids astray. I'm firmly convinced that drugs and violence correlate to the breakdown of the family. We substitute materialism for spending time with the kids. My wife and I, we're there for the kids. It's a twenty-year commitment. A lot of things our ancestors figured out weren't so stupid, and we're throwing them out the window, we're throwing out the baby with the bathwater.

Mr. Connors also leans toward the belief that family values are universal, saying, "Find me someone who disagrees with family values." But others in the school—for example, Beth Hedges—are reluctant to identify common family values as a stable, core belief among students or adults:

> I'm a child of the fifties. When I came here and got a whiff of the cultural differences of these children, their global perspective and their lifestyle, I knew that I needed to hold back in terms of putting out anything. . . . I think he [Mr. Connors] knows that by putting it out there he's putting himself up for some criticism and some challenges.

The school's principal, Dr. Clark, while not wholly disagreeing with the con-cept of family values, remembers taking a different approach to teaching about values:

> I recall doing an English project, and having the kids prioritize what was important in their lives and the lives of their family. Then we sorted out what seems to be the values that your family has. It's a sorting process and an identifying process rather than my being up there and saying, "This is what your family's values should be."

Mr. Connors uses personal stories to show his students moral absolutes, such as family values, to live by; similar to the flow charts, the stories teach one les-son through one perspective. In contrast, Crick's use of stories opens up new possibilities for rethinking the place of both historical and personal narrative in the classroom.

WATERLANDS, SCENE 2:
MORAL STORYTELLING IN THE CLASSROOM:
CRICK FAMILY VALUES

Mr. Crick's break with the traditional narrative of history is motivated by and connected to rupture in his personal life. As he begins to stray from the formal curriculum of his classroom, he tells the students stories of his life and his ancestors. He relives his life in a search for meaning and simultaneously allows the students to access history in a fundamentally new way.

Reorientation

Mr. Crick begins, "When I was your age, children, the Second World War was raging, and every night we'd hear the bombers overhead on their way to Germany. Things were approaching a climax, you might say; but I have to tell you children, there were other climaxes that were happening that seemed far more important." Through this introduction Mr. Crick positions himself in relation to a major world event that affected his life, but admits that it was peripheral to the excitement of discovering the world as a teenager in the Fens, in England.

He relates for the students how he and Mary, then his girlfriend and now his wife, would have sex every day on the way to school. The girls are uncomfortable with the story. The boys, however, are intrigued and motivated to ask questions. "Why did you have to do it on the train," one of them asks. "We didn't have a car," replies Mr. Crick. "Why didn't you go to a motel, that's what I do," says another boy. Mr. Crick answers, "There were no motels in the Fens, and you have to remember it was flat country, everything was visible to God and to our parents."

Mr. Crick introduces the children to his father and to his brother Dick, who is mentally retarded. The children are curious about this and Mr. Crick replies, "To really explain, we need to back it up, back to 1911." The students and Mr. Crick are suddenly transported back in time, and find themselves in a carriage going down a dirt road in England, on their way to Mr. Crick's grandfather's mansion. One of the students asks Mr. Crick why he is doing this. He replies, "Does anybody know, anybody want to guess?" Judy says, "It's like history, but you're showing us; you're a part of history too."

WATERLANDS, SCENE 3: MY LIFE AS AN OPEN TEXT

Back at school, students have started complaining about Mr. Crick's class, particularly the girls who are disturbed by the stories about sex. The principal, who is skeptical about the subject of history, confronts Mr. Crick, "How is teaching about history going to get them a job? Besides, you're not even teaching the curriculum. You're telling these children stories." Mr. Crick replies, "We're not just in the business of turning out good job prospects. What matters is what we teach them about life and how to live it." Like Mr. Connors, Mr. Crick sees himself as a moral guide for children and recognizes that history is a teacher. But Mr.

Crick's history is individual and subjective; it does not attempt to impose frameworks on history or to dictate morals.

The principal's warning has affected Mr. Crick, and he attempts to return to a standard teaching of the French Revolution. Slides flash on the screen: Marie Antoinette, La Bastille, Place de la Revolution, the guillotine. He stops at the guillotine, and begins an explanation of how it was considered a step forward: a more humane way of killing people. But he slips and becomes lost back in his story, back in the Fens.

He and Price are standing in his childhood bedroom as bombers fly overhead. Price asks, "What is that?" Mr. Crick replies, "It's 1943, Price, remember there's a war on." In this scene, Price experiences World War II, not from the perspective of a general, a president, or a prime minister but through the eyes of a sixteen-year-old boy. Suddenly, Crick snaps back to the present. "My wife, she took a baby. We've never been able to have children. Mary says it's God's punishment. But last week when I arrived home, there was a baby. Mary said the baby was from God and that we had been forgiven. But the baby was not hers, it was not ours. After we returned the child, she left me. A week later I came home to a note and an empty house."

When the principal, Lewis, hears about these latest stories, he "retires" Mr. Crick. Price, who has transformed himself from Crick's nemesis to his friend, feels sorry for him; he regrets that he did not stop the others from going to the principal, and says, "First the stories bothered me, but then I realized you were doing it for yourself, that's okay." Crick replies, "Strange, I thought I was telling them for you." In this exchange, Crick problematizes the purpose and meaning of history, both practically, within his classroom, and theoretically: Why do we tell these stories? Who are they for? Whose purpose do they serve? Crick's exchange with Price, and the questions it forefronts, echo the concerns of multicultural educators who question the metanarrative of history and its representations (such as the literary canon), instead emphasizing how the stories we tell can be remobilized to question and challenge existing power/knowledge relations (Bennett 1999; McCarthy, Dolby, and Valdivia 1997; Nieto 1994).

Repositioning

The whole school assembles in the auditorium to say good-bye to Mr. Crick. The principal thanks him for twenty years of dedicated service to the school and turns the podium over to him for his farewell speech. Mr. Crick uses the opportunity to finish the story, to connect the past to the present as a way of searching for meaning for himself and his students.

Tom and Mary's illicit sex on the train has resulted in pregnancy, and they sneak off to see an old woman, living in a rundown shack on the edge of town, for an illegal abortion. Martha takes Mary into the shack and tells Tom to wait outside. As Tom hears Mary scream over and over again in excruciating pain, he can no longer stand still. He runs into the nearby reeds, throws himself on the ground, and cries, pounding his fists into the muddy water. At that moment, his life ends. One story ends and another begins. His life is not linear and neither is history. It is a yarn that spins endlessly, often without explanation, without cause, without reason. At the close of the story, Crick completes his repositioning of himself in relation to his students. While teaching the standard curriculum, he saw himself as a dispenser of knowledge and of wisdom. But that position is no longer valid. He cannot claim to understand history, to explain it, but simply to retell it and reinterpret it, alongside his students. He says, "In response to your earlier question, Price, about the end of history. There are as many ways for the world to end as there are people. In one life there can be more than one ending, there has been in mine. How can I help you? I can't. I'm done. I'm retired. I'm history. But at your age, Price, at your age."

Crick no longer asks Price to accept his stories without comment but to question them and to actively engage with them as stories, not as immutable facts. He also gives his students agency to put forward their interpretations, to engage with history, to validate their own understandings and to trust their own stories.

There Are as Many Ways for the World to End as There Are People: History as Multiple Stories

Like Mr. Connors, Mr. Crick teaches who he is. His view is that history is a complex, fantastical myth told by many people who bring their subjectivity to the story. The world begins and ends in different ways because there are multiple ways of looking at the world and numerous realities; there is no metanarrative that explains his life, his family's history, or the French Revolution. There is only the retelling of tales. Mr. Crick uses a nonlinear method of reading his own life: it does not progress or flow in a singular line, but it ruptures, it breaks, and it begins again. There is no forward march, no simple cause and effect: such an explanation misses the complexity of the Crick family story and of the story of history. Mr. Crick's story does not close neatly and succinctly.

In the final scene of the film, he has found Mary, walking by the water in the Fens. He sees her in the distance and heads toward her. Is this an ending, a new beginning, or something else? Multiple interpretations are possible. There is no universal law that predicts how these lives will spin. As Mr. Crick rereads his own life in a moment of crisis, he can no longer sustain the grand narrative of history. He must teach it differently. And for that he is fired.

Telling a Different Story

Mr. Connors's use of flow charts is an attempt to structure and order history and the world, to see life as a grand narrative. But what is lost in this monolithic structure is the reality of conflicting views, of multiple perspectives and of the local specific conditions of history. Within Mr. Crick's perhaps unintentional strategies lie ideas that can be explored to create new ways of teaching history, new ways of mobilizing the stories of the past.

In Crick's historical narrative, the individual perspective and the practices and lives of everyday people become the center. Those who occupy center stage in Mr. Connors's world become minor, even peripheral characters in Mr. Crick's. By starting there, in the local and the quotidian, it is far easier to draw out the multiple perspectives and realities that shape our world. The core of Mr. Crick's historical narrative rests in the everyday; it refocuses attention on those who have been marginalized by grand narratives, and at the same time questions and problematizes the very construction of "history." The issues of perspective, power, and agency are forefronted in Mr. Crick's engagement with history: How do we define "The French Revolution"? How do we understand the impact of World War II on two adolescents (and others like them) to whom the war was a backdrop for growing up?

Crick's approach embodies what Linda Levstik terms "perspectival history," which asks, as she explains, "Why are some voices heard and not others? How is the past manipulated for present purposes? How might different historical voices help us make better sense, not just out of the past, but out of the present?" (49). Such an approach to teaching history goes beyond "tolerance" or "acceptance" models (Nieto 1994) that attempt to simply add in content about people and histories who are "different." Instead, the focus of inquiry is on the actual construction of the history itself, the creation of the historical canon, and the implications of this construction for multicultural practices.

Mr. Crick's practice also points to a different way of using personal stories in the classroom. Mr. Connors uses stories, like the story of his father, to teach moral lessons, to give students absolutes to live by. They are modernist stories that have a beginning, middle, and end; they teach a lesson. In contrast, Mr. Crick's stories exemplify a "messy text" (Marcus 1994); they do not outline universal laws and resist trying to draw moral conclusions from actions.

By leaving the stories of history open-ended, Mr. Crick allows a place for students to enter and create their own interpretations and their own meaning. There *are* instances in which Mr. Crick transgressed: it may have been inappropriate for him to share his sexual history with his students. However I draw attention to these stories not for their content, but to examine the way in which they are constructed. Mr. Crick could have told his students his story and concluded with a message that they should not have premarital sex or an abortion. But he did not and could not. Mr. Crick did not because drawing moral conclusions is not important; allowing students to enter history and to develop their own interpretations is. He could not because morality is not at issue; it is not the frame of reference with which he examines his life.

Finally, Mr. Crick's practice changes the relationship between teacher and student. Mr. Connors sees himself as dispensing knowledge to students and modeling appropriate moral behavior. He says, "It's not just a matter of knowing facts, but also . . . of having wisdom." In contrast, Mr. Crick relinquishes that position, instead relocating himself as a facilitator of students' learning. He is not able to convey the truth to his students because no such truth, no such story, exists. His approach to teaching history represents what Levstik (1997) calls an apprentice-ship, "in which teachers and learners engage in a dialogue that results in the co-construction of historical meaning in the classroom" (48). Yvonne Lincoln and Norman Denzin (1994) might refer to this type of teacher as a *bricoleur* who is "trying to cobble together a story that we are beginning to suspect will never enjoy the unity, the smoothness, the wholeness that the Old Story had. As we assemble different pieces of the Story, our *bricolage* begins to take not one, but many shapes" (576).

To teach history in this manner, in a public high school, is of course to take a risk. As Levstik notes, teaching perspectival history through an apprenticeship model "suggests that children learn to challenge assumptions, ask sometimes uncomfortable questions, demand support for assertions, and develop support-able interpretations of the past" (1997, 50). But, as Beth Hedges comments, it is necessary to question both how we create knowledge from history, and subse-quently how we teach it:

> I was brought up in the more traditional manner, that history was essentially the deeds of men. My approach lately has been more toward common people's history, women's history, minority history, and oral history. I do wonder how I would teach U.S. history now. I don't think I would teach it the way I have taught it. Branching out necessitates that you get away from the lecture method. You just cannot lay out history in that didactic manner and teach those issues. The kind of history I would teach now allows for much more hands-on, more involvement. It also affirms stu-dents and tells them that what you have already experienced, what you have already learned, is important.

To eschew a grand narrative means to resist setting out a uniform formula for all to follow; change cannot be dictated simply through large-scale rewriting of curriculum. But the questions posed by Mr. Crick and Price need to be addressed: For what purpose do we teach history, and whose interest does it serve? How can we mobilize the stories of history in a different way? Mr. Crick does not provide an ideal model, but aspects of his philosophy and pedagogy can be read as sparks, as suggestions that point us in a new direction. In giving up some control over history and our classroom, we do risk, as Beth Hedges warns, "chaos." But the "Old Story" is gone. The new one cannot be contained within frames, flow charts, or moral tales.

ACKNOWLEDGMENTS

I would like to thank John St. Julien and the editors of this collection for helpful comments on earlier drafts of this article.

NOTES

1. Dialogue quoted in re-creations of scenes from the book and film *Waterland* may be approximate, and at times combinations of the two sources.
2. Mr. Connors begins each day's lesson with a quote taken from the book *Deep Thoughts,* which is based on the sketch from television's *Saturday Night Live.*

REFERENCES

Bennett, C. 1999. *Comprehensive Multicultural Education: Theory and Practice.* Boston: Allyn and Bacon.

Crichlow, W., S. Goodwin, G. Shakes, and E. Swartz. 1990. "Multicultural Ways of Knowing: Implications for Practice." *Journal of Education* 172, no. 2:101–17.

Denzin, N. 1994. "The Art and Politics of Interpretation." In *Handbook of Qualitative Research,* edited by N. Denzin and Y. Lincoln, 500–515. Thousand Oaks, Calif.: Sage.

Gates, H. L. Jr. 1992. "The Transforming of the American Mind." *Social Education* 56, no. 6: 328–33.

Gyllenhaal, S., director. 1992. *Waterland.* Los Angeles: Columbia Tri-Star Film.

Levstik, L. 1997. "'Any History Is Someone's History': Listening to Multiple Voices from the Past." *Social Education* 61, no. 1:48–51.

Lightfoot, S. 1983. *The Good High School: Portraits of Character and Culture.* New York: Basic Books.

Lincoln, Y., and R. Denzin. "The Fifth Moment." In *Handbook of Qualitative Research,* edited by N. Denzin and Y. Lincoln, 575–86. Thousand Oaks, Calif.: Sage.

Loewen, J. W. 1995. *Lies My Teacher Told Me: Everything Your American History Textbook Got Wrong.* New York: New Press.

Marcus, G. 1994. "What Comes (Just) After 'Post'?" In *Handbook of Qualitative Research,* edited by N. Denzin and Y. Lincoln, 563–74. Thousand Oaks, Calif.: Sage.

McCarthy, C., N. Dolby, and A. Valdivia. 1997. "The Uses of Culture: Canon Formation, Post-colonial Literature and the Multicultural Project." *International Journal of Inclusive Education* 1, no. 1:89–100.

Nieto, S. 1994. "Moving beyond Tolerance in Multicultural Education." *Multicultural Education* 1, no. 4:9–12, 35–38.

Swift, G. 1983. *Waterland.* New York: Heinemann.

9

MULTICULTURAL DISCOURSE IN TEACHING EDUCATION

The Case of One Integrated Teaching Methods Block

Lalita Subrahmanyan, Steve Hornstein, and Dave Heine

St. Cloud State University

In this chapter we will discuss issues and experiences related to the integration of multiculturalism into the curriculum for an elementary education teaching methods block—hereafter referred to as the "block"—in a four-year teacher education program at St. Cloud State University, a large teaching university seventy miles northwest of Minneapolis in the state of Minnesota. We will first elaborate the theoretical premises on which the block is grounded in the context of the available literature. Then we will describe the curriculum of the block as a whole, along with those specific curricular engagements that speak directly to issues of multicultural education. Finally, we will use data we have collected from the block by way of student papers, student self-evaluations, and student journals, along with instructor evaluations and reflections, to engage in a discussion of issues that have arisen out of our efforts.

For purposes of this paper, we use the term *preservice teacher candidates* to mean all university students in the teacher certification program. We also use the term *students* or *student-interns* for the students in the block. For students in the elementary schools, we will use the term *children* or *elementary school children*. For teachers in the public schools in whose rooms our students have their field experience, we will use the term *cooperating teachers*. For our colleagues at the university we use the term *university faculty*.

Several years ago, Steve Hornstein, with a background in social studies and mathematics education, and Dave Heine, with expertise in reading and language arts, set out to create the integrated methods block in elementary education using a declared child-centered and inquiry-based perspective. In 1994, Lalita Subrahmanyan, with a background in social studies and language arts methods in India and a doctoral degree in the social foundations of education from the United States, joined the team. In this chapter, we focus on our experiences in the block from that time until the fall of 1998, when the university switched to the semester system. At present a new program is being developed to fit the changed licensure structure in the state of Minnesota.

The block consisted of the following courses: Reading, Language Arts and Social Studies Teaching Methods, Classroom Management, and a Seminar in Inclusion. The objectives of the block were primarily to develop in preservice teachers the ability to use an integrated thematic approach to teaching elementary school children all areas of curriculum, focused specifically on the three above-mentioned disciplines. Our task as instructors was to model for preservice teachers an inquiry-based holistic perspective: to help them see how democratic classroom environments enable independent learners to conduct individualized inquiry and obtain multiple perspectives on various issues, and to evaluate their learning according to whether or not their goals as well as those of the instructors were being met. We did this in two ways: through the curriculum, methods, and assignments for the block; and through carefully selected field sites in which students completed a three-and-a-half-week, all-day field experience. Within this context of inquiry, the central strand was inclusion, defined in our block according to Sleeter's and Grant's fifth and broadest category,[1] as education that is multicultural and social reconstructionist (1994). Education conceived under this category is considered inclusive of all children regardless of race, class, gender, ability, age, or sexual orientation.

The logistics of the block were fairly simple. In the quarter before they began student teaching, teacher education majors registered for all courses within the block (i.e., for fourteen quarter credits), which were scheduled from 8:00 A.M. to 3:00 P.M. After five to six weeks of in-class instruction, the students were placed in elementary level classrooms for three and a half weeks for the entire school day. They then returned to the university for the last week and a half. During the field experience, student interns were expected to follow the teachers' schedules. For the most part, we placed our students in select classrooms in rural, suburban, and urban settings with teachers whom we knew—from our graduate program or otherwise—to have a philosophy of teaching similar to ours. This ensured that our students were able to see the application of the theories and concepts that they were exposed to through books, articles, and discussions, and to try out some of the same techniques that were modeled in the block.

Our Department of Teacher Development, as it is called, is part of the College of Education in a university that is the leading institution in the state system with a teaching, rather than research, focus. Since this university is situated in the Midwest, our students are mainly from small, rural and suburban "monocultural" communities. Few of them have had any experience with cultural diversity issues and indeed, for many of them, their undergraduate work at our university is their first experience outside their hometowns. We also have a small, but growing, number of nontraditional students who have moved into teaching after other life experiences. Whereas almost all our students may have had some exposure to issues of special education and gender diversity, most of them have not had any experience in critically examining equity issues based on ideas of critical pedagogy.

The overall context in the College of Education is very favorable for integrative and transformative approaches to teacher education such as ours. The National Council for the Accreditation of Teacher Education (NCATE), one of the leading accreditation agencies, now requires all colleges of education to explicate what is called a "knowledge base," which underlies their programs. The philosophical framework or knowledge base for our college embraces a constructivist vision of learning. Educators are seen as transformative professionals, capable of basing their instruction upon learners' personal knowledge, integrating multiple perspectives, and conducting interdisciplinary collaboration. Our knowledge base also fits readily with the concept of "teacher as researcher," an idea that has acquired tremendous importance in the recent literature on education (Richardson 1994; Roth 1994; Wilson, Miller, and Yerkes 1992; Wong 1995). The central aspect of this teacher-as-researcher inquiry that we would like our students to conduct is inclusion, again broadly conceived to include children/people of all races, ethnic origins, abilities, classes, genders, languages, religions, and backgrounds.

THE CONTEXT OF INQUIRY

What is inquiry? And how does it connect with multicultural education as discussed in the literature on teacher education? Inquiry, as we see it, is grounded in the theory of constructivism, which posits that children learn through construction of meaning from interacting in an environment (Brooks and Brooks 1993). Constructivists also contend that knowledge is "temporary, developmental, socially and culturally mediated, and thus non-objective" (Brooks and Brooks 1993, vii). These notions of knowledge and learning transform the teacher's role from that of a banker holding and doling out information to that of a facilitator who creates a stimulating environment of learning. Therefore, as Nel Noddings (cited in Brooks and Brooks 1993) concluded, constructivist teaching "recognizes the power of the environment to press for adaptation, the temporality of knowledge, and the existence of multiple selves behaving in consonance with the rules of the various subcultures" (6). In summary, inquiry enables learners to internalize and reshape information that they engage based upon their previous experiences and understandings.

It is obvious to us that constructivist teaching is very closely related to multicultural education and that the infusion of multicultural education is not merely a political decision—it is a sound educational one as well. Carla M. Mathison and Russell Y. Young called the relationship between constructivism and multicultural education a "mighty pedagogical merger" (1995). First of all, the assumption in constructivism of learner power is closely related to Paulo Freire's critical pedagogy, the concept that forms the foundation for education that is multicultural and social reconstructionist (Sleeter and Grant 1994). Such a pedagogical approach is geared toward making learning relevant to the current life experiences and realities of learners, and empowering them to become transformative citizens in a democracy. Learning theorists and psychologists use the term *cognitive filters* for those realities—personal thoughts, beliefs, and experiences—based upon which individuals act and operate. Multicultural educators define cognitive filters in broader terms, to include culture—languages, worldviews, and cognitive styles—as factors that influence the realities of people's experiences, their perceptions, and hence, their learning. Thus, constructivism and multicultural education complement each other: one emphasizes the need to look at learners as unique individuals, the other sees individuals as members of groups. In our block, we included both the above elements under our interpretation of inquiry.

MULTICULTURALISM IN TEACHER EDUCATION

Teacher education programs are in the unique position of being able to develop thinking in future teachers that encompasses and integrates both these approaches. Hence, scholars of multicultural education have strongly emphasized the need for infusing constructivism and multicultural education into teacher education, and are advocating that constructivism and multicultural education be the basis of any program in teacher education. Grant (1994) used a different framework by examining how teacher education programs include multicultural education. He then compared them to Sleeter and Grant's five approaches and found that they too, like K–12 education, were premised on a wide range of theoretical perspectives: on the one hand, a very functionalist approach of multiculturalism as the teaching of exceptional children; on the other, a more critical-conflict, theory-based view of education that is multicultural and social reconstructionist.

But why multiculturalism in teacher education at all? The main argument presented for this in the research was the changing ethnic demographics of children in K–12, and students in teacher education programs. While public school children are becoming more ethnically, socially, and linguistically diverse, prospective teachers continue to be predominantly English-speaking, middle-class, European Americans (Fox and Gay 1995). In addition, in the present technological and information age, the world in general has "become smaller" and is changing. For all children and adults—even those who live in small, isolated communities—education that is not global and social reconstructionist is an anachronism. In a recent national survey of multicultural education requirements in teacher certification, Elizabeth E. Evans, Carol T. Torrey, and Sherri N. Newton (1997) discovered that twenty-five out of the fifty-one states have some state requirement for multicultural education. However, the authors concluded that there were several problems inherent in these requirements, such as the lack of infusion into all aspects of teacher development, vagueness of the criteria, and the consequential difficulty of analyzing whether the criteria were being implemented. In fact, vague criteria could easily result in great variability in how teacher certification programs were actually fulfilling the requirements. One fact, however, was encouraging. Accreditation agencies like NCATE have begun to expect teacher certification programs to include multicultural education. As a result, some states reported that they were revising their programs to include these requirements. Yet the question remains: How was multicultural education defined, and how did that definition influence its implementation?

In other words, what did multicultural and social reconstructionist education look like? And how could teacher education programs be conceived to develop educators who are multicultural and socially reconstructionist? The model closest to the ideal might be constructed like the University of California, Los Angeles, program that Jeannie O. Oakes (1996) describes, which included multicultural competencies infused into the entire program both at the university and through the urban field experience. Other programs included those described by Barbara S. Shade (1995) about a Wisconsin program in which cultural competency was sought to be developed in preservice teachers even in contexts that are highly monocultural. As we went down the list, we found descriptions of a small number of programs in which multicultural education is covered in groups of courses. However, the overwhelming majority of the research reports that discussed curriculum for teacher education were descriptions of individual isolated courses designed specifically for multicultural education.

An overview of the literature on multicultural teacher education revealed that the following strategies were most successful in ensuring that a teacher education program was truly multicultural in its orientation:

1. Multiculturalism was most effective when it was infused throughout the teacher education program in a highly integrated manner. The surveys of teacher education programs conducted by Michael Vavrus (1994) and Gloria Ladson-Billings (1995) have suggested that this was the weakest area. A subfinding was that stronger links were needed between foundations and methodology courses in order to achieve this integration.
2. Multiculturalism should be included in the curriculum for teacher preparation in a manner designed to empower teachers so as to ensure their continued development in it rather than to intimidate them and turn them away altogether from tackling it (Finney and Orr 1995; McCall 1995).
3. Constructivist learning approaches such as autobiographies proved very useful with students in teacher education programs because they helped empower them as learners, while simultaneously modeling for them approaches that they could emulate (Jackson 1992; Kroll and LaBoskey 1996).
4. The field experience should be restructured to ensure that preservice teachers have at least one field experience in a diverse setting. In fact, some programs stressed an immersion experience in a diverse community in an attempt to counter the dysconscious racism that many students from monocultural communities often felt (Mahan 1982; Noordhoff and Kleinfeld 1991).
5. Scholars and teacher-education practitioners both emphasized the importance of culturally relevant teaching and situated pedagogies (Ladson-Billings

1990). Teaching pedagogy that was very specific to race, class, and gender avoided the platitudes and generalities of generic pedagogy. In our experience this has been essential because of students' tendencies to define inclusion in manners that were least uncomfortable for them.

6. Utilizing models of exemplary practice of teachers who have successfully implemented multicultural teaching strategies with culturally diverse children was seen as most useful (Foster 1989; Henry 1992).

In this chapter we have examined our block against the background of the above recommendations for teacher education, keeping in mind Sleeter's and Grant's (1994) five categories of the different kinds of multicultural education.

THE BLOCK: GOAL SETTING AND ASSESSMENT

As stated earlier, the integrated methods block consisted of fourteen credits and included five courses in reading, language arts and social methods, classroom management, and a seminar in inclusion. The framework of the block was that of inquiry, as defined by Kathy S. Short, Jerome H. Harste, and Carolyn B. Burke (1995) and included both instructor's goals and outcomes as well as learner's goals and outcomes. We divided the components of our block into several themes, and the instructors defined our outcomes and objectives in each of these areas. These themes included inquiry, the nature of public schools, child-centered learning, democratic classrooms, and so on. (See excerpt from our syllabus, fig. 1.) At the same time, students were required to set goals for themselves, which were discussed with us in the second or third week, subsequently revisited at various points during the quarter, and revised based upon various experiences. Students were also required to generate questions about content and process issues in each of those areas, questions that were also revised. In addition to overall course goals and questions, students were expected to set goals for each of their assignments. These questions and goals formed the basis for students to evaluate their work and that of their peers on individual assignments and on the block as a whole. These goals and questions, as well as the assessments we detail next, formed the basis for the creation of a portfolio by each student.

Our system of assessment was based upon principles of constructivism, and was therefore both formative and summative. Assessment for individual assignments and for the block as a whole was conducted by the students, either individually or in groups, by peers, by one of the instructors, and in case of experiences in the field, by the cooperating teacher as well. We tried to set aside grading by developing standards that reflected transformative teaching. Students were responsible for documenting how they met the standards in order to go further in the program, on to student teaching. Students who did not submit satisfactory work were often asked to repeat an assignment, and if there was a pattern in a set of problems, they were encouraged to take an "incomplete" and to examine the problems seriously even if it meant rethinking their commitment to teaching. Some of them were allowed to repeat the field experience or complete their assignments more thoroughly during the next quarter. However, a few of them

---

Goal Setting: Integrated Block

Name_____

General Goals for Methods Students:
1) To grow in the understanding of learning theory and philosophies of education.
2) To develop a personal perspective on schooling based on a sense of long-term and short-term goals and to develop methodologies appropriate to those goals.
3) To develop an understanding of child-centered learning, teaching and schooling.
4) To grow in the ability to create inclusive, multicultural classrooms.
5) To develop ways to use these experiences as you move from being students to being "transformative professionals."

In addition to the above listed general goals, the following themes will run through the course:

Theories of Learning
The Nature of Public Schools
Assessment, Evaluation and Grading
Social Studies
Reading
Language Arts
Community Building and Classrm. Mgmt.
Classroom Discipline
Curriculum Integration

Inclusive/Multicultural Education
Child-Centered Education
Politics in Schools and in Education
Whole Language
Democratic Classrooms
The Role of the Teacher
Inquiry
Curriculum Planning and Development

Student Goals:
On the following page please type any general goals you have for this quarter that are not included in the general goals listed above. In addition, please list the most pressing questions you have about each of the course themes listed above. (Feel free to cluster some of the themes as they are not all separate topics. You need respond only to the clusters rather than to the individual questions.)

Fig. 1.

ended up leaving the program because they could not cope with the intensity of the work or found that they could not sustain their interest in the profession. One of our biggest struggles was to keep the student workload down to a reasonable level in consonance with the practical constraints the students faced. Many were nontraditional students with family responsibilities, or working-class students who needed to hold outside jobs to support themselves. However, we felt that the work in this block, as in student teaching, did need to reflect the heavy and intense work that good elementary educators do.

THE BLOCK: ASSIGNMENTS

Over the years we used some or all of the following major assignments for the block that focused primarily on inclusion:

Living Social Studies

The Living Social Studies project was a small-group assignment in which students conducted historical research on a local issue represented by a historical site, event, or artifact using primary sources with an emphasis on seeking out the multiple perspectives represented by those responsible for or affected by the issue. We also asked our students to situate the issue in its larger historical context in American and/or world history. To help students think through the interrelationship of presentation to content we asked that they present their work in some form other than a traditional research report.

As an example of our Living Social Studies project one group of students began by investigating the history of the St. Cloud Children's Home (a juvenile residential facility operated by the Catholic Charities of the Diocese of St. Cloud). They quickly discovered that the present-day Children's Home was originally an orphanage located thirty miles west of St. Cloud and was established to "take in" the children who had not been adopted at the terminus of the "orphan trains." At this point the students chose to refocus their project from the Children's Home to the orphan trains of Minnesota. Through books, letters, diaries, and interviews the students sought the perspectives of the orphans themselves, the families who adopted them, and the people who organized the whole operation. To capture and share the drama of this event they chose to create a short play letting the historical characters tell their own stories.

The Inclusion Project

The Inclusion project was designed to help students identify issues related to inclusive classrooms and to develop the tools to research those issues. In this project, groups of students chose a topic related to inclusion as defined in the block and developed a question they would like to research. They then conducted the research by using multiple resources, including primary and secondary sources, print and/or web sources, teachers and other personnel at their schools, and community members, as appropriate. Often topics were sparked by classroom incidents and reflected a need by our students to make sense of the theoretical arguments presented at the university with the pragmatic considerations of life in public schools. Students presented their work in the form of a publication that became a resource for all their classmates.

The Choices Project

The Choices project gave our students the opportunity to investigate any topic of importance to them. Although we built choice into *every* project, we felt it was important that our students found space within our curriculum to pose questions and seek answers to their own concerns. Some of our students had difficulty with this project. They were used to, and initially comfortable with, being told what to learn. This changed as our students took a more active role in setting their own goals for projects and assessing their own learning. We placed no restrictions on their topics, trusting that they knew what it was they still needed to learn. Often our students chose topics of personal interest that would not normally be covered in our teacher preparation program, including interviewing techniques, teachers' unions, and how school principals evaluate candidate resumes.

Reading Assignments

Over the years, we used two textbooks to form the basis of the students' knowledge and for class discussions on inclusion. For special education we used Greg L. Lang and Chris B. Berberich's *All Children Are Special* (1995); for discussions of race, class, and gender we used Sonia Nieto's book *Affirming Diversity* (1996), or *The Dream Keepers,* by Gloria Ladson-Billings (1994). Issues of class, gender, and sexual orientation were discussed as offshoots of the issues of culture, language, and ability. In addition, we used articles such as Lisa Delpit's "The Silenced Dialogue: Power and Pedagogy in Educating Other Peoples' Children" (1988) to help students see the broader issues of how power, privilege, and pedagogy interrelate. Our social studies textbook, *If This Is Social Studies, Why Isn't It Boring?* (Steffey and Hood 1994), in which all but a few of the authors are classroom teachers, provided a wealth of strategies that teachers could use to teach multiple and multicultural perspectives in child-centered and democratically run classrooms.

Students worked in groups to read and discuss the content of the books and share information with the others, sometimes in the form of what we call a "progressive jigsaw." In this model, each group of students reads, discusses, and presents its section only after the previous group has completed its task. Within the umbrella concept of inclusion, discussions centered around critical issues such as bias, prejudice, exclusion, and social action, and focused on teacher attitudes, philosophy, and strategies for antibias teaching.

Walking Journals

Walking journals (Heine 1988) provided students the opportunity to pose and discuss issues and topics through written dialogue. Each journal was circulated among four students and one of the block professors. The student read the past entries and then either participated in that ongoing discussion or began a new topic before passing the journal on to the next student. Later we used e-mail journals, which eliminated the problem of late or misplaced notebooks. Students were asked to read and post entries a minimum of twice each week. One professor participated in each journal. Our intent was not to lead or direct the discussion; we consciously worked at avoiding authoritative and evaluative language that may have privileged our responses. Like the students, we responded to other's ideas, and posed tentative insights that invited critical response. By providing space for students' voices within our curriculum we hoped to demonstrate the importance of creating classroom environments where children's voices are sought after, valued, and celebrated.

Focus Study

This was an inquiry project that students were expected to complete with the children of the classroom in which they were placed. In the focus study, children and teachers collaborated to complete the steps of the inquiry cycle as described by Short, Harste, and Burke (1995). They chose an overall theme; explored it in order to gradually develop focused issues and questions; collected and organized ideas and data in large and small groups; shared and presented their findings; reflected on strategies; and evaluated their learning processes and products.

The focus study provided an excellent opportunity for our students to apply all the key concepts they had learned through their peer-level projects and the readings for the class: democratic education, learner choice, multiple perspectives, hands-on learning, children as critical thinkers, problem posers, problem solvers, and so on. We found that the focus study also provided a natural context of exploring issues of equity and social action. For instance, one student conducted an inquiry on water in a grades 1–3 multi-age classroom. For one of the activities, children chose to test the water in their school building and in their homes for heavy metals. They found out that the water did not meet the safety standard in two rooms in their school and convinced the administration to replace the water fountain in those rooms. They also wrote a note to parents about ways to avoid water waste, for publication in the school Parent-Teacher Association newsletter.

The Field Experience

Research has shown that students, especially white students with little or no experience with cultural diversity, benefit greatly by participating in a field experience or internship in a setting culturally different from their own (Gomez and Tabachnick 1992; Diez and Murrell 1991). According to various scholars, students who were placed in immersion experiences in various diverse communities demonstrated greater multicultural competencies than students placed in monocultural settings. As stated briefly earlier, in our block, we have developed partnerships with select cooperating teachers, many of whom are graduate students in our program, and pursue a similar inquiry-oriented approach to teaching. A few of these placements were in culturally diverse classrooms in the nearby metropolitan twin cities of Minneapolis and St. Paul. Therefore, not all our students in the block had a cultural immersion experience.

While we have understood the virtues of giving students field experience in a culturally diverse classroom, we realize that much of the literature on field experiences has focused on cultural diversity as race, ethnicity, and at most, class. Since inquiry, multiple perspectives, and democratic education were the cornerstones of our block, we hoped that our objectives of making students aware of education that was multicultural and social reconstructionist could be achieved, theoretically, in any classroom. Moreover, the practical concerns of students, especially nontraditional students, such as distance between their homes and internship sites, and concerns of the instructors, such as the quality and availability of the cooperating teachers, outweighed the concern that the classroom be culturally diverse. We also felt that we should give students control over the extent of cultural risk they wish to take by choosing settings that were very different from their own personal experience. It was very important to us that our students learn to teach in multicultural and social reconstructionist ways even in classrooms where the children were not racially diverse. Thus, given that our typical student was very unlikely to actively seek out a job in a setting culturally different from the one he or she had grown up in, we believed that our objectives were very realistic. Later on in the chapter, we will share our own reflections about the same issue.

Student Portfolio

The capstone project of our integrated block was the student portfolio, in which students documented their growth during the quarter and which was used as a summative assessment of their learning and development as teachers. The portfolio consisted of the following:

1. Students' goals and questions as expressed at the beginning of the quarter, as well as subsequent revisions in each identified area, one of which was inclusion.

2. Students' statements of their philosophies of education and autobiographical accounts of their own education—again, as expressed at the beginning of the quarter, with two revisions: one at midterm and another at the end of the quarter.

3. A final paper, which, as we stated earlier, helped students document how they had met the assessment standards for the block. In this paper, students described in detail their learning under the themes, and included documentation from those components of the block that had helped them gain insights. The students could document their learning by attaching relevant materials from self-, peer, cooperating teacher, or instructor assessments of their projects; class notes of discussions, along with their own comments; excerpts from various readings, with their own comments; or documents of learning in the field (e.g., lesson plans, videotapes, children's work, etc.). This documentation provided a sort of proof of learning on the one hand, but was primarily a wonderful window into the process of learning. Students gave us copies of the evaluations and assessments for our records.

THE BLOCK AS EDUCATION THAT IS MULTICULTURAL AND SOCIAL RECONSTRUCTIONIST

As we stated earlier, *inquiry* was the model used in the block at multiple levels. Students conducted inquiry projects in small groups at peer level; they also conducted inquiries with children during their field experience. Their learning in the block as a whole could also be interpreted as a process of inquiry in which they brought their prior knowledge, engaged in new learning, and reflected on that process. For us as instructors, the block was an inquiry into our teaching methods. First, we came with our notions and ideas about multicultural education. Second, we engaged with students in different roles as classroom instructors and field supervisors. Third, we collected and organized data and ideas during the quarter, and finally, we conducted ongoing reflections on the block upon what we had learned about teaching, what areas we felt we had been successful in, as well as in which areas we thought we could grow further.

Our notions of inclusion clearly have stemmed from Sleeter and Grant's (1994) ideas that the cultures of oppressed groups should be included in the discussion of multicultural education in a context of social action. This puts teachers in a position of responsibility to teach antioppression activism rather than merely nonoppressive practices. By broadening the definition of inclusion and multicultural education to encompass various cultural groups—based on race, ethnicity, ability, class, age, and gender—we avoided what Carmen Montecinos (1995) describes as a conceptualization of culture that assumes it to be a self-contained, fixed whole, made up of coherent patterns impermeable to influences, and attempts to reduce an ethnic group's social life to "master narratives" that then subsume every particular specific viewpoint.

We used the framework of inclusion in the context of social reconstructionism in the preparation of teachers who we hoped would empower children to be active members/participants in a democratic society, while at the same time affirming the multiplicity and diversity of perspectives. To achieve this goal we stressed community building and the idea of developing strong classroom cultures and communities. We examined ideas of *communitarian* versus *representative* democracies, with emphasis on consensus building as an alternative to the simple majority vote. We also examined the dynamic social relations between groups, and among individuals as members of overlapping cultural groups. At the same time, we tried to protect the idea of individual learner choices—of what children would like to learn and how they would like to learn it. According to Sleeter and Grant (1994), democratic education is a very essential component and characteristic of multicultural education. We modeled this democratic approach through the choices we gave our students in the topics they chose for research, as well as by having students set up criteria for the assessment of their assignments—criteria that held them accountable for achieving their objectives as well as ours.

As stated earlier, this idea of inclusion was connected to both multicultural education and curriculum principles. As Martin (1994) has said, linking teacher education with multicultural perspectives to constructivism helps us avoid the pitfalls that cause "issues of diversity [to] have often been viewed as problems rather than as opportunities to re-conceptualize the nature of the learning environment" (78). Through our model of inquiry, we were able to show how knowledge is constructed in all disciplines, how the scientific method works, how historians, mathematicians, social scientists, linguists, authors, and readers create meaning. And in fact, we tried to show students how inquiry is a natural process by which all human beings—children and adults—learn new information or solve problems. Such an approach provided us with a framework within which knowledge could be seen as both individually and socially constructed. It also helped us model the development of various perspectives, and provided for learner empowerment while at the same time maintaining the integrity of our objectives as instructors.

Finally, we tried to integrate ideas of multicultural education into every component of the block in very specific ways. When we taught the theoretical aspects of inquiry as a curricular framework, multiple perspectives were naturally included when the inquirer worked with other colleagues on collaborative projects. Sleeter (1995) recommended that in order to help white students learn multicultural and social reconstructionist pedagogy, it was essential that they begin to view things from all perspectives. In our Living Social Studies project, one of the stipulations was to obtain multiple perspectives during the collection of data from primary sources. We ensured through this that students saw history as the construction of "stories" and narratives from the perspectives of the individuals/ groups who had lived those experiences, not merely as a study of "facts and figures" from the past.

In language arts and reading methods students are expected to learn how to analyze and respond to various children's books. One of the ways in which we undertook this was to have them read several books and conduct "literature circles" to prepare response matrices with analytical, critical, intertextual, and cultural responses to the books. Responding to literature critically entailed looking for hidden messages that may be stereotypical. Cultural response meant that students had to examine the cultural context of the story. In another assignment, students conducted a reading intervention project in the field in which they developed a detailed case study of one student's reading problems. One area we explored was the cultural context of the problem: family support for literacy, family literacy activities, English as a second language, and so on. The students themselves also wrote children's books, and used the above response matrix to self-evaluate their books as well as to evaluate each other for peer assessment. Students realized that writing a children's book within a multicultural context is not that easy. One student, Paul, discovered that it is not sufficient to merely paint the characters in the book a brown color and believe that one's objectives of writing a multicultural book have been fulfilled!

REFLECTIONS AND INSIGHTS

Paul's insight was one example of our success with raising multicultural awareness in students. The strongest theme that emerged from an examination of students' self- and peer evaluations was this articulation of their awareness of the need and importance of multiculturalism. They also realized that multiculturalism should be integrated into the fabric of education and should not be viewed as an "add-on." Claudia was one of a number of students who felt that multicultural education must be pervasive, which means it must be an integral part—at the core—of the curriculum. Students also expressed that after the block they felt that had a better understanding of how the classroom could be more culturally inclusive. Marlena said, "As far as multicultural education goes, I learned that it is far more than hanging posters on the wall that include different cultures and ethnic groups. It is more than just acknowledging other holidays, also." Becky said that the answer she found was "really quite simple. Child-centered education, multicultural/inclusive education, whole language and inquiry are not things that need to be 'included' in the classroom. They become part of the way the classroom is organized and the curriculum taught."

We were also pleased to see that students recognized the need for and power of learning about multiple perspectives. Neil expressed this eloquently in his self-assessment for the Living Social Studies project: "We told the story of the Farmers' Market in such a way that people saw the diversity, learned some background, lived it through our eyes (from our perspectives) and, hopefully, will have the urge to go and experience this cultural icon themselves." The Living Social Studies project was perhaps the most direct and the most effective project to help achieve our instructor objectives of teaching what history is about, and how multiple perspectives are important. As Ruth stated so powerfully, "What I want my students to learn through living history is how vulnerable history really is, and that it can be told differently by different people and still be accurate. Meaning that we are all unique individuals looking at and experiencing life all quite differently." Many students also felt that working in cooperative groups helped them see multiple perspectives within their peer group itself, something they had not thought of earlier. To quote another student, Heidi, "Participating in this Choices project, I have gained insights into other people's perspectives on the same event.... We need to listen to each other and try to understand other people's perspectives."

How many students out of the ones we have had will actually use multiple perspectives and teach social-action-based multicultural education remains to be seen. We believe that multiple perspectives may indeed be high priority for some of them, and we certainly once had a small, dynamic group of students who were convinced that social action was an important part of education. Some of the questions that students asked with respect to inclusion were excellent. For instance, one student linked the politics of educational funding and the issue of support groups and programs for persons with disabilities. Another student wrote that she once asked the physical education teacher at her school how that person would feel about having a special-needs student in the class. She was not at all happy with the response she got. "I got a typical response, 'It will be OK.' I then asked how they would change their curriculum to have the student involved. But that person just stood there and didn't answer at first. Later the teacher said, 'I would have to know the kind of disability before I would be able to answer that.' I thought the person was being very honest."

For the most part, however, there were very few reflections on how education could be multicultural in monocultural classrooms in ways other than the introduction of multiple perspectives. In monocultural settings, the discussion on inclusion tended to focus mainly on special education students. For instance, many students picked special education as their topic in the Inclusive Education project, and none ever attempted to examine issues of sexual orientation.

Since democratic education and community building were given a great deal of importance in the block, the latter was an essential point of focus for student reflections. Almost all students reflected on how community building is essential and how different teachers used different strategies to build community in their classrooms. Students learned a great deal about classrooms as caring communities from various articles and books we used at different times, among them "The

Song Of Inmates" (Wigginton 1993–94) and *The Challenge to Care in Schools* (Noddings 1992). They recognized that classrooms that foster a sense of caring, honesty, and respect for all members have few classroom management problems, and that even those can be tackled easily before they become too serious. Students also realized that it was not easy in some cases to build a strong feeling of community in the classroom. In one instance in an inner-city metropolitan school where our students were placed, the teacher felt strongly that the school should be a safe place for the children, and yet our students recognized the difficulties and challenges in building that environment of safety and caring. Other buildings in our region were also seen as challenging not because of their location, but because they had a large number of transitional children who attended the school anywhere from three weeks to three months.

The idea of using autobiographies has been extolled in the literature as one of the newest strategies in helping change attitudes toward a variety of issues. Racism, sexism, and other social justice issues often are very sensitive, and autobiographies are seen as an effective way of raising people's consciousness about them. In our block, Steve Hornstein and Lalita Subrahmanyan started off the discussion on racism and prejudice in education with accounts of their personal experiences with anti-Semitism, racism, and sexism as students and as teachers. Lalita Subrahmanyan also discussed from a personal perspective other issues of inclusion, such as students with special dietary requirements on account of religion, culture, or health. At this time, as at others, all of us brought in our international experiences from India, Malaysia, and the United Kingdom. Students then shared their own experiences of bias and prejudice, usually based on class or gender. Others remembered the racism of their grandparents and parents and the difficulties they had negotiating a racist home when their own notions of race had been changed through education. The voices of the children in Nieto's *Affirming Diversity* (1996) and their accounts of the strategies their teachers used that worked for them complemented our autobiographical discussions very effectively. Students were also very keen on learning specific classroom strategies to deal with issues of diversity and prejudice. Last year we used Ladson-Billings's book *The Dreamkeepers* (1994) and learned about the features of culturally relevant teaching. In addition to our general focus on inclusion in discussion and in the projects and assignments outlined above, we conducted specific discussions on inclusion in subject areas such as language arts. For instance, how does the writing process work differently when children are second-language learners of English? How can we assess the reading of children so as to distinguish between a child from, let us say, Laos, who has a reading disability and one who just needs more time to learn English as a second language?

One outcome of our extensive discussions on good multicultural practice in class using Ladson-Billings's and Nieto's books was that students improved greatly in their ability to recognize and appreciate good multicultural practices in their field experiences. They were thus able to critique existing practices, sometimes using extremely sophisticated analysis. For instance, one student was very upset when she attended a meeting for developing an individual educational plan for an African-American child and saw that whereas all the school professionals present were white, the parent was African American and working class. She strongly felt that the school should have encouraged the mother to bring an advocate with her, because in her perception this would have demonstrated the school's willingness to recognize and correct the imbalance of power that tended to silence the mother. According to her, the school had not acknowledged the parent as its partner in the life and learning of the child.

Students were well aware of their lack of power, both as interns and student teachers as well as later on, as first-year and nontenured teachers. Thus they were often worried whether teaching multicultural issues would become controversial if parents, administrators, or school districts did not support them fully. This is, perhaps, the biggest concern for most beginning teachers, and one that prevents them from taking up controversial issues. One of our students shared, in a self-evaluation of his children's book, that he had planned to write a book about a gay family but during authors' circles his group dissuaded him from doing so, saying that he would not be able to share it during his field experience. Moreover, many of our students planned on working mainly in rural or suburban districts, which they expected would be rather conservative.

We found, however, that the few students who self-identified as minority tended to be more aware and conscious of the need for multicultural education of the social reconstructionist category. They also shared their personal experience working with our white students. For instance, our Japanese student, Tomoyo, wrote extensively not only about race and ethnicity in education, but also about inclusion in a broad sense. She felt that although she got a lot better about expressing her opinion in a large group, she still left feeling uncomfortable, but admitted that the small group work had gone very well.

As instructors we have spent a great deal of time reflecting on the block we have designed and implemented over the last few years. Our biggest struggle has been to create democratic models that emphasize choice but challenge learners to make informed and uncomfortable decisions. We are afraid that when we give too many choices, our students pick those options that they are most comfortable with and refuse to challenge themselves with unknown territory. We know that giving learners choices is sound pedagogy, but which choices are students who have lived all their lives in small, rural monocultural settings likely to make? One of us once had an experience with a student who was not in this block who said, "I am very uncomfortable with the idea of racial diversity. I intend to teach only in a small town near my home county. I have created a couple of multicultural units in my course on human relations. That is all I plan to teach about that topic." Such approaches have sometimes sorely tempted us to set up strict requirements for students to demonstrate specific competencies in multiculturalism before allowing them to graduate.

We have not had students in this block actually express such feelings. But there have been others. For instance, we have had students claim that they are, and that everyone should be, color-blind. "Why shouldn't all students recite the Pledge of Allegiance?" they ask. Or, "Why shouldn't everyone learn standard English? Children who speak black English use so many profanities. How can we allow profanities? We should emphasize the commonness of all children, we should think of all of them as American. They have to learn to be Americans, don't they?"

Therefore, does giving students choices help us achieve our objective of developing awareness that is multicultural and social reconstructionist? For instance, we have found that given open choices in our Inclusion project, students tend to ask what they consider "safe" questions: about gender, special education, and the like, rather than controversial ones about racism, or, rarer still, homophobia. As a result of this, the last quarter we taught the course, we decided to drop the inclusive education assignment. However, that shortchanged the inclusive education component of the course, since we lost a valuable context in which to share perceptions on inclusion of specific groups: gender, class, and so on.

Another area of struggle we have is in attempting to change deep-seated student assumptions and stereotypes that tend to affect their attitudes within a short span of time—the eleven weeks of the quarter. As we saw earlier, students reported that they were much more aware of the importance of multicultural education, and yet student learning about the nuances of inclusion was still a struggle. And this struggle continues despite what we consider very effective practice. In one instance, students had read about, discussed, and commented upon Nieto 1996, and Delpit's (1988) redefinition of family involvement in schools. Despite that, students who had chosen the topic, "How do we get parents involved in children's education?" for their Choices project fell back easily upon their original definition of parent involvement as attendance at school conferences and volunteer work in classrooms. During their inner-city field placement, we had to constantly remind them not to judge inner-city parents using the same criteria used for families in suburban or rural settings!

Finally, there has constantly been a struggle between our prescribed task of teaching educational methods and the perceived need to teach school curriculum content—that is, Minnesota history and geography, or writing. This should be no surprise, since the two are so closely related. Still, it seems very problematic that students come to us with little or no understanding of what history is really about, and little or no knowledge of diverse social, religious, and cultural practices. As a result, along with teaching students ways in which diverse social and religious customs can readily be part of a curriculum for grades 1–6, we also find ourselves needing to teach them where to find information on these topics, again from multiple perspectives. In fact, so strong is our recognition of the problem that in the future we are thinking of requiring an assignment through which students will learn content information about another culture. One of us has successfully tried out such an assignment in another class and believes it works well in requiring students to find out more about a culture other than their own, and share the information with their peers.

SUMMARY AND CONCLUSIONS

In summary, we believe that it is essential that teacher-education programs develop multicultural skills, attitudes, and values in preservice candidates regardless of whether the children they ultimately teach are Caucasian or of other cultures. It is also essential that teacher education programs develop positive skills, attitudes, and values in preservice teachers with regard to education that is inclusive of all people and perspectives. However, it is even more essential that white preservice candidates who see themselves as either "having no culture" or as future teachers employed in monocultural settings appreciate the diversity within and between cultures, especially with regard to race, class, and gender. It is also imperative that these same candidates recognize that children in settings that are monocultural are often most in need of good multicultural education because their only sources of information are television and movies—sources notorious for their misrepresentation and stereotyping of people.

The process of developing such transformative teacher education programs, however, is slow and difficult. What we learned and were fairly successful with in our block was our decision to provide at peer level all the experiences with inclusion and multiple perspectives that we expected them to teach children once they became teachers. The insights our students derived from the Living Social Studies project on the importance of multiple perspectives is a telling example of that success. Another example is the sense of community that we were able to build among the students through cooperative work, and peer review, as well as by giving them the power to set goals and criteria for assessment of projects and assignments. The strong sense of empowerment they felt made them see the importance of giving the same experiences to children.

Still, empowering students in this manner creates its own paradox. Empowerment is necessary if students are to genuinely understand and embrace reconstructionist pedagogy. At the same time, such empowerment allows students to continue to choose "safe" or noncontroversial areas to study. For example, one group wished to study the inclusion of "fat" children in classroom activities. Such a topic, although possibly revealing a genuine concern for students' feelings (and a possible personal issue as well), completely avoids the issues of ethnicity, language, culture, power, and ability that have been the focus of the block all quarter long.

So herein lies the paradox: If we insist on a topic of which we approve, we demonstrate that reconstructionist pedagogy still allows those in power (namely the instructors) to force students to consider only the ideas the instructors see as valid. On the other hand, not pushing for appropriate content abrogates our responsibility for having students consider the content we see as vital.

We have tried to walk this line by allowing the topics to go forward, and trying to help the students see the societal issues of sexism, gender, and media marketing that could be a part of this concern. Ultimately the students have produced such bromides as "Try to make sure they are included in all activities" and "Have class meetings to talk about people's feelings." Although we have been clearly disappointed with the results, we are as yet unsure about what we could do with a similar request in the future. This paradox becomes even more problematic as we try to challenge students' ideas about inclusion with respect to ethnicity, religion, language, and class. Most of these were due to strong and highly ingrained feelings in our students about such concepts as "the American way," and the liberal notions of choice and opportunity. To expect students to be able to question those foundational concepts during the course of one quarter is admittedly unrealistic. And this is something we talk about in class when they express difficulty with unlearning sixteen years of education based on the idea of America as a "melting pot" of cultures.

Another consequence of this idea of assimilation was that our students had not been exposed to much information about diverse ethnic, religious, or other cultural groups. They were thus afraid that in their attempt to be inclusive they might offend someone on account of their ignorance of that person's culture, or their own prejudices and stereotypes. The area of multicultural content is therefore one that has been a constant challenge.

What does the future of integration of multicultural education in our teacher education program look like? The last three years have been one of flux, with the university moving to semesters and the state to a new licensure. At present it appears that all teacher education programs in the state that had been training teachers for grades 1–6 in four years will now be preparing teachers to teach in three additional grade levels within the same length of time. This does not bode well for education that is multicultural and social reconstructionist, since it gives us much less time to focus on the special competencies teachers need to become democratic, transformative educators who are multicultural and social reconstructionist in orientation. It also allows much less time for helping students understand the content of different subject areas such as mathematics, science, history, and geography from multiple perspectives in order for them to translate their own understanding into meaningful experiences for young children. We who teach transformative specialty graduate and undergraduate courses on gender and science, inquiry, and current issues in education fear that the undergraduate curriculum may not scratch the surface in these essentials for teachers to help them even see the need for further in-depth understanding.

On a more positive note, the new licensure has given us the opportunity—and has forced us to think deeply about the need—to infuse and integrate multicultural discourse into each and every aspect of our new program. One way we have planned to do this is through two major course focuses at each end of our program: a curriculum course at the beginning, and a foundations course at the end, during student teaching. We will try to achieve integration through the rest of the program by having our students complete the last two semesters (i.e., one year of the program) as a cohort with the same group of instructors and cooperating teachers in professional development school settings. During our temporary program for students who are in transition between quarters and semesters, we have been trying out several options within the professional development school model, and our experiences have been very positive. Of course, as in any institution of higher education with academic freedom, a great deal will depend upon who the instructors are, and what perspectives they bring to education that is multicultural and social reconstructionist. Whatever the philosophical framework or organizational structure may be, one thing is clear: Multicultural discourse in teacher education is no longer just a necessity. It is a given.

NOTE

1. Sleeter and Grant, in their book *Making Choices for Multicultural Education* (1994), discuss five approaches that are based on a range of educational and sociological theories from functionalism and theories of assimilation on the one hand to critical pedagogy on the other. Stated in that order, they are: teaching the exceptional and culturally different, human relations, single-group studies, multicultural education, and education that is multicultural and socially reconstructionist.

REFERENCES

Brooks, J. G., and M. G. Brooks. 1993. *In Search of Understanding: The Case for Constructivist Classrooms.* Alexandria, Va.: Association for Supervision and Curriculum Development.

Canella, G. S. 1994. "Preparing Teachers for Cultural Diversity: Constructivist Orientations." *Action in Teacher Education* 16, no. 3:37–45.

Damon, L., J. Duffield, J. Goetz, M. Marlow, and S. Nathenson-Mejia. 1997. *Preparing Teachers for Tomorrow: A Constructivist Approach.* Paper presented at the conference of the American Association of Colleges of Teacher Education, Phoenix, Ariz., February.

Diez, M., and P. Murrell. 1992. *Assessing Abilities of Expert Teaching Ppractices in Diverse Classrooms.* Unpublished manuscript, Alverno College, Milwaukee, Wisc.

Delpit, Lisa D. 1988. "The Silenced Dialogue: Power and Pedagogy in Educating Other People's Children." *Harvard Educational Review* 58, no. 3:280–98.

Evans, E. D., C. C. Torrey, and S. D. Newton. 1997. "Multicultural Education Requirements in Teacher Certification: A National Survey." *Multicultural Education* 4, no. 3:9–11.

Finney, S., and O. Jeff. 1995. "'I've Really Learned a Lot, But . . . ': Cross-Cultural Understanding and Teacher Education in a Racist Society." *Journal of Teacher Education* 46, no. 5:327–33.

Foster, M. 1989. "'It's Cookin' Now': A Performance Analysis of the Speech Events of a Black Teacher in an Urban Community College." *Language in Society* 18:1–29.

Fox, W., and G. Gay. 1995. "Integrating Multicultural and Curriculum Principles in Teacher Education." *Peabody Journal of Education* 70, no. 3:64–82.

Gomez, M. L., and B. R. Tabachnick. 1992. "Telling Teaching Stories." *Teaching Education* 4: 129–38.

Grant, C. A. 1994. "Best Practices in Teacher Preparation for Urban Schools: Lessons from the Multicultural Teacher Education Literature." *Action in Teacher Education* 16, no. 3:1–18.

Heine, D. A. 1988. *Teaching as Inquiry: A Sociosemiotic Perspective of Learning.* Doctoral dissertation, Indiana University. UMI Dissertation Express, 8916397.

Henry, A. 1992. "African Canadian Women Teachers' Activism: Recreating Communities of Caring and Rresistance." *The Journal of Negro Education* 61:392–404.

Jackson, S. 1992. *Autobiography: Pivot Points for the Study and Practice of Multiculturalism in Teacher Education.* Paper presented at the annual meeting of the American Educational Research Association, San Francisco.

Kroll, L. R., and V. K. LaBoskey. 1996. "Practicing What We Preach: Constructivism in a Teacher Education Program." *Action in Teacher Education* 18, no. 2:63–72.

Ladson-Billings, G. 1994. *The Dreamkeepers: Successful Teachers of African American Children.* San Francisco: Jossey-Bass.

———. 1995. "Multicultural Teacher Education: Research, Practice, and Policy." In *Handbook of Research on Multicultural Education,* edited by J. A. Banks and C. A. M. Banks, 747–59. New York: Simon and Schuster.

Lang, G., and C. Berberich. 1995. *All Children Are Special: Creating an Inclusive Classroom.* York, Maine: Stenhouse.

Mahan, J. 1982. "Native Americans as Teacher Trainers: Anatomy and Outcomes of a Cultural Immersion Project." *Journal of Educational Equity and Leadership* 2:100–110.

Martin, R. J. 1994. "Multicultural Social Reconstructionist Education: Design for Diversity in Teacher Education." *Teacher Education Quarterly* 21, no. 3:77–89.

Mathison, C., and R. Young. 1995. "Constructivism and Multicultural Eeducation: A Mighty Pedagogical Merger." *Multicultural Education* 2, no. 4:7–10.

McCall, A. L. 1995. "We Were Cheated! Students' Responses to a Multicultural, Social Reconstructionist Teacher Education Course." *Equity and Excellence in Education* 28, no. 1:15–24.

Montecinos, C. 1995. "Culture as Ongoing Dialog: Implications for Multicultural Teacher Education." In *Multicultural Education, Critical Pedagogy, and the Politics of Difference,* edited by C. E. Sleeter and P. L. McLaren, 291–308. Albany, N.Y.: State University of New York Press.

Nieto, S. 1995. *Affirming Diversity: The Sociopolitical Context of Multicultural Education.* New York: Longman.

Noddings, N. 1992. *The Challenge to Care in Schools: An Alternative Approach to Education.* New York: Teachers College Press.

Noordhoff, K., and J. Kleinfeld. 1991. *Preparing Teachers for Multicultural Classrooms: A Case Study in Rural Alaska.* Paper presented at the annual meeting of the American Educational Research Association, Chicago.

Oakes, J. 1996. "Making the Rhetoric Real: UCLA's Struggle for Teacher Education That Is Multicultural and Social Reconstructionist." *Multicultural Education* 4, no. 2: 4–10.

Richardson, V. 1994. "Conducting Research on Practice." *Educational Researcher* 23, no. 5: 5–10.

Roth, K. 1994. "Second Thoughts about Interdisciplinary Studies." *American Educator* 18, no. 1: 44–48.

Shade, B. 1995. "Developing a Multicultural Focus in Teacher Education: One Department's Story." *Journal of Teacher Education* 46, no. 5: 375–80.

Short, K. G., and J. C. Harste, with C. Burke. 1995. *Creating Classrooms for Authors and Inquirers.* Portsmouth, N.H.: Heinemann.

Sleeter, C. 1995. "Reflections on My Use of Multicultural and Critical Pedagogy When Students Are White." In *Multicultural Education, Critical Pedagogy, and the Politics of Difference,* edited by C. E. Sleeter and P. L. McLaren, 415–38. Albany, N.Y.: State University of New York Press.

Sleeter, C. E., and C. A. Grant. 1994. *Making Choices for Multicultural Education: Five Approaches to Race, Class, and Gender.* New York: Macmillan.

Steffey, S., and W. J. Hood. 1994. *If This Is Social Studies, Why Isn't It Boring?* York, Maine: Stenhouse Publishers.

Vavrus, M. 1994. "A Critical Analysis of Multicultural Education Infusion during Student Teaching." *Action in Teacher Education* 16, no. 3:46–57.

Wigginton, E. 1993–1994. "A Song of Inmates." *Educational Leadership* 51, no. 4:64–71.

Wilson, S. M. 1995. "Not Tension but Intention: A Response to Wong's Analysis of the Researcher/Teacher." *Educational Researcher* 24, no. 8:19–22.

Wong, E. D. 1995. "Challenges Confronting the Researcher/Teacher: Conflicts of Purpose and Conduct." *Educational Researcher* 24, no. 3:22–28.

10

Beyond Eurocentrism

Implications of Social Epistemology
for Mathematics Education

Ram Mahalingam

University of Michigan

> The master took a stick and asked his disciple: Tell me whether this is a stick or not? If you say yes it is a stick, I will hit you to prove that this is indeed a stick. If you say it is not a stick, then also I will hit you to show you are wrong!
>
> —Zen koan

This Zen koan exemplifies the paradox in the Eurocentrism debate. I could easily imagine myself in the place of the disciple facing the question, "Is there Eurocentrism in the historiography of mathematics?" If I say no, then I am turning a blind eye to the hegemony of Eurocentric bias—something obvious in the historiography of mathematics. If I say yes, then I am turning a blind eye to the hegemony of the elitism in subaltern mathematics. Paradoxically, what is considered as subaltern in the development of mathematics is marginal and hegemonic at the same time, depending on from which side we are looking at the issue.

Zen koans are supposed to force disciples to change their frame of reference, leading to the path of enlightenment. I intend to follow the Zen path to face this paradox. I hope you will forgive me for doing so, especially when enlightenment is not a fashionable term in postmodern times.

The discussion in this paper is in three parts. First, I will briefly review the key arguments in the multiculturalism debate in mathematics education. Using Indian mathematics as an example, I will argue for the need to reconceptualize the issues. Second, I will examine the issues raised by scholars of the sociology of mathematics (such as Restivo) and their relevance to the multiculturalism debate. Third, I will discuss the possibility of applying social epistemology to address

189

the issue of multiple social realities and the paradox that is inherent in the Eurocentrism debate.

KEY ARGUMENTS IN THE EUROCENTRISM DEBATE

Critics of Eurocentrism have questioned the Eurocentric bias in the historiography of mathematics primarily on two accounts. First, Eurocentric bias in the historiography of mathematics does not credit the contributions of non-European or subaltern cultures. Second, Eurocentrism has created an exotic "other" by "orientalizing" (Syed 1985) the cultural experience, the cultural products, and the contribution of "others"; as a result, the contributions of mathematics from outside European cultures are devalued (Joseph 1987). Although I agree with the critics of Eurocentrism about the marginal status of the subaltern's contribution, I find the Eurocentrism versus subalternism dichotomy problematic.[1] Before elaborating, I should point out the impact of the Eurocentrism debate on multicultural discourse. Facts and figures from various cultures, such as descriptions of Hindu mathematics, abound in multicultural curriculum materials, but without any critical examination of the sociocultural and historical contexts in which they were produced.

Problems with the Eurocentrism versus Subalternism Dichotomy

Two issues that I found problematic are of relevance to multicultural discourse. First, the Eurocentrism debate portrays a monolithic subaltern and a monolithic Europe. Second, by portraying a monolithic subaltern, we fail to scrutinize the intracultural variation of a culture in the production of knowledge and its legitimation. In the process, we often inadvertently engage in a multicultural discourse that is counterproductive and in danger of thwarting the goals of multiculturalism.

According to Frantz Fanon (1965), the notion of "Europe" is the construction of the "third world." It is important to remember this observation, especially when we encounter Eurocentrism in postcolonial times. The constitution of Europe was consolidated with colonialism. Now we overlook the central role historical events and crises played in our internalization of the very notion of Europe. As an extension of such internalization, the Eurocentrism debate also presumes the existence of a unified Europe without examining the multicultural realities of Europe. Cornel West (1993) eloquently pointed out this problem in his criticism of Eurocentrism, asking, "What do we mean by Eurocentrism? Which particular mind do you have in mind? Which classes of Europe you have in mind [*sic*]? Certainly Sicilian peasants don't have the same status as Oxbridge elites. . . . the very terms themselves are for me not analytical categories, they are categories to be analyzed with a nuanced historical sense and also a subtle social analysis. By subtle social analysis, I mean powerful descriptions of persuasive explanation of wealth, and status and prestige" (7).

In addition, we are in danger of portraying the subaltern as a monolithic society. Instead, one has to examine the role of power in social relations as reflected in knowledge production (Foucault 1972) and the appropriation of knowledge in practices of various social groups according to gender, caste, and class. Paradoxically, in the name of multiculturalism, without such frames of reference, we end up legitimizing another elite mathematics.

To illustrate my point, I will first describe the sociohistorical roots of medieval Indian mathematics. Indian mathematics, as it is known in the history of mathematics, is the product of an elite, hierarchical society. The caste relations and boundaries are well defined. Brahmins (the priest caste) and Shatriyas (warrior caste) primarily form the coterie of the elites. All prominent medieval mathematicians were from this elite upper class, irrespective of their religious background. The Sudras (laborers), Daliths ("untouchables"), and women were denied any forms of education that would improve the status of their life. Discriminatory social practices prevented the participation of these groups in any formal schooling. Only Brahmins and Shatriyas were allowed to pursue any form of higher learning. The Hindu code prescribed by Manu, the ultimate Hindu law giver, laid out the code in unambiguous terms:

> Women should especially be guarded against addictions, even trifling ones, for unguarded women would bring sorrow upon both families.... Knowing that their very own nature is like this, as it was born at the creation by the Lord of Creatures, a man should make the utmost effort to guard them. The bed and the seat, jewelry, lust, anger, crookedness, a malicious nature, and bad conduct are what Manu assigned to women. (Doniger 1991, 198)

> He [the priest] should not recite [Vedas] indistinctly, nor in the presence of Sudras. (83)

> A Sudra should not amass wealth even if he has the ability, for a Sudra who amasses wealth annoys priests. (250)

Manu's laws reflect the worldview of the Indian elites, and prescribe the ways in which the state should control the knowledge production and dissemination. The exclusion of Daliths and women from the participation of knowledge production was not sporadic but institutionalized. What is typically called "Indian mathematics" is in this regard actually the mathematics of the upper-caste elites of India. The Indians at the margins not only did not participate in the acknowledged mathematics, but the various forms of mathematics that they produced were not even recognized by the elite Indian mathematicians as something valuable. The medieval Indian mathematics reminds me of Plato's condemnation of the materialists "who saw in geometry only what was immediately useful to the artisans and mechanic" (Smith 1951).[2]

I do not think things have changed that much today in India. Even today, the mathematics that is produced and practiced by those at the margins is not recognized as part of Indian mathematics. I will give two examples of mathematics in practice in the lives of those in the margins.

Example One—Kolam

Kolam is the name for the rice-flower drawings executed by Tamil women on the floors of buildings. These drawings involve complicate understanding of geometric patterns and spatial reasoning (see figs. 1, 2, and 3). This art form is practiced exclusively by women. They learn how to draw *kolam* from their mothers, sisters, or grandmothers. To become a competent *kolam* artist, one needs to have both geometrical knowledge and strategic understanding of how to transfer this knowledge into actual practice. The artist has to make many decisions on the spot depending on the available space so that she can reduce the size in proportion to the availability of space. Thus, the practice of drawing *kolam* is a complex mathematical activity involving an intuitive and strategic understanding of spatial reasoning.

Since *kolam* is something only women do, the enriched mathematical understanding required to draw a *kolam* is not valued and therefore not legitimized as part of any mathematical discourse.

Example Two—Pallanguzhi

Pallanguzhi is a traditional game that can be played by two people. Each player has seven cups (something like muffin tins), and each cup contains six beads (see fig. 4). The player has to distribute the beads, one in each cup, in a clockwise direction. When she has distributed all the beads, she then picks up the next cup and starts again until she reaches an empty pocket. Then the player takes the beads in the cup that is next to the empty cup. The game continues until all cups are emptied. Again the players start the game with whatever beads they have won. If one player cannot fill all the cups in her side, she fills as many cups as possible. The game continues.

This game involves a complex understanding of distribution and the regrouping of numbers, and an excellent memory for recognizing various positions of the game (as for chess). For each possible starting position, an expert player knows how many beads she will get if she chooses to start with a particular cup. An expert player would know where to start to get the maximum number of beads at any point in the game.

Pallanguzhi is played mostly by women, and they share an expert knowledge of the game among themselves. Whenever my parents played this game, my mother knew when to stop the game so that my father did not go bankrupt.

Both *kolam* and *pallanguzhi* show how the production and practice of certain forms of knowledge are marginalized along the dimension of gender. Given the ambience of an Indian society based on Manu Dharma, one would find several marginalized epistemologies along the dimensions of class and caste. It is not surprising that none of these games or *kolam* drawings are used in Indian curriculum to teach mathematics even today.

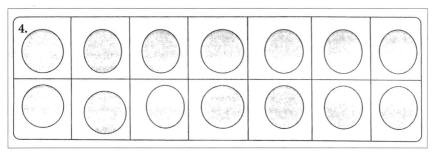

Figures 1–4. Kolam and Pallanguzhi.

IMPLICATIONS OF THE EUROCENTRISM
VERSUS SUBALTERNISM DICHOTOMY

The implications of a multicultural discourse that rests on a unified notion of the subaltern and of Europe are several. Such a multicultural discourse is a self-defining experience for American society and for the subaltern. The notion of a unified Europe enables the "New World" to consolidate its intellectual legacy. For the subaltern, it becomes possible to envision a cohesive and contradiction-free glorious past that was pristine and pure but which was corrupted by invaders. In fact, for the subaltern, the self-defining moment transforms itself into a discourse of national identity. For example, when the People's Party—a Hindu fundamentalist party—won an election in India, instead of incorporating *kolam* or *pallanguzhi* in math curriculum textbooks were written glorifying Vedic mathematics as the mother of all mathematics.[3] The textbooks consciously engage in building a national and religious identity based on the glorious past. Under these circumstances, how should we propose an informed educational policy to realize the egalitarian goals of multiculturalism? Is it possible to envision an educational policy for a global epistemic discourse?

THE SOCIOLOGY OF MATHEMATICS AND EUROCENTRISM

Traditionally, these sorts of questions have been addressed by scholars of sociology of knowledge. Within the discipline of mathematics, the situation is peculiar. The emerging scholars of sociology of mathematics, such as Restivo and other social constructivists, have to fight a different battle, spending most of their energy fighting the absolutist notions of mathematics.

Social constructivists argue that mathematics is a sociocultural product that has to be understood in the matrix in which it is produced, practiced, and transmitted. Restivo (1994) refers to two kinds of constructivism. "Weak constructivism" accepts a unity among mathematical truths that often underlies our efforts to trace various cultural expressions. "Strong constructivism" sees both the objective status and the content of mathematics as culturally constructed. Being a strong constructivist, Restivo argues that a sociological turn is necessary to attack a priori notions of mathematics. He points out that even bringing psychology to the philosophy of mathematics will not help unless we recognize that psychology is a truncated form of sociology and anthropology. He reiterates the need for taking a "sociological turn."

Taking the sociological turn means recognizing that "rational" is synonymous with "social" and "cultural" as an explanatory account. As soon as we replace psychologism with sociological imperative, rationality (as a privileged explanatory strategy) and epistemology (as a philosophical psychologistic theory of knowledge) are nullified (Restivo 1994, 218).

Similarly, another group of strong social constructivists (Asher 1991; D'Ambrosio 1994) identifies ethnomathematics as a category that is outside

Western mathematical practice. They valorize various forms of mathematical expression embedded in different cultures and settings for their enriched intuitive understanding of mathematics in practice. Asher documents several forms of mathematics that emerge from various art, kinship, and cultural expressions; D'Ambrosio designates ethnomathematics as the mathematics of other cultures.

Both strong constructivists and advocates of ethnomathematics have made considerable progress in establishing the sociocultural roots of mathematics. They have not, however, elaborated on the issues related to intracultural variations in knowledge production and legitimation.

Although I am sympathetic to Restivo's sociological imperative and social constructivists' agenda in general, most of their energy is spent on establishing the sociocultural roots of mathematics instead of on providing a critical framework. This framework is needed in order to investigate the complexities of sociocultural arrangements and power relations in the production and transmission of mathematics along complex dimensions such as race, caste, gender, and class. I am not trying to portray the theoretical formulations of social constructivists as trivial. Rather, I wish to point out that we need to go beyond battling the hegemony of absolutist notions of mathematics.

Merely establishing the cultural roots of mathematics does not address the central question, "Whose knowledge are we talking about?" Why, within a cultural group, are certain forms of mathematical knowledge dominant? For example, in places like India, the marginalized epistemologies are both visible and illegitimate in spite of the fact that those epistemic agents outnumber the members of the dominant social group.

In Steve Fuller's social epistemology (1988), I see a possibility for a framework to address the issue of how to develop strategies to mainstream the marginalized epistemologies in any given social setting. I do not mean to imply that social constructivists oppose such an agenda. Instead, their focus and energy has been directed elsewhere.

SOCIAL EPISTEMOLOGY AND ITS IMPLICATIONS FOR MATHEMATICS EDUCATION

Social epistemology, as outlined by Fuller, is an inquiry to improve knowledge production and distribution in any social system. Fuller attempts to address the shortcomings of both classical epistemology and the sociology of knowledge.

Classical epistemology is normative in the sense that it proposes that knowledge claims and justifications are universal. So, for a multiculturalist, classical epistemology is problematic. Traditionally, sociologists of knowledge are concerned with problems in accepting knowledge claims that serve the interests of specific groups. These two disciplines—epistemology and sociology—are in conflict with each other since classical epistemology presupposes that social acceptance of certain forms of knowledge has equal benefit for all, and hence has no net effect on the distribution of power. In contrast, sociologists of knowledge are concerned with the inequalities in the distribution of power associated with acceptance of such claims of value-free knowledge. Sociologists are skeptical about the objective knowledge claims presupposed by classical epistemology.

The tension between these two disciplines is exemplified in mathematics education in any discourse between social constructivists and absolutists. As a result of this tension, most social constructivists are questioning the value-free, neutral status of mathematics. In any culture, social acceptance of the inequalities in the distribution of power and the denial of epistemic status to those who are at the margins are linked. With legitimation of knowledge comes covert distribution of power. How are we going to address the problem of granting epistemic warranty?

According to Fuller, arguments such as "knowledge production is context dependent and contingent or open-ended" from New Wave sociologists are problematic for two reasons: (1) they presume that the knowledge producer has full control over his knowledge production and utilization, and (2) any knowledge producer is relatively free to tailor any knowledge claims to his specific situation. For example, "the epistemic ambassadors" of a subaltern are free to co-opt various forms of knowledge produced and practiced by those at the margin without even acknowledging their origins. Therefore, we would not be surprised to hear claims about *kolam* as Indian mathematics that do not give due credit to the women who produced, practiced, and transmitted that knowledge for years, and not to hear mention of the history behind the silenced epistemic discourse.

Social epistemology as proposed by Fuller is a normative epistemology that is sociologically informed. He envisions a social epistemologist who can be an epistemic policy maker and who is sensitive to multiple social realities. A social epistemologist would like to show how the products of our cognitive pursuits are affected by changing the social relations in which knowledge producers stand in relation to others. If certain kinds of knowledge product are desired, then the social epistemologist could design a scheme for dividing up the labor that would be likely to efficiently bring it about. If the society is already committed to a certain scheme for dividing up cognitive labor, the social epistemologist would indicate the knowledge products that are likely to flow from that scheme (Fuller 1988, 3).

Moreover, a social epistemologist would not merely be interested in various ways knowledge is produced. By aligning himself with "naturalistic approaches to knowledge" he will also be conscious of the variety of products that pass for knowledge itself in various sociocultural settings; consequently, he engages in any social discourse without worrying about "getting into the right frame of mind" (3).

How Can We Apply Social Epistemology in Multicultural Discourse in Mathematics Education?

I make four modest proposals as a way to resolve the paradox in the Eurocentrism debate. In addition, I argue that the subaltern person should also be an active participant in the multicultural discourse, with the courage to examine her cultural legacy and knowledge systems in relation to existing social relations instead of merely complaining about Eurocentric bias.

First, since multiculturalism is a movement concerned about empowerment, we need to go beyond the Eurocentrism debate. If we are interested in providing epistemic warranty to various kinds of mathematics produced in various cultures, we should actively examine those cultural products in conjunction with the differential status of the knowledge producers.

Second, such a framework will also force the epistemic ambassadors of any subaltern to critically examine their own history and their intellectual legacy. That is, the elites of any subaltern culture should have to account for the inequalities in the legitimation of various forms of knowledge that are practiced by those in the margins.

Third, social epistemology can provide a framework for a global epistemic discourse without losing sight of the intra- and intercultural variations in mathematical products and the kinds of mathematical knowledge that are produced and practiced in different cultures. At the same time, we should resist any attempts to merely burden students with facts and figures from various cultures as a reaction to Eurocentric bias. Instead, those artifacts could be used to engage in a debate about various kinds of mathematics and their status within a culture.[4]

Fourth, we should go beyond both ideological (Eurocentrism versus subalternism) as well as epistemological (context-free versus context-dependent) dichotomies to realize the goals of multiculturalism.[5] Instead we should focus on knowledge in practice, in relation to power, racism, sexism, and casteism, to further our understanding of the ways in which we can develop an equitable global epistemic policy.

Such an epistemic policy would challenge the tendency to portray a monolithic Europe or subaltern to offset the goals of multiculturalism. We have witnessed what happened in Nazi Germany with such consolidation and with its national identity rhetoric. It is also happening in India, where "national identity" is cultivated through a rhetoric of a pristine, monolithic golden past, free of any contradictions. Such a consolidation is detrimental to the realization of the goals of multiculturalism. To counter such attempts, we should engage in a global epistemic discourse that would bring the ethics of education to the foreground by listing its goals, such as preferring empowerment and participatory democracy to meritocracy (Gowri 1994). I sense an urgency to take the multiculturalism debate beyond ideological and epistemological dichotomies.

In conclusion, coming back to the Zen koan, we need to go beyond Eurocentrism versus subalternism or context-dependent versus context-free dichotomies to overcome the problem of multiple social realities. Social epistemology could be a useful framework for the understanding of various kinds of knowledge production in conjunction with the social relations in which they are produced and practiced. Through its use we can expand the scope of multiculturalism so that it is also relevant to subaltern.

I wish to thank Dr. Carl Johnson and Dr. Steve Fuller for their valuable comments on earlier drafts of this paper.

1. I use the word *subalternism* instead of *orientalism* in order to bring the self-defining attempts of the "other" into multicultural discourse.
2. Plutarch remarks on Plato: "Plato's indignation at [using mathematics for practical purposes] and his invections against it as the mere corruption and annihilation of the one good of geometry, which was thus shamefully turning its back upon the unembodied objects of pure intelligence" (Smith 1951, 90).
3. *Vedas* are the canonized religious texts of Hinduism.
4. A similar proposal is made by Nel Noddings in her provocative 1994 paper.
5. See also Delpit (1993), who has discussed the issue of power in deciding what is good for poor children and children of color.

REFERENCES

Ascher, M. 1991. *Ethnomathematics: A Multicultural View of Mathematics.* Belmont, Calif.: Wadsworth.
D'Ambrosio, U. 1994. "Ethnomathematics, the Nature of Mathematics and Mathematics Education." In *Mathematics, Education and Philosophy: An International Perspective,* edited by P. Ernest, 230–42. London: Falmer Press.
Delpit, L. 1993. "The Silenced Dialogue: Power and Pedagogy in Educating Other People's Children." In *Beyond Silenced Voices: Class, Race, and Gender in United States Schools,* edited by L. Weis and M. Fine, 119–39. Albany, N.Y.: State University of New York.
Doniger, W., and B. Smith. 1991. *The Laws of Manu.* London: Penguin.
Fanon, F. 1965. *The Wretched of the Earth.* New York: Grover.
Foucault, M. 1972. *Archeology of Knowledge,* translated by A. M. Sheridan. New York: Pantheon.
Fuller, S. 1988. *Social Epistemology.* Bloomington: Indiana University Press.
Gowri, A. 1994. "Ethnomathematics and Ethics of Enculturation." Paper presented at the Society for Social Studies of Science annual meeting, New Orleans.
Joseph, G, 1987. "Foundations of Eurocentrism in Mathematics." *Race and Class* 28, no. 3: 13–28.
Noddings, N. 1994. "Does Everybody Count? Reflections on Reforms in School Mathematics." *Journal of Mathematical Behavior* 13: 89–104.
Restivo, S. 1994. "The Social Life of Mathematics." In *Mathematics, Education and Philosophy: An International Perspective,* edited by P. Ernest, 209–20. London: Falmer Press.
Said, E. 1985. "Orientalism Reconsidered." *Race and Class,* 27, no. 2: 1–15.
Smith, D. 1951. *History of Mathematics,* vol. 1. New York: Dover.
West, C. 1993. *Beyond Eurocentrism and Multiculturalism,* vol. 2. Monroe, Maine: Common Courage.

11

IS THE MULTICULTURALIZATION OF MATHEMATICS DOING US MORE HARM THAN GOOD?

Rochelle Gutiérrez

University of Illinois, Urbana-Champaign

Few people would deny that mathematics is an important skill that should be acquired and applied by *all* citizens. However, there is great debate in the mathematics education community about how best to teach and reach all students.[1] At times the debate has centered around issues of tracking (whether or not schools should group students according to their perceived abilities),[2] and at other times around issues such as curriculum standards (creating a common curriculum that focuses on problem solving, reasoning, communications, and connections).[3] With increased proportions of nonwhite school-aged children in the United States, the debate recently has come to focus on student culture and the curriculum (whether and how to incorporate the needs of a diverse student population).

More specifically, "multicultural mathematics" has been offered as a potential solution for the low performance in mathematics exhibited by students of color.[4] In a general sense, multicultural mathematics is a form of mathematics education that focuses school curricula on the contributions of non-Europeans. It draws largely upon the work of ethnomathematicians who have documented the mathematical activities of cultures outside of the United States (especially third world countries). Such activities include the African counting game commonly known as *mancala* and the Yoruba numeration system that uses twenty (not ten) as its base (Zaslavsky 1979, 1994). Though there is inconsistency in the use of the term *ethnomathematics,* it is regarded generally as the recognition that mathematics exists beyond the school walls and beyond a Eurocentric view. Multicultural mathematics is concerned with infusing ethnomathematical perspectives into mathematics education. However, it generally is not connected to the sociology of mathematics, which concerns itself with the global construction and representation of knowledge.

The basic debate surrounding multicultural mathematics has three major perspectives. Proponents (primarily educators and some cultural anthropologists) suggest that if students were to realize that a great deal of the mathematics they learn in school was developed in Asia and Africa, they would be more interested in mathematics and could take greater pride in the achievements of their people.[5] Opponents (primarily mathematicians), however, suggest that multicultural mathematics is nothing more than a watered-down version of "real mathematics" and that examining mathematics "in context" leads to an emphasis on context in absence of pure mathematics.[6] Furthermore, sociologists of mathematics suggest that the debate needs more carefully to consider whose mathematics is being created, represented, and consumed (Bloor 1994; Restivo 1994). I discuss distinctions between (and conflations of) the terms *multicultural mathematics, ethnomathematics,* and *sociology of mathematics* later in this chapter.

Early on, multicultural mathematics created great optimism for addressing the needs of our increasingly diverse (ethnic/racial/linguistic) student population. Unfortunately, that optimism has not translated into concrete improvements. Recent studies indicate that the gap in mathematical performance between whites and students of color persists (Secada 1992; Tate 1997b). And the debate surrounding multicultural mathematics continues, with recently added perspectives from the sociology of mathematics (Bloor 1994; Restivo 1994). A decade ago, Derek Woodrow (1989) reviewed the response to multiculturalism by mathematics educators and concluded that the initial emphasis was on a search for mathematical content. I assert that this pattern continues today and has the potential to do us more harm than good.

In this chapter, I provide a critical analysis of how mathematics educators and researchers are incorporating the goals of multicultural education into the mathematics curriculum. I show how the pattern of borrowing from a tradition in social studies/history leads to a version of multicultural mathematics that is limiting at best and which has great potential to keep teachers from meeting the needs of an ethnically and linguistically diverse student population. As a means to exploring the specific manner in which multicultural mathematics can be seen as doing more harm than good, I introduce the term "attractive distracter." I argue that the current form of multicultural mathematics becomes an attractive distracter because it keeps our eyes on mathematics content and away from sociocultural processes and power relations in classrooms and in society, areas in which we greatly need to improve. I argue that in place of the current *multiculturalized* mathematics, we need to move toward a *critical and antiracist* mathematics education that embraces the broader definition of multiculturalism.[7] Such a critical and antiracist mathematics education has as its foundation a deep examination and understanding of teachers' belief systems and working realities, the social construction of knowledge, and power relations in a global society.

I begin with an exploration of the roots of multicultural mathematics as located in ethnomathematics, and not the sociology of mathematics. It is important to understand such origins for two reasons. First, the terms *ethnomathematics, multicultural mathematics,* and *sociology of mathematics* are often blurred, which contributes to problems in educational practice. Second, the borrowing of mathematical content from ethnomathematics has influenced greatly the manner in which multicultural mathematics has been applied to classrooms in the United States as well as the limitations that it may hold for the future.

THE ROOTS OF MULTICULTURAL MATHEMATICS

In contrast to traditional depictions of mathematics as a universal, value-free, and objective discipline, multicultural mathematics builds its foundation upon ethnomathematics, which has at its center the culture of those persons doing mathematics in their natural context. Although examined by a few researchers before 1950, according to Paul Gerdes (1994), ethnomathematics really did not become a recognized field until the late 1970s and early 1980s. For the most part, ethnomathematics was developed by mathematicians and educators in countries outside of the United States, especially within third world countries (e.g., Mozambique). The growing resistance to racist, postcolonial prejudices in math served as a catalyst for the documentation of ethnomathematics.[8]

Developed over a decade ago by Ubiritan D'Ambrosio and the International Study Group on Ethnomathematics (D'Ambrosio 1985), there is still some disagreement about what constitutes ethnomathematics or how it should be applied. For example, D'Ambrosio (1990) relies on etymology and defines ethnomathematics generally as "the art or technique (tics) of explaining, understanding, coping, with (mathema) the sociocultural and natural (ethno) environment' (22). Attempting to be specific, but failing to define his terms, Gerdes (1994) includes in ethnomathematics the following eleven versions: indigenous mathematics, sociomathematics, informal mathematics, mathematics in the sociocultural environment, spontaneous mathematics, oral mathematics, oppressed mathematics, nonstandard mathematics, hidden/frozen mathematics, folk mathematics, and mathematics codified in know-hows. The fact that Gerdes includes sociomathematics and mathematics in the sociocultural environment in the general category of "ethnomathematics" is further evidence of the blurring of the terms I mentioned earlier. The main contribution of ethnomathematicians, such as D'Ambrosio and others, has been their ability to document diversity in the manner in which mathematical knowledge is created, transmitted, diffused, and institutionalized within different cultural systems. The inclusion of this knowledge begins to challenge a vision of mathematics as created solely by mathematicians in Europe.

Ethnomathematicians recognize that at least two distinct areas of mathematical literacy exist: (1) school mathematics, and (2) mathematics of a given cultural group (D'Ambrosio 1985). That is, when children are a very young age they possess the mathematical knowledge of their cultural group; however, when they begin to attend school on a regular basis, this knowledge is replaced with school knowledge, which is valued more by the system.

For our purposes, ethnomathematics is seen as a research field, where a cultural-anthropological approach is applied to the study of mathematics. As such, ethnomathematics is not directly related to teacher education or teaching and the implications we can draw from such research currently are limited. However, one goal of ethnomathematics is to acknowledge the mathematics studied by people outside of school and to move away from a Eurocentric view of the curriculum.

For some students, especially Latinos, Native Americans, and African Americans, schooling in America follows postcolonial patterns whereby school knowledge is expected to replace cultural (or home) knowledge. As such, several researchers and educators have suggested that teachers need to begin incorporating more ethnomathematics into the curriculum in order to give students a better chance to relate to the material at hand and to build upon the knowledge of mathematics learned outside of formal education (Zaslavsky 1996). This infusion of ethnomathematics into the curriculum (and referred to by educators as multicultural mathematics) not only recognizes that Western mathematics may be only *one* of many mathematics (Bishop 1989), but (in theory) it values the knowledge that students bring to school.

The recent embracing of students' diverse cultures (Nieto 1996) and home knowledge is an improvement on deficit models witnessed over the past three decades (Weiner 1993). However, student culture generally has been incorporated into mathematics in a manner similar to social studies (Gutiérrez and Rosiek 1994), with an emphasis on content integration, not social transformation or other goals of multicultural education (Banks and Banks 1997). The main contribution of ethnomathematics is its documentation of the societal and cultural aspects of mathematics as a whole.

While the goals of multicultural mathematics are similar to those of ethnomathematics, there are some differences worth noting. First, very little of the research conducted on mathematics used by everyday peoples is situated in the United States (Secada 1994). As a result, multicultural mathematics tends to borrow directly from the knowledge base created by ethnomathematicians, but its relationship to citizens is not direct. Second, multicultural mathematics tends to be supported by a framework created within the multicultural education movement. That is, proponents of multicultural mathematics (e.g., Ladson-Billings 1995; Zaslavsky 1996) tend to refer to (and align with) Banks and Banks (1997) and others who have delineated the major goals of multicultural education as they relate specifically to equity within and outside of the U.S. school. Unlike ethnomathematics, multiculural mathematics is developed primarily by educators and educational researchers who take into consideration educational theories when depicting the student and her learning environment. For the most part, their efforts tend to be directed toward teachers and educational researchers, not mathematicians or anthropologists.

While multicultural mathematics tends to focus on mathematical end products of different cultures, sociologists of mathematics are concerned with the social histories and social worlds embodied in mathematical objects (e.g., Restivo

1994). Relatively new to the field of mathematics education, sociologists of mathematics challenge the idea that mathematicians alone possess the ability to determine what *is* and what is *not* mathematics. Using a social constructivist model, they suggest that all mathematics is social, that ideas become communicable concepts only when they can be shared, and that current views of mathematics currently limit the field's ability to address global problems (including equity). Though there is not sufficient space to adequately address the finer points of the sociology of mathematics or ethnomathematics, I offer these distinctions to provide the reader with a context for my argument.[9] For the most part, however, I focus my analysis on multicultural mathematics, as it is the form most commonly represented and consumed by educators concerned with equity.

Exploring Multicultural Mathematics as an Attractive Distracter

[A]lthough scholars and researchers have continued a line of inquiry related to multicultural education, the development of multicultural practice has lagged significantly.... What passes for multicultural education in many schools and classrooms is the equivalent of food, fiestas, and festivals.

—Gloria Ladson-Billings, "Making Mathematics Meaningful in Multicultural Contexts"

The term "attractive distracter" refers to a phenomenon I first experienced while in college. While preparing for one of the many standardized tests required for graduate study, I took a review course in which the staff helps devise strategies for the kinds of problems one will encounter on the actual test. In this class, I remember the section leader telling us about different ways the test makers try to "trick" the test taker. One of these tricks was what our section came to call "the attractive distracter." The attractive distracter was an incorrect answer that usually occurred at the beginning of a series of answers, may have been partially correct, and served to distract you from the correct (and often more complete or appropriate) answer. Though that was a long time ago, I continue to reflect on that class, as I since have encountered many "attractive distracters" in my life.

I apply this term *attractive distracter* to the current form of multicultural mathematics as it is enacted in classrooms with an increasingly diverse student population. I argue that the current form of multicultural mathematics becomes an attractive distracter because it keeps our eyes on mathematics content and distracts us from sociocultural processes within classrooms (e.g. teacher-student interactions) that reflect power relations in society. I will examine the manner in which multicultural mathematics is both attractive and distracting.

I do *not* argue in this paper that the incorporation of either the history of mathematics or activities that highlight the contributions of different cultures in mathematics is not useful. Rather, I suggest this information should be seen as a necessary but insufficient piece of a larger whole. My main concern is that multicultural perspectives of math are being envisioned and addressed in a primarily content-oriented manner with little regard for the social reality of teaching or the politics of knowledge construction.

THE ATTRACTIVENESS OF MULTICULTURAL MATHEMATICS EDUCATION

As noted earlier, the performance levels of students of color, female students, and the poor persist at levels lower than can be explained by factors outside of school (Oakes et al. 1990; Secada 1992; Tate 1997b). Therefore, a focus on mathematics teaching that incorporates the contributions of different cultures and that seeks to engage a wider audience is clearly useful. Beyond this general aim to make mathematics more accessible to a wider group of people, there are other benefits to the current form of multicultural mathematics.

Encouraging Social and Dynamic Views of Mathematics

At a very basic level, multicultural mathematics challenges the long-held myth that mathematics is acultural. When the history of mathematics and mathematics from a global perspective are explored, students of all backgrounds can begin to view mathematics as a field that is continually being created, by different peoples, often times concurrently. While Dee Stander (1989) indicates that students' attitudes about mathematics do not change with the introduction of historical content, this use of questionnaires as a means for assessing "attitudes" is called into question by the work of Stanic and Hart (1995) who found contradictory information about students' attitudes when comparing data from questionnaires and interviews. Furthermore, the move away from a Eurocentric view of math has the potential to change students' attitudes about themselves (e.g., as competent mathematicians and members of society). According to Volmink (1994), socially situating mathematics uncovers strong hegemonic processes at work in society. If students are to ever see themselves as *owning* mathematics, they must also see themselves as *creating* it. Without acknowledging that school math has an inherent cultural bias, students from cultures not aligned with European traditions will be at a disadvantage for obtaining an adequate/effective education, but will have few opportunities for realizing why. Beverly Anderson (1990) underscores this point, suggesting that presenting mathematics without cultural, political, or historical references contributes to a process of convincing people of color they are "biologically, intellectually, and/or psychologically incapable of understanding mathematics" (352).

In addition, the inclusion of ethnomathematics in the curriculum provides a specific context rather than an abstract setting, moving us in the direction of recommendations by math educators to situate mathematics in real-world contexts (NCTM 1989).[10] Recognizing that mathematics is grounded in social activity and that contradictory ideas become competing theories may facilitate among teachers a greater inclination for students' views and cultures to come into play (Nickson 1989). An emphasis on the sociocultural nature of mathematical knowledge also supports a move away from traditional forms of mathematics teaching (e.g., an emphasis on rote memorization, proofs, and algorithms) and opens the door for more active (e.g. hands-on, project-based) and constructivist forms of learning.

Relating to a Diverse Student Population

Multicultural mathematics, with its current emphasis on the contributions of different peoples to the creation and implementation of mathematical knowledge, also aligns with America's increasingly diverse student population. For dominated minorities, reform-oriented curricula (including knowledge about the history and cultural achievements of people of color) have been associated with increased achievement patterns (Cummins, cited in McCarthy 1993). When mathematics texts include information that recognizes the many perspectives and accomplishments of different cultural groups, there is a greater likelihood that students' personal interests will be met. Anderson's (1990) work with college students in New York and Newark provide us with some proof. For example, taught a non-Eurocentric mathematics curriculum, his students exhibited more positive and self-assured attitudes about mathematics, greater persistence and achievement in algebra courses, and greater rates of participation in subsequent mathematics courses when compared to their peers.

Affirming Diversity

Not only does multicultural mathematics recognize the heritage of our diverse U.S. society, it also (in theory) affirms diversity. In direct contrast to previous deficit theories of student failure, multicultural mathematics attempts to address the student in a positive manner, encouraging teachers to build upon the knowledge and experiences that students bring to the classroom (Moll and Gonzalez 1994). Rather than promote a color-blind approach to teaching, multicultural mathematics emphasizes the cultural aspects of mathematics. As such, it provides opportunities for students to be "experts" on the curriculum, a position students rarely hold.

THE DISTRACTIVE POTENTIAL OF MULTICULTURAL MATHEMATICS

Similar to the attractive distracters that are present on standardized tests, at first glance, multicultural mathematics appears to be a good answer to the low performance levels that we witness among students of color. However, a closer look at the implementation of multicultural mathematics indicates that the recent multiculturalization may not be sufficient to stimulate improvement for all students in mathematics.

While exposure to a variety of perspectives on mathematics may be useful for extending students' conceptions of mathematics and/or their conceptions of knowledge, it fails to address many issues that have been associated with student learning. In fact, the emphasis on curriculum in the absence of a critical analysis of student identity, racism, teacher beliefs, schooling conditions, or dominance in society does a disservice to the potential of a new knowledge base to help create a more humane society. In reality, the (current) multiculturalization of mathematics serves as an attractive distracter in several ways.

Narrowly Defining Audiences

First, because recommendations for the multiculturalization of mathematics are often tied to making mathematics more relevant to an increasingly diverse (racial/ethnic/linguistic) student population, many teachers have interpreted multicultural mathematics as something to be saved for classrooms in which there is a significant population of students of color (Ladson-Billings 1995). The implication is that white, middle-class students cannot benefit from learning about other cultures or from exploring the political dimensions of race in our society. This approach also disadvantages female students and students in poorly funded schools, both of whom are marginalized in society but who may not be empowered by current efforts to multiculturalize mathematics that focus on ethnic contributions.

The primary model that has been applied by teachers is a student-centered, constructivist one: students will bring to class those cultural and experiential artifacts that are important to explore within mathematics. However, this particular constructivist model ignores the fact that not all U.S. classrooms will have students whose experiences or ideas differ from the dominant white perspective currently presented in mathematics classrooms and society at large. Even if all classrooms possessed the reservoir of knowledge/experience needed to enact multicultural mathematics, relying on students to offer relevant information is limited by the facts that most school-aged students lack: (1) the critical thinking skills necessary to discern what their needs are and how they relate to their position(s) in society, and (2) the power to control classroom processes (an issue I discuss later).

Furthermore, efforts to create a multicultural mathematics curriculum have tended to take place in the elementary grades (Zaslavsky 1979, 1996). This focus on early years of schooling has the danger of perpetuating stereotypes about non-Eurocentric contributions to mathematics as "primitive."

Deflecting (Current) Political Situations

By assuming that students' self-concept and disposition toward mathematics will improve once they have been exposed to ancestral contributions, multicultural mathematics focuses on history and distracts students from thinking about mathematics in ways that help them see their current situation. In the words of Peter McLaren (1994), "We have been standing at the crossroads of a disintegrating culture for the last two decades where we have witnessed a steady increase in the disproportionate level of material wealth, economic dislocation, and intergenerational poverty suffered by African-Americans, Latinos, and other minorities" (193).

Though this prevalence of poverty among certain U.S. groups is widely accepted by the general public, multicultural mathematics tends not to address such issues.[11] The current multicultural mathematics curriculum may convince students of the value of mathematics created by their ancestors, then subsequently leave them wondering what members of their culture have done lately (Woodrow 1989). That is, most multicultural mathematics curricula do not situate the mathematics in a social context that allows students to see the connection between the development of mathematics as a field and the low participation and achievement rates they currently experience.

Moreover, the focus within multicultural mathematics is, for the most part, apolitical. That is, even though teachers are encouraged to include and refer to ancient peoples who have created and used mathematics, rarely are students exposed to the status of people in these ancient times or the manner in which mathematics is used to promote capitalism (Anderson 1990) and the subordination of third world countries (Woodrow 1989). In researching the use of mathematics by ancient cultures, John Volmink (1994) indicates that mathematics has always been owned by a privileged class, explaining, "While there is an acknowledgment that mathematics is a pan-human activity, there is no evidence either in the history of mathematics or in mathematical practice today, to support the belief that, within a particular cultural context, mathematics was widely practised by the majority. The social arrangements of early civilizations were such that only the rich, the powerful, the influential, had access to mathematical knowledge. At times there was almost a conspiracy to keep the codified mathematical knowledge as secret as possible" (51).

While Volmink may be referring only to documented (written) mathematical knowledge and not mathematics known and practiced by people in everyday life, it is this "knowledge" that exists in history books and reference materials and is most readily available for inclusion in multicultural mathematics curricula.

Perpetuating Stereotypes about Cultural Groups

Because multicultural mathematics has been conceptualized with an emphasis on the history of different countries and their peoples (and tends to import research from populations seen as "exotic" by most Americans), most of the materials available for consumption depict single, homogeneous cultures such as the Mayans in Mexico, and the Egyptians in Africa (Escalante and Dirmann 1990; Zaslavsky 1979, 1996). While ancient countries may have been more homogeneous, modern states are increasingly diverse.

Students in today's classrooms come from a number of different ethnicities; single individuals often draw from more than one race/ethnicity. By encouraging teachers to incorporate the history of Africa to be more inclusive of blacks or the history of Mexico to be more inclusive of Latinos, the implication is that *all* blacks will relate to African representations and *all* Latinos will relate to Mexican representations. In fact, Latinos from Argentina or Chile may have little more perspective on (or identification with) Chicano history (especially colonialization) than their non-Latino classmates. It is my experience that students with heritage in the Dominican Republic choose to identify with Latinos. And yet, because of their skin color and the social construction of race in the United States, the African-American experience will often be projected onto them. An important lesson for teachers: merely surveying one's class is not a good indication of students' identities.

Even knowing students' racial/ethnic backgrounds is limiting. For instance, knowing that her students are Chicano may encourage a teacher to incorporate examples from Mexico. Yet, assuming that all Chicanos will benefit from historical (or even current) references to Mexico ignores the fact that Chicanos identify to differing degrees (at times contradictory within an individual) with their cultural heritage (Burciaga 1993) and their positions in society (Villenas 1986)— exhibiting the "multivocality" described by McCarthy (1993). Furthermore, this approach fails to recognize that much of Mexico's written history caters to the Spaniards, not the perspectives of indigenous populations with which many Chicanos choose to identify (Castillo 1994). Moreover, in their eagerness to affirm diversity, there is the potential danger for teachers to expect students of color to be spokespeople for their ethnic/racial group.

Recent work by critical race theorists underscores the point that race has been poorly constructed as a static and essentialist category (Ladson-Billings 1998; Parker 1998; Tate 1997a). Asking teachers to incorporate multicultural mathematics without problematizing the categories of race, culture, gender, and identity leaves teachers relying on curriculum materials to address the needs of students. As such, the current multiculturalization of mathematics distracts teachers from seeing diversity *within* ethnic groups (and individuals) and may, subsequently, encourage them to perpetuate stereotypes. In addition, multicultural mathematics fails to address the white ethnic identities of students. In doing so, it maintains the potential to reduce ethnic groups of color to deviant status or categories of "other" (McLaren 1994).

Ignoring the Social Reality of Teaching and Learning

Perhaps most important, however, is the role that multiculturalization of mathematics plays in the development of socially conscious teachers and a democratic education system.[12] Though many of the proponents of ethnomathematics document the cultural and contextual influences of mathematics in an anthropological (Saxe 1991) and even sociological (e.g., Restivo 1994) sense, for the most part, mathematics education is not part of their projects. As a result, much of the content and approaches that eventually are imported into multicultural mathematics ignore the social reality of teaching and learning in U.S. schools. By *the social reality of teaching*, I mean the influence of teacher beliefs/knowledge, institutional racism, and teacher-student interactions on students' access to knowledge construction and participation in mathematics.

With respect to individual teachers, the multiculturalization of mathematics distracts those who feel compelled (either intrinsically or merely to remain "politically correct") to address issues of equity but who are unwilling to think about their role in perpetuating the underrepresentation of women, the poor, and students of color at higher levels of mathematics in school and in positions of power in the world.[13]

From educational research, we know that mathematics teachers tend to implement only those standards/practices that are consistent with their beliefs (Thompson 1984). My own research has shown that when teachers do not agree with the philosophy underlying certain reforms, they carry them out in a way that is consistent with their beliefs but is not obvious to administrators (Gutiérrez 1996). Ignoring these beliefs can have serious implications for the development of a truly multicultural mathematics experience for students. Allow me to explain.

Most preservice teachers are white and middle-class, aspire to teach in settings similar to the small towns in which they grew up (Zimpher and Ashburn 1992), and fail to recognize race or racism as significant factors in society or in the education of students of color (Sleeter 1993). How can students be expected to truly engage in a critical examination (or even reasoning) about the construction and meaning of mathematical knowledge if that reasoning poses a threat to the privilege or belief systems of their white teachers? Such critical mathematical reasoning on the behalf of students is not likely to be met with positive teacher-student interactions. In fact, because teachers maintain a position of power over students, efforts to encourage students to engage in multicultural mathematics could have the unintended consequence of further marginalizing them from the system and disadvantaging them in later teacher assessments. The potential damage of negative teacher interaction and assessment is further exacerbated by the sequential nature of the mathematics curriculum (and tracking practices) in U.S. schools, whereby a student's achievement in one course can continue to influence her placement and achievement in future courses.

The importance of teacher beliefs and positive teacher-student interactions cannot be overstated. Among other things, teachers' beliefs (about students, mathematics, teaching, and learning) influence classroom processes and therefore the kinds of opportunities students have to exhibit their full potential. In studying high school math departments across the United States, I have found that certain teacher beliefs (including stereotypes about low-income students and students of color) are strongly associated with teacher-student relationships, the kinds of mathematics that are provided to students, and eventual student outcomes (Gutiérrez 1996, and in press). For example, although teachers often lacked concrete knowledge about the lives of students, they had well-developed ideas about students of color. Common images of students' lives were those portrayed in the media: that students of color live in gang-ridden areas, that they are responsible for the care of their younger siblings, that their parents work more than one job and are not at home during the evening, and that their parents (and other family members) lack the educational background (or language skills) to assist with homework. When they believed their students lacked such home supports, these teachers decided not to assign homework or to require class materials. It has also been found that teacher-student interactions and academic interactions in a seventh-grade classroom of African-American and white students influenced the levels of achievement they experienced in mathematics (Stanic and Hart 1995).

The importance of classroom processes on students' opportunities to learn mathematics or exhibit their full potential is further suggested by Yando and colleagues (cited in Reyes and Stanic 1988). These researchers studied the influence of race, socioeconomic status (SES), and gender on the problem-solving skills of eight-year-olds and found that low-SES students performed better than high-SES students on tasks that required creativity, while high-SES students performed better than low-SES students on tasks that aligned with school activities. By continuing to limit the creativity involved in mathematics activities, schools continue to ensure low performance from low-income students and perhaps others.

Bill Atweh, Robert Bleicher, and Tom Cooper (1998) studied the social context of two Year-9 mathematics classrooms in Australia and found that teachers' conceptions of students from different socioeconomic backgrounds and genders influenced greatly their teaching decisions and communication styles. This research illustrates that teachers conduct their classrooms in accordance with what they perceive to be students' abilities and needs, focusing on formal and abstract mathematics for students whose trajectory is perceived to be professional careers and emphasizing concrete mathematics for students they view as potential consumers. Atweh and colleagues suggest that in attempting to make mathematics relevant to the lives of students, there is a danger of teachers exacerbating, not mitigating, differences in mathematics achievement. More research needs to be conducted on classroom processes as they relate to race, gender, and socioeconomic status if we are to truly address equity issues in mathematics education.

I have discussed some of the ways in which teachers' beliefs and interactions with students have been found by researchers to influence low performance among many students of color. Common sense suggests others. For example, if teachers do not already understand the development of mathematical knowledge from a global perspective, if they do not realize their position in society or the manner in which power and privilege play out along lines of race, class, and gender, then the inclusion of multicultural mathematics materials is not likely to challenge their beliefs about students and their capabilities. Neither is such an emphasis likely to produce pedagogies that will benefit these students most. Instead, well-intentioned teachers who work in constraining environments (an issue I discuss later) are likely to overestimate the potential of a multicultural curriculum to "empower" students whose histories align with the social contexts presented in mathematical activities and exercises.

Clearly, a greater focus needs to be placed on teachers' complex belief systems, including beliefs about mathematics, beliefs about the teaching and learning of mathematics, beliefs about students (e.g. what they are capable of doing, how their histories contribute to the teaching and learning process), and conceptions of privilege and power in society. Getting teachers to see their role in student learning in mathematics requires more than exposure to cultural contributions of different groups of students. Like Leone Burton (1994), I take the position that (among other things) content *and* pedagogy are responsible for discrimination in school mathematics. Unfortunately, like previous efforts to make mathematics more accessible to culturally and linguistically diverse students, current efforts to "multiculturalize" mathematics ignore the complex system of teacher beliefs through which new reforms are filtered.[14]

Beyond the individual teacher, multicultural mathematics also distracts us away from powerful forms of institutional racism at work in the U.S. education system. One strong example is tracking—the process of grouping students into courses or levels based on ability judgments by their teachers and performance on standardized tests. Oakes and colleagues (1990) make a strong case for such institutional racism in reporting that in comparison to white and higher-income students, students of color and lower-income students are disproportionately represented in low-ability mathematics and science classes; are more likely to attend schools with limited mathematics and science programs; have more limited resources (e.g., access to computers); tend to receive instruction from the least-qualified mathematics and science teachers, using the most outdated textbooks; and tend to have teachers who focus on behavior, not learning. Moreover, U.S. schools continue to perpetuate a sequential mathematics curriculum that requires students to have a prerequisite set of basic skills before allowing them to move onto more advanced topics. Other institutional policies, such as school funding—which is based on property taxes—further exacerbate the gap between the rich and the poor (Kozol 1991).

In addition to the kinds of institutional racism present in the educational system, teachers are constrained by their general working conditions. The recent intensification of their work lives (Hargreaves 1994) means teachers have little time to reflect on the nature of mathematics presented to students, to have meaningful relationships with their students, to have deep conversations with colleagues about mathematics teaching and learning, or to effectively critique reform efforts in mathematics. In fact, because teachers are pressed for time, they tend to have little option other than to carry out a predesigned curriculum.

Assuming Expertise among Teachers

An emphasis on multicultural mathematics content also assumes teachers possess sufficient knowledge about mathematics and the contexts in which it is used by other cultures, or that they can easily attain this knowledge from workshops or textbooks. In fact, Stander (1989) notes that teachers are largely untrained in the use or substance of issues such as the history of mathematics. Moreover, if we aspire to develop a multicultural mathematics that encourages students to debate and reason about the environment around them (Frankenstein 1990; NCTM 1989; Secada 1994), we must recognize it requires a great deal of sophistication on the part of teachers to explore with students issues of knowledge construction, history, power, race, and class without resorting to oversimplification, stereotyping, or defense of the status quo.[15]

Most teachers, having had little opportunity to explore mathematics in nontraditional ways, benefit from simplifying the tasks they are given. My experience with preservice teachers in secondary mathematics is that they focus on the contributions of certain ethnic groups to the exclusion of the mathematics at hand (Gutiérrez 1997). For example, when asked to develop educational materials that recognized ethnic and racial diversity in U.S. students, mathematics was no longer central to the activity.[16] Instead, activities such as sharing recipes from different cultures (manipulating simple fractions as the recipes are doubled and halved) were seen as appropriate for high school students. These preservice teachers' interpretations of the task send messages to students that either one does mathematics *or* one addresses the sociocultural needs of students, not both. Similarly, in studying the discourse of bilingual mathematics classrooms, Lena Khisty (1995) found that although teachers sprinkled Spanish into their lessons, it was rarely used when teachers were explaining or discussing the mathematical aspects of an activity. Again, the hidden message for native Spanish speakers is that language and mathematics are not integrally linked. Moreover, by conducting classes primarily in English, teachers unwittingly deny native Spanish speakers the opportunity to create mathematics in their own language. To overlook the lack of expertise within some teachers is to place too much weight on a multicultural curriculum to influence the learning experiences of students.

Toward a Critical and Antiracist Mathematics Education

Where might we turn, then, for future directions in the development of multicultural mathematics education? I draw on the perspectives of Derek Woodrow and Cameron McCarthy to develop the foundations of a critical and antiracist mathematics education. Woodrow (1989) describes antiracist mathematics as a "multicultural approach to mathematics which is particularly vigilant on matters of racism" (227). For Woodrow, school mathematics always entails a certain degree of indoctrination because value judgments are continually made by teachers. He suggests that instead of ignoring values or mirroring the "natural order of things" in society, mathematics might be used to explore such issues as the cost of feeding the world versus the cost of continuing to supply weaponry. Woodrow's emphasis on values allows us to move multicultural mathematics beyond an apolitical stance toward an approach that aligns with social and global transformation.

Cameron McCarthy (1993) offers us the concept of critical multiculturalism, describing it as "radical definition of school knowledge from the heterogeneous perspectives and identities of racially disadvantaged groups—a process that goes beyond the language of 'inclusivity' and emphasizes relationality and multivocality as the central intellectual forces in the production of knowledge" (290). Currently, Woodrow's example assumes an "either/or" perspective (either one feeds the world or one supplies weaponry) within a static time frame, and assumes we do not already have the capacity to feed the world. McCarthy's concept of heterogeneous perspectives allows us to push the definitions of "feeding the world" and "supplying weaponry" in ways that allow mathematics to be modeled and explored from a number of different viewpoints in society.

Now, if we rely upon a framework that validates Western mathematics as the standard of rationality (as multicultural mathematics tends to do), it becomes difficult to address global equity. Here is where the sociology of mathematics becomes useful. Restivo (1994) provides a convincing argument that a closed system of mathematics (one that is isolated from social worlds or other mathematical worlds) prevents the flow of information and cuts off mathematics from the stimulus of external problems. In his words, "If pure mathematicicans have to rely entirely on their own cultural resources, their capacity for generating innovative, creative problems and solutions will progressively deteriorate. As a consequence, the results of pure mathematical work will become less and less applicable to problems in other social worlds" (214).

Though Restivo recognizes the need for some closure in the field (especially as it facilitates innovation and progressive change), he recommends a balance between open-mindedness and closure.

Restivo's criticism of the closed structure of mathematics aligns with visions of a critical/antiracist mathematics education as well as with the perspective of others concerned with the state of ethnomathematics. For example, D'Ambrosio (1997) criticizes current forms of ethnomathematics for focusing on "small achievements and practices in non-Western cultures that resemble Western mathematics" (15), thereby perpetuating Western mathematics as the standard of rationality. It is clear that if we are to use mathematics to address issues of power and equity, we need to consider seriously the perspectives from sociologists of mathematics.

I have already mentioned the usefulness of McCarthy's notion of critical multiculturalism and Woodrow's sense of antiracist mathematics, especially as they align with the sociology of mathematics. How might this relate directly to teachers and the kinds of pedagogies that will maximize a critical and antiracist multicultural mathematics? Emerging theories on white teacher identity and privilege (Cochran-Smith 1995; Lawrence and Tatum 1997; McIntyre 1997; Tatum 1994) as well as dominance (Applebaum 1998) afford us another avenue through which to bridge multiculturalism and mathematics.

Though few researchers have been successful in getting teachers to fully realize the prevalence of race and racism in society (Cochran-Smith 1995; McIntyre 1997; Sleeter 1996), our efforts to encourage such exploration should not be abandoned.[17] My current work with a high school mathematics department in Chicago indicates that one of the characteristics of effective teachers of Latino students is the ability to recognize race and racism in society (Gutiérrez, in press). Unlike most white teachers of students of color, mathematics teachers at this high school do not ascribe to the universal stance that "kids are kids, teaching is teaching, and learning is learning" (Haberman 1996, 747). These teachers understand that students of color are often presented with negative images of themselves in the media and from society at large.

How does race play out in the classroom? Forms of discourse is one prominent area. Addressing this very issue, sociologists of mathematics indicate the need for mathematics teachers to facilitate classroom discourse that disturbs dominant modes of thought and reasoning while at the same time empowering students with the tools for participating in the dominant language of mathematics.

It is clear that teachers need to examine their position(s) in society before they can facilitate students exploring and reasoning about the world around them.[18]

The goal of raising teachers' consciousness, however, is not to produce teachers without prejudice, even though this goal is commonly embraced by those enacting a multicultural mathematics curriculum. Rather, such efforts are intended to make teachers aware of their (dominant) positions in society, of the taken-for-granted practices, values, and frames of reference from within a white, Eurocentric tradition so that they can better understand that such a position is just one among many possible—and one that continues to oppress others. Furthermore, creating individual teachers without prejudice is not likely to address the forms of institutional racism I discussed earlier. In fact, Barbara Applebaum (1998) reminds us that racism tends not to be of the explicit nature we have come to recognize (as something that someone does *to* someone else), rather, it comes in the form of implicit norms and is intricately related to power.

IMPLICATIONS FOR POLICY MAKERS AND TEACHER EDUCATORS

The purpose of my comments is not to insult those researchers or practitioners who are attempting to make mathematics more multicultural. Rather, I raise my concerns to provide direction for future improvements. To summarize, my main concerns about multicultural mathematics are that (1) it ignores teachers' beliefs and the social reality of teaching; (2) it imports ethnomathematical content alongside Western mathematics without questioning the social construction of knowledge; (3) it does not adequately address global issues of equity and power. Mathematics should be more than just multicultural in its content; it should embrace the spectrum of goals in multiculturalism and critical pedagogy. As educators and researchers, we should continue to rethink our approach to mathematics, with an eye on equal outcomes, not just equal access (Secada 1991).

I hesitate to offer specific recommendations for policy makers—who often fail to acknowledge the political and social context of schools (Anyon 1997)—or for teacher educators, who have developed what Lilia Bartolome (1994) calls a "methods fetish." However, some general recommendations move us closer to the development of a critical and antiracist mathematics education.

At one level, practicing teachers need to be exposed to ethnomathematics if they are to begin to address the cultural experiences of their students. However, as I have argued here, mere exposure has the potential to do more harm than good. Teachers also need to understand the history that accompanies ethnomathematics and its relations to the sociology of mathematics. Such understanding is critical to getting teachers to move beyond Western mathematics as the standard of rationality. Without such understanding, teachers may eliminate racial hegemony only to perpetuate cultural hegemony (D'Ambrosio 1997).

Moreover, teachers need to become familiar with their own personal histories and to understand how these are linked to power relations in society. They also need to become more aware of how their current working realities challenge their efforts to apply new knowledge or their understandings of positionality. In fact, I suspect that students may benefit more from teachers who provide opportunities to explore issues of racism and the social construction of knowledge throughout history or who engage them in debates about forms of dominance in the world (especially dominance between students and teachers[19]) than from workshops that introduce new pedagogies or incorporate ethnomathematics content alongside traditional content.

For the education of preservice teachers, it seems important to require a course in the sociology of mathematics and to structure into the curriculum exercises that facilitate reflection about mathematics and power in a global society. Such courses might also go a long way toward educating the faculty who teach within teacher education programs, and who themselves have had little opportunities for reflection or professional development.

Devising effective mechanisms for practicing teachers, however, is more difficult. Because of the social reality of teaching, which is fairly isolating and time pressured, it is difficult to structure such opportunities. Traditional workshop and in-service formats are not likely to be sufficient. Instead, we must find ways to sustain conversations among and between teachers about the role that mathematics can play in creating a more humane society. Developing strong partnerships between university faculty and local schools is one place to start.

Though efforts to rethink mathematics (its content and pedagogical forms) are likely to be met with the resistance of previous reforms, there are a number of reasons to be hopeful that a critical and antiracist mathematics education could take root in the future. First, our classrooms are becoming populated with increasing proportions of nonwhites, rendering forms of mathematical teaching that have failed in the past even more futile. Second, emerging research on critical race theory, white identity, and dominance reveals greater complexity in the issues surrounding schooling for students of color than research on intergroup relations of the 1970s. Third, with technological advances such as the Internet, information can be shared more widely and more efficiently than ever before. And, with technology, such information draws on an even greater number of perspectives in the world.

We should be pleased that mathematics educators are beginning to rethink the development of mathematical knowledge with the goal of better supporting an increasingly diverse student population. Previous generations of mathematicians have been unwilling/unable to address these issues. However, we should avoid being "distracted" by the "attractive" qualities of approaches that fall short of achieving our original goals: improved performance and, ultimately, global transformation. We need to move beyond a model that considers ethnicity a static variable and culture as a homogeneous experience lived by "others." We need to move toward a model that recognizes power relations in society.

NOTES

1. See, for example, Apple 1992a, 1992b; Cuevas and Driscoll 1993; NCTM 1989; Romberg 1992.
2. Among others, see Oakes et al. 1990.
3. For a debate on the merits of the National Council of Teachers of Mathematics (NCTM) curriculum and evaluation standards, see Apple 1992a, 1992b; Romberg 1992; see also Tate 1995.

4. I recognize that multicultural mathematics is constantly evolving. However, I refer in this chapter to the current form, which borrows mathematical content from ethnomathematics.
5. Among others, see Zaslavsky 1994, 1996.
6. See, for example, Thomas 1996.
7. The broader definition of multiculturalism to which I refer is educational reform that supports equity at an international level.
8. In fact, though the United States also presents a colonial model for indigenous peoples such as Amerindians, most of the research conducted on everyday mathematics is situated outside of the United States (Secada 1994).
9. For an excellent presentation of sociological and philosophical perspectives on mathematics, see Ernest 1994.
10. The presence of a social context alone, however, is insufficient to develop students' ability to understand and generalize in other contexts (Boaler 1993).
11. A noted exception is the curriculum developed by Marilyn Frankenstein (1990, 1995) that emphasizes a consciousness of sex, race, and class issues in today's society.
12. See Woodrow 1997 for an insightful discussion of democracy and its relationship to mathematics education.
13. Of course, teachers should not focus their goals solely on student achievement in school mathematics. McCarthy (1993) reminds us that increased levels of education do not necessarily translate into increased job prospects for students of color.
14. See, for example, Oakes and Guiton 1995 for a discussion of politics and human decision-making that accompany tracking policies in schools.
15. Adler (1997, 1998) presents a wonderful analysis of a teacher who struggles with her goals to provide opportunities for knowledge construction by all students while also encouraging participation by diverse students in the school mathematics curriculum.
16. Secada (1994) found similar patterns among textbook publishers.
17. The ability to get preservice or working teachers to consider race may have more to do with current conceptions of professional development and methods of measuring beliefs and practices than with the actual immutability of teacher thought and practice.
18. Though the current move toward teacher reflection about self and positionality in society is on the rise, the concept of reflection and action (*conscientizacao*) was developed long ago by Paulo Freire (1970). Moreover, the call for teachers to consider their own biographies and enculturation as a means for preparing to teach students of color in urban schools was suggested almost a decade ago by Carl Grant (1991).
19. See for example, Bartolome 1994.

References

Adler, J. 1997. "A Participatory-Inquiry Approach and the Mediation of Mathematical Knowledge in a Multilingual Classroom." *Educational Studies in Mathematics* 33, no. 3: 235–58.
———. 1998. "A Language of Teaching Dilemmas: Unlocking the Complex Multilingual Secondary Mathematics Classroom." *For the Learning of Mathematics* 18, no. 1: 24–33.
Anderson, S. E. 1990. "Worldmath Curriculum: Fighting Eurocentrism in Mathematics." *Journal of Negro Education* 59, no. 3: 348–59.
Anyon, J. 1997. *Ghetto Schooling: A Political Economy of Urban Educational Reform.* New York: Teachers College Press.
Apple, M. W. 1992a. "Do the Standards Go Far Enough? Power, Policy, and Practice in Mathematics Education." *Journal for Research in Mathematics Education* 23, no. 5: 412–31.
———. 1992b. "Thinking More Politically about the Challenges before Us: A Response to Romberg." *Journal for Research in Mathematics Education* 23, no. 5: 438–40.
Applebaum, B. 1998. "Raising Awareness of Dominance: Does Acknowledging Dominance Mean One Has to Dismiss the Values of the Dominant Group?" Paper presented at the National Academy of Education annual meeting, Palo Alto, Calif.

Atweh, B., R. E. Bleicher, and T. J. Cooper. 1998. "The Construction of the Social Context of Mathematics Classrooms: A Sociolinguistic Analysis." *Journal for Research in Mathematics Education* 29, no. 1: 63–82.

Banks, J. A., and C. M. Banks, eds. 1997. *Multicultural Education: Issues and Perspectives.* Boston: Allyn and Bacon.

Bartolome, L. I. 1994. "Beyond the Methods Fetish: Toward a Humanizing Pedagogy." *Harvard Educational Review* 64, no. 2: 173–94.

Bloor, D. 1994. "What Can the Sociologist of Knowledge Say About 2 + 2 = 4?" In *Mathematics, Education and Philosophy: An International Perspective,* edited by P. Ernest, 21–32. London: Falmer Press.

Boaler, J. 1993. "Encouraging The Transfer of 'School' Mathematics to the 'Real World' through The Integration of Process and Content, Context and Culture." *Educational Studies in Mathematics* 25:341–73.

Brown, T. 1994. "Describing the Mathematics You Are Part Of: A Post-structuralist Account of Mathematical Learning." In *Mathematics, Education and Philosophy: An International Perspective,* edited by P. Ernest, 154–62. London: Falmer Press.

Burciaga, J. A. 1993. *Drink Cultura: Chicanismo.* Santa Barbara: Joshua Odell Editions.

Burton, L. 1994. "Whose Culture Includes Mathematics." In *Cultural Perspectives on the Mathematics Classroom,* edited by S. Lerman, 69–83. Dordrecht: Kluwer Academic Publishers.

Castillo, A. 1994. *Massacre of the Dreamers: Essays on Xicanisma.* New York: Plume.

Cochran-Smith, M. 1995. "Uncertain Allies: Understanding the Boundaries of Race and Teaching." *Harvard Education Review* 65, no. 4: 541–70.

Cuevas, G., and M. Driscoll, eds. 1993. *Reaching All Students with Mathematics.* Reston, Va.: National Council of Teachers of Mathematics.

D'Ambrosio, U. 1985. "Ethnomathematics and Its Place in the History and Pedagogy of Mathematics." *Educational Studies in Mathematics* 5, no. 1: 44–48.

———. 1990. "The Role of Mathematics Education in Building a Democratic and Just Society." *For the Learning of Mathematics* 10, no. 3: 20–23.

———. 1997. "Where Does Ethnomathematics Stand Nowadays?" *For the Learning of Mathematics* 17, no. 2: 13–17.

Ernest, P. ed. 1994. *Mathematics, Education, and Philosophy: An International Perspective.* London: Falmer Press.

Escalante, J., and J. Dirmann. 1990. "The Jaime Escalante Math Program." *The Journal of Negro Education* 59, no. 3: 407–23.

Frankenstein, M. 1990. "Incorporating Race, Gender, and Class Issues into a Critical Mathematical Literacy Curriculum." *Journal of Negro Education* 59, no. 3: 336–47.

———. 1995. "Equity in Mathematics Education: Class in the World Outside the Class." In *New Directions for Equity in Mathematics Education,* edited by W. G. Secada, E. Fennema, and L. B. Adajian, 165–90. Cambridge: Cambridge University Press.

Freire, P. 1970. *Pedagogy of the Oppressed.* New York: Continuum.

Grant, C. A. 1991. "Culture and Teaching: What Do Teachers Need to Know?" In *Teaching Academic Subjects to Diverse Learners,* edited by M. M. Kennedy. New York: TC Press.

Gerdes, P. 1994. "Reflections on Ethnomathematics." *For the Learning of* Mathematics 14, no. 2: 19–22.

Gutiérrez, R. 1996. "Practices, Beliefs, and Cultures of High School Mathematics Departments: Understanding Their Influences on Student Advancement." *Journal of Curriculum Studies* 28, no. 5: 495–530.

———. 1997. "School Teachers' Belief Systems as a Context for Exploring the 'Mathematics for All' Reform Agenda." Paper presented at the American Educational Research Association annual meeting, Chicago.

———. In press. "Advancing Urban Latino Youth in Mathematics: Lessons from an Effective High School Mathematics Department." *Urban Review.*

Gutiérrez, R., and J. Rosiek. 1994. "The Need For Subject Matter Specificity in Multicultural

Education Research: The Case of Mathematics Education." Paper presented at the American Educational Research Association annual meeting, New Orleans.

Haberman, M. 1996. "Selecting and Preparing Culturally Competent Teachers for Urban Schools." In *Handbook of Research on Teacher Education: A Project of the Association of Teacher Educators,* 2nd ed., edited by J. Sikula, 747–60. New York: Macmillan.

Hargreaves, A. 1994. *Changing Teachers, Changing Times: Teachers' Work and Culture in the Postmodern Age.* New York: Teachers College Press.

Khisty, L. 1995. "Making Inequality: Issues of Language and Meaning in Mathematics Teaching with Hispanic Students." In *New Directions for Equity in Mathematics Education,* edited by W. G. Secada, E. Fennema, and L. B. Adajian. Cambridge: Cambridge University Press.

Kozol, J. 1991. *Savage Inequalities: Children in America's Schools.* New York: Crown.

Ladson-Billings, G. 1995. "Making Mathematics Meaningful in Multicultural Contexts." In *New Directions for Equity in Mathematics Education,* edited by W. G. Secada, E. Fennema, and L. B. Adajian, 126–45. Cambridge: Cambridge University Press.

———. 1998. "Just What Is Critical Race Theory and What's It Doing in a Nice Field Like Education?" *The International Journal of Qualitative Studies in Education* 11, no. 1: 7–24.

Lawrence, S. M., and B. Tatum. 1997. "White Educators as Allies: Moving from Awareness to Action." In *Off White: Readings on Race, Power and Society,* edited by M. Fine, L. Weis, L. C. Powell, and L. M. Wong. New York: Routledge.

McCarthy, C. 1993. "After the Canon: Knowledge and Ideological Representation in the Multicultural Discourse on Curriculum Reform." In *Race, Identity and Representation in Education,* edited by C. McCarthy and W. Crichlow, 289–305. New York: Routledge.

McIntyre, A. 1997. *Making Meaning of Whiteness: Exploring Racial Identity with White Teachers.* Albany: State University of New York Press.

McLaren, P. 1994. "Multiculturalism and the Post-modern Critique: Toward a Pedagogy of Resistance and Transformation." In *Between Borders: Pedagogy and the Politics of Cultural Studies,* edited by H. Giroux and P. McLaren. New York: Routledge.

Moll, L. C., and N. Gonzalez. 1994. "Lessons from Research with Language Minority Children." *Journal of Reading Behavior* 26: 439–56.

NCTM (National Council of Teachers of Mathematics). 1989. *Curriculum and Evaluation Standards for School Mathematics.* Reston, Va.: National Council of Teachers of Mathematics.

Nickson, M. 1989. "What is Multicultural Mathematics?" In *Mathematics Teaching: The State of the Art,* edited by P. Ernest, 236–40. New York: Falmer Press.

Nieto, S. 1996. *Affirming Diversity: The Sociopolitical Context of Multicultural Education.* New York: Longman.

Oakes, J., and G. Guiton. 1995. "Matchmaking: The Dynamics of High School Tracking Decisions." *American Educational Research Journal* 32, no. 1: 3–33.

Oakes, J., T. Ormseth, R. Bell, and P. Camp. 1990. *Multiplying Inequalities: The Effects of Race, Social Class and Tracking on Opportunities to Learn Mathematics and Science.* Santa Monica: Rand Corporation.

Parker, L. 1998. "Race is . . . Race Ain't: An Exploration of the Utility of Critical Race Theory in Qualitative Research in Education." *International Journal of Qualitative Studies in Education* 11, no. 1: 25–41.

Restivo, S. 1994. "The Social Life of Mathematics." In *Mathematics, Education and Philosophy: An International Perspective,* edited by P. Ernest, 209–20. London: Falmer Press.

Reyes, L. H., and G. M. A. Stanic. 1988. "Race, Sex, Socioeconomic Status, and Mathematics." *Journal for Research in Mathematics Education* 19, no. 1: 26–43.

Romberg, T. 1992. "Further Thoughts on the Standards: A Reaction to Apple." *Journal for Research in Mathematics Education* 23, no. 5: 432–37.

Saxe, G. B. 1991. *Culture and Cognitive Development: Studies in Mathematical Understanding.* Hillsdale, N.J.: Lawrence Erlbaum.

Secada, W. G. 1991. "Diversity, Equity, and Cognitivist Research." In *Integrating Research on Teaching and Learning Mathematics,* edited by E. Fennema, T. P. Carpenter, and S. J. Lamon, 17–53. Albany: State University of New York Press.

————. 1992. "Race, Ethnicity, Social Class, Language, and Achievement in Mathematics." In *Handbook of Research on Mathematics Teaching and Learning,* edited by D. A. Growns. New York: Macmillan.

————. 1994. "Towards a Consciously Multicultural Mathematics Curriculum." In *Reinventing Urban Education: Multiculturalism and the Social Context of Schooling,* edited by F. L. Rivera-Batiz, 235–55. New York: IUME Press.

Sleeter, C. 1993. "How White Teachers Construct Race." In *Race, Identity and Representation in Education,* edited by C. McCarthy and W. Crichlow, 157–71. New York: Routledge.

————. 1996. *Multicultural Education as Social Activism.* Albany: State University of New York Press.

Stander, D. 1989. "The Use of the History of Mathematics in Teaching." In *Mathematics Teaching: The State of the Art,* edited by P. Ernest, 241–46. New York: Falmer Press.

Stanic, G. M., and L. E. Hart. 1995. "Attitudes, Persistence, and Mathematics Achievement: Qualifying Race and Sex Differences." In *New Directions for Equity in Mathematics Education,* edited by W. G. Secada, E. Fennema, and L. B. Adajian, 258–76. Cambridge: Cambridge University Press.

Tate, W. 1995. "Economics, Equity, and the National Mathematics Assessment: Are We Creating a National Toll Road?" In *New Directions for Equity in Mathematics Education,* edited by W. G. Secada, 191–206. Cambridge, Mass.: Cambridge University Press.

————. 1997a. "Critical Race Theory in Education: History, Theory, and Implications." *Review of Research in Education* 22: 195–247.

————. 1997b. "Race-ethnicity, SES, Gender, and Language Proficiency Trends in Mathematics Achievement: An Update." *Journal for Research in Mathematics* 28, no. 6: 652–79.

Tatum, B. D. 1994. "Teaching White Students about Racism: The Search for White Allies and the Restoration of Hope." *Teachers College Record* 95, no. 4: 462–76.

Thomas, R. 1996. "Proto-mathematics and/or Real Mathematics." *For the Learning of Mathematics* 16, no. 2: 11–17.

Villenas, S. 1986. "The Colonizer/Colonized Chicana Ethnographer: Identity, Marginalization, and Co-optation in the Field." *Harvard Educational Review* 66, no. 4: 711–31.

Volmink, J. 1994. "Mathematics by All." In *Cultural Perspectives on the Mathematics Classroom,* edited by S. Lerman, 51–67. Dordrecht: Kluwer Academic Publishers.

Weiner, L. 1993. *Preparing Teachers for Urban Schools: Thirty Years of School Reform.* New York: Teachers College Press.

Woodrow, D. 1989. "Multicultural and Anti-Racist Mathematics Teaching." In *Mathematics Teaching: The State of the Art,* edited by P. Ernest, 229–35. New York: Falmer Press.

————. 1997. "Democratic Education: Does it Exist—Especially for Mathematics Education?" *For the Learning of Mathematics* 17, no. 3: 11–16.

Yando, R., V. Seitz, and E. Zigler. 1979. *Intellectual and Personality Characteristics of Children: Social-Class and Ethnic Group Differences.* Hillsdale, N.J.: Lawrence Erlbaum.

Zaslavsky, C. 1979. *Africa Counts: Number and Pattern in African Culture.* New York: Lawrence Hill.

————. 1994. "'Africa Counts' and Ethnomathematics." *For the Learning of Mathematics* 14, no. 2: 3–7.

————. 1996. *The Multicultural Math Classrooms: Bringing In the World.* Portsmouth, N.H.: Heinemann.

Zimpher, N. L., and E. A. Ashburn. 1992. "Countering Parochialism in Teacher Candidates." In *Diversity in Teacher Education,* edited by M. Dilworth, 40–62. San Francisco: Jossey-Bass.

Part III

POLICY

12

Multiculturalism and the Academic Organization of Knowledge

Marc Chun
Columbia University

Susan Christopher
Patricia J. Gumport
Stanford University

Over the past two decades, scholarship about the social construction of knowledge has moved along several trajectories. While one strand of this work laments the sustained tensions that erupted in the "culture wars" in undergraduate education,[1] another draws attention to the often obscured linkages between knowledge and power and articulates a critical role for academic knowledge in the creation of a democratic society.[2] Taken together, perhaps the greatest enduring contribution of this body of work is the way it has problematized long-standing assumptions about what counts as legitimate knowledge within the academy.[3] In exploring how areas of academic knowledge emerge and become legitimated, scholars have also observed how knowledge workers in emerging areas have struggled to gain credibility for their work (e.g., in alternative medicine) whereas others have had near unquestioned acceptance (e.g., in biochemistry).

To complement this large body of work on the legitimacy of knowledge, we turn to a discussion of the organization of academic knowledge. This perspective illuminates the contested nature of knowledge areas, as well as the politics of their relative valuation within the academy. The academic location of any particular knowledge area is not a given; thus, decisions about how and where academic knowledge is organized may be revealing. Should accounting be located in the more central economics department, or placed further on the periphery in the business school? Should social work be incorporated into the more traditional sociology department, or placed on its own as a professional program?[4] Different answers to these questions would undoubtedly create dramatically different academic landscapes.

Historically, academic knowledge work has aspired to ideals of inquiry that promote the notion of a disinterested and objective search for "truth." Knowledge work and its evaluation strive to be, in a word, *apolitical*. Relying on the process of the scientific method or the vernacular of being "scientific," a widespread belief is that both the process of producing the knowledge should be interest-free. Moreover, areas of knowledge work that collectively endeavor to produce and disseminate seemingly apolitical knowledge are considered more legitimate academically, in part because they reflect many taken-for-granted values found within the larger society and within the culture of higher education. Once they become institutionalized as components of the academic landscape, they can more readily escape the public scrutiny that is popularized by wider social critics.[5]

Here we suggest that the way academic organizations locate and label knowledge can be seen as inherently political in nature.[6] For the purposes of this essay, we maintain that there are personal, cultural, social, and economic influences that shape the content and the categories of academic knowledge, and that all knowledge is linked to political interests.[7] We do this to consider the links between political interests, knowledge, and the academic context. Our thesis is that the politics of some fields remain invisible and hidden (whether strategically or unconsciously), enabling adoption and institutionalization; on the other hand, the politics of other fields are highlighted and made apparent, undermining their incorporation, and leaving them more vulnerable to being discredited as "unscholarly."

In other words, we maintain that the dynamics of the organization of academic knowledge illuminate the politics of knowledge. To that end, in this chapter, we focus on multiculturalism, and consider two levels of analysis. First, by contrasting the organizational locations of two bodies of knowledge—multiculturalism and technology—we argue that the more explicitly political nature of the former results in more contentious debates about its legitimacy. This, in turn, suggests the privilege assigned to supposedly value-neutral knowledge (such as technology), even when it too has clear links to advocates outside of academe. Second, we examine the challenges in organizing multiculturalism by considering two specific forms it has taken as identifiable academic units within the curriculum—gender studies and ethnic studies[8]—and we explore the political struggles around content and epistemology, both internal to multicultural programs, as well as between multiculturalism and the larger academic context.

This two-stage approach—somewhat likened to first peering through a microscope, and then increasing the magnification to take an even closer look—helps to demonstrate the recursive nature of the politics of knowledge as manifested at several levels in the organization of academic organization. Moreover, this approach ultimately motivates our final discussion wherein we conclude that a more explicit recognition of the political character of multicultural knowledge work could lead to the radical transformation of the academy.

BRINGING THE ACADEMIC ORGANIZATION OF KNOWLEDGE INTO FOCUS: MULTICULTURALISM AND TECHNOLOGY

Our first view of the academic organization of knowledge helps to illuminate the dynamics of knowledge politics by considering the ways higher education has organized knowledge in two domains: technology and multiculturalism.[9] We have selected technology and multiculturalism not only to highlight ideological differences with respect to the relationship between knowledge and modernity, but also to demonstrate the contrasts between the two areas that reveal fundamental differences in how academic knowledge is coded and understood, and how the influence of external interests is constructed. Ultimately, what we seek to illustrate is the political nature of the organization of academic knowledge with respect to the links between academia and outside interests. We argue that these links are seen as problematic when the connections to external agents are made explicit, and even more so when an academic unit has a link to a *political* external agent—defined here as being, or perceived as being, in opposition to the status quo and prevailing political interests.

Technology is a key element of modernism, and it is accepted dogma that advancements in technology are directly and causally linked to the social progress modern society advocates. Technology is generally accepted as a tool to make people and social processes more efficient, and as a means to facilitate the functional needs of society. Because programs in technology are ideologically consistent with the status quo, economic advancement, and academic entrepreneurship (Slaughter 1990), their establishment in universities as degree-granting academic programs is readily accepted, and not contested as political (Gumport and Chun 1999).[10]

In contrast, programs in multiculturalism claim that political standpoints are inescapably linked to academic knowledge. Whether focusing on non-Western societies, women, ethnic and racial minorities, or members of disadvantaged social classes, multicultural programs emerge from critical analyses of situated identities, identity politics, and the power relations of groups of people. In contrast to the purportedly politically neutral programs (such as technology), these programs endeavor to destabilize universal knowledge and have subversive objectives. They not only draw attention to social groups and social processes that have previously been ignored or marginalized by the traditional configuration of academic work, but in many cases they explicitly criticize or critique the status quo and may even seek to transform the structure altogether. Critics assert that such politics disrupt the march toward progress, and as such these politics are therefore seen as antimodern.

In several ways, multiculturalism and technology have emerged on the academic landscape with similar trajectories. On some campuses, both of these knowledge areas have been structured as autonomous academic units as well as integrated, to some extent, into the traditional areas of disciplinary knowledge. Any given English or history department, for example, is likely to have incorporated multicultural perspectives into the curriculum (e.g., with readings representing a broad range of voices and perspectives) or to have areas of study that focus on technology (e.g., the study of the history of technology).[11]

Yet when the locations of technology and multiculturalism are juxtaposed, it becomes clear that they have attained somewhat different degrees of incorporation and institutionalization. For instance, with respect to integration into the academic core, some schools have adopted a technology requirement, since it is widely assumed that computer literacy is fundamental for life in the twenty-first century. By contrast, efforts to require students to take courses that address issues of race, class, or gender have been met with greater opposition and have been far more contentious and problematic.[12] Academic organizations more readily embrace the seemingly apolitical areas of knowledge than the explicitly political areas.

The preliminary findings from a series of case studies of colleges and universities indicate that this pattern persists across sectors of public higher education (Gumport, forthcoming).[13] While there has been the continual and unproblematic addition of technology-related departments and degree programs, there have been greater controversies with respect to the status of multicultural programs (not only where to place the programs, but whether or not even to have them). In other words, the value in adding technology programs is expected and taken for granted by the academic organization, whereas the value of the expansion of multicultural programs is seen as uncertain and disputed.

Across the research universities, comprehensive colleges, and community colleges in this study, technology programs tend to be supported at least in part by partnerships with industry. Technology companies provide funding for the programs, internships for students, and expertise for the campus (for example, with company employees serving as adjunct faculty or sitting on program advisory boards).[14] The influence of technology is perhaps most evident in the way in which the organization of knowledge maps onto specific career options: new degree programs in "cytotechnology" or "computer-human interaction" obviously reflect a knowledge structure that is meaningful to industry as producers of hardware and software, as well as to industry as the subsequent employers of graduates. In addition to this blurring of ideological and epistemological borders between the academy and industry, some campuses have even dissolved the physical boundary: they invite companies to set up shop on campus in technology "incubators" where corporate personnel work with academics on new technology projects.

In contrast, academic units focusing on multiculturalism follow the topography of individual and group identities, and their educational goals stem from sociopolitical movements rather than the economic interests of private industry.[15] In some cases, accusations have been made that these programs reflect an anti-intellectual campaign for political correctness or the uninvited influence of external, radical groups. Still, in other cases, multicultural academic units are seen as a means to help students to prepare to live and work in an increasingly pluralist society. Although there are indeed outcomes that are highly valued by partici-pants in multicultural programs (e.g., access to social and career networks, fund-ing—particularly from foundations—for curricular transformation), for the most part the multicultural programs have nowhere near the level of financial support or infusion of resources as does technology, nor the same clear and direct link to internships and employment opportunities.[16]

Many have questioned whether or not such areas of knowledge should be part of the traditional academic landscape, let alone part of the academic core (evi-denced by their struggles for inclusion as required course work). Ongoing debates have considered where multicultural programs should be located within the cam-pus landscape: as full-fledged departments or as interdisciplinary programs, as degree-granting majors or as minor fields within an existing discipline. However, their typical location as separate programs (sometimes without degree-granting ability or designated faculty lines) serves to reinforce a marginal position as a peripheral "other."

These patterns with respect to technology and multiculturalism help to reveal the knowledge politics of the contemporary academic organization. At some level, the campus's academic landscape reflects an organization of knowledge driven by criteria that privilege new programmatic areas that appear consistent with the tra-ditional ideology of apolitical knowledge. Programs that purportedly reflect value neutrality, progress toward modernity, and objective scholarship are more readily adopted—even when they are heavily influenced by economic relations with agencies outside of the academy. In other words, the influence of industry has an obvious and direct effect on the content and oversight of the academic pro-grams.[17] Although the curriculum is traditionally thought to be the sole province of the faculty, it can be argued that the college's or university's authority in the cul-tural space of knowledge work is diminished when industry assumes a role in dic-tating its content.

Nonetheless, the development of these programs and the partnerships with industry are not seen as a challenge to the campus's authority.[18] The discourse of "adaptation" and "external pressures" is rejected, and these changes are instead seen as "synergy," "opportunity," and "progress." At some level, even though these technology programs demonstrate the corporatization of the academy and illus-trate an interest in supporting "profitable" knowledge work, they are not con-structed as such.[19]

In contrast, those knowledge areas that are more overtly political have a more tenuous relationship with the academy. The adoption of multicultural programs has been framed in terms of a response to the political pressures from an increas-ingly diverse student population, and, in some cases, in relation to the research interests of faculty who brought a progressive political consciousness to create new areas of study. Because multicultural programs are tied to explicitly political interests, they have been subject to greater scrutiny as to whether or not the sub-ject matter meets scholarly standards. Lacking the economic power and allies of private industry, these multicultural programs are more vulnerable to the whims of local campus and internal knowledge politics.

In other words, the influence of external pressures (which shape the valuation of knowledge areas in academic settings) evokes differential responses. Economic influences are tolerated—or even expected, given the role of the academy in career preparation—while oppositional political influences are eschewed as inappropriate in their rigor or utility for career preparation. The central point, then, is that although both areas of knowledge have links to external pressures, those of technology are masked (or framed as an "opportunity"), while those of multiculturalism are highlighted and made explicit as problematic.[20] As will be discussed in the concluding section, these distinctions have profound implications for the academic organization of knowledge, which becomes most contentious when a unit has an explicit link to a *political* external agent.

LOOKING WITHIN MULTICULTURALISM: THE CASES OF ETHNIC STUDIES AND WOMEN'S STUDIES

So far in this chapter, we have clustered together all areas of knowledge that would fall within "multiculturalism," broadly defined. Here, we seek to unpack this notion. While there may be no simple or easily accepted definition of multiculturalism, the term generally refers to the collective fields of African-American (or black) studies, Asian-American studies, Chicano or Latino studies, and Native American studies, as well as women's studies and queer studies.[21] We note here, however, that multiculturalism is frequently assumed to be synonymous with race or ethnic studies, in the same way that the "diversity" of a student body or faculty is most often operationalized through the categories of race or ethnicity.[22] When race and ethnicity dominate the discourse of multiculturalism, other dimensions of difference (namely gender, sexuality, and class) may be seen as less salient.

The notions of identity and difference are central components of multiculturalism, as are the links between these notions and an oppositional epistemological standpoint that is based on a particular set of cultural histories, experiences, and behaviors; this standpoint is specifically contrasted with that of elite, Western, heterosexual, and male identities. We use the term *knowledge politics* in two ways: (1) to refer to the alliances between multiculturalism and the broad social movements that advocate a political stance in opposition to racism, classism, sexism, heterosexism, and the like, and (2) to refer to the internal political struggles of academic interest groups who compete with one another to establish scholarly legitimacy for different forms of knowledge.

In order, then, to illuminate the knowledge politics related to the organization of multiculturalism, we consider two areas of knowledge that fall under the broad umbrella of multiculturalism—ethnic studies and women's studies. The primary foci of these two areas are race and gender, respectively.[23] Without overlooking the degree to which the central concepts of race and gender have been integrated into traditional disciplinary knowledge, we consider here the empirical phenomenon whereby the labels of ethnic studies and women's studies have been attached to interdisciplinary programs with distinct organizational histories and identities. We consider the parallel development of these two areas, comparing and contrasting the struggles they have faced. Despite many similarities in the way these two areas have evolved, they have generally been institutionalized as separate and distinct organizational forms. Initially, this separation may be explained by pointing to the racism that has pervaded women's studies and the sexism that has pervaded ethnic studies.[24] But we may also look at organizational features that serve to perpetuate their distinct locations within the academy. Furthermore, we will argue that the epistemological critiques offered by multicultural knowledge work may be obscured by the perceived need to define knowledge as politically neutral.

In this section, we draw attention to two distinct dimensions of multicultural knowledge politics that have implications for the way multicultural knowledge has been organized. First, we point to the ways in which the concepts of race and gender have been introduced as *subject matter;* this dimension presupposes no particular epistemological standpoint nor means of analysis, but describes the knowledge work that has emerged about women and people of color. The second dimension is a *critical epistemology*, which describes gender studies and ethnic studies in terms of alternative standpoints that provide new, different, and (most important here) oppositional theoretical analyses. We then focus on how these dimensions of knowledge work shape the particular ways in which these forms of multicultural knowledge have been organized as academic units of knowledge within higher education.

Historically, ethnic studies emerged as an extension of the civil rights movement. As new knowledge about people of color was "discovered" and a new awareness of racial differences developed, scholarly attention turned to the concept of race and racial differences as subject matter. In response to the long-standing dominance of white scholars who created knowledge based on their own experience (without making racial identity problematic), one of the main goals of ethnic studies was to increase the representation of "minority" experiences, as both the creators of knowledge and as new objects of study. Race and ethnicity became central categories of analysis in new and ever-expanding research and teaching contexts that had previously neglected or excluded these concepts.

Set in the particular context of U.S. history, the discourse derived from ethnic studies—as well as from the larger political movement out of which it arose—has been dominated by attention to the experiences and perspectives of African Americans. Nonetheless, ethnic studies is grounded in an epistemological assumption of *multiple* standpoints that coalesce around socially constructed racial categories. It is clear that multiple perspectives are fundamental to the study of race and ethnicity, such that a scholar in ethnic studies might choose a particular racial perspective to adopt, but would not deny the relevance of multiple perspectives that stand in opposition to whiteness.

By comparison, women's studies also grew out of a political movement (usually referred to as second-wave feminism), and developed as "the academic arm of the feminist movement" (Howe 1972, 162). Utilizing the concept of gender as a category of analysis and initially highlighting differences between men and women, between male and female, and/or between masculinity and femininity, this knowledge represented a new subject within academic knowledge. In roughly the same time period in which ethnic studies developed, women's studies expanded as a field, as awareness of women's experiences (and of the previous exclusion of their experiences from academic knowledge) increased.

Thus, the concept of gender has emerged as a *binary* social construction, based on biological assumptions about sexual differences. Putting aside the intriguing claims made by Anne Fausto-Sterling (1985) and others that there may actually be five distinct sexual categories in humans, the prevailing view of gender is as a binary category of analysis. Combined with the demographic fact that women represent a majority of the U.S. population, rather than a minority identity, the category of "woman/women" has a somewhat different stance in relation to "man/ men" than does any one particular racial or ethnic category to "white." In other words, both ethnic studies and women's studies as subject areas are predicated on a notion of "otherness" in relation to the dominant referent. Historically, however, "other" has been defined within ethnic studies in terms of the multiple standpoints from which race is analyzed, while it is defined within women's studies as a binary analytic category.[25] While these distinctions do not mean that ethnic studies and women's studies are wholly or inevitably incompatible areas of study, their central analytical concepts represent clearly distinct forms of knowledge.

The second dimension of multiculturalism that is illustrated by this examination of ethnic studies and gender studies is the *critical epistemology* embedded in each. The concepts of race and gender have not been incorporated merely as objective concepts or subject matter, but rather as categories of analysis that are tied to particular epistemological standpoints. These standpoints are oppositional in nature. While merely adding knowledge about gender or race into the curriculum or into other knowledge units has been fairly noncontroversial, the incorporation of the concomitant critical standpoints in relation to gender and race has been extremely contentious. To the degree that ethnic studies and women's studies represent both a critique and a transformation of existing knowledge, they have provoked widespread resistance. Few would argue that issues of race or gender should be denied or excluded outright; even defenders of the traditional canon would not claim that scholarship and teaching should focus only on white men. Furthermore, it has not been problematic to add race or gender as long as traditional knowledge claims are preserved: as long as new knowledge is merely additive and not critical, existing knowledge claims remain unchanged.[26] However, both ethnic studies and women's studies developed as curricular forms that similarly offer epistemological critiques of the ways that race and gender have been integrated into scholarship.

Just as in the prior discussion of multiculturalism and technology, it is when the *political* aspects of these epistemological standpoints are made explicit that the knowledge work becomes problematized. In the areas of both ethnic studies and women's studies, scholars are frequently accused of promoting mere partisanship or propaganda in ways that call into question the academic legitimacy of their specific claims about race or gender. When knowledge work is accused of being political in this partisan sense (read: biased), issues about the validity of the knowledge itself are raised; to the degree that external constituencies that have an interest in this knowledge work are also viewed as explicitly political, the conferral of academic legitimacy is less likely. For example, work that provides an Afrocentric analysis of literature written by black authors might make explicit the political goals of the civil rights movement, leaving the literary critic vulnerable to accusations of serving political rather than scholarly interests.[27] In another example, women's studies scholarship that is grounded in the subjective standpoint of women's experiences in the workplace in order to challenge previous understandings of the nature of work could be similarly discredited, accused of merely advocating social change rather than seeking "truth" or "impartial" knowledge. In these examples, and across many forms of multicultural knowledge work, controversy erupts when the inherently transformative potential of the epistemological standpoint is made explicit.

To review, these two areas of multicultural studies have been similarly institutionalized along two dimensions, adding new subjects of study, specifically the concepts of race and gender as categories of analysis, and providing a critical epistemology that seeks to transform existing disciplinary knowledge. Having discussed the relatively unproblematic yet separate way in which the concepts of race and gender have been incorporated into knowledge work as *subject matter*, and the fairly contentious way in which their respective *epistemological standpoints* have criticized and transformed the traditional paradigms of knowledge work, we now turn to a discussion of the *organization* of multiculturalism knowledge work.[28]

For the most part, women's studies programs have developed as separate academic units. They may assume different names (e.g. "women's studies," "feminist studies," "gender studies"—and even "women and gender studies"), each of which has complex symbolic implications.[29] And, over the past decade, they have given increasing attention to race, class, culture, and sexuality, as noted above. Still, they are organized most obviously to focus on *knowledge about gender*.

On any given campus, the organization of ethnic studies may take a variety of organizational forms, typically separating out the different areas or combining them together in idiosyncratic ways.[30] For example, there might be separate programs in African-American studies, Chicano studies, and Asian-American studies, or there might be one academic unit that facilitates their comparative study. Nevertheless, the organizing principle for these units is generally understood to be *knowledge about race or ethnicity*. The key point here is that ethnic studies and women's studies are distinct from and structurally separate from one another; they may be allied and they may have parallel organizational structures, but they are nevertheless different entities.[31]

The case of knowledge work by and about women of color most poignantly illustrates the implications of this separation.[32] From this epistemological standpoint, the concepts of race and gender are, by definition, inextricable; knowledge workers who embody this intersection may remain relative "outsiders" in relation to both academic domains. This suggests that multicultural knowledge work must transcend the existing organizational categories in order to create more effective coalitions among multicultural knowledge workers.

To more fully understand the academic organization of knowledge, we may want not only to consider the way the various areas within multiculturalism do or do not form linkages, but also to look at linkages across the larger academic institution. Although stand-alone programs or departments in ethnic studies and women's studies exist somewhat autonomously, they are also linked to other parts of the academic organization as a whole. In a pragmatic way, they are linked to other units because they are typically staffed by faculty who have primary affiliations in other departments.[33] In this way, we can see that multicultural programs are subject to the norms and institutional practices of the larger context of higher education. While these organizational features might promote links between individual multicultural programs on one hand, and traditional disciplines on the other, they do not readily facilitate links between women's studies and ethnic studies.

Important linkages also exist between these academic units and the larger social movements from which they have emerged. These links need to be considered, of course, in a historical context. As noted earlier, programs in ethnic studies and women's studies maintain their ties to the larger movements for civil rights and feminism, respectively. In turn, these movements for social change have links to one another and share many common ideologies, but nonetheless represent separate political phenomena.[34]

We now arrive at a normative question about how such academic knowledge *should* be organized. Having reviewed a number of powerful rationales for the development of women's studies and ethnic studies as separate academic units, we see how the complex political relationships within multiculturalism problematize any easy generalizations about the organization of multicultural knowledge. However, just as these separate academic units initially had different goals (e.g., to reveal sexism on the one hand and racism on the other), together they sit in opposition to the traditional standpoint of universal knowledge claims within a positivist framework. They share common elements as critical, oppositional projects that are tied to liberation studies and to the politics of emancipation. In reference to our discussion of multiculturalism and technology—because all of these forms of academic knowledge are explicitly linked to external political influences—they also face similar resistance from conservative critics. It may also be that their internal political relationships limit their ability to act in coalition toward a collective goal of transforming academic knowledge.

We claim, however, that ultimately it is the highly institutionalized structure of the university that provides the strongest influence preventing such a coalition. The dominant ideology of the academy embraces and rewards the assumption that universities should be organized academically by content area (which leads to separate academic units of race and gender), rather than being organized by epistemological position (in which case, these programs—all of which share an explicitly political way of knowing—would more readily be linked). In other words, a program is organized and justified as a legitimate academic unit based on the subject matter as a knowledge base, rather than epistemological standpoint or perspective.

It may be helpful at this point to reflect briefly on the nature of conservative critical responses to multiculturalism. Other scholars have reviewed these in great detail,[35] but we point out here that these responses challenge the epistemologically political nature of multicultural knowledge work while also serving to perpetuate many myths about multiculturalism. Inspired, at least in part, by the reactionary rhetoric of "political correctness," the following myths have emerged: (1) multiculturalism is merely a call for pluralism, in which multiple voices are included without any understanding of cultural differences or systems of inequality; (2) multiculturalism promotes a theory of relativism whereby no conclusions may be drawn about the meaning of cultural differences; (3) multiculturalism is simply a reflection of identity politics, such that knowledge may be derived only from firsthand experience; (4) multiculturalism is aimed at denigrating Western culture; and finally, (5) multiculturalism is antiintellectual.

This final myth, accusing multiculturalism of promoting anti-intellectualism in higher education, is often tied to conservative critiques that portray ethnic studies and women's studies as attempts to politicize previously apolitical domains and to contaminate universal knowledge claims through partisan self-interests. These critics ground their claims in the traditional values of academic freedom, and characterize multiculturalism as a threat to existing scholarship that is grounded in positivistic objectivity; they often assume that legitimate scholarship should be free from any cultural, personal, or political interests, while masking their own interests.[36]

All of these critiques represent attempts to delegitimize, destabilize, and dismiss multicultural knowledge work. Moreover, they imply that scholarly and political goals are necessarily mutually exclusive, as though one who does multicultural knowledge work from an epistemological standpoint that is inherently political must sacrifice any claims to sound or rigorous scholarship.

In response to this, scholars of multiculturalism claim that because their work aspires to be liberatory and emancipatory scholarship, it is necessarily both political and scholarly. In turn, these scholars may not achieve widespread acceptance and legitimacy to the degree that their knowledge work is located on the periphery and not within the boundaries of core academic knowledge. If it is true that only knowledge meeting traditional standards is likely to be incorporated at the center (which symbolizes the most important and most valuable form of academic knowledge), then scholars with aspirations to locate themselves there are more likely to obscure the critical epistemological standpoint of their work. Their need to justify their organizational autonomy in the study of content areas (e.g., race and gender) that are politically neutral analytical categories and therefore legitimate in scholarly terms reinforces the marginalization of critical epistemological critiques. In other words, multicultural scholars find that the current system requires that knowledge be organized in ways that reflect neutral, apolitical subject areas, and not around critical epistemological perspectives. However, doing so dictates that they put aside and thus put at risk the political purposes, meanings, and implications of their knowledge and their knowledge work.

IMPLICATIONS AND CONCLUSIONS

This chapter has discussed the politics of the academic organization of knowledge in a number of ways. By first comparing the fields of technology and multiculturalism as newly incorporated areas within the academic landscape, we explored how both areas have links to external interests, and focused on the ways in which explicitly *political* connections give rise to resistance and controversy. Much of this can be attributed to the fact that unlike the case of technological knowledge, the addition of multicultural knowledge introduces an epistemological critique that is both oppositional and potentially transformative.

Conventional scholars assume that knowledge work must aspire to be politically neutral, objective, and universal; this conservative position stands in stark contrast to the goals of multicultural knowledge work. Nonetheless, because the conservative approach occupies a relatively privileged position within academic organizations, these norms of apolitical knowledge dominate the discourse about what counts as legitimate academic work.

Those who have benefited from this academic system (where seemingly apolitical knowledge is valued and rewarded) are thus more inclined to reject the critical, oppositional standpoints that challenge and subvert these norms. In fact, they may be unable (rather than just unwilling) to "see" the validity of such explicitly political knowledge, and therefore believe that legitimate knowledge should be apolitical, or at least not used to advance partisanship or the particular self-interests of oppositional groups. In other words, those who created the system and benefit from the system (or, some might claim, created a system *from which* they benefit) are unlikely to be attuned to ways in which the existing system is harmful, disempowering, oppressive, or, in a word, *political.*

In contrast, those who are disempowered are quite likely to clearly perceive the inherently political nature of the system. For example, academic women are likely to have personal experiences that illustrate how the system has been historically grounded in racism and sexism. Thus, the political nature of all academic knowledge is relatively indisputable to those who have been least likely to benefit from the aforementioned academic reward system.

When taken together, the two levels of analysis presented in this chapter help to illuminate the relationship between the organization of academic knowledge and the relative legitimacy of that knowledge. As discussed, the distance from the core, the degree of integration into disciplinary-based knowledge units, and the relative location vis-à-vis other areas of knowledge work bring into focus what we describe as "knowledge politics."

Some authors have discussed how "revenue generating potential" or "proximity to the market" provides protection from being eliminated (Slaughter 1993; Gumport 1993). In a complementary way, we propose that *proximity to partisan politics* puts it in jeopardy. In other words, as discussed, when a knowledge area or knowledge work has clear links to sociopolitical movements, its appropriate location in the academy is controversial and the quality of the scholarship is more readily questioned. The examples from this chapter demonstrate how these two trends often move together and support one another. The adoption of an area of knowledge such as technology—which has close proximity to the market but perceived distance from politics—is unproblematic; the adoption of multiculturalism—with less proximity to the market but explicit proximity to oppositional politics—is disputed.

There are numerous ways in which these insights can provide practical implications with respect to the curriculum. If multiculturalism is to realize its aims as a radical social project, then there needs to be an explicit recognition of the political dimension of multicultural knowledge work alongside deliberation as to the preferred *organizational locations* of multicultural knowledge.

First, multicultural scholars would need to reject the logic that politics and scholarship are mutually exclusive, and instead embrace the assumption that multiculturalism can embody both elements simultaneously. Doing so will enable them to advance the understanding of how particular interests underlie scholarship of all forms. Moreover, they may adopt a discourse that embraces and affirms (rather than denies and rejects) the importance of the political character of multicultural knowledge work. This would require a fundamental redefinition of scholarship—not only to make clear how knowledge is political (including, for example, the areas of technology with their linkages to industry, as discussed above), but also to affirm the ways in which political knowledge is valid and valuable. As they do this, they may be working against institutionalized silences that are found in the traditional disciplines.

Second, the separated units in the existing configuration of multicultural knowledge should consider the ways in which it may be feasible to build upon their shared critical epistemological stance. The organization of academic knowledge highlights the saliency of specific subject matter categories (as department names, course titles, major and distribution requirements), but obscures the epistemological standpoints of knowledge and pedagogy. This organizational practice has made possible oversight of academic programs and peer review for scholars working in the same field, even if the specialized subject matter interests vary. Yet those whose interests and expertise do not fit neatly into a department may seek cross-departmental affiliations. This is common for feminist scholars as well as for faculty in technology programs; as an example of the latter, the computer science department at Stanford University includes faculty members from electrical engineering, philosophy, psychology, linguistics, and medicine, all of whom have joint or courtesy appointments.

If the goal of multiculturalism is to form collaborative links and coalitions across interdisciplinary knowledge boundaries, then the traditional divisions of knowledge into departments may hinder these purposes. Unlike the aforementioned example of technology, in which the links are based on mutual subject matter foci, a common thread across multicultural knowledge work is critical epistemology. Hence, a configuration of the academy in which knowledge units are organized along epistemological lines may provide greater opportunities for collaboration between multicultural scholars at the local level. Such an organizing practice may in turn transform the way knowledge work is conducted and organized. For instance, if scholars who share a critical epistemological standpoint could be located together, regardless of their subject matter interests, teaching and research may find some unexpected synergies.

Of course, for emerging fields of study that fall under the rubric of multiculturalism, academic legitimacy is not at all assured. For example, currently queer studies is facing many of the same struggles encountered by other areas of multicultural scholarship. Queer studies scholars must grapple with how they organize their knowledge work and how they construct links to the politics of the larger gay rights movement, while trying to establish the scholarly legitimacy of their knowledge work. Some of the issues of positioning and location are not unlike those encountered by earlier generations of feminist scholars (Gumport 1988, 1990; Butler and Walter 1991).

Perhaps there are also lessons to be learned for multiculturalism from the relative absence of some areas of knowledge work, such as the case of Marxist studies. Although Marxist scholars have established themselves in pockets of ethnic studies, women's studies, and even in some departments (e.g., economics, political science), there are virtually no departments of Marxist studies. When Marxist scholars are members of traditional departments, they may represent an extreme position along an array of theoretical perspectives within that department. Although this organization of knowledge permits different perspectives on a common subject matter within an academic unit, it may also be seen as stifling academic work for faculty and students who seek different parameters in the social location for their academic work. Often, Marxist scholars experience great difficulty in hiring and tenure given the political nature of the work and their epistemological commitments, and in some cases are treated as tokens (in much the same way as other scholars of multiculturalism). It is possible that the organization of Marxist studies as a separate unit would permit a meaningful way for scholars (who alternatively would have been located in various disciplines and departments on campus) to coalesce around their shared epistemological standpoint and theoretical perspective. Moreover, surrounded by other scholars who understand and value the explicitly political nature of their knowledge work and their epistemological position, Marxist scholars would find more local support to expand what counts as legitimate scholarship.

This is not to deny that faculty do affiliate across departmental or disciplinary lines to form political coalitions. These connections are real and meaningful in faculty's own lives and in the development of their scholarship; nevertheless, these links are often masked in the curriculum and hidden from students,[37] who are left to figure these issues out on their own, since the academy does not "teach the conflicts," as observed by Graff (1992).

In conclusion, the study of the organization of academic knowledge provides an opportunity to recall that the particular configuration of knowledge units within the academy is the product of historical circumstance. Recognizing this, it is possible to imagine other ways in which knowledge might be organized. We have argued here that all knowledge is political; the comparison of technology and multiculturalism demonstrates that the political implications of some knowledge areas are downplayed, while those that are oppositional are made explicit. By considering how ethnic studies and women's studies—both of which have strong political links and critical epistemological orientations—have been organized separately, we explored how the explicit recognition of the political character of multicultural knowledge work reveals important considerations about the legitimacy of academic knowledge. A politically explicit knowledge organization could have profound implications for emergent fields of study and for the students and faculty members who toil as knowledge workers. Finally, we suggest that future discussions about the politics of knowledge take into account a series of questions: How might the traditional disciplines be reorganized in line with the political implications of their epistemological claims? What is the role of multiculturalism in the reorganization of disciplinary knowledge? How might new knowledge be granted legitimacy within an organizational context that made knowledge politics explicit? What would such an organization signal about suitable categories for educating future generations of scholars? How might the faculty reward system be revised to take into account the political character of knowledge work? While the answers remain elusive, the potential transformation of the academic may depend on our careful consideration of such questions.

Notes

1. See Arthur and Shapiro 1995 and Berman 1992.
2. See Carlson and Apple 1998.
3. For an account of substantive and reactive knowledge growth in higher education, see Metzger 1987. For descriptions of struggles for academic legitimacy, see Gumport 1988, 1990, 1993; Christopher 1995; and Chun 1999. For a discussion that defines the conceptual domain of social epistemology, see Fuller 1988.
4. While these examples could be seen within the confines of curriculum, we intend here to refer not only to sets of courses, but more broadly to the organization of academic knowledge in a variety of configurations.
5. The organization of academic knowledge can also be seen as instrumental in reifying organizational identity. Given the pervasive societal expectation that the most elite colleges and universities should be protected as rarefied intellectual environments committed to the pursuit of objective truth, it is not surprising to find that they attempt to make central that which garners the highest cultural cachet. To that end, the organization of academic knowledge generally reflects a heuristic that centers the most seemingly apolitical at the core, and locates the explicitly political at the periphery. In this way, not only can the core be insulated from the potential deleterious effects of the periphery (or, at least, to maintain the *perception* that the core is so insulated), but it also enables the organization to demonstrate that it places the highest value on the creation and transmission of apolitical knowledge.

   Thus, the disciplines reflecting the traditional liberal arts and sciences core are made central. This is evidenced in a number of ways: courses from these disciplines are required through general education and distribution requirements, faculty resources are allocated in an enduring manner, and the discourse about the strength and importance of these programs is reiterated in official campus documents, formal proclamations and public addresses.
6. It is often noted that in the language of Eskimos there are many different words for *snow,*

each with its own nuanced meaning and referent. Here, we note that we only have one word for *political*, although—as will be evident throughout this chapter—we think it is important to clarify our different uses of this single term.

7. It is useful to mention our starting assumptions: Rather than taking for granted that academic knowledge advancements are linear and self-propelled, we suggest that observable changes in the academic landscape are historically contingent and highly contested, with legitimacy and institutionalization not assured. Additionally, we explicitly acknowledge the role of agency and structure in the process of organizing academic knowledge.

8. In this chapter, we will use the more generic term *academic unit* to refer to the formal organizations of knowledge, such as departments, interdisciplinary programs, and research centers.

9. In this chapter, we use *technology* to mean, generally, information technology as an area of academic knowledge.

10. This is not to suggest that technology is ideologically apolitical or culturally value-free. Indeed, many have raised important concerns and critical questions: Who controls the trajectory of developments in technology? Who benefits from the adoption and use of technology? Who can legitimately influence the way technology progresses?

11. Additionally, both multiculturalism and technology may shape the pedagogy: teaching and learning may be responsive to different cultural traditions, and computers may be used for library research or writing programs.

12. This may seem particularly surprising in the contemporary era of "selective consolidation prompted by resource constraints" given that programs in technology often require large investments of funds, while programs in multiculturalism do not (Gumport 1993).

13. The research project focuses upon a stratified sample of nine public colleges and universities to examine how they have reshaped their academic organizations to respond to changing environmental pressures as well as knowledge change in selected fields. Data sources include documents, interviews, and quantitative institutional data (Gumport, manuscript in preparation)

14. The close linkages between industry and academia are generally not seen as cause for concern, and may even signal the campus's ability to be "cutting-edge."

15. We refer here to the civil rights movement, second-wave feminism, and the gay rights movement, for example.

16. It should be noted that it can be argued that programs in technology are more capital-intensive, and in fact require such huge investments of resources to even exist. The seeming ultimate irony—which deserves study beyond the scope of this chapter—is that in cases of budgetary cutbacks and retrenchment, it is more likely for inexpensive programs (such as multiculturalism) to be cut.

17. Industry's influence is felt not only indirectly as the "end consumer" (by hiring the college or university graduates), but now also more directly as consultants or participants in actually developing and determining curriculum.

18. We refer specifically here to the aforementioned research study (Gumport, in preparation), and a series of interviews with administrators.

19. Here, it is crucial to note that we make no claim that the incorporation of technology-related programs is in any way antithetical to the goals of higher education. Indeed, the legacy of the land-grant university has been explicitly to adopt and advance such programs. The point is to consider the way in which the links to external pressures are constructed as unproblematic.

20. Not to belabor the point, but it should be noted that we do not assume here that economic and business interests are not political; rather, they are not *constructed* as political (even though the role of an external agent in the shaping of the curriculum is inherently political).

21. The notion of multiculturalism has also been distorted in various ways: romanticized in the notion that diverse groups within society can coexist harmoniously if only there is mutual understanding, dismissed through the rhetoric of "political correctness," obscured in the notion of identity politics (whereby all members of particular racial or gender categories are

assumed to have identical views), and oversimplified in programs that alternately highlight the desultory aspects of culture (e.g., heroes and holidays, food and fashion) and exoticize these "cultural traditions."

22. We use the terms *race* and *ethnicity* together to signify the broadest sense of the many socially constructed categories that are relevant to this discussion, but note here that they are not synonymous; the term *race* is the more common referent, for reasons that will be noted below. We use the term *ethnic studies* in an inclusive way, to refer to the area of academic knowledge that incorporates both race and ethnicity, as well as particular forms of culture.

23. Admittedly, if we label these as separate entities we risk falling into two common traps found in the discourse of multiculturalism: (1) pitting discussions of race against those of gender, and (2) assuming that the critical discourses of gender and race do not already coexist in the same academic unit. Our intention, however, is to point out similarities in the ways these areas of study have developed and to consider how they are also different.

24. The irony of this observation is fairly obvious, especially in light of contemporary postmodern work that analyzes race and gender (as well as class, sexuality, etc.) as simultaneous and interlocking concepts (see hooks 1984, and Collins 1990, for example).

25. It is important to note that this is a historical characterization that is useful for this argument, but has been disputed within feminist scholarship. A more contemporary portrait would reveal that knowledge in women's studies has overwhelmingly rejected an essentialized notion of woman in recognition of differences among women, both in relation to gender itself as well as in relation to the categories of race, class, and sexuality; this has resulted in the proliferation of multiple standpoints within women's studies. Similarly, issues of gender are much more likely to be addressed in contemporary work within ethnic studies.

26. See Christopher 1995, for an analysis of additive, critical, and transformative categories of knowledge in relation to the incorporation of a gender studies distribution requirement at Stanford University.

27. Keep in mind that framing these as mutually exclusive is a reflection of prevailing ideological constructs and not an assumption of these authors.

28. A somewhat rhetorical question remains: If the work of these two knowledge projects has advanced along such similar paths, why has there not been a substantial number of cases of programs in "multicultural studies"?

29. See Boxer 1998 for a comprehensive analysis of these historical developments, including a discussion of "men's studies."

30. As a case in point, Stanford University's recently formed ethnic studies program (named "The Program in the Comparative Studies in Race and Ethnicity") links some, but not all, existing programs together. The women's studies program (named "The Program in Feminist Studies"—see Christopher 1995 for a brief institutional history of this program) is not included in this organizational unit, although many of its affiliated faculty members are also allied with various ethnic studies programs. It is important to note that this description of organizational location is not intended to deny that there is a rich and growing tradition of knowledge work and scholarship that sits at the intersections of race and gender, either combining these elements as subjects of study and/or taking an epistemological position that puts both race and gender in the foreground. Our point is, rather, that there are very few instances in which race and gender have been linked in the more formal structure of academic organizations.

31. A notable exception to this generalization is San Francisco State University's program that focuses on women of color as a core organizing concept (Boxer 1998).

32. The title of an important contribution to this line of theory makes a highly relevant point: "All the Women Are White, All the Blacks Are Men, But Some of Us Are Brave" (Hull et al. 1982).

33. For instance, a faculty member of an Asian-American studies program may be appointed and reviewed for promotion within the department of history, but have only teaching responsibilities within the Asian-American studies program.

34. It is interesting to consider here the more recent emergence of queer studies (or gay and lesbian studies) as an academic knowledge unit that is similarly derived from a broader social movement and is also organized separately, yet in close alignment with other multicultural areas. (In this case, queer studies is more likely to be aligned with women's studies or gender studies.) To the degree that this emerging field of study has confronted both racism and sexism while attempting to focus on critical analyses of sexuality, we can see obvious parallels to the knowledge areas described above. To the degree that queer studies becomes more firmly institutionalized in the form of autonomous academic units, its proponents must navigate internal political conflicts within multiculturalism as well as resistance from multiculturalism's external critics.

35. See Gless and Smith 1992; Carnochan 1993; and Graff 1992, for example.

36. See Graff 1992.

37. As for students, the traditional epistemology is so dominant that it is, ironically, hidden from them. The traditional epistemology has become taken for granted and is the default mode, so students must therefore actively search for courses that embrace an oppositional, critical, or multicultural perspective. However, the multicultural perspective need not be set up to counter the default. That is, for example, if undergraduates are supposed to understand Western civilization as well as non-Western civilization, do they need to learn about these sequentially? This common order and arrangements presents a process of learning and *un*learning (as has been elaborated by feminist scholars, this is the process of learning first in the father tongue, then "unlearning" that in order to give voice to the mother tongue). Rather, students can instead be taught from a critical perspective at the outset, so as to understand the cultural differences as well as the epistemological/political implications of different traditions. Such an approach is consistent with the multicultural goals of analyzing cultural differences without subscribing to the adversarial presumptions of Western versus non-Western, Anglo versus "ethnic," and men versus women.

REFERENCES

Alcoff, L., and E. Potter, eds. 1993. *Feminist Epistemologies.* New York: Routledge.

Arthur, J., and A. Shapiro, eds. 1995. *Campus Wars: Multiculturalism and the Politics of Difference.* San Francisco: Westview Press.

Berman, P, ed. 1992. *Debating P.C.* New York: Bantam Doubleday Dell.

Berube, M. and C. Nelson, eds. 1995. *Higher Education under Fire: Politics, Economics, and the Crisis of the Humanities.* New York: Routledge.

Boxer, M. J. 1998. *When Women Ask the Questions.* Baltimore: Johns Hopkins University Press.

Butler, J. E., and J. C. Walter. 1991. *Transforming the Curriculum: Ethnic Studies and Women's Studies.* Albany: State University of New York Press.

Carlson, D., and M. W. Apple, eds. 1998. *Power/Knowledge/Pedagogy.* Oxford: Westview Press.

Carnochan, W. B. 1993. *The Battleground of the Curriculum: Liberal Education and American Experience.* Stanford, Calif.: Stanford University Press.

Christopher, S. 1995. *Required Knowledge: Incorporating Gender into the Core Curriculum.* Ph.D. dissertation, Stanford University, Stanford, Calif.

Chun, M. 1999. *When Social Worlds Collide: Boundary Politics and the Production of Knowledge.* Ph. D. dissertation, Stanford University.

Collins, P. H. 1990. *Black Feminist Thought: Knowledge, Consciousness, and the Politics of Empowerment.* New York: Routledge.

Fausto-Sterling, A. 1985. *Myths of Gender: Biological Theories about Women and Men.* New York: Basic Books.

Fuller, S. 1988. *Social Epistemology.* Bloomington: Indiana University Press.

Gless, D. J., and B. H. Smith, eds. 1992. *The Politics of Liberal Education.* Durham, N.C.: Duke University Press, 1992.

Graff, G. 1992. *Beyond the Culture Wars: How Teaching the Conflicts Can Revitalize American Education.* New York: W. W. Norton.

Gumport, P. J. 1988. "Curricula as Signposts of Cultural Change." *Review of Higher Education* 12, no. 1: 49–62.

———. 1990. "Feminist Scholarship as a Vocation." *Higher Education: The International Journal of Higher Education and Educational Planning* 20, no.3: 231–43.

———. 1993. "The Contested Terrain of Academic Program Reduction." *Journal of Higher Education* 64, no. 3: 283–311.

———. Manuscript in preparation. *Academic Restructuring: Institutional Change and Knowledge Reorganization in Higher Education.*

Gumport, P. J., and M. Chun. 1999. "Technology and Higher Education: Opportunities and Challenges for the New Era." In *American Higher Education in the 21st Century: Social, Political, and Economic Challenges,* edited by P. Altbach, R. Berdahl, and P. J. Gumport, 370–95. Baltimore: Johns Hopkins University Press.

hooks, b. 1984. *Feminist Theory: From Margin to Center.* Boston: South End Press.

Howe, F. 1972. "Women's Studies and Social Change." In *Myths of Coeducation.* Bloomington: Indiana University Press.

Hu-DeHart, E. 1993. "Rethinking America: The Practice and Politics of Multiculturalism in Higher Education." In *Beyond a Dream Deferred: Multicultural Education and the Politics of Excellence,* edited by S. Tyagi and B. Thompson, 3–17. Minneapolis: University of Minnesota Press.

Hull, G., P. B. Scott, and B. Smith, eds. 1982. *All the Women Are White, All the Blacks Are Men, But Some of Us Are Brave: Black Women's Studies.* New York: Feminist Press.

Metzger, W. 1987. "The Academic Profession in the United States." In *The Academic Profession: National, Disciplinary, and Institutional Settings,* edited by B. Clark, 123–208. Berkeley and Los Angeles: University of California Press.

Slaughter, S. 1990. *The Higher Learning and High Technology.* Albany: State University of New York Press.

———. 1993. "Retrenchment in the 1980s: The Politics of Prestige and Gender." *Journal of Higher Education* 64, no. 3:250–82.

13

THE HAUNTING OF
MULTICULTURAL EPISTEMOLOGY
AND PEDAGOGY

Nancy Lesko
Columbia University

Leslie Rebecca Bloom
Iowa State University

We have to relate ourselves somehow to a social world that is polluted by something invisible and odorless, overhung by a sort of motionless cloud. It is the cloud of givenness, of what is considered "natural" by those caught in the taken-for-granted, in the everydayness of things.

—Maxine Greene, *Releasing the Imagination*

If haunting describes how that which appears to be not there is often a seething presence, acting on and often meddling with taken-for-granted realities, the ghost is just the sign, or the empirical evidence if you like, that tells you a haunting is taking place.

—Avery Gordon, *Ghostly Matters*

As these opening quotations suggest, the social world in which we live is polluted by injustices that are taken as "normal"; haunting occurs to meddle with these damaging, taken-for-granted realities. It is this problematic social world that multicultural educators address, often making teaching a site of discomfort. We feel this discomfort when we wrestle with the taken-for-granted realities (e.g.: structural oppression, hierarchical understandings of difference, persistent injustice) that are the focus of intervention in the multicultural classroom. To feel the discomfort as a multicultural educator is to acknowledge that you have been visited by a ghost wishing to disrupt normative multicultural epistemology and practice.

According to sociologist Avery Gordon (1997), haunting is the way ghosts call attention to injustices in order to move those who are haunted to different epistemologies from which they may act differently in the presence of injustice. Therefore, suggests Gordon, if we want to study and change social life and its damaging effects, "we must learn how to identify hauntings and reckon with ghosts, learn how to make contact with what is without doubt often painful, difficult and unsettling" (23). This chapter is about our process of learning to identify the ghosts that haunted our multicultural education classrooms and our attempts to interpret the meanings of their presence. With Gordon, we understand haunting as signifying both a form and process of knowledge and we therefore use the concept of haunting as a trope for interpreting the epistemology and pedagogy of multicultural teacher education.

Gordon explains that there are three characteristic features of hauntings, and we have used these three characteristics to organize this chapter. The first characteristic is that "the ghost imports a charged strangeness into the place or sphere it is haunting, thus unsettling the propriety and property lines that delimit a zone of activity or knowledge" (63). If you are being haunted, she continues, you first have the recognition that a profound social phenomenon is persistently addressing itself to you, distracting and disturbing your daily life, often messing it up and leaving in its wake an uneasy feeling. For us, the "charged strangeness" that suggested a haunting, as we will analyze below, was particularly apparent to us in our efforts to teach about difference as a central epistemological framework of multicultural education. It was through the discomfort we experienced from being haunted that we came to see how our teaching maintained and even fostered the normalized epistemologies of difference we had tried to disrupt. The second characteristic of haunting is that "the ghost is primarily a symptom of what is missing. It gives notice not only to itself but also to what it represents. What it represents is usually a loss, sometimes of life, sometimes of a path not taken. From a certain vantage point the ghost also simultaneously represents a future possibility, a hope" (63–64). As we will illustrate below by analyzing our pedagogical practices, we came to understand how ghosts representing "paths not taken" are particularly salient in multicultural education. Specifically, we explore how the pedagogical experiences we participated in with our students limited the kinds of knowledge that could and could not be constructed in the classroom. Third, Gordon explains, "the ghost is alive, so to speak. We are in relation to it and it has designs on us such that we must reckon with it graciously, attempting to offer it a hospitable memory *out of a concern for justice*. Out of a concern for justice would be the only reason one would bother" (64). In our conclusion, we take up the challenge to reckon graciously with the ghosts and accept that being haunted may have helped us move toward a better understanding of how to teach in ways that enhance the struggle for social justice—which is, after all, the goal of multicultural education.

INTERROGATING MULTICULTURAL EDUCATION EPISTEMOLOGY:
CHARGED STRANGENESS, UNSETTLED KNOWLEDGE,
AND UNEASY FEELINGS

> When a ghost is haunting a story about intellectual storytelling, what is important is not to be afraid. (Gordon 1997, 59)

When we began teaching multicultural education in 1991 and 1992, we believed that if we revealed the "truth" to our students about tracking, racism, and classism in disciplinary practices and the second-class education given to many youth (but especially to youth of color), they would be outraged and quickly replace their false beliefs about the reliability of tests, the factual bases for tracking, and the naturalness of "boys being boys" with new, correct facts and ideas. We soon found ourselves feeling uncomfortable with our teaching and began to talk to each other about what we were each doing in our secondary school multicultural education courses at Indiana University.[1] In our discussions, we asked ourselves if we were teaching our students to think like us. Is the purpose of the course to clone ourselves and our thinking about race, class, gender, religion, and sexuality? These were the initial troubling questions about our courses that voiced an awareness that our approaches to multiculturalism worked toward reproduction, toward identity and duplication, and thus away from difference. Additional questions emerged in our conversations: Why, when we aim to teach about difference, do we end up reinforcing sameness? How does our teaching result in essentialized views of people of color or of poor people, and a reaffirmed assuredness among our predominantly white students of the correctness of their knowledge? How was it that our pedagogical approach to multiculturalism seemed to promote a new orthodoxy, a new authoritative knowledge of life in schools (Ellsworth 1992; Berlak 1994)? These questions, which we now interpret as signs of being haunted, started us on a path of dialogue and reading that helped us to interrogate the epistemologies of our pedagogical practices.[2]

The Epistemology of the Real

Deborah Britzman and colleagues (1993) characterize the general epistemological orientation to multicultural education as a preoccupation with supplying students with "accurate" and "authentic" representations. "Good realism" is offered as a remedy to the "bad fictions" of stereotypes. A related stance emphasizes that prejudice, racism, and sexism are due to a lack of knowledge, or error in thinking, a belief regularly repeated among our preservice teachers.[3]

Recent reconceptualizations, however, emphasize that "ignorance" is an effect of particular knowledge, not an absence of knowledge (Henriques et al. 1984; Scott 1992). This reformulation of the production of prejudice assumes a link between knowledge and power, rather than an idealist view of correct knowledge as liberation from power. For example, Stuart Hall (cited in Britzman 1991, 231) critiques the belief in the power of "the real" to educate and transform, saying, "The notion that our heads are full of false ideas which can, however, be totally dispersed when we throw ourselves open to 'the real' as a moment of absolute authentication, is probably the most ideological conception of all."

These ideas helped us begin to see our reliance on "the real" in our multicultural teacher education as located in a positivist approach to knowledge, learning, and classroom pedagogy. We understand positivism as an ontological and epistemological stance that asserts that there are truths to be known and taught, and that these truths exist independently of knowers and of other ideas. Much to our dismay, we saw that the positivist epistemology promoted a reliance on realism and rationality as a central method for teaching, and rationality was likewise a central expected learning outcome of the course. As a result, we expected rational conversations to lead to "correct" thinking among our students.

Our readings and conversations also helped us to understand how we relied on a positivist view of learning in which ideas have a separate, autonomous existence apart from our students and our interpretations (Maher 1991). The effect of this epistemology was to make our students "objects" of our knowledge who either became identical to us by assimilating our knowledge or remained nonidentical and therefore (in a dualistic knowledge system) completely "other" to us (Young 1990). This is how rationality and realism functioned in our multicultural education classrooms. Thus, we began to understand the influence of positive epistemology and how it produced particular kinds of knowledge and knowledge relations. Our "achievements," then, were familiar dualisms that only permitted good/bad positions, real/fictional readings, and bias/truth in evaluations.

As our conversations continued and we began to write about multicultural education, we also became more aware of how the teaching of multicultural education is grounded in a modernist fantasy in which its main character, the teacher, is engaged in a heroic and solitary act (Farber et al. 1994; Dalton 1995). We saw how, by assimilating the assumption of the rationality of students and teachers, and by endorsing rational persuasion as a staple pedagogical strategy, we taught from an epistemological stance that fashions the teaching of multicultural education as a dramatic narrative sounding something like this: ". . . and once the conquering has taken place, either in terms of the students or administration, then there is the possibility of a 'happily ever after' existence" (Weber and Mitchell 1995). This fiction arrives at the dénouement that occurs when students stop resisting and do what the teacher asks. The happy ending is achieved when students come to new understandings, among which are being supportive of multicultural curricula and topics in schools, understanding oppression, understanding perspectives different from their own, and becoming committed to social justice in education.

This clearly modernist narrative of teaching, with its linear and hero-centered form, chafed against our feminist theoretical understandings and lived experiences (see, for example, Bloom 1998). Even the narratives of problems teaching multiculturalism that we read (Ahlquist 1991, 1992; Allsup 1995; Berlak 1994; Boyle-Baise 1995; Britzman 1995; Carlson 1995; Roman 1993; Sleeter 1994; Tatum 1994; Watkins 1994) failed to complicate the basic linear plot, and teacher as hero and primary knower in the classroom. Our understandings of the links between knowledge and power made this view of teaching suspicious, as did our feminist critiques of the teacher as masculinized hero. Despite our misgivings and dissatisfactions—Is this all there is supposed to be?—we recognized that we were teaching within the framework of this narrative of multiculturalism. But before we were able to articulate alternatives, we decided to make sense of the actual pedagogical approaches we were using, and try to come to terms with how they were fashioned, and why they felt haunted.

Toward this end, we examined two of the pedagogical mainstays of our multi-cultural courses—the course reading selections and a one-day visit to an urban school—for the kinds of discussions and learning they authorized, and for what remained undisturbed, unexamined, and polluted.

INTERROGATING MULTICULTURAL EDUCATIONAL PRACTICE: PEDAGOGICAL LOSS AND PATHS NOT TAKEN

> If you let it, the ghost can lead you toward what has been missing, which is some-times everything. (Gordon 1997, 58)

The Haunting of Multicultural Readings

During the 1991–93 academic years we used different course readings in our multicultural classes, but we had similar expectations of what they would ac-complish. Nancy (Lesko) drew on empirical accounts, often social scientists' descriptions, of school practices to counter white students' general assumptions that schools are meritocratic, fair, and impartial institutions. Competing expla-nations for patterns of student failure in schools were read, so that students got a sense of the ongoing research and policy discussions on inequality, culture and schooling.

A central reading, for example, was Shirley Heath's *Ways with Words* (1983), a text characterized variously as a "classic" in teacher education (De Castell and Walker 1991) and a "seminal study" (Zeichner 1996, 144). This ethnographic study demonstrates how groups of people's values, social relations, uses of time and space, and language patterns varied, and how the literacy practices of poor whites and blacks clashed with the values, relations, and language-use patterns of middle-class families and middle-class teachers in their local schools. Heath's contention that students fail because of cultural conflicts between their home and school "ways with words" was juxtaposed with other accounts of racial and eco-nomic inequalities outside and inside schools (e.g., Ogbu 1987).

Nancy expected that readings such as Heath (1983) and Ogbu (1987), as well as writings by Rist (1970), Baldwin (1985), McIntosh (1988), Bigelow (1991), hooks (1993), and Christensen (1994), would convince many students of the exis-tence of institutionalized racism and classism in schools; she expected that these readings would be interpreted by her students as she had read and understood them in the 1970s. Like Christine Sleeter's (1995a) acknowledgment that her central pedagogical strategies are formulated to echo her own processes of learning, Nancy's approach drew from her own history and education. However, the students responded differently to *Ways with Words*. For example, some were outraged that the African-American Trackton families kept newborn children with them constantly and provided no scheduled nap times or feeding times.[3] They believed that the families were negligent rather than culturally different. This was one of the many "interpretive stand-offs" Nancy experienced: the failure of students to read and interpret from a similar perspective to hers, and to the author's of a text. Such stand-offs were perplexing to Nancy and all too often were a stopping point for discussion. With some students, only Nancy's authority (in the form of graded assignments) could lead to some consideration of Heath's, Ogbu's, and others' views. That is, the teacher's power could he used to "force" discussion of certain topics, but such use of classroom authority to enforce interpretive considerations was at odds with Nancy's beliefs that the classroom should foster open dialogue.

Leslie (Bloom) drew on life histories and personal narratives, ethnographic studies, documentary videos, novels, panel discussions and guest speakers as ways to examine multiple perspectives on social inequalities, culture, and schooling. One key text was David Schoem's *Inside Separate Worlds: Life Stories of Young Blacks, Jews, and Latinos* (1991), a book consisting of life stories written by undergraduate students taking a course entitled "Ethnic Identity and Inter-group Relations" taught by Schoem at the University of Michigan. The authors examine such issues as family life, schooling experiences, neighborhoods and friendships, ethnic and religious identities, and understandings of dominant culture, marginality, and their own places within these issues.

Inside Separate Worlds was a particularly compelling text for many students, both because its stories were poignant and personal and also because it was written by college people their own age and in academic circumstances akin to theirs. Leslie's goals in including this book were to break down negative stereotypes by showing the complex cultural contexts of the lived experiences of the "other" and to raise students' consciousness about the structural inequities of youth their own age. If they understood these inequities, she reasoned, they would never be able to blame minorities for their own poverty—their inability to "pull themselves up by their own bootstraps."

However, what most students took away from this book was the comfort of knowing that "under the skin, we are all alike and have the same hopes and dreams"—an often repeated statement in students' papers about the book. The students delighted in having located ways that those who have been oppressed or marginalized shared certain values with them, and they took comfort that they could claim that there is a universal sameness that binds all humans. Their interpretations elided ways that predominantly white, Christian institutions had structurally excluded and undermined these young minority authors. Furthermore, they were harshly critical of the teachers discussed in the book whom some of the authors vividly described as having sabotaged their academic achievements and participation. Some of Leslie's students asserted that had these teachers taken a multicultural course, this sabotage would not have happened, whereas others argued that it was "natural" for there to be some racist teachers, and that they (the students), of course, were different.

In both cases, our students failed to replace their false beliefs with the realist truths we allegedly provided in the texts, calling into question Diane Hoffman's (1996) belief in the power of ethnographies and case studies to successfully reformulate multicultural education. In Nancy's class, the students' judgments that the Trackton families had "bad" child-rearing practices often solidified beliefs that black families are deviant. Rather than promoting the idea of positive difference or nonjudgmental understanding, students remained within an interpretation "that defines what is different as inherently inferior" (Rothenberg 1994, 296). Contact with text-based information about different cultural norms and practices could not by itself foster a new way of seeing the world.

In Leslie's class, the students' interpretations that the essays in *Inside Separate Worlds* prove that people are the same regardless of race, ethnicity, or religion reveal an investment in the view of the "generic human" underlying classical liberal thought (Ellsworth 1992, 102), a view that comes seemingly from nowhere. It is also a colonizing interpretation, one that seeks to assimilate the margins into the center so that "the Other can never speak as Other" (Mohan 1995, 273). This response to the book likewise engages in what Ruth Frankenberg (1993) calls a discourse of "color/power evasiveness":

> What becomes clearer about color evasiveness, then, is that more than evading questions of difference wholesale, this discursive repertoire selectively engages difference, evading questions of power. While certain kinds of difference or differentiation can be seen and discussed with abandon, others are evaded if at all possible . . . power evasion involves a selective attention to difference, *allowing into conscious scrutiny even conscious embrace those differences that make the speaker feel good* but continuing to evade by means of partial description, euphemism, and self-contradiction those that make the speaker feel bad. (1993, 152, 156–57; emphasis added)

Leslie's students' evasion of the authors' statements about their systematic disempowerment by institutions such as public schools, combined with her students' enthusiastic acceptance of similarities, illustrates Frankenberg's (1993) theory that the differences that are embraced are those that make the speaker feel good.

Further, as Elizabeth Minnich (1994, 305) suggests, such responses to difference are attempts to hold onto universal ideals, another eighteenth-century Enlightenment legacy:

> It is the loss of universal ideals that they fear. . . . To admit the differences between us as other than equal variations on a single theme is to admit that injustice is not an

aberration. In the areas on which we focus under the complex term "diversity," injustice is indeed foundational.... To insist on diversity ... is to shake the forms and frames and modes of knowledge which derived from and served the unjust orders—but which some still think of as the only grounds for any kind of judgment. Even as people who cannot conceive of any other valid grounds for judgment may ... share concern—about hate crimes and poverty and violence and abuse, they *feel* that concern as a fear of chaos, of a loss of control and order and safety.... Their concern leads them to crave certainty, and they retreat to whatever it is they are most sure they know. (305)

And finally, Emmanuel Levinas warns us that such responses to differences can be interpreted as an active process of the self assimilating the other, explaining that "the fundamental problem concerns the way in which knowledge—and therefore theory, or history—is constituted through the comprehension and incorporation of the other.... In Western philosophy, when knowledge or theory comprehends the other, then the alterity of the latter vanishes as it becomes part of the same. This [is] 'ontological imperialism.'... The relation with the other is accomplished through its assimilation into the self" (Levinas, cited in Young 1990, 12–13).

Using the insights of Frankenberg, Rothenberg, Minnich, and Levinas, we see that realist texts, although an important component of multicultural education, are unlikely to disturb universal ideals that people are all the same ("we're all human") and that U.S. social structures and schools are neutral. Injustice remains an aberration, not a structural reality.[4]

Our point in analyzing these interpretive "stand-offs" is not to criticize these students, but rather to illustrate the effects of Western Enlightenment epistemology on accepted approaches to teaching about difference. In other words, despite our firmest intentions to do otherwise, as multicultural educators, we perpetuated discourses integral to white male dominance, specifically the use of binary pairs such as us/them, self/other, normal/deviant, and neutral/biased, in thinking and discussion about social groups and social inequities. Critics have pointed out how these dualities in language and thought are legacies of particular social orders and power arrangements in which the valued term of each pair flows from and supports the given distribution of resources and power (Haraway 1989; Scott 1990; Young 1990). These binarisms are hierarchically ranked, polarly opposed, and the less valued terms "serve the higher, in a relation of dominance, mastery, or control" (Code 1991, 274). Part of changing social inequalities, then, is destabilizing the certainties of such oppositional categories, something we did not accomplish through course readings while under the epistemological spell of realism and positivism. Being haunted helped us to recognize that while our texts imparted knowledge and even produced knowledge, they did not have the capacity to transform student thinking in the ways that being haunted eventually did for us. In the next section, we explain how for us, the class activity of a visit to an urban school was similarly haunted and had similar effects of reconfirming the "bad fictions" of our students regarding difference.

The Haunting of Multicultural Experience

The kinds of experiences our students have had prior to attending Indiana University are significant in shaping their beliefs and expectations when they enter the multicultural classroom. About two-thirds of the students come to the university from small towns (under 15,000 people) that are predominantly white and largely Christian, in Indiana or from adjoining states. Most are between nineteen and twenty-one years old. Only about one-fifth of the students have attended elementary and secondary schools with any significant population of students of color, although there were poor students in every school. In a secondary education class, there is usually a fairly equal distribution of males and females. Classes may have two or three Jewish students who are often from urban areas and/or out of state. In our view, a mix of conservatism and Christianity dominates our undergraduate teacher education students. Some students say that the issues of the course (e.g. racism, homophobia, and sexism) make them feel "picked on" and discriminated against because the "liberal attitudes" that structure the course often conflict with their religious and political beliefs.

Because personal experience, the ground upon which one becomes a teacher (Britzman 1991), is considered important to teacher education, and because so many students come from monocultural areas and live at school in predominantly white dormitories—what is called "living in a white bubble" (Feagin and Vera 1995, 138)—one of the required activities for all multicultural classes is a one-day field trip to a nearby urban high school or middle school. Charter buses ferry the classes early in the morning to the city, dropping students off at schools whose populations are working class, poor and multiethnic, but predominantly African American and European American. Each college student is assigned to a school student, often one who is perceived as "model" by the school administration. They spend the day "shadowing" the student, attending classes and eating lunch together. The stated purpose of the trip is for the preservice teachers to get acquainted with one secondary school student and to observe her experiences during one day in an urban school. It is important to note that this field experience is mandated, organized, and paid for by the teacher education program, and all course instructors are required to participate, two facts that highlight the value placed on this realist experience.

For many students this school visit is deemed the "high point of the course" because being in a school feels qualitatively different (and better) from the abstractness of reading and class discussion. Although experience visiting an urban school and talking with one inner-city student is supposed to lead to compassion for or active advocacy of historically subordinate groups of students (because of the belief that personal knowledge of an individual or a situation will counter stereotypes and false beliefs), we find that this activity has no more power to effect change than do the "vicarious experiences" produced by ethnographies or autobiographies. Indeed, many students in our classes returned from their one-day field trip in an ethnically mixed urban school adamantly expressing their revulsion at the lack of teaching they observed, the lack of discipline among the students, and the lack of safety they felt as they walked the police-patrolled halls. Although the students' interpretations of the urban school field trip are various, they tend to fall into the same types of responses they had to the texts: (1) these "kids" are the same as "we" were in high school (speaking of the students' disinterest in their courses and interest in music, dating, etc.); (2) these "kids" are totally different—for example, because they do not seem to respect teachers and seem undisciplined; (3) there is little worthwhile learning occurring in urban classrooms. For many, such experiences reinforced the desire to remain in the familiar—to graduate and teach in the "white bubble."

Although some university students have meaningful contacts with the secondary school students of different backgrounds, in general we think the field trip fails to call into question previous beliefs, assumptions, stereotypes, and fears about "urban schools." This failure is linked to what can be understood as an unacknowledged desire to maintain a color-/power-evasive discourse that allows university education students to categorize comfortably the students in schools either as just like themselves or as deviant. That is, they either assimilate/universalize them or mark them as deviant. To maintain this dualism, positive difference is not a possible response to the "kids" and the situations they encounter. The field trip is *supposed* to be an event whereby false ideas about inner-city schools and "kids" are dispersed. The trip is *supposed* to make visible—that is, real—what we have introduced in the classroom: schools are inequitably funded along racial and class lines; these material realities harm students in their everyday lives and their future expectations; the "inner city" should not be a code or euphemism for "dangerous-to-whites" or "all-black." However, as Cameron McCarthy and colleagues (1997) and Henry Giroux (1996) maintain, the predominance of television and print media in people's lives not only serves to reinforce the association of urban black youth with violence and poor white youth with laziness and apathy, but also makes it very difficult (and all the more imperative) for educators to challenge these hegemonic conceptions.

Classroom discussions after the trip rely upon, and intend to build upon, students' experiences and observations during this important day. Further, discussions attempt to reexamine what students understand about what they have seen and what they believe. However, we find that the field trip further essentializes and distances students from what they have seen. As a manifestation of positivist epistemology, the field trip becomes assimilated into existing frameworks of knowledge, rather than problematizing students' knowledge frameworks. Thus, a "personal experience" created by the teacher education program does not have the positive effects promised, and, yet again, race and power structures are evaded. Furthermore, the way the field trip is constructed produces the students, and us, as authorized voyeurs-for-a-day. We may legitimately enter and critique the classroom and school lives of "inner-city" youth and teachers; this privilege rests in our position as university people from a predominantly white institution. No wonder we returned troubled by our mandated participation in the school! No wonder the activity was haunted by disruptive ghosts!

Our problems with this field trip are clarified by understanding that "experience ... is *produced,* rather than simply *registered"* (Rattansi 1992, 33). Thus, experience cannot simply be used or referred to as some unchanging entity that will connect students to truths about racism or inequality. Joan Scott (1992), a feminist historian, clarifies the epistemological problems of using "experience" as uncontestable evidence or the beginning of explanations:

> [T]he evidence of experience, whether conceived through a metaphor of visibility or in any other way that takes meaning as transparent, reproduces rather than contests given ideological systems.... The project of making experience visible precludes critical examination of the workings of the ideological system itself, its categories of representation (homosexual/heterosexual, man/woman, black/white as fixed immutable identities), its premises about what these categories mean and how they operate, its notions of subjects, origin, and cause.... It is not individuals who have experience, but subjects who are constituted through experience. *Experience in this definition then becomes ... that which we seek to explain....* To think about experience in this way is to historicize it as well as to historicize the identities it produces. (25–26; emphasis added)

Using Scott's analysis that experience must be what people seek to understand, and that their understanding must encompass the logic of the ideological system that produces and supports racism, sexism, classism, and homophobia, we maintain that the focus of multicultural teacher education must shift from *presentations* of experiences of "others," as the field trip does, to *examinations* of the construction of identities, subjectivities, and experiences. This understanding shifts the curriculum focus from imparting "realistic truths" about historically oppressed groups to interrogating how systems of meaning work—systems that result in people seeing and believing that the world is made up of "blacks" and "whites," "women" and "men," and "gays" and "straights."

GRACIOUS RECKONING AND CREATING HOSPITABLE WELCOMES

> It is no simple task to be graciously hospitable when our [classroom] is not familiar, but is haunted and disturbed. It could require an effort to which our manners are not yet accustomed. It could require a different sort of receptiveness and welcome. And out of a "will to heal," or *out of a concern for justice?* Well, yes, but that leaves everything of a precise nature of the hospitality to be decided. (Gordon 1997, 58)

While we did not consciously encourage our classroom spaces and course activities to be haunted, our recognition of the seething presence of ghosts was an important and transformative event in our teaching lives. Drawing again from Gordon (1997), we now can see that being haunted is a particularly wonderful opportunity for those working toward social justice in a world of "bloodless categories, narrow notions of the visible and the empirical, professional standards of indifference, institutional rules of distance and control, [and] barely speakable fears of losing the footing that enables us to speak authoritatively and with greater value than anyone else who might" (21). The honor of being haunted may be particularly important in multicultural education, where "our methods have thus far been less than satisfactory for addressing the very nature of things and the problems it is our responsibility to address, leaving us not yet making something new enough out of what are arguably many new ideas and novel conditions" (21). Therefore, as Gordon argues, we must recognize that "a different way of knowing and writing about the social world, an entirely different mode of production still awaits our invention" (21).

Being haunted alerted us to the necessity for us to find new modes of production and different ways of knowing and teaching in our multicultural classrooms. Further, our subsequent examination of the epistemologies underlying our pedagogical practices and our interrogation of the course readings and field trip activity described above helped us to reckon with the ghosts who haunted our multicultural classrooms. Through this analytic reckoning, we became cognizant of how we reproduced dualistic thinking by reinforcing "us/them" oppositions and how we produced a classroom dynamic that resulted in interpretive stand-offs. Reckoning with the ghosts was also a self-reflexive process that challenged us to acknowledge that our teaching of multiculturalism was flawed, not only by its emphasis on imparting realisms that were intended to replace students' "sincere fictions" (Feagin and Vera 1995) regarding schooling, but by its assumption that experience could change hegemonic patterns of interpretation. We came to more clearly see that we were trying to model a stance that we implicitly or explicitly wanted students to adopt. When they took a different position, the conversational possibilities soon ran out. They interpreted the world as neutral, fair, and getting better. We interpreted the world as a place filled with structural inequalities and growing poverty, violence, and homelessness among children and youth (Books 1998). When our students adopted the "other" position, our mutually "factual" (albeit opposing in substance) interpretive stances ended further discussion. They had their version of reality and we had ours. Even when we were successful, when students could analyze inequities and biases, we found ourselves worried that all we desired and taught for was the duplication of our own thinking.

That we rejected the students' assimilation of our ideas as well as their active participation in classroom discussions when they did not assimilate our ideas suggested to us that the dissatisfaction of teaching multiculturalism was not going to be resolved by changing only the pedagogical strategies. Rather, our experiences of being haunted and learning to reckon with the ghosts helped us to see that in order to teach from the postpositivist, antirealist epistemological stance that we so desire, we must learn to make the classroom a place where "arriving at some predetermined destination remains less important than struggling for some ethical end" (Collins 1998). To make the classroom a site of struggle, then, replaces the goal of imparting realisms and truths. When the classroom is a site of struggle for justice, ghosts are hospitably received. Having come to believe that being haunted can be a catalyst for rethinking multicultural education, we offer our understandings of how to reframe multicultural education classrooms to make them more hospitable for the ghosts. More hospitality can be shown, we conclude, in three connected ways: with a more dialogical approach to classroom pedagogy, a focus on the production of student interpretations, and, finally, with the acceptance by multicultural educators of a pedagogy of risk.

First, a more hospitable approach to ghosts may be to employ a dialogical theory of knowledge to classroom pedagogy in place of a positivist, realist theory of knowledge. A dialogical approach means that any idea, concept, or utterance is interrogated for the necessary presence of other ideas, forming a chain of connotative associations. Bakhtinian dialogism is particularly helpful here, for as Mikhail Bakhtin (1981) explains, "Everything means, is understood, as a part of a greater whole—there is constant interaction between meanings, all of which have the potential of conditioning others. Which will affect the other, how it will do so and in what degree, is what is actually settled at the moment of utterance. This dialogic imperative . . . insures that there can be no actual monologue" (425).[5] As a form of classroom pedagogy, dialogism can be employed in classroom discussions to interrogate students' and teachers' utterances so that together they may begin to understand the historical, cultural, and sociological assumptions and discourses on which they individually and collectively make their knowledge claims. We draw on Paulo Freire's (1970, 86) placement of dialogue at the center of education, with its aim to understand "the thought-language with which men [*sic*] refer to reality, the levels at which they perceive that reality, and their view of the world." The point of a dialogical approach is that there are no *positive* terms or ideas or understandings; all meanings are sets of relations.[6] These relations must be interrogated as a core element of conversation in teaching multiculturalism. But we also agree that Freire's understanding of dialogue must be made more complex (Whitson 1988; Weiler 1991).

A second particularly hospitable approach includes an emphasis on multiple interpretations in student writing assignments. As Donna Haraway (1989) argues, it is through interpretation that we can learn to consciously examine the fictioning of our worlds and the fashioning of knowledge. In our graduate curriculum courses, where we have tried this strategy of multiple interpretations, we have each asked students to write several interpretations of one "text" or phenomenon (the subject of texts have included learning to write, mathematics teaching, and reforming teacher education). The students write one interpretation using a realist perspective, one a feminist, and the third a poststructuralist. We then use the students' interpretations as primary discussion sources in class, in which all participants critically examine each interpretation and the layers of interpretations contained within each account. Finally, students are asked to read across their three accounts and examine the elements used in the production of each interpretation. According to our course evaluations and anecdotal comments, students find this strategy very helpful in understanding the production of interpretations.

For teaching multicultural education differently, this practice of producing multiple interpretations may include asking students to write a conventional interpretation and a critical postpositivist interpretation of a "text." The final part of the assignment could be an analysis of significant differences between the two interpretations—that is, an examination of the production of each of the interpretations and the fashioning of knowledge within them. This comparison/contrast will probably involve analyzing language choices; observing the presence or absence of color/power evasion (and evasions of gender, sexuality, religion, and class); and examining the assumptions of rationality, autonomous facts existing independently of knowers as well as other unstated assumptions.

Gordon, too, encourages the production of interpretations and the interrogation of our knowledge and memories through what she calls "ghost stories," stories that "not only repair representational mistakes, but also strive to understand the conditions under which a memory was produced in the first place, toward a countermemory, for the future" (1997, 22). Thus, the production of multiple interpretations and the "ghost stories" they produce are hopeful in that they do have the potential to help us rethink those hegemonic assumptions that reside in memory; they may lead toward a refashioning of the world that has the potential to engender social justice.[7]

Finally, just as we believe educators must reformulate classroom strategies and writing assignments to manifest a nonpositivist epistemology in order to make more hospitable places for ghosts, we believe that educators need to guard against inflated expectations for how dialogical teaching and the production of interpretations will work. That is, we will need to continue to struggle against the heroic version of teaching with its images of progress, breakthrough moments, and happy-ever-after endings. Multicultural education, therefore, becomes what Lawrence Grossberg (1994) calls a "pedagogy of articulation and risk:

> [T]he risk of making connections, drawing lines, mapping articulations, between different domains, discourses, and practices, to see what will work, both theoretically and politically ... to multipl[y] connections between things that have [apparently] nothing to do with each other ... speaks to the conditions of exile and displacement ... to conditions of homelessness and restlessness in terms of a renewed commitment to theory that is motivated by the desire to displace established orthodoxies.... It is a pedagogy that demands of students ... simply that they gain some understanding of their own involvement in the world, and in the making of their own future. (18)

An emphasis on the dialogic character of knowing and meaning and the pedagogical emphasis on interrogating the production of interpretations shift the epistemological and pedagogical ground of multicultural teacher education. As Grossberg states, it is pedagogy that demands of students, and of teachers, that they "gain understanding of their involvement in the world"—their involvement in producing interpretations that are always in relation to the interpretations of others and their involvement in concrete actions that follow from particular renditions of their shared world. Such a view of teaching and learning could transform "everyone's sense of belonging, affiliation, and self" (Fraser 1995, 83). It could also, we hope, inspire a commitment to social justice because it has the potential to shake students' beliefs in the binary categories that have organized human relations and thinking for too long.

Thus, gracious reckoning with the ghosts who haunted our multicultural classrooms ultimately has brought us to new understandings of the relationships possible in teaching multicultural education. Initially a destabilizing process, being haunted and finally learning to reckon with the ghosts has been personally transformative, affirming Avery Gordon's assertion that "following the ghosts is about making a contact that changes you and refashions the social relations in which you are located" (22). Therefore, as teachers of multicultural education, as postpositivists, and as feminists committed to social justice, we hope that you will join us in our dedication to making a hospitable reception for the ghosts that may haunt your classrooms.

ACKNOWLEDGMENTS

The authors wish to thank Lynne Boyle-Baise for helpful comments on earlier drafts and Rebecca Schmidt for editing this manuscript. For another interpretation of these issues, see Lesko and Bloom (1998).

NOTES

1. This three-credit course is typically taken during the first or second semester of teacher education coursework, generally by second- or third-year students. It is a required course, developed in the early 1980s. Each semester, seven or eight sections of the secondary school multicultural education course are offered, and three or four sections of an elementary school version; enrollment in each section is capped at thirty-five students. Most sections are taught by associate instructors, with two to five full-time faculty members also teaching. There are ongoing discussions about whether the separate course should be continued, expanded to a two-semester course, or the ideas dispersed across other teacher education courses.

2. See Sleeter 1995b for a review of critiques of multiculturalism, and Ladson-Billings 1995 for a review of multiculturalism in teacher education. Our characterization of "mainstream" American multicultural teacher education is grounded upon knowledge of research and scholarship in the area, and upon familiarity with popular, widely used textbooks. There is, of course, conceptual diversity in the field. Our account draws largely on McCarthy's (1993) analysis of three different approaches to multicultural education, which he labels "cultural understanding," "cultural competence," and "cultural emancipation." Although the approaches differ, McCarthy contends that they all "attach an enormous significance to the role of attitudes in the reproduction and transformation of racism" (292). Henriques (1984) critiques such an attitudinal approach to racism because it posits *individuals* as the unit in which prejudice occurs and assumes that individuals are rational beings whose attitudes can be changed through better reasoning. Our discursive approach attempts to avoid the problems of rationalist and individualized accounts of racism. A discursive approach understands racism and sexism as structured into language, conceptual categories, and knowledge (which are, in turn, woven into relations of power). This view is equally influenced by post-

structuralist and postcolonialist work (Donald and Rattansi 1992). Another approach to overcoming rationalist and individualist assumptions is a psychoanalytic understanding of the sources of prejudice (Bhabha 1994).

3. Trackton is the name of one of the U.S. communities studied by Heath and described in *Ways with Words* (1983). It is a small working-class, African-American community in the central area of the Piedmont Carolinas.

4. Certainly, in both of our classes, there were students who did seem to follow our expectations and changed their views of schooling practices in relation to nonmainstream students. However, we emphasize here the majority of the students, those who challenged our approach by responding outside our expectations. We are aware that these effects of our teaching are not to be expected or found in all similar circumstances. We are also aware that the particular mix of our own backgrounds as teachers, our pedagogical approaches, our students' perspectives, and American institutional and historical contexts are all involved in producing these responses. Teachers and students in different situations might have different encounters. We acknowledge the set of factors that likely affects our pedagogical efforts, although in this paper we focus upon the discursive relationships created through two teaching events.

5. According to Holquist (1990, 22), dialogism is not another dualism, but "a necessary *multiplicity* in human perception. The multiplicity manifests itself as a series of distinctions between categories appropriate to whatever is being perceived on the other." In addition, factors of situation and relation come into play, making for multiplicity.

6. These ideas are developed in relation to conceptions of curriculum and censorship in Whitson 1988, 1991, and in the fields of moral and epistemological theory in Code 1991.

7. The problem of ontological imperialism remains. Can people know in a way that does not violate the "other" as "other"? Can they come into relationships with otherness without dominating it via theory, history, or other conceptual manifestations of power? We cannot answer these questions at this time, but we will continue to ask ourselves whether a dialogical knowledge and pedagogy can no longer be imperialistic.

REFERENCES

Ahlquist, R. 1991. "Position and Imposition: Power Relations in a Multicultural Foundations Class." *Journal of Negro Education* 60, no. 2: 158–69.

———. 1992. "Manifestations of Inequality: Overcoming Resistance in a Multicultural Foundations Course." In *Research and Multicultural Education: From the Margins to the Mainstream,* edited by C. A. Grant, 89–105. London: Falmer Press.

Allsup, C. 1995. "What's All This White Male Bashing?" In *Practicing What We Teach: Confronting Diversity in Teacher Education,* edited by R. J. Martin, 79–94. Albany: State University of New York Press.

Bakhtin, M. M. 1981. *The Dialogic Imagination: Four Essays,* translated by C. Emerson and M. Holquist, edited by M. Holquist. Austin: University of Texas Press.

Baldwin, J. 1985. "A Talk to Teachers." In *The Graywolf Annual Five: Multicultural Literacy,* edited by R. Simonson and S. Waler, 3–12. St. Paul, Minn.: Graywolf Press.

Berlak, A. 1994. "Antiracist Pedagogy in a College Classroom: Mutual Recognition and a Logic of Paradox." In *Inside Out: Contemporary Critical Perspectives in Education,* edited by R. A. Martusewicz and W. M. Reynolds, 37–60. New York: St. Martin's Press.

Bhabha, H. K. 1994. *The Location of Culture.* London: Routledge.

Bigelow, B. 1991. "Discovering Columbus, Re-reading the Past." In *Rethinking Columbus,* edited by B. Bigelow, L. Christensen, S. Karp, B. Miner and B. Petersen, 6–9. Milwaukee, Wisc.: Rethinking Schools.

Bloom, L. R. 1998. *Under the Sign of Hope: Feminist Methodology and Narrative Interpretation.* Albany: State University of New York Press.

Books, S., ed. 1998. *Invisible Children in the Society and Its Schools*. Mahwah, N.J.: Lawrence Erlbaum.

Boyle-Baise, L. 1995. "Teaching Social Studies from a Multicultural Perspective." In *Developing Multicultural Teacher Education Curricula*, edited by J. M. Larkin and C. E. Sleeter, 159–70. Albany: State University of New York Press.

Britzman, D. P. 1991. *Practice Makes Practice: A Critical Study of Learning to Teach*. Albany: State University of New York Press.

———. 1995. "Is There a Queer Pedagogy? Or, Stop Reading Straight." *Educational Theory* 45, no. 2: 151–65.

Britzman, D. P., K. Santiago-Valles, G. Jimenez-Munoz, and L. M. Lamash. 1993. "Slips That Show and Tell: Fashioning Multiculture as a Problem of Representation." In *Race, Identity, and Representation in Education*, edited by C. McCarthy and W. Crichlow, 188–200. New York: Routledge.

Carlson, D. L. 1995. "Constructing the Margins of Multicultural Education and Curriculum Settlements." *Curriculum Inquiry* 25, no. 4: 407–31.

Christensen, L. 1994. "Unlearning the Myths That Bind Us: Critiquing Fairy Tales and Films." In *Rethinking Our Classrooms: Teaching for Equity and Justice*, B. Bigelow, L. Christensen, S. Karp, B. Miner, and B. Petersen, 8–13. Milwaukee: Rethinking Schools.

Code, L. 1991. *What Can She Know? Feminist Theory and the Construction of Knowledge*. Ithaca, N.Y.: Cornell University Press.

Collins, P. H. 1998. *Fighting Words: Black Women and the Search for Justice*. Minneapolis: University of Minnesota Press.

Dalton, M. 1995. "The Hollywood Curriculum: Who is the "Good" Teacher?" *Curriculum Studies* 3, no. 1: 23–44.

De Castell, S. and Walker, T. 1991. "Identity, Metamorphosis, and Ethnographic Research: What 'Kind' of Story Is *Ways with Words*?" *Anthropology and Education Quarterly* 22, no. 1: 3–20.

Donald, J., and Rattansi, A., eds. 1992. *"Race," Culture and Difference*. Newbury Park, Calif: Sage.

Ellsworth, E. 1992. "Why Doesn't This Feel Empowering? Working through the Repressive Myths of Critical Pedagogy." In *Feminisms and Critical Pedagogy*, edited by C. Luke and J. Gore, 90–119. New York: Routledge.

Farber, P., E. F. Provenzo, and G. Holm, eds. 1994. *Schooling in the Light of Popular Culture*. Albany: State University of New York Press.

Feagin, J. R., and H. Vera. 1995. *White Racism: The Basics*. New York: Routledge.

Frankenberg, R. 1993. *White Women, Race Matters: The Social Construction of Whiteness*. Minneapolis: University of Minnesota Press.

Fraser, N. 1995. "From Redistribution to Recognition? Dilemmas of Justice in a 'Post-socialist' Age." *New Left Review* 212: 68–93.

Freire, P. 1970. *Pedagogy of the Oppressed*, translated by M. B. Ramos. New York: Continuum.

Giroux, H. A. 1996. *Fugitive Cultures: Race, Violence, and Youth*. New York: Routledge.

Gordon, A. F. 1997. *Ghostly Matters: Haunting and the Sociological Imagination*. Minneapolis: University of Minnesota Press.

Greene, M. 1995. *Releasing the Imagination: Essays on Education, the Arts, and Social Change*. San Francisco: Jossey-Bass.

Grossberg, L. 1994. "Introduction: Bringin' It All Back Home—Pedagogy and Cultural Studies." In *Between Borders: Pedagogy and the Politics of Cultural Studies*, edited by H. A. Giroux and P. McLaren, 1–25. New York: Routledge.

Haraway, D. 1989. *Primate Visions: Gender, Race, and Nature in the World of Modern Science*. New York: Routledge.

Heath, S. B. 1983. *Ways with Words: Language, Life, and Work in Communities and Classrooms*. New York: Cambridge University Press.

Henriques, J. 1984. "Social Psychology and the Politics of Racism." In *Changing the Subject: Psychology, Social Regulation and Subjectivity*, edited by J. Henriques, W. Hollway, C. Urwin, C. Venn, and V. Walkerdine, 60–89. London: Methuen.

Henriques, J., W. Hollway, C. Urwin, C. Venn, and V. Walkerdine, eds. 1984. *Changing the Subject: Psychology, Social Regulation and Subjectivity.* London: Methuen.

Hoffman, D. M. 1996. "Culture and Self in Multicultural Education: Reflections on Discourse, Text, and Practice." *American Educational Research Journal* 33, no. 3: 545–69.

Holquist, M. 1990. *Dialogism: Bakhtin and His World.* New York: Routledge.

hooks, b. 1993. "Transformative Pedagogy and Multiculturalism." In *Freedom's Plow: Teaching in the Multicultural Classroom,* edited by T. Perry and J. W. Fraser, 91–97. New York: Routledge.

Ladson-Billings, G. 1995. "Multicultural Teacher Education: Research, Practice, and Policy." In *Handbook of Research on Multicultural Education,* edited by J. A. Banks and C. A. McGee Banks, 747–59. New York: Macmillan.

Lesko, N., and L. R. Bloom. 1998. "Close Encounters: Truth, Experience and Interpretation in Multicultural Teacher Education." *Journal of Curriculum Studies* 30, no. 4: 375–95.

Maher, F. 1991. "Gender, Reflexivity and Teacher Education: The Wheaton Program." In *Issues and Practices in Inquiry-oriented Teacher Education,* edited by B. R. Tabachnick and K. Zeichner, 22–34. London: Falmer Press.

McCarthy, C. 1993. "After the Canon: Knowledge and Ideological Representation in the Multicultural Discourse on Curriculum Reform." In *Race, Identity, and Representation in Education,* edited by C. McCarthy and W. Crichlow, 289–305. New York: Routledge.

McCarthy, C., A. Rodriguez, S. Meecham, S. David, C. Wilson-Brown, H. Godina, K. Supryia, and E. Buendia. 1997. "Race, Suburban Resentment, and the Representation of the Inner City in Contemporary Film and Television." In *Off White,* edited by M. Fine, L. Powell, L. Weis, and M. Wong, 229–41. New York: Routledge.

McIntosh, P. 1988. "Unpacking the Invisible Knapsack of White Privilege." Unpublished paper, Wellesley Center for Research on Women, Wellesley, Mass.

Minnich, E. K. 1994. "'Prisoners of Hope': Even When We Have Tried to Go Further Than It Turns Out We Yet Can, We Have Not Simply Failed." *NWSA Journal* 6, no. 2: 299–307.

Mohan, R. 1995. "Dodging the Crossfire: Questions for Postcolonial Pedagogy." In *Order and Partialities: Theory, Pedagogy and the "Post-colonial,"* edited by K. Myrsiades and J. McGuire, 261–84. Albany: State University of New York Press.

Ogbu, J. U. 1987. "Variability in Minority School Performance: A Problem in Search of an Explanation." *Anthropology and Education Quarterly* 18, no. 4: 312–34.

Rattansi, A. 1992. "Changing the Subject? Racism, Culture, and Education." In *"Race," Culture and Difference,* edited by J. Donald and A. Rattansi, 11–48. Newbury Park, Calif.: Sage.

Rist, R. C. 1970. "Student Social Class and Teacher Expectations: The Self-fulfilling Prophecy in Ghetto Education." *Harvard Educational Review* 40, no. 3: 411–51.

Roman, L. 1993. "'On the Ground' with Antiracist Pedagogy and Raymond Williams' Unfinished Project to Articulate a Socially Transformative Critical Realism." In *Views Beyond the Border Country: Raymond Williams and Cultural Politics,* edited by D. L. Dworkin and L. G. Roman, 158–214. New York: Routledge.

Rothenberg, P. 1994. "Rural U: A Cautionary Tale." *NWSA Journal* 6, no. 2: 291–98.

Schoem, D. 1991. *Inside Separate Worlds: Life Stories of Young Blacks, Jews, and Latinos.* Ann Arbor: University of Michigan Press.

Scott, J. W. 1990. "Deconstructing Equality-versus-Difference; or, The Uses of Post-structuralist Theory for Feminism." In *Conflicts in Feminism,* edited by M. Hirsch and E. Fox Keller, 134–48. New York: Routledge.

———. 1992. "Experience." In *Feminists Theorize the Political,* edited by J. Butler and J. W. Scott, 22–40. New York: Routledge.

Sleeter, C. E. 1994. "Multicultural Education, Social Positionality, and Whiteness." Paper presented at the annual meeting of the American Educational Research Association, New Orleans.

——— 1995a. "White Preservice Students and Multicultural Education Coursework." In *Developing Multicultural Teacher Education Curricula,* edited by J. M. Larkin and C. E. Sleeter, 17–30. Albany: State University of New York Press.

————. 1995b. "An Analysis of the Critiques of Multicultural Education." In *Handbook of Research on Multicultural Education,* edited by J. A. Banks and C. A. McGee Banks, 81–94. New York: Macmillan.

Tatum, B. 1994. "Teaching White Students about Racism: The Search for White Allies and the Restoration of Hope." *Teachers College Record* 95, no. 4: 462–76.

Watkins, W. H. 1994. "Multicultural Education: Toward a Historical and Political Inquiry." *Educational Theory* 44, no. 1: 99–117.

Weber, S., and C. Mitchell. 1995. *"That's Funny, You Don't Look Like a Teacher!" Interrogating Images and Identity in Popular Culture.* London: Falmer Press.

Weiler, K. 1991. "Freire and a Feminist Pedagogy of Difference." *Harvard Educational Review* 61, no. 4: 449–74.

Whitson, J. A. 1988. "The Politics of 'Non-political' Curriculum: Heteroglossia and the Discourse of 'Choice' and 'Effectiveness.'" In *Contemporary Curriculum Discourses,* edited by W. F. Pinar, 279–330. Scottsdale, Ariz.: Gorsuch Searisbrick.

Whitson, J. A. 1991. "Post-structuralist Pedagogy as Counter-hegemonic Praxis (Can We Find the Baby in the Bathwater?)." *Education and Society* 9, no. 1: 73–86.

Young, R. 1990. *White Mythologies: Writing History and the West.* London: Routledge.

Zeichner, K. 1996. "Educating Teachers for Cultural Diversity." In *Currents of Reform in Preservice Teacher Education,* edited by K. Zeichner, S. Melnick and M. L. Gomez, 133–75. New York: Teachers College Press.

14

HYBRID DISCOURSE PRACTICES
AND THE PRODUCTION OF
CLASSROOM (MULTI)CULTURES

George Kamberelis
Purdue University

In this chapter, I construct a sketch of how hybrid discourse practices can function within quotidian classroom activities to exert powerful positive effects on students' thinking, social development, and critical consciousness by helping them fuse authoritative and internally persuasive discourses (Bakhtin 1981). That these practices and effects are important for moving beyond paternalistic, imperialistic, and "it's-a-small-world-after-all" forms of multiculturalism has been demonstrated by critical social and cultural theorists of (e.g., Appadurai 1996; Bakhtin 1986; Bhabha 1994; McCarthy 1998; Soja 1996; Volosinov 1973; Zizek 1999).

Mikhail Bakhtin celebrated the counterhegemonic potential of the interanimation of different character and narrator discourses (and their attendant ideologies) in the novel. It is but a minor shift to imagine how the interanimation of heterogeneous voices over the course of an episode of literature, science, or history discussions could similarly result in counterhegemonic pedagogy that could produce emancipatory classroom (multi)cultures.

In the sections that follow, I first outline the theoretical framework that informs my empirical work on the production and effects of hybrid discourse practices for constructing classroom (multi)cultures. Next, I outline an analytic framework for understanding the forms and functions of hybrid discourse practices. Then I illustrate how hybrid discourse practices actually function in classrooms by discussing two different examples of this discursive phenomenon. In the first example, I demonstrate how one African-American fourth grade teacher enacted and allowed children to enact hybrid discourse practices to help build linkages between the culturally familiar discourses of their homes, peer groups, and communities and the culturally distant discourses of literary interpretation.

In the second example, I show how two fifth-grade children melded popular registers and genres with scientific ones as they slowly and tentatively built "scientist identities."

In my analyses of these two examples, I highlight (a) the ways in which various speech genres were laminated onto one another; (b) how these laminations were constitutively related to shifts in the registers and participation structures of discourse; and (c) what pedagogical effects seemed to result from these various laminations and shifts. I show how many of these laminations involved the disruption of fairly traditional discourse patterns (e.g., initiation-response-evaluation sequences, lectures, laboratory talk and practice) with more dynamic forms of talk and social interaction. I also discuss the consequences these disruptions seemed to have for student participation and learning.

THEORETICAL INTRODUCTION: HYBRIDITY AND HYBRID DISCOURSE PRACTICES

Largely because they are rooted in essentialist and standpoint epistemologies and presume pragmatic short-term outcomes, much theory and research on multiculturalism has focused on the "democratic" cohabitation of "intact" cultural formations. Although in some ways a noble goal, it is incompatible with the hybrid character of most cultural formations in the United States today. To understand multiculturalism and to generate less hegemonic multicultural practices in American schools thus requires theories of culture and of discursive practice that foreground hybridity and its effects.

Although hybridity (and thus discursive hybridity) is a buzzword in contemporary educational discourse, few scholars or practitioners have explicitly explained how it may function as a resource for learning and teaching. More specifically, few examples exist in the literature on effective teaching and learning that describe or explain the strategic use of discursive hybridity to reconceive and deploy cultural artifacts, participation structures, and pedagogical activities to produce new and more productive forms of classroom learning.

My understanding of hybridity derives primarily from work in several disparate domains, including postcolonial feminist studies, cultural studies, and Mikhail Bakhtin's translinguistics. From these perspectives, the ideas of the person and of knowledge shift from semifixed, autonomous essences to polysemic sites of articulation for multiple subjectivities and knowledges continually achieved in relation with other subjectivities and knowledges through discursive and material practices.

Gloria Anzaldúa (1987) refers to such sites of articulation as *mestiza* sites (an Aztec word meaning "torn between ways"), and she argues that individual and collective selves are "product[s] of the transfer of the cultural and spiritual values of one group to another. Cradled in one culture, sandwiched between two cultures, straddling all three cultures and their value systems, *la mestiza* undergoes a struggle of flesh, a struggle of borders, an inner war" (78). Such individuals and collectives are constantly engaged in inner wars because they have taken up and are taken up within incommensurable social/cultural spaces. In a similar though not identical move, Homi K. Bhabha (1994) uses the term "cultural hybrid" to describe the process of reinscription and relocation that emerges out of being "in-between a plurality of practices that are different yet must occupy the same space of adjudication and articulation" (57). Joining the chorus, Laurence Grossberg (1992) claims that, in this in-between space, "the subaltern is different from the identifications on either side of the border but they are not simply the fragments of both" (3). Stuart Hall (1990) refers to this general problematic by the term "diaspora identities," and he characterizes them as constantly producing and reproducing themselves anew through their responses to difference and opposition and by means of their idiosyncratic appropriation of available narratives and material practices. Similarly, Donna Haraway (1991) coined the term "cyborg identities" to refer to what she sees as individual and collective identities constituted in and through the fusion of multiple-outsider (or partial-outsider) identities. Similarly, Cameron McCarthy (1990, 1998) has argued convincingly for viewing identities as "nonsynchronous," constituted through complex laminations of diverse and dynamic vectors of cultural and social positioning (e.g., social class, race, gender, ethnicity, regionality, language use, sexual orientation, and so on).

Foregrounding issues of power and its relation to knowledge even more overtly, Linda Alcoff (1988) and other theorists have used the construct of "positioning" to construe identity. According to this perspective, raced, classed, or gendered identities involve positioning oneself at the intersection of various identity axes within a changing historical context of identity markers. Being black, Latina, working class, or a woman (or various combinations of these and other social categories), for example, is to take up a position within a moving historical context, to choose how to interpret this position, and to imagine how to alter the context that made such positioning available in the first place. This way of thinking about identity seems to avoid reducing agency to the intentions of a homunculus while also escaping antihumanist assaults on the very notion of agency by reconceptualizing identity as the activity of positioning oneself within (and against) existing social and cultural networks and ideologies. Instead, identities are recognized as multiple, complex, porous, and shifting sets of positionings, attachments, and identifications through which individuals and collectives understand who they are and how they are expected to act across a range of diverse social and cultural landscapes (Hall 1996).

Whereas Anzaldúa, Alcoff, Bhabha, Grossberg, Hall, Haraway, and McCarthy have discussed hybridity primarily in relation to individual (and sometimes collective) social identities, others have focused more directly on the concept of culture. Renato Rosaldo (1989), for example, has argued that culture should be viewed in terms appropriate to the current world—a world marked by increasing globalization, cultural dynamism, and social heterogeneity. In such a world, cultures are perhaps best conceived *not* as essentialized and bounded spaces but as complex sites constituted by multiple interactions and flows among material and cultural artifacts including speech styles, social norms and values, and aesthetic tastes. Deploying this basic binary, Rosaldo contrasted traditional approaches to culture with postmodern approaches. He used the metaphor of the art museum to describe traditional approaches to culture. According to this metaphor, cultures are stable entities to be preserved for all time in their original form. In contrast, Rosaldo used the metaphor of the garage sale to describe postmodern approaches to culture. According to this metaphor, cultures are continually changing as "cultural artifacts flow between unlikely places, and nothing is sacred, permanent, or sealed off" (44). African-American youth culture, which incorporates tropes from blues, jazz, hip-hop, Christianity, Islam, family lore, cultural history, U.S. advertising culture, Latino culture, and many other social formations and cultural traditions, is a key example of a postmodern cultural formation. To understand the cultures of many U.S. classrooms, which are constituted by many such hybrid cultural formations, further requires interrogating the interactions and flows that occur among them. Relevant artifacts of exchange within these flows would include the discourse practices from all of these cultures, especially the discourse practices that are emblematic indicators of cultural identity within each of them (Ferdman 1990).

Focusing more on the productive historical trajectories of language in use, Bakhtin argues that to understand actual language and its effects we must view the various languages used in any interaction in terms of each other and their self-organizing interactions, the ways in which they are "hybridized" so that an "interminable" dialogue is created among them. Such hybridization "demands an enormous effort: it is stylized through and through, thoroughly [strategic]. . . . This is what distinguishes it from the frivolous, mindless, and unsystematic mixing of languages . . . characteristic of mediocre prose writers [and much everyday conversation]. In such hybrids, there is no joining together of consistent language systems, merely a random combination of brute elements out of which languages are made" (Bakhtin 1981, 366). Central to Bakhtin's conception of hybridized discourse is its strategic nature. It is not code-switching for code-switching's sake or style-switching for style-switching's sake. Rather, it is the strategic deployment of the resources from different discursive worlds to forge new codes and to achieve new and richer forms of intersubjectivity and shared understanding.

Discursive hybridization, then, is a dynamic, strategic, and self-organizing communicative practice that involves the layering of two or more discourse styles and/or speech genres onto one another within a given speech event or stretch of discourse. For example, a teacher may laminate a personal narrative onto an ongoing initiation-response-evaluation (I-R-E) sequence in order to drive home a key point. Similarly, a physicist may laminate a dramatic performance of subatomic movement where she plays the character, if you will, of a subatomic particle in order to demonstrate or make more accessible the meaning of abstract equations (Ochs, Gonzalez, and Jacoby 1994).

When such laminations occur, they also invoke changes in the participant roles of the discourse—or who gets to talk, to whom, from what perspective, in what circumstances, and for what purposes. For example, if a teacher laminates a dramatic performance onto an I-R-E sequence focusing on vocabulary acquisition, she has also reconfigured her role (from didact to entertainer), as well as her personal/social relationships with her students (from more formal to more intimate). She has also expanded the range of participant roles available to students. They become ratified as more dialogic participants (not just listeners and responders), and they are ratified to "pitch in" contributions of their own.

Besides causing shifts in participant roles, hybrid discourse practices also cause shifts in the registers or social languages that occur within social interactions. For example, one teacher with whom I have worked ventriloquated the social language of the judiciary in the context of staging and managing a mock trial of the O. J. Simpson case. These shifts functioned to link disparate and sometimes competing worlds of meaning and practice, expanding both the semantic and pragmatic potential of these worlds.

Let me expand upon why hybrid discourse practices might be important for understanding classroom discourse and learning. First, hybrid discourse practices function to foreground, amplify, and clarify the *meanings* of discourse. Foregrounding, amplification, and clarification are all central to good teaching and learning processes. Thus, hybrid discourse practices may be a particularly productive pedagogical tactics. Second, hybrid discourse practices function to rekey discursive practices and meanings in contextualized, playful, ironic, parodic, or analogic ways, all of which have been shown to contribute to learning (e.g., Booth 1974; Duranti and Goodwin 1992; Forman, Minick, and Stone 1993; hooks 1994; Lakoff and Johnson 1980; Lave and Wenger 1991; Rosaldo 1989; Tedlock and Mannheim 1995; Vygotsky 1978; Zizek 1999). A third function of hybrid discourse practices is to forge relations of affirmation or negation between and among multiple social discourses and identities. The foregrounding of such relations facilitates the development of metalevel understandings of the concepts and meanings under study. It also allows children to "try on" new social identities or inhabit new subject positions. Such experimentation with or tentative grasping of discourse roles within multiple communities of practice is central to learning and the development of expertise. That this is the case has been supported by recent work on "signifying practices" in classrooms (e.g., Jeffries 1994; Kamberelis and de la Luna 1996; Lee 1993). This general idea has also been supported by recent work on cultural identity (Appadurai 1996; Bhabha 1994; Conquergood 1991; Grossberg 1992, 1998; Spivak 1988).

Hybrid Discourse Practices and Classroom Research: Loosening the Lid of the I-R-E

As many researchers of classroom discourse have argued (e.g., Cazden 1998; Hicks 1995; Luke 1995), the analysis of classroom talk needs to pay much more attention to the discursive and social practices within which texts are produced, distributed, and consumed. In this regard, the presumed homogeneity of classroom discourse implicit in the ubiquitous initiation-response-evaluation (I-R-E) speech genre has recently collapsed under the weight of research that has shown the wide range of heteroglossic registers, speech events, and speech genres that occur and interact in classrooms (e.g., Gee 1996; Gutiérrez 1993; Kamberelis 1998; Kamberelis and de la Luna 1996; Wells 1993). This research has demonstrated how linkages among various discourses and practices affect teaching/ learning processes in productive ways. For example, Wells (1993) shows how the I-R-E is reconfigured to accomplish a number of different classroom functions depending upon the tasks and goals at hand. If one expands the notion of the I-R-E to include all forms of triadic discourse as Wells has done, then this genre can be viewed as encompassing a wide range of quite heteroglossic "speech activities" (Gumperz 1982). Although the basic structure of the I-R-E may be reasonably consistent across activities, its functions may vary considerably. Several researchers (e.g., Hicks 1995; Longo 1994; Wells 1993) have pointed out that the I-R-E as the "unmarked case" of classroom discourse often coexists with other genres or forms of talk associated with inquiry-based learning, open discussion, popular understanding, and even carnivalistic interactions.

As Norman Fairclough (1992) has argued, when you look really closely at classrooms or at texts, much of the discourse you see there is "bumpy discourse" that reflects the juxtaposition of discourses from different social and cultural worlds. It is common, for example, for these juxtapositions to include the more formal institutional discourses of science or social studies or literary criticism with more personal and informal discourses from experience, the media, and various local cultures, including youth culture. Such "bumpy" heterogeneity may be especially common among younger students. It may also be particularly prevalent in classrooms inhabited by children whose community-based discourses differ significantly from formal institutional discourses. And it may be particularly prominent in classrooms constituted at the intersections of multiple axes of diversity. Additionally, it may be that teachers can laminate various discourses within single classroom events in ways that bring them into productive dialogue that has noticeable effects both on children's learning and their abilities to analyze and criticize the very notion of discourse practice itself.

ANALYTIC TOOLS FOR STUDYING HYBRID DISCOURSE PRACTICES

Many analytic constructs are useful for understanding the forms and functions of hybrid discourse practices. The ones most useful for my particular purposes in this chapter include speech genres, registers (or social languages), and footings. Each of these constructs is outlined briefly in the sections that follow.

Speech Genres

Bakhtin (1986) defined speech genres as discursive forms that organize utterances into coherent ensembles of structures and practices. A speech genre "is not a form of language, but a typical form of utterance; as such the genre also includes a typical kind of expression that adheres in it. . . . [Speech] genres correspond to typical situations of speech communication, typical themes, and consequently, also to particular contacts between the *meanings* of words and actual concrete reality under certain typical circumstances" (87).

Bakhtin goes on to argue that all utterances are constructed not from individual words but from speech genres. "We speak only in definite speech genres, that is, all our utterances have definite and relatively stable typical *forms of construction of the whole*. Our repertoire of oral (and written) speech genres is rich. We use them confidently and skillfully *in practice*, and it is quite possible for us not even to suspect their existence *in theory*" (78). Although Bakhtin posits speech genres as the fundamental templates and building blocks of discourse, he is careful not to represent them as static or ossified structures, but ones that are continually reconstituted within new contexts and in the hands of new users. "A genre lives in the present," he notes, "but always remembers its past" (1984, 104).

As such, genres are historically and ideologically saturated "aggregate[s] of the means for seeing and conceptualizing reality" (Bakhtin and Medvedev 1985, 137). Genres are indexical, signaling the ideologies, norms, values, and social ontologies of the communities of practice in which they typically function. Indeed, it is central to Bakhtin's theory of genres that the thematic and stylistic construction of texts embody ideological values rooted in sociocultural-historical contexts (Bakhtin and Medvedev 1985, 21). No elements of texts are pure form; they also populate the texts with ideological intentions or value orientations. In the appropriation of genres, then, people also appropriate these ideologies as obvious and familiar, as horizons against which their actions and the actions of others make sense.

Bakhtin's discussion of how speech genres mediate identity practices and the social discourses within which they are embedded provides a powerful framework for describing the particular discursive practices through which people construct their social knowledges and identities. Such a theoretical framework helps demonstrate precisely how young people take up certain subject positions through the enactment of certain speech genres. Central here is an examination of the typified forms of discourse (i.e., speech genres) that people deploy when responding to others or to tasks. This articulation of speech and event provides insights into what kinds of knowledges are enabled (and constrained) by what kinds of discursive practices and frames, as well as what kind of frames are familiar and/or preferred for understanding and talking about what kind of experiences.

Registers

Registers (or social languages) are stretches of discourse and configurations of meaning that are typically associated with particular social contexts or domains of practice (Bakhtin 1986; Gee 1996; Halliday and Hasan 1989; Wertsch 1991). According to Halliday and Hasan (1989), registers are comprised of particular configurations of field, tenor, and mode. *Field* refers to the topic of the discourse, or what is happening in and through the discourse. *Tenor* refers to who is taking part in the discourse, including their personal relationships, role statuses, attitudes toward each other, and so on. *Mode* refers to the role language is playing in the discourse, including the semiotic organization of the discourse, its medium of exchange, and its function in the context in which it occurs.

Registers vary in relation to speech genres in fairly systematic ways. For example, "legalese" permeates briefs, closing statements, and the courtroom activity of lawyers. All speech and discourse communities have their own quasi-unique registers that index particular social contexts and function to construct particular kinds of social identities. These identities are implicitly signaled by the verbal and nonverbal behaviors of people who invoke the registers.

Footings: Production Formats and Participation Frameworks

Erving Goffman was interested in how language indexed and constituted social alignments and positions between people. This interest was most clearly expressed in his notion of *footing*, which is "the alignment we take up to ourselves and others present as expressed in the way we manage the production or reception of an utterance. A change in our footing is another way of talking about a change in our *frame* for events" (1974, 128). A good example of a change in footing is when a parent is playing with a child but begins reprimanding him or her when things get a bit rough or something is broken. Another example is Bateson's (1972) nip that becomes a bite when the interactional frame between primates shifts from play to fighting.

Goffman's notions of frames and footings suggest the need to examine the multiple roles played by speakers and hearers, and how roles shifts have constitutive effects on the dynamics of the discourse situation itself. As he struggled to understand how footings were enacted and negotiated, Goffman questioned certain assumptions about conversation as calculated turn taking enacted by felicitous and egalitarian partners. In this regard, he saw the need to rethink the notions of speaker and hearer. For example, he argued that the notion of the *speaker* is far too simple to capture what actually happens in real-time discourse. To problematize the notion of the speaker, he suggested that this construct be reenvisioned as a "production format," which includes the roles of *author, animator, principal*, and *figure*. An *author* is a person or party who constructs the message; an *animator* is a person or party who delivers the message; a *principal* is a person or party whose interests are represented in the message; a *figure* is a person or party that is the topic of the message. A given individual or collective can, in principle, function in one, two, three, or all four of these roles. However, many instances of talk divide these roles. Together, the author, the animator, the principal, and the figure constitute an analytic matrix for understanding how the production of messages is a complexly organized set of practices with multiple roles and relations.

To problematize the folk-linguistic model of the *hearer*, Goffman called attention to the fact that most talk has multiple participants, which he called a "participation framework." Within any participation framework there often exist multiple participants, only some of whom are message targets. For example, there are both addressed and nonaddressed participants. Addressed participants are those who are expected to attend to messages. Nonaddressed participants are those who are official hearers but whom the speaker is not addressing directly. There are also ratified participants and nonratified participants. Ratified participants are those actually addressed by the speaker both verbally and visually, some of whom may be expected to respond. Nonratified participants are those for whom messages are not intended but who may hear them anyway (e.g., those who overhear, eavesdroppers, even bystanders who simply witness the talk).

According to Goffman's theory of footings, talk no longer flows through a single conduit connecting speaker and hearer. Multiple threads of talk may crisscross on a complex verbal/visual landscape. For example, there may be *by-play*, which is nonfocal talk between ratified participants. There may also be *cross-play*, which is nonfocal talk between ratified and nonratified participants and bystanders. And there may be *side-play*, which is nonratified talk between bystanders or eavesdroppers.

By situating talk in particular social activities and roles, Goffman moved beyond the linguistic model of the speaker-hearer dyad, replacing it with a complexly textured communication situation involving multiple and often simultaneous forms of participation in talk. Imagining the ways talk is subordinated to activity in many situations (e.g., medical examinations, service encounters, mechanics diagnosing and repairing an engine), Goffman concluded that the unit of analysis needed for understanding talk is situated social activity rather than a narrower notion like speech act or speech event.

KEY EXAMPLES OF THE FORMS AND FUNCTIONS OF HYBRID DISCOURSE PRACTICES

Lotto Luck: "I Better Play 5-0-3"

The first example of hybrid discourse practices that I will analyze and discuss comes from a year-long classroom ethnography that I conducted in a culturally and economically diverse fourth-grade classroom. This example was initiated by an African-American fourth grade teacher (whom I will refer to as Mrs. D) during a classroom literacy event. During this event, Mrs. D laminated a personal experience narrative onto children's struggling attempts to define the vocabulary word *fortune*. Important for my larger argument is the fact that this act was embedded within a complex literacy event that was constituted in and through the situationally generated juxtaposition of at least eighteen basic speech genres within less than ten minutes of classroom interaction. This literacy event was the first event that occurred in relation to a short story entitled *A Sign in Mendel's Window*. The transcript of the event is 527 lines long. Before analyzing in detail one of the most crucial instances of discourse hybridization that occurred within this event, I will briefly outline the speech genre shifts that occurred during the entire event.

This speech event began as a teacher monologue on previewing strategies (1). Previewing then gave way to an I-R-E on word attack skills (2). This was followed by another I-R-E on previewing strategies (3). Then Mrs. D initiated a round-robin reading of the story (4). After one child read the first sentence of the story—"They called Kosnov a town"—she initiated another I-R-E on finding main ideas (5). This I-R-E gave way to another I-R-E on analogic relations when a student (Brenda) pointed out the author's use of analogy (6). This I-R-E was followed by more round-robin reading (7), onto which was laminated a long I-R-E on the meaning of the word *town* and the ideas of community and community cohesion (8). This was followed by more round-robin reading (9), onto which Mrs. D laminated a teacher monologue on summarizing strategies and their relation to identifying main ideas (10). This was followed by more round-robin reading (11), onto which Mrs. D enacted the most crucial lamination of the whole literacy event, her "good fortune" story (12), which I unpack in greater detail below. An I-R-E on the meaning of the term *good fortune* was then laminated onto this story (13). This was followed by an I-R-E on the definition of the word *butcher* (14), onto which was quickly laminated a lively and comical monologue/performance about meat processing and distribution (15). From this, Mrs. D segued seamlessly to an I-R-E on the significance of the "For Rent" sign in Mendel's window (16). Next, she initiated a discussion of key vocabulary words relevant to describing the characters in the story (17). The event ended with an I-R-E in which children predicted what would happen next in the story (18).

As I mentioned, the most crucial lamination in this literacy event occurred when Mrs. D told her "good fortune" story. This lamination, along with several that surrounded it, are displayed below. Each major speech genre shift is indicated by bold typeface. All transcription conventions appear in the appendix that follows this essay.

> T: **O.K., so imagine this.** = Now we know that this story's gonna be about this very important sign because it was mentioned in the title. {And the first thing that happens} One of the most important things that happens with that sign is what? Summarize. (0.5) We *know* we got to focus in on that *sign*, it was mentioned in the *title*. We *know* we have to concentrate on what happens with that sign. What Mendel *does*. Because he's a main character. = His name's mentioned in the title as well. ((*Mrs. D strokes her chin.*)) (0.5) What do we focus in on? {What} What's the significance of the sign? = Summarize, Brenda. (?)
>
> Brenda: {The sign} Mendel put the sign in his window.
>
> T: You're teaching the class and we can't hear you. = If you're going to teach it, you have to speak louder.
>
> Brenda: Mendel put the sign in his window.
>
> T: . . . **Next sentence, please.**
>
> Lauren: "Had (10.0)" ((*Some children begin mumbling in the background. They seem to be trying to help Lauren out. Mrs. D waits for about 10 seconds before she tries to help.*))
>
> T: F, O, R, do you know that word?
>
> Lauren: /For/ /toon/. (1.0)

T: Say it again, sweetheart.

Lauren: /For/ /toon/.

T: O.K., now, for-toon, that's a good guess. "Had for-toon." Can someone on your
team help you figure out what that word

[

Ss: (XXX). *((Kids on her team try to help Lauren decode the word "fortune."))*

[

T: means.

Student: Fortune?

T: Fortune = "Had fortune . . ."

Lauren: " . . . come knocking on their door."

T: O.K., what is fortune? (2.0) Usually fortunes are *good*. What is good fortune? (2.5)
= **I almost had good fortune.** (1.0) I played 5-0-3, my old address, for the lotto
last night. = It was 5-0-*2*. = Darn it. *((Mrs. D frowns and snaps her fingers.))* *Fifty
cents.* = I could've had *two hundred dollars.* Good fortune. = I wanted to have
good fortune. = What does that mean? *((Several students mumble inaudible
responses.))* But I didn't have good fortune. *((One student has his hand raised,
but Mrs. D does not call on him.))* (0.5) And I don't play often, but I kept seeing
5-0-3, 5-0-3, 5-0-3, an' I thought, "that's my old address where I grew up. = I
better play 5-0-3." **What does good fortune mean?** = Good fortune? *((Mrs. D
asks this question in a very soft voice. A woman walks into the room and Mrs. D.
interrupts her questioning to greet her.))* Good morning, Dr. B. How are you?

[

Dr. B: Good morning.

S: Good fortune? *((It is unclear whether this student directs this question to herself or
has assumed Mrs. D's role.))*

T: Terra? *((Student comments on visitor's very nice clothes. Teacher answers, "Oh, yes,
always." Mrs. D and Dr. B both laugh.))*

Terra: To get a lot of money, perhaps.

T: To get a lot of money, perhaps. That's one example of good fortune. = What else
could be good fortune? *((Teacher raises her index finger indicating that they've
come up with one example so far.))* Give me other examples. (2.0) Now we're giving examples and from the examples, we should be able to come up with a
meaning. Tommy?

Tony: Good luck.

T: Good luck? Uh-huh. Good luck. Give me an *example* though (1.0). {Lots} Getting
lots of money would be good luck, good fortune. = I didn't get that money. =
Didn't have that good fortune. Jamal?

Just prior to telling this story, Lauren had been struggling to read the word
fortune. Mrs. D and several children at Lauren's table scaffolded her attempts
to sound out the word. With this help, Lauren arrived at the correct pronuncia-
tion and completed the sentence she was reading. Then Mrs. D asked the question, "O.K., what is fortune?" Ii is important to note that this was not a genuine

question but a *signal* that a story or lecture was to follow. This form of signaling was extremely common in Mrs. D's classroom, and the children were so used to it that they seldom raised their hands to bid for speaking turns. As it turns out, a past-event personal narrative followed.

The shift from round-robin reading and I-R-E to personal storytelling was also marked by a change in the teacher's register, and an analysis of register (i.e., field, tenor, and mode) contributes to understanding the structure and function of this hybridization. The *field* shifted from that of formal schooling to that of conversational storytelling. The focus of talk thus shifted from understanding the meanings of words and text on their own terms to how these meanings fit into the wider worlds of personal experiences and social relations. Mrs. D used the experience of almost having "good fortune" to anchor the text world of the folktale in the familiar world of everyday life.

As Mrs. D began her story, the *tenor* of discourse also shifted. Her role status as an authority figure and knowledgeable expert gave way to the role status of a raconteur with personal experience relevant to the meanings of the literary text. Whereas the students had been positioned as readers, listeners, and ratified respondents before Mrs. D began her story, they were now authorized to be more active participants in the event and to participate in it, truly or vicariously.

Finally, the *mode* of discourse also shifted when the story was introduced. The paradigmatic I-R-E mode was suspended or displaced by the narrative mode. There were several linguistic indicators of this shift. In the I-R-E mode, language functions to package information efficiently both for consumption and assessment. Its primary features include question-answer adjacency pairs, logical connections between propositions, evaluative comments, and a discipline-based lexicon. In the narrative mode, language functions to affect an audience both rhetorically and aesthetically. Its features include a more conversational lexicon, the temporal sequencing of events, reported speech, more body language, faster-paced prosody, and various tropes such as repetition, imagery, and metaphor. Indeed, many of these features entered the discourse of this speech event as soon as Mrs. D began to tell her good fortune story. For example, her speech style became rapid, lively, and conversational. She repeated the numbers of her old street address five times. She reported her own past speech. And she punctuated her speech with animated gestures. Not surprisingly, this complex constellation of changes that constituted Mrs. D's register shift had the effect of increasing her audience's interest and attention.

With shifts in speech genre and register also came shifts in participants' footings or the "participation framework" and the "production format" of the ongoing discourse. Although the "rim" of the discourse frame remained the same—that is, participants were still talking about a particular literary text—the "innermost activity" of the frame shifted from a recitation script to personal storytelling/audiencing, and the "involvement" (Tannen 1989) of all participants thickened and became more complex. Prior to the introduction of the good fortune story, Mrs. D or various children functioned almost exclusively as animators of the basal story or the teacher's manual. They were neither the authors, nor the principals, nor the figures of either of these texts. When Mrs. D laminated her good fortune story onto round-robin reading and a recitation script, however, the production format of discourse was altered significantly. Mrs. D immediately became not only the animator but also the author, the principal, and the figure of discourse. That she assumed these roles was marked linguistically by first-person pronouns and reports of her own past speech. Note, for example, that she said, "an' I thought, 'that's my old address where I grew up. I better play 5-0-3.'" That she became the principal of discourse is further reinforced by her preceding statement, "And I don't play often," which betrays her sense that playing the lottery is frivolous and not something that she does routinely.

With changes in the production format of discourse came changes in its participation framework. As I already mentioned, Mrs. D's lamination of a past event narrative onto the recitation script of classroom interaction escalated the students' interests and attention. Indeed, much more "by-play" occurred during Mrs. D's story than had gone on before. Some of this "by-play" involved children's own stories of good fortune. Several children also raised their hands, hoping to contribute some stories of their own. Although they were never nominated to hold the floor officially in this instance, on other occasions Mrs. D often welcomed such personal contributions. This resulted in the construction of a palimpsest of mutually reinforcing contextualization cues relevant to the comprehension and analysis tasks at hand. Additionally, this creation of multiple layers of context for anchoring word meanings and text meanings often led to further discussion both within and outside the "official world" of classroom learning. For example, later in the day, several children "signified" on Mrs. D's good fortune narrative by telling their own good fortune narratives during lunch and recess. As they did so, each story became more elaborate and more compelling than the one it followed, and many stories were linked back to *A Sign in Mendel's Window* and to Mrs. D's good fortune story. In their ongoing efforts to exploit the tensions between the authoritative discourses of text and classroom and the internally persuasive discourses (Bakhtin 1981) of their own lives, children continued to construct their knowledge of vocabulary and text meaning far beyond the bounds of the language arts activity in which the tension began.

Kids Just Gotta Have Fun: "Pass the Scalpel"

The discourse example that I will analyze next comes from a yearlong classroom ethnography that I conducted in a culturally and economically diverse fifth-grade classroom led by a European-American teacher whom I will refer to as Ms. G. The example occurred within an interaction between two boys in the context of a biology activity. The biology unit of which this activity was a part focused on the characteristics, habits, and habitats of owls. The specific activity in question was a laboratory exercise in which children dissected "owl pellets" and reconstructed the skeletons of the animals contained within them. The unit began with children viewing an educational video, *Ecology and the Barn Owl*, which provided an abundance of information about the physical features and habits of the barn owl, including a long section on owl pellets. Ms. G followed up this video with a discussion of the scientific method, relevant informational texts that children could use as resources for the unit, and an introduction to the owl pellet dissection activity. For the next three weeks, children worked largely on dissecting their pellets, reconstructing the skeletons therein, and writing reports on barn owls that included a section on their digestive habits and a section on their personal response to their dissecting experience.

During the viewing of the video, students were active audience members, often oohing and aahing at what they saw. At the end of the video, Ms. G asked students questions based on the video (e.g., What is an owl pellet? Is it dirty?) in a fairly typical I-R-E fashion. She then explained that the students would be dissecting owl pellets. They became increasingly active. Several side conversations broke out around the room. A few students made faces that mimicked what a barn owl looks like as it readies itself to purge a pellet. What appeared chaotic at first blush was actually highly productive anticipatory activity for the work that would follow. Ms. G paired up students for the dissection activity. Kyle and Ezekiel—whose interactions I will analyze—were paired as a team. The teacher then had students line up to receive their dissection trays and tools. Kyle's desk was the closest one in the room to where the trays were, but several other students got in line in front of him. Ezekiel became frustrated and yelled at him. What follows is a transcript of the beginning of Kyle and Ezekiel's dissecting work together.

> *((Kyle seems oblivious to Ezekiel yelling at him. He walks back to his desk slowly. He holds up the tray and inspects it from different angles. He sets the tray down on his desk.))*
> Kyle: I'll be the researcher and you be my assistant, O.K.?
> Ezekiel: O.K., Doctor.
> Kyle: Scalpel. *((He extends his hand.))*
> Ezekiel: Scalpel. *((He places scalpel in hand.))*
> Kyle: Heh heh, this smells like my dentist, heh heh, heh heh. *((apparently impersonating Beavis of the* Beavis and Butthead *TV show))*
> Ezekiel: You're weird, Beavis. *((apparently impersonating Butthead))*
> Kyle: Oh, look, I see something.
> Ezekiel: Cool, what is it?
> [
> Kyle: Yeah, I think I've got something.
> Ezekiel: Be careful not to hit a vein.
> [
> Rachel: What have you guys got? *((She is not part of their group but has wandered over to see what they found.))*
> Ezekiel: Bones. Lots of bones ha ha ha ha ha! *((He sounds like a mad scientist.))*
> Rachel: We've got lots of bones too.
> Ezekiel: So go back to your table and do your own stuff. I'm assisting a great doctor and don't want to be disturbed.

Kyle: I think we got a skull, Ezekiel.

Ezekiel: Yeah, that's a skull alright.

Kyle: I'm going in. *((He then makes a sound as if he were using a saw or similar tool.))*

Ezekiel: Cool.

Kyle: I could easily crush these bones. *((He enacts a kind of Arnold Schwarzenegger voice.))*

((This comment refers back to a warning given by the teacher earlier, "Be gentle. Don't slam with your tools like this. Don't pull too hard with your tweezers 'cause you'll break the bones. And the skull is the most fragile part." About a minute passes during which both students barely speak. They seem incredibly focused, and when they do talk, they utter barely audible sounds of concentration [e.g., hmm, umph]. During this time, the two exchange tools and Ezekiel takes on the role of dissector [but not doctor, as will be shown below].))

Ezekiel: Jenga, jenga, jenga. *((As he carefully uses the scalpel, Ezekiel provides commentary on his own actions that come from the television advertisement for the children's game Jenga, which requires exceptional manual dexterity.))*

Eric: What are you guys doing?

Kyle: I'm the doctor, and he's my assistant.

Eric: Cool.

Ezekiel: Beam me up, Scottie. I've got something new to show you. I think it's a hip bone. *((enacting his best Scottish accent))*

Kyle: You got it all wrong, Scottie is the one with the accent. Dr. McCoy has a dry voice.

Ezekiel: Oh. Well, let's get back to work. Let's see what this belongs to. *((Kyle and Ezekiel go to consult a classroom poster of rodent skeletons in an attempt to determine what animal the bone belonged to.))*

Ezekiel: I think it's a field mouse.

Kyle: Nah, it looks like a vole.

Ezekiel: I don't think so.

Kyle: Who's the real surgeon here?

Ezekiel: Oh yeah, I forgot. *((Interestingly, he flashes my assistant what seems to be an ironic gesture of collusive solidarity.))*

During this short snippet of interaction, a long segment of which involved relatively silent concentrated work, at least nineteen speech genres or speech genre fragments were laminated onto one another. The interaction began with a veiled command and consensual reply (1). This was followed by a snippet of surgical discourse similar to that which occurs on medical television programs such as *ER* (2). This surgical discourse gave way to a locally situated *Beavis and Butthead* reenactment (3). This reenactment was disrupted when Kyle thought that he has made an important scientific discovery (4), and it was followed by a medley of hybrid discourse that combined science talk (5) with surgery discourse (6) with interruptions from a nonratified party (7) with "mad scientist" talk (8) with a response to the intrusive nonratified party (9) with more surgical talk (10) with a task-related Arnold Schwarzenegger–like comment (11). A bit later in the interaction, Ezekiel engaged in self-regulatory talk derived from a television commercial (12). This was interrupted by a question from another bystander (13), which was followed by an explanation (14). Then Ezekiel initiated a task-related *Star Trek* dialogue to report the important discovery of a hip bone (15). This was followed by a clarification statement (16), which gave way to a debate about the kind of animal the bone belonged to (17). The debate ended with a conversational exchange when Kyle "pulled rank," claiming authority because he was, after all, the surgeon and Ezekiel was but a mere assistant (18). In what appears on the surface of things to be a concession, Ezekiel closed the interaction with an ironic gesture of solidarity and affirmation to my research assistant, thus disrupting the "play frame" they had maintained all along (19).

These shifts across multiple speech acts, speech genres, and speech genre fragments were accompanied by register shifts (i.e., shifts in the field, tenor, and mode of discourse). For example, the field shifted back and forth across surgery and the operating room, popular television, and conversation. The tenor of the interaction was fairly consistent with Kyle inhabiting a subject position of greater power and prestige than Ezekiel. This was indexed, for example, by Ezekiel's utterance, "I'm assisting a great doctor and don't want to be disturbed." As an aside, their relationship in this interaction was consistent with their relationship in other activities. Moreover, Kyle typically commanded more social prestige in the classroom than Ezekiel. Although consistent, however, the tenor of the relationship between these two boys was unstable and fragile. This was indexed in a variety of ways including Ezekiel's comment, "You're weird, Beavis," Ezekiel's performance of surgery even while in the official role of assistant, and Ezekiel's ironic sidelong glance at my assistant. Nevertheless, these disruptions were often sutured over, and Kyle was typically repositioned as the more powerful and more knowledgeable of the two. His demonstration of expert knowledge with respect to *Star Trek* characters and his response to Eric about being the "doctor" are examples of this repositioning.

What are the footings of the participants in this interaction and how do they shift? During most of the surgical discourse segments and popular media segments, Kyle and Ezekiel seemed to be animators and principals but not really the authors of their discourse. Additionally, they tended to function as both addressed and ratified participants for each other. Kyle and Ezekiel also seemed to be the figures of their discourse, even though they referred to each other with fictional appellations (e.g., Doctor, Beavis). Although their words came from elsewhere, they adequately marked their intense involvement in the coordinated activity of dissecting and their commitment to the task. They appropriated discourse from popular sources, but they reanimated it to express their scientific identities and task commitments.

Importantly, Kyle and Ezekiel's alignment toward each other and with respect to the task involved the productive use of power. In bringing popular surgical discourse to bear on their science "work," they were able to manage and control the scientific activity in which they were engaged in ways that they could not were they merely "being themselves." That this was the case is suggested by the fact that Kyle and Ezekiel seemed to inhabit all positions of the production format toward the end of this transcribed segment when they inhabited the roles of classroom scientists and argued about the identity of the hip bone they had found. Finally, Kyle and Ezekiel also seemed to become authors, principals, and figures when they addressed nonratified participants. What is important is that their investments in the doctor and assistant subject positions became less playful and more overdetermined when they were drawn into cross-play with these nonratified persons. Testimony to this fact was Ezekiel's command, "So go back to your table and do your own stuff. I'm assisting a great doctor and don't want to be disturbed." Among other things, this suggests that framing their dissecting activity as surgery allowed them to inhabit subject positions that were familiar, that were close cousins of the target subject position of "scientist" demanded of the task, and that moved them toward increased familiarity and competence with thinking, being, acting, and talking science. However, framing their positions as surgeon and surgeon's assistant seemed to make it difficult to maintain an equal distribution of their productive use of power through discourse hybridization. In general, the circulation of power flowed toward Kyle more than it flowed toward Ezekiel. This pattern was both reinforced and disrupted by the boys in a variety of ways. For example, it was reinforced when Ezekiel publicly maintained that he was "assisting a great doctor." It was also reinforced by Kyle when he "pulled rank" and said, "Who's the real surgeon here?" In contrast, this pattern of circulation was disrupted when Ezekiel interpellated Kyle into the role of Beavis, when he did the actual work of surgery while maintaining the role of assistant, and when he undercut Kyle's authority by casting an ironic sidelong glance at my assistant. This pattern was also disrupted by Kyle when he broke from his surgeon frame and slid into his Beavis frame. In all of these examples and many others in the corpus of data, these reinforcements and disruptions of participant alignments were accomplished by shifts in speech genres and registers (social languages). All of these various shifts had visible effects on the levels of engagement experienced by the students, the kinds and amounts of active learning that occurred, and the circulation of power within the interactions. These various changes, in turn, had significant effects on how children positioned themselves and were positioned by others in future classroom events. For example, early in the year, Kyle's artsy antics were read as a sign of his "oddness" and contributed to his status as an "outsider" to most social and cooperative learning groups. Later in the year, these same antics were read as a sign of his rich knowledge of popular culture and his creative genius, and he was often enlisted as an "insider" and valuable resource in academic and social activities. Also important here were changes in Ms. G's stance toward children's hybrid discourse practices throughout the year and its concomitant effects on children's subject positionings. Early in the year, she tended to silence discursive voyages into popular cultural terrain. As the year progressed, however, she allowed and even encouraged such voyages. When I called her attention to this change, she told me that she had come to realize not only that the children's hybrid discourse practices were often productively task-related but also that they allowed children to "show off" their knowledge, creativity, and prowess. She also mentioned that, for some children, allowing their investments in popular culture to become part of classroom life opened up opportunities for "social acceptance" and "social growth."

DISCUSSION

There are several reasons why these analyses of hybrid discourse practices are important for understanding the productive possibilities of hybridized discourse for producing and sustaining classroom (multi)cultures. First, hybrid discourse practices are potentially powerful learning and teaching tactics because they amplify and contextualize the meanings of the materials and tasks at hand. Hybrid discourse practices are often deployed when children are either having trouble understanding a meaning or a task or when they seem disengaged, and they are often effective in solving these problems. For example, when children were dissecting their owl pellets, hybrid discourse practices seemed to help build important bridges between familiar knowledges, practices, and identities and less familiar scientific ones. Similarly, Mrs. D's hybrid discourse practices seemed to facilitate children's attempts to read more strategically and to acquire knowledge about literary analysis.

A second reason why hybrid discourse practices are important for understanding the possibilities of classroom learning and community building is that they seem to disrupt traditional power relations and passive forms of student participation—both between student and teacher and between more knowledgeable/powerful and less knowledgeable/powerful peers. In both examples that I analyzed, hybrid discourse practices resulted in a communicative context that was more conversational and less hierarchically structured. For example, even as he remained in the official role of the surgeon's assistant, Ezekiel was empowered to do the work of surgery as evidenced by his ironic glance at my assistant. Similarly, many children were afforded more and more varied forms of participation in the discussion of *A Sign in Mendel's Window* after Mrs. D told her good fortune story. They interrupted her more, their speech overlapped more, and they had more side conversations. Thus, hybrid discourse practices seems to create what Bhabha (1994); Gutiérrez (1993); Gutiérrez, Baquedano-López, and Alvarez 1998); and Soja (1996) have referred to as a "third space," a space wherein the productive power of social heteroglossia allows for productive disruptions of the more static scripts that both teachers and students bring to classroom events and try to maintain or enforce.

Although this notion of a "third space" has both transformative potential and explanatory power, it also has some inherent problems. More specifically, it seems to overdetermine the negative dimensions of control and facilitation by teachers or more experienced student peers, the positive dimensions of student resistance, and the idea that it is always good to wrest power from teachers or more experienced peers and to decenter more recitative modes of interaction. Evidence from the work I have presented here suggests that the "third space" need not be constituted solely out of conflict between teachers and the students' incommensurable scripts or agendas. It also suggests that the enactment of more controlled modes of interaction can be productive and even *critical* at times, and that an interaction between more and less controlled modes of interaction may be most productive. Explanations of improvisation in jazz often follow a similar logic. For example, "[j]azz innovator Miles Davis is known to have told band members: 'You need to know your horn, know the chords, know all the tunes. Then you forget about all that and just play'" (Sanjek 1990, 411). The creative integration of elements and forms in both jazz and classroom discourse requires both intimate knowledge of relevant cultural tools and a highly differentiated sense of traditional forms. Without having mastered these requirements, it is difficult, if not impossible, to "just play."

Contemporary U.S. classrooms are incredibly complex (multi)cultures that are continually reconstituted in the interactions and flows among multiple discourses, various participation structures, and self-organizing chains of utterances and actions. Within such (multi)cultures, classroom discourses are intertextually dense and locally situated accomplishments. Teaching in such contexts poses serious new challenges, and meeting these challenges may require revisioning pedagogical practice as an improvisational enterprise that necessarily involves moving in and out of more didactic and more dialogic modes of interaction and constructing heterogeneous discourses through the interanimation of speech genres, registers, production formats, and participation frameworks from diverse social contexts.

More important, then, than asking what the *best* forms of social interaction in classrooms are or who should *own* them is asking how and why certain forms of talk and social interaction are deployed, in what situations, for what purposes, and with what effects. In this regard, Mrs. D often initiated voyages into the "third space" on her own, with quite powerful effects. She also allowed or encouraged the "underlife" activity of the classroom to produce new forms of knowledge and social interaction. Sometimes children took over the interactional space of the classroom and she "went with it," capitalizing on their knowledge, enthusiasm, and energy, not worrying about forging links back to the official tasks at hand. She also reined in lively interactions when the children strayed too far from their ostensible topic or ceased being productively engaged. Similar patterns occurred in the peer interactions. Indeed, the short snippet of dialogue between Kyle and Ezekiel that I analyzed is an example of situated self-organizing activity in which more calculated and more improvisational moves interacted, and in which there was a collusion of serious play that integrated transgression, irony, and parody.

A third reason why hybrid discourse practices are important is that they seem to help children forge productive linkages between the sometimes contradictory worlds of school and everyday life. These linkages help them simultaneously to make sense of the new and deconstruct/reinterpret the familiar. Put another way, and building upon Carol Lee's (1993) work on "signifying," hybrid discourse practices help children forge productive linkages between strategies for constructing personal relevance and strategies for distanciated critical analysis. Forging such reciprocal linkages is extremely important. It is not enough for teachers simply to help children connect with knowledge and texts personally. In fact, children can do that pretty well on their own. Nor is it enough simply to teach interpretive and critical skills and strategies. Both are required, and to do both requires constructing "fictional equations" between everyday and disciplinary/professional knowledges, practices, and identities. James Gee (1996) coined the term "mushfake" to refer to such equations, and he argued that "mushfake" provides children with at least some insight into how certain forms of discourse carry with them certain forms of cultural and symbolic capital in particular contexts while others do not. Perhaps more important is that these equations do not discount the validity of children's everyday discourses and practices. Rather, through their participation in classroom talk and interaction, children are allowed to construct utterances, acts, literacies, and identities that fuse everyday modes of appropriating and repopulating the structures and meanings of texts with more school-based modes. This fusion may be a necessary condition for the production of internally persuasive (Bakhtin 1981) classroom (multi)cultures.

In this regard, it seemed that the hybridized discourse of Kyle and Ezekiel—which combined science talk, popularized surgical talk, and Beavis and Butthead–speak with other tropes from popular culture—helped them increasingly to inhabit the physical and conceptual space of biological research and writing. This example of discourse hybridization thus signals the importance both of irony as a learning trope and of taking seriously children's intense investments in the discourses and practices of popular culture and youth culture.

Mrs. D's various acts of discourse hybridization also seemed to accomplish the dual goals of helping children personally connect with relatively new and unfamiliar knowledge and discourse and develop critical analytic skills relevant to literary interpretation. These connections were often facilitated by invoking and exploiting various tropes of popular culture and youth culture. In the "good fortune" story, for example, she drew children into her personal narrative about playing the state lottery both to help them understand a particular vocabulary word and to help them develop more encompassing strategies of deriving meaning from context. Contextualized as they were in popular culture and everyday life, these new knowledges and strategies helped children probe more deeply into the meanings and significance of the text they were reading. As indexed by the hybrid discourse practices of Kyle and Ezekiel, Mrs. D's discourse hybridization signals the need to take children's investments in popular culture and youth culture very seriously when negotiating internally persuasive classroom (multi)cultures.

To summarize my conclusions, the examples of hybrid discourse practices that I analyzed were particularly effective in facilitating children's ability to deploy familiar knowledges and skills from everyday life to learn the knowledges and skills requisite for competence in various disciplinary domains of practice. More generally, within various actions and interactions constituted by hybrid discourse practices, children either "took up" or were imaginatively and materially interpellated into subject positions that had previously perhaps lain beyond both their "lived" and their "imagined" landscapes for self. In deploying tropes from their home cultures and from youth cultures, the children constructed imaginative and dramatistic worlds of meaning that flowed into and interacted with the worlds of meaning indexed by the texts they were reading or writing.

Before closing I would also like to note some of the implications that this research on hybrid discourse practices has for understanding classroom (multi)-cultures. Too much classroom research has slavishly applied received analytic frameworks to map and explain student learning and teacher-student interactions. One result of this has been the overdetermination of structural dimensions of classroom life and a certain blindness to more self-organizing dimensions. The examples that I have shared suggest that teaching and learning are simultaneously systematic and unpredictable. They are constructed in the interplay of structure and improvisation because classrooms are incredibly complex, dynamic, and heterogeneous social spaces that are continuously constituted and reconstituted in the interplay of centripetal and centrifugal forces.

If, instead of superimposing received analytics onto classroom interactions, we begin to view classroom interactions more genealogically (Foucault 1977) or more rhizomatically (Deleuze and Guattari 1987), then we might begin to see them not as prefigured and linear but as complex, multivalent, and partially self-organizing. More important, we might begin to "see" the creative and pedagogically productive possibilities inherent in the intermingling of heterogeneous discourses within "literature discussions," "science talk," "history reenactments," and so on. Hybridized discourse practices are often divergent (and/or convergent) paths to the construction of academic knowledge rather than evidence that individual children *do not* possess any. This means that more serious inquiry is required to understand how hybridized discourse practices constitute classroom cultures and what counts as "school knowledge" in the late twentieth century. Knowledge generated from such inquiry should help teachers negotiate classroom interactions in ways that allow children from diverse backgrounds more opportunities for successfully and comfortably participating in formal, institutional discourses (e.g., Gutiérrez, Baquedano-López, and Alvarez 1998; Ladson-Billings 1992; Lee 1993; Willet, Solsken, and Wilson-Keenan 1998).

Re-visioning hybrid discourse practices as discursive sites for change wherein "cultural artifacts flow between unlikely places, and nothing is sacred, permanent, or sealed off" (Rosaldo 1989, 44) bears a strong family resemblance to what Michel de Certeau (1984) called "the art of making do." In describing what he meant by this term, de Certeau made a useful distinction between "places" and "spaces." Places, according to de Certeau, define or delimit fields of activity and are governed by principles of proper usage. In contrast, spaces result from the productive transformation of places. Composed of self-organizing interactions among various elements, spaces are realized by the ensemble of activities deployed within them. For example, city parks in the United States, which were originally places defined by urban planning for strolling and perhaps playing softball, are commonly transformed into spaces by various groups of immigrants who construct temporary makeshift soccer fields in them or claim them as sites for ethnic festivities. Similarly, certain discursive spaces may be produced by appropriating and subverting the meanings and functions of discourses and texts (places constituted by systems of signs). For example, with an eye toward their own liberation, many African-American slaves learned to read by secretly engaging with written texts designed by whites to perpetuate their oppression. As Henry Louis Gates, Jr., so aptly put it, "the first slave to read was the first to run away" (1988, x). Such forms of "reading" constituted acts of "spatial practice" that entailed decolonizing discourses and texts, for the purposes of black people, by overlaying new meanings on discourses and texts that already had—and retained—certain meanings of their own. In general, spatial practices generate hybrid discourses in which the uppermost inscriptions provide commentaries on the ones beneath them, with each inscription enriching the meaning(s) of the others. These complex laminations function to reconfigure traditional or mainstream resources to serve the needs and goals of people and groups for whom those resources were neither developed nor intended. Revising exclusive traditions through spatial practices often makes them more inclusive.

In this regard, a particularly useful consequence of de Certeau's understanding of the relations between places and spaces is that it disrupts the distinction between authentic and inauthentic. At the same time, it avoids prefiguring the nature and tempo of the spatial practices of particular places (e.g., using parks, reading texts, talking in classrooms). A written text or a social interaction may be spatially practiced in many ways, in multiple directions, and for many purposes. By definition, no single discourse practice can correspond to a "proper" use of a discursive place, and there are no exemplary uses of such places. Rather, discourse acts as means of transportation (*metaphorai*) in the shuttling that constantly transforms places into spaces and spaces into places. In this regard, hybrid discourse practices are particularly efficient and powerful vehicles for "rearticulating the real" (Deleuze and Guattari 1987).

REFERENCES

Alcoff, L. 1988. "Cultural Feminism versus Post-structuralism: The Identity Crisis in Feminist Theory." *Signs: Journal of Women and Culture* 13, no. 3: 405–36.
Anzaldúa, G. 1987. *Borderlands/La Frontera: The New Mestiza*. San Francisco: Spinsters/Aunt Lute.
Appadurai, A. 1996. *Modernity at Large: Cultural Dimensions of Globalization*. Minneapolis: University of Minnesota Press.
Bakhtin, M. M. 1981. *The Dialogic Imagination,* translated by C. Emerson and M. Holquist. Austin: University of Texas Press.
———. 1984. *Problems of Dostoevsky's Poetics,* edited and translated by C. Emerson and M. Holquist. Minneapolis: University of Minnesota Press.
———. 1986. *Speech Genres and Other Late Essays,* translated by V. W. McGee. Austin: University of Texas Press.

Bakhtin, M. M., and P. N. Medvedev. 1985. *The Formal Method in Literary Scholarship: A Critical Introduction to Sociological Poetics,* translated by A. J. Werhle. Cambridge, Mass.: Harvard University Press.

Bateson, G. 1972. *Steps to an Ecology of Mind.* New York: Ballantine.

Bhabha, H. K. 1994. *The Location of Culture.* London: Routledge.

Booth, W. 1974. *A Rhetoric of Irony.* Chicago: University of Chicago Press.

Cazden, C. 1998. *Future Directions for the Study of Classroom Discourse: A Conversation with Courtney Cazden.* Panel presented at the annual meeting of the American Educational Research Association, San Diego.

Conquergood, D. 1991. "Rethinking Ethnography: Towards a Critical Cultural Politics." *Communication Monographs* 58: 179–94.

de Certeau, M. 1984. *The Practice of Everyday Life,* translated by S. Rendall. Berkeley and Los Angeles: University of California Press.

Deleuze, G., and F. Guattari. 1987. *A Thousand Plateaus: Capitalism and Schizophrenia,* translated by B. Massumi. Minneapolis: University of Minnesota Press.

Duranti, A., and C. Goodwin, eds. 1992. *Rethinking Context: Language as an Interactive Phenomenon.* Cambridge: Cambridge University Press.

Fairclough, N. 1992. *Discourse and Social Change.* Cambridge: Polity Press.

Ferdman, B. M. 1990. "Literacy and Cultural Identity." *Harvard Educational Review* 60, no. 2: 181–204.

Forman, E. A., N. Minick, and C. Stone, eds. 1993. *Contexts for Learning: Sociocultural Dynamics in Children's Development.* Oxford: Oxford University Press.

Foucault, M. 1977. *Discipline and Punish: The Birth of the Prison,* translated by A. M. Sheridan-Smith. Harmondsworth, England: Penguin.

Gates, H. L. Jr. 1988. *The Signifying Monkey: A Theory of African-American Literary Criticism.* New York: Oxford University Press.

Gee, J. P. 1996. *Social Linguistics and Literacies: Ideology in Discourses,* 2d ed. London: Taylor and Francis.

Goffman, E. 1974. *Frame Analysis.* New York: Harper and Row.

Grossberg, L. 1992. *We Gotta Get Out of This Place: Popular Conservatism and Postmodern Culture.* New York: Routledge.

———. 1998. *Identity and Cultural Studies: Is That All There Is?* Unpublished manuscript, University of North Carolina at Chapel Hill.

Gumperz, J. J. 1982. *Discourse Strategies.* Cambridge: Cambridge University Press.

Gutiérrez, K. D. 1993. "How Talk, Context, and Script Shape Contexts for Learning: A Cross-case Comparison of Journal Sharing." *Linguistics and Education,* 5, no. 3/4: 335–66.

Gutiérrez, K. D., P. Baquedano-López, and H. H. Alvarez. 1998. "Language Practices: The Radical Middle in the Third Space." Paper presented at the annual meeting of the American Educational Research Association, San Diego.

Hall, S. 1990. "Cultural Identity and Diaspora." In *Identity: Community, Culture, Difference,* edited by J. Rutherford, 222–37. London: Lawrence and Wishart.

———. 1996. "Who Needs 'Identity'?" In *Questions of Cultural Identity,* edited by S. Hall and P. du Gay, 1–17. London: Sage.

Halliday, M. A. K., and R. Hasan. 1989. *Language, Context, and Text.* Oxford: Oxford University Press.

Haraway, D. 1991. "A Cyborg Manifesto: Science, Technology, and Social Feminism in the Late Twentieth Century." In *Simians, Cyborgs, and Women: The Reinvention of Nature,* 149–81. London: Routledge.

Hicks, D. 1995. "Discourse, Learning, and Teaching." In *Review of Research in Education,* vol. 21, edited by M. W. Apple, 49–95. Washington, D.C.: American Educational Research Association.

hooks, b. 1994. *Teaching to Transgress: Education as the Practice of Freedom.* New York: Routledge.

Jeffries, R. B. 1994. "The Trickster Figure in African-American Teaching: Pre- and Postdesegregation." *Urban Review* 26: 289–304.

Kamberelis, G. 1998. "Children Talking Science: Productively Laminating Popular and Academic Speech Genres." Paper presented at the annual meeting of the American Educational Research Association, San Diego.

Kamberelis, G., and L. de la Luna. 1996. "Constructing Multiculturally Relevant Pedagogy: Signifying on the Basal." In *Forty-fifth Yearbook of the National Reading Conference,* edited by D. J. Leu, C. K. Kinzer, and K. A. Hinchman, 329–44. Chicago: National Reading Conference.

Ladson-Billings, G. 1994. *The Dreamkeepers: Successful Teachers of African American Children.* San Francisco: Jossey-Bass.

Lakoff, G., and M. Johnson. 1980. *Metaphors We Live By.* Chicago: University of Chicago Press.

Lave, J., and E. Wenger. 1991. *Situated Learning: Legitimate Peripheral Participation.* Cambridge: Cambridge University Press.

Lee, C. D. 1993. *Signifying as a Scaffold for Literary Interpretation.* Urbana, Ill.: National Council of Teachers of English.

Longo, D. 1994. "The Dialogic Process of Becoming a Problem Solver: A Sociolinguistic Analysis of Implementing the NCTM Standards." Paper presented at the Ethnography of Education Research Forum, University of Pennsylvania, Philadelphia.

Luke, A. 1995. "Text and Discourse in Education: An Introduction to Critical Discourse Analysis." In *Review of Research in Education,* vol. 21, edited by M. W. Apple, 3–48. Washington, D.C.: American Educational Research Association.

McCarthy, C. 1990. *Race and Curriculum.* London: Falmer Press.

———. 1998. *The Uses of Culture: Education and the Limits of Ethnic Affiliation.* London: Routledge.

Ochs, E., P. Gonzales, and S. Jacoby. 1994. "'When I Come Down, I'm in the Domain State': Grammar and Graphic Representation in the Interpretive Activity of Physicists." Paper presented at the Third Annual Crisis of Text Symposium, San Diego.

Rosaldo, R. 1989. *Culture and Truth: The Remaking of Social Analysis.* Boston: Beacon Press.

Sanjek, R. 1990. "On Ethnographic Validity." In *Fieldnotes: The Making of Anthropology,* edited by R. Sanjek, 385–418. Ithaca, N.Y.: Cornell University Press.

Soja, E. W. 1996. *Thirdspace: Journeys to Los Angeles and Other Real-and-Imagined Places.* Oxford: Blackwell.

Spivak, G. C. 1988. "Can the Subaltern Speak?" In *Marxism and the Interpretation of Culture,* edited by C. Nelson and L. Grossberg, 272–313. Urbana: University of Illinois Press.

Tannen, D. 1989. *Talking Voices: Repetition, Dialogue, and Imagery in Conversational Discourse.* Cambridge: Cambridge University Press.

Tedlock, D., and B. Mannheim. 1995. *The Dialogic Emergence of Culture.* Urbana: University of Illinois Press.

Volosinov, V. N. 1973. *Marxism and the Philosophy of Language,* translated by L. Matejka and I. R. Titunik. Cambridge, Mass.: Harvard University Press.

Vygotsgy, L. S. 1978. *Mind in Society: The Development of Higher Psychological Processes.* Cambridge, Mass.: Harvard University Press.

Wells, G. 1993. "Reevaluating the I-R-F Sequence: A Proposal for the Articulation of Theories of Activity and Discourse for the Analysis of Teaching and Learning in the Classroom." *Linguistics and Education* 5: 1–37.

Wertsch, J. V. 1991. *Voices of the Mind: A Sociocultural Approach to Mediated Action.* Cambridge, Mass.: Harvard University Press.

Willet, J., J. Solsken, and J. Wilson-Keenan. 1998. "Constructing Hybrid Language Practices During Family Visits in an Elementary Classroom." Paper presented at the annual meeting of the American Educational Research Association, San Diego.

Zizek, S. 1999. *The Zizek Reader,* edited by E. Wright and E. L. Wright. Oxford: Blackwell.

Appendix: Transcription Key

T indicates teacher
S(s) indicates unidentified student or students
Boldface indicates major speech genre shift
underline marks emphatic stress
CAPS mark very emphatic stress
: indicates a lengthened vowel sound (extra colons indicate greater lengthening)
(X) indicates a word that was inaudible and could not be transcribed (extra Xs indicate additional words)
((italicized double parentheses)) contain contextualizing commentary
{brackets} indicate a false start
= indicates utterances latched on to one another without perceptible pauses
[Left square bracket between lines indicates overlapping speech

15

REAPING THE
HARVEST OF SHAME

Racism and Teaching in a Time of
Radical Economic Insecurity

(Lessons from a High School Mass Media Course)

Glenn M. Hudak

Pace University

INTRODUCTION

What can be more important for high school students than the study of popular media such as TV, film, and photography? For students are submerged in a sea of media images and representations that frame, to a growing extent, their conceptions of self and society. Yet schooling in general remains silent with regard to student media experiences. Media theorist Todd Gitlin writes (1985) that "the presence of the media is such that we don't reflect on the meanings or study them; we swim in them.... We swim in its world even if we don't believe in it" (333). Within this context, the important question to ask is not, What are the media doing to adolescents? but rather, What are adolescents doing with the media? Indeed, research indicates that most students have an active rather than a passive relationship with the media. Far from accepting what is offered to them wholesale, most make discriminating judgments, selecting those elements that speak to them and rejecting those that do not.

The point is that students (and teachers) appropriate and incorporate selective media discourses into their conception of self and society. Popular media (TV, film, and radio) are part of the students' personal knowledge of the world; furthermore, it is possible to claim that they are literate with regard to popular media. Students actively decode the symbolic world in which they are immersed.

It is legitimate to wonder how they (and teachers) actually *use* media-related knowledge and skills within the classroom context.

At issue are the definitions of legitimate knowledge found in the classroom, and the power to legitimate one specific knowledge form over another. As such, the heart of the debate over media in schools lies in a number of issues revolving around the legitimacy of popular culture and the role of students' (and teachers') personal knowledge within the curricular context.

Within the classroom the curriculum is not a static body of knowledge predefined for student consumption. Instead, the knowledge found within the classroom "is produced in the process of interaction, between teacher and learner at the moment of classroom engagement" (Lusted 1986, 4–5). As such, our concerns must focus on how the interactions between student/teacher, within the historical context of the institution of school, produce an academic discourse, that is, a particular way of talking and thinking about media.

In an effort to capture the concrete material conditions that give rise to the formation of an academic discourse, this essay will reflect upon, reexamine, and extend with new material my previous research (see Hudak 1995) on the formation and politics of classroom knowledge as a mode of social knowing. To this end, this essay will revolve around a case study of the incidents occuring within the context of a single high school mass media course, particularly as they pertain to issues of race. Here my intent is to amplify and examine two complex microprocesses occurring within the classroom context:

In part 1, I will examine the micropolitics—those struggles and negotiations between teacher and students—in the formation of school knowledge. For, as Homi Bhabha argues, "negotiation is what politics is all about. And we are always negotiating even when we don't know we are negotiating: we are always negotiating in any situation of political oppression or antagonism" (1990, 216). Indeed, this study demonstrates that the social production of an academic discourse is not a smooth, monolithic process. Instead, an academic discourse is constituted through a struggle over whose knowledge is to be included (and excluded) in classroom discussions—that is, whose knowledge is deemed legitimate. Of importance then is my focus on relations of power in the formation of school knowledge, particularly in a situation (such as the mass media course) where multiple voices (i.e., teacher's and students') come together as a moment of technological interdisciplinarity in the concrete creation of an academic discipline.

In part 2, I will extend and reflect upon the case study in an effort to draw out implications and difficulties pertaining to the teaching of mass media to high school students. Here I want to highlight a classroom incident revolving around issues of race. The incident involves the classroom showing of the documentary film *Harvest of Shame*. After this film was shown, several students made racist comments. While the teacher acknowledged the racism of the student comments to me in private, it struck me as odd that he did not address (in some fashion) the students' comments publicly. Within the context of the study, then, I want to use these incidents to segue into the personal politics woven into the fabric of teacher motivations in the negotiation of classroom knowledge. Specifically, I want to draw our attention to the perceived *terror* felt by this teacher in confronting the issue of racism (and sexuality) in class, and explore further the possible reasons for his unwillingness to engage students. As such, I close by pointing out the tight connection between issues revolving around race, the ways in which "job security" frames teachers' decisions, and the moral courage needed to surmount existential, social, and economic barriers.

THE CASE STUDY

The setting for the study was a high school mass media course that was offered at a medium-sized school with a total enrollment of approximately 1,800. The high school was located in a city with a population of 250,000. The media course had an enrollment of twenty-four students, thirteen of whom were male and eleven female. No students of color were enrolled in the course. All students came from middle-income families, and about half anticipated enrolling at a university after graduation. The course was offered as an elective within the English department. Only high school juniors and seniors (eleventh and twelfth grades) were allowed to register for the course. There were no other formal prerequisites. Throughout the study the instructor is identified as "Mr. Albert" (a pseudonym).

In the conceptual orientation for this study, I define the learning process in terms of the formation of an academic discourse. Michel Foucault's (1981) discussion of the formation of discourse within the institutional setting provides an overall framework for the study. Here, the production of a discourse entails an actual *struggle* between two opposing forces. Generally speaking, this struggle is played out in terms of the institution versus the individual or group. The power of the institution resides in its ability to act in such a manner as to control, select, or organize knowledge. In essence, institutions tend to *contract* the parameters of legitimate knowledge by controlling access to, and the flow of, information. On the other hand, social forces exist that seek to be infinitely open, to *expand* the parameters of legitimate knowledge by including knowledge forms not officially sanctioned by established institutions. This tension between forces of expansion and contraction ultimately defines a set of rules that in turn give direction to a particular way of talking and thinking about a subject (i.e., a *discourse*).

To operationalize a Foucaultian model of discourse production, I translated the tension between forces of expansion and contraction into the tension created between internal (school) and external (student) knowledge. Based on data obtained and current research into classroom life, I found that the teacher in this study controlled classroom information. Essentially, the teacher acted as a force of contraction, but because of student familiarity with the media, I found that students attempted to include their opinions in the classroom discussion. That is, students acted to expand what could be said. Thus, a struggle between student and teacher emerged over whose knowledge would be discussed and considered legitimate.

The struggle between forces of contraction and expansion was described in terms of the boundary strengths between student and school knowledge. Here a "weak" boundary between internal (school) and external (student) knowledge meant that students were able to draw upon and use their knowledge during classroom discussions. In this instance, a weak boundary indicates that the parameters of legitimate knowledge had expanded to include student knowledge. On the other extreme, a strong boundary between internal and external knowledge means that student responses to teacher inquiries were restricted to information presented in class, and that students had limited access to their own knowledge. In this instance, a strong boundary indicates that the parameters of legitimate knowledge tended to contract, that is, to exclude student knowledge from classroom discussions regarding the media. The struggle that occurred was then between students' attempts to include their opinions in discussions and the teacher's attempts to control students by restricting their opinions. As we shall see, out of this struggle three rules were created that defined the learning process.

The data for the study was collected for the entire length of the course—a full semester, January through June. The course met five days a week for fifty minutes each day. The total contact time with members of the class was approximately 105 hours.

Material was organized by establishing a broad taxonomy of teacher approaches to the study of the media. During the course of the semester, data revealed that the teacher tacitly approached the media from three distinct knowledge orientations: common-sense, cultural, and technical orientations.

Common-Sense Orientation: An Incident to Set the Stage

The analysis of common-sense orientation revealed that the boundary strength between internal (school) and external (personal) knowledge was weak. This meant that in general discussions characteristic of this orientation, students were encouraged to draw from their own knowledge of the media. Mr. Albert, the teacher, asked students to state their opinions and to be open-minded when listening to the views of others. He stated that in general discussions there were no explicitly right or wrong answers and that each student was entitled to his opinion. Relatively speaking, students appeared to have enjoyed this discussion format for the following reasons: (a) given student familiarity with the media, they were able to give off-the-cuff answers; (b) the classroom discourse included student opinions and thus student knowledge was granted legitimate status; and (c) the legitimacy of student knowledge allowed the students to control some aspect of the classroom discourse by interjecting comments into the discussion.

However, by the second lesson an incident occurred that came to constitute the first prohibition on the classroom discourse. After the film *Why Man Creates* was shown, Mr. Albert initiated a discussion. In the midst of this discussion a student called out, "The film was dumb!" This comment was followed by a moment of silence in the classroom. Then other students voiced their dissatisfaction with the film. The agenda that Mr. Albert had planned for the lesson came to a sudden halt.

Mr. Albert's response to this student's comment was surprising, given the understanding that student opinion was to be honored. Mr. Albert silenced the class by publicly reprimanding the student. This incident tacitly led to the establishment of a rule (rule 1) for proper protocol during classroom discussion: students were not to challenge or question Mr. Albert's agenda. The reprimand of the student graphically conveyed to others that not all student comments were legitimate. Students could draw from their own experiences; they could state their opinions; however, they could not question or critique the material presented by Mr. Albert. The establishment of rule 1 essentially contracted the parameters of legitimate knowledge by prohibiting certain aspects of students' knowledge.

Cultural Orientation: An Incident Revolving around Sexuality

The cultural orientation was characterized as being a relational mode of knowing. Its logic is synthetic in that it attempts to bring together and synthesize the various dimensions of media practices through the integration of several academic disciplines. As the analysis revealed however, the promise of the cultural orientation was never realized in media course.

For example, during one lesson on the history of photography, the film *This Is Edward Steichen* was shown. The film revealed, among other aspects of Steichen's life, that his wife was a great deal younger than he was. After the film was shown, Mr. Albert attempted to discuss Steichen's perspective on photography. Students, however, had a different agenda in mind. They asked, "How could she kiss him?" As Mr. Albert attempted to refocus the discussion on Steichen's philosophy, students continued to talk among themselves about Steichen, the "dirty old man." This difference in interest led to a disruption of Mr. Albert's agenda, a disruption that students appeared to have enjoyed.

The disruption led to two further prohibitions (rules) on classroom practices. Tacit rule number 2 was that students were to direct their comments to Mr. Albert, and not to talk among themselves. As student collaboration increased the student's ability to include their comments into the discussion, it also increased student control over the discourse and reduced Mr. Albert's ability to control the agenda for the discussion session. Rule 2, then, sought to fragment student communication collaboration. If students could not talk among themselves, then it was possible to avoid further disruptions. Tacit rule number 3 was that students were to keep their comments "clean." Sexuality appeared to be one topic that brought students together and led to student disruptions of the agenda. By prohibiting the discussion of issues involving sexuality from the discourse, some of the impetus for collaboration could be reduced. Taken together, rules 2 and 3 continued to contract the parameters of legitimate knowledge by further limiting student behavior and increasing the strength of the boundary between internal and external knowledge.

In order to enact rules 2 and 3, Mr. Albert appeared to increase the tempo of discussions. Increased tempo transformed the character of the discussion sessions from a relatively informal format to question-and-answer sessions. In prior lessons, student responses to Mr. Albert were characterized as rambling off-the-cuff statements. Increased tempo limited the amount of time available for response. Hence, student responses were compressed and usually limited to a word or a short phrase. (For example, "When was the first photograph developed?" The response was "1848.") The result of increased tempo truncated the relational aspect of the cultural orientation. Students were not asked to reflect on the cultural social foundations of the media. Instead, the discourse was reduced to the identification of discrete facts. Rules 2 and 3 not only limited student actions and knowledge, but transformed the essential character of the cultural orientation by removing reflection and synthesis from the pedagogical process.

By the last lessons of the cultural orientation, parameters of legitimate classroom knowledge had contracted to such an extent that student knowledge had been virtually defined out of the discussion. As a result, the social relations between teacher and students deteriorated to the point where each responded to the other at times as adversaries. This gap between the teacher and students was not bridged during the remaining lessons in the cultural orientation.

Technical Orientation: An Incident Revolving around Race

The pattern of contraction continued throughout the technical orientation. The analysis revealed that the boundary strength for initial technical knowledge lessons was strong. This meant that discussions now focused almost exclusively on information presented within the classroom; there was little evidence of students drawing from their own experiences. However, these lessons were met with moderate student enthusiasm for the material. There were a number of reasons for this occurrence. First, students did not have to discuss the "boring" sociocultural foundations of the media any longer. Second, the instrumentality of the technical orientation appeared to match student expectations of what a media course should cover, that is, how to make videotapes and films. Third, the analytic procedure used to disseminate technical information about production processes appeared to be compatible with student expectations. Students had little difficulty taking apart production procedures and identifying specific technical terms. Since this method was familiar to students, they were able to anticipate questions that Mr. Albert would have normally asked. The result was greater student control over the terrain of the discussion. Taken together, there appeared to be a compatibility among students' expectations, teacher agenda, and the primary method for study of the technical aspects of production. In essence, students and teacher were moving in the same direction. As a result, there was no evidence of student resistance during initial lessons, and the gap between students and teacher appeared to have been momentarily bridged. The key to these successful lessons appears to have been new control, a new approach to the media, and, most important, an increase in student access to and control over parts of the discussion.

The breakdown of student enthusiasm corresponded with a continual contraction in the parameters of legitimate knowledge. As lessons progressed, there was a marked increase in the amount of class time used for the showing of films, and a decrease in time for discussion. Decreased discussion time meant that the discussion itself had to be compressed in order for Mr. Albert to remain on his schedule. Hence, the tempo of the discussion increased. As in the case of cultural knowledge lessons, increased tempo meant that discussions had to become very focused. There was no longer time for students to collaborate among themselves. Student responses had to be compressed to a single word or phrase. They could not ask questions; they could not reflect on material presented. With reflection and collaboration removed from classroom discussion, the promise of the technical orientation was never achieved. That is, the instrumentality of the technical orientation was depleted from the discourse. Students did not learn "how to" construct a video or film. Instead, they identified discrete technical terms.

The contraction of parameters literally squeezed the fundamental instrumentality of this orientation out of the picture. With it went student incentive for studying the technical aspects of production. Students no longer had any legitimate avenue for introducing their opinions into the discussion. They were once again backed into a corner where the only mode of including their opinions was to resist Mr. Albert. The analysis revealed that both overt and covert resistances emerged at this point of mutual antagonism.

It is important to document the concrete manifestation of student antagonism within the classroom context, specifically as it pertains to issues revolving around race. I present the data from three class periods within the technical orientation to illustrate points being made:

Field notes from 2/16:

As class begins, students are restless and noisy. Mr. Albert tells them repeatedly to settle down. Eventually, they listen. Mr. Albert tells them that they are going to view the film *T.V. News: A Measure of the Medium*. He writes on the board: "Anchor, Reporter, News Director, Film Editor." The film is then shown. Students are quiet. Part way through the film an African-American student enters the class to pick up some A.V. equipment that Mr. Albert had used previously. This equipment is located in the front of the classroom. As this student walks past a row of desks, several students begin to cough very loudly. The student picks up the equipment and leaves quickly. During this, Mr. Albert is sitting at the back of the classroom reading.

Field notes from 2/17 and 2/18:

On 2/17, Mr. Albert shows part 1 of *Harvest of Shame*. On 2/18, he shows the second part. Part 1 of the film depicts the plight of migrant workers and families living in the southeastern part of the United States from 1959 and 1960. In this part, the poverty of the migrant is contrasted with the callousness and lack of sympathy of the farm owners. The poverty is presented in graphic detail. We see poor sanitation facilities, poor eating facilities, low wages, no benefits, no job security. This utter poverty is contrasted with the very comfortable life of the farm owners. One owner states, "This race of people likes this type of life. They're gypsies. They like the free life." This particular speaker raises race horses. The sad truth is that his horses are treated with more care and dignity than the migrants he employs.

The majority of migrants interviewed in this film are African American. In part 1, an African-American woman describes the difficulty she has in getting food for her children. She is almost in tears as she explains, "Amid the fields of plenty, my children are starving." At this point in the film, one student yells out: "Yass sir, baby!" I hear other students laugh. It is hard to tell how many laugh since the room is dark. This comment tears me away from the film and I begin noticing the students around me. One is sleeping with his head on his desk. Others also sit with their heads on their desks; I cannot tell if they are watching the film or if they are asleep. Mr. Albert is sitting near the doorway reading a book.

At the end of this class Mr. Albert, obviously bothered, makes a comment to me. "Can you feel the racism in this group? It is like this every year. They don't seem to understand or care."

As in the case regarding sexism, mentioned earlier under the heading of cultural knowledge, I was puzzled as to why Mr. Albert did not bring up the issue of race and prejudice during the discussion that took place after this film. But instead the discussion took the following tone:

Mr. Albert: Steve, how is an editorial different from straight news?
Steve: Uh, I don't know.
Mr. Albert: Mary Beth?
Mary Beth: It is an opinion . . . one-sided.
Mr. Albert: Right. Documentaries show the real thing, both sides. (The class is quiet.
   Mr. Albert calls on another student.)
Mr. Albert: Why did they initially show this film on Thanksgiving day?
Student: To make an impression.
Mr. Albert: To juxtapose images of Thanksgiving and food with images of starving.
Scott (calls out): Can what is shown on TV actually influence what is happening?
   Like schools? Like ads on the army?
Mr. Albert: That seems possible. Okay, tomorrow, part 2. . . .

On 2/18 the second part of the film is shown. This part is concerned with the education of migrant children. The narrator attempts to show the problems these children face in gaining an education. A major problem brought out in the film is the transient aspect of their parents' occupation. The children are never settled long enough to receive a continuous education.

In one scene, an African-American child is interviewed. The narrator inquires about the child's age. The child, obviously shy, hesitates and then states: "I'm five." A moment later: "No. I'm six." During this scene, a few students giggle and shake their heads. The situation is similar to that which occurred the day before. Again we find a lack of sympathy toward the subjects of this film. I might add that while some students laughed during the film, others found it anything but interesting;

during the film, Mr. Albert had to wake up students. When the film came to an end there were many yawns. Several students did not bother to lift their heads up from their desks. None appeared eager to discuss the film.

Yet a small discussion did occur. Led by Mr. Albert, this discussion focused on the following questions: "How did editing affect the film?" "What was the effect of filming in black and white rather than color?" Again, we find a discussion emphasizing the technical aspects of film production. Of importance was the absence of any discussion on the content of the film itself.

With regard to the lessons of 2/16, 2/17, and 2/18, the following points need to be brought out:

First, Mr. Albert's handling of the situation clearly suggests similarities with previous situations found under cultural knowledge. We notice Mr. Albert's silence. Unless his agenda is challenged (as in the lesson on Edward Steichen), Mr. Albert's response to comments pertaining to sexuality and race is that of silence. Also, we find a continued commitment to the separation of adult knowledge and school knowledge. Mr. Albert is more than willing to comment to me, the researcher, about what is happening, yet as far as communications with his students go, he remains constant in his refocusing on the identification of technical terms. Mr. Albert can be seen as fearful of bringing in controversy and perhaps breaking institutional norms, thereby threatening his position at the school. He clearly does not want to risk mishandling a situation that might result in problems with parents or the school administration.

Second, based on my data, I am not able to state with any degree of certainty whether or not the coughs, remarks, and laughter are truly indicative of student attitudes. These comments and gestures persisted for three days, however, and I feel obligated to come to some understanding of the situation. One might be inclined to label these occurrences as coincidental, for the fact that a black student entered the classroom on 2/16 and coughing follows may or may not be related to the incidents of the following two days. As we look over what occurred, it seems hard to dismiss these events as purely coincidence, however.

It seems evident that the gestures and comments were meant to be noticed by Mr. Albert, as well as by others in the class. On all three days these comments and gestures were clearly heard and seen throughout the room. If these instances were related to some situation external to classroom events, one could speculate that students would have kept comments to themselves or would have been more secretive. Yet comments were made loudly, and there was no embarrassment shown on the part of the students involved. The comments/gestures came across as bold, callous, and defiant. These incidents suggest a gap was once again created between teacher and students.

Rarefaction and the Safe Discourse:
An Incident Revolving around Normalization

While gaps were identified within both the cultural and technical orientations, there was also evidence to suggest that both teacher and students actively sought to bridge this gap (though the motivation for doing so was quite different for each). The pattern of contraction indicates that the parameters of legitimate knowledge were radically reduced for each knowledge orientation and that the discourse was essentially constituted through a process of rarefaction. This concept, which is adopted from Foucault, is defined as "those internal procedures which deplete meaning from the discourse. They constitute a growing scarcity, a dwindling of meaning in that . . . the discourse reveals not plenitude of meaning, but scarcity" (Foucault 1981, 46). The important point is that the struggle over control of the discourse actually leads to a depletion of meaning. For each knowledge orientation there is evidence to show that the struggle between student and teacher led to a strengthening in the boundary between internal and external knowledge. For the common-sense and cultural orientation, this process of contraction was initiated by student attempts to include their knowledge into the classroom agenda. In the technical orientation the process of contraction was initiated by the teacher's overuse of films. The result of these conflicts was that for the cultural and technical orientations, the domain of legitimate classroom knowledge came to consist solely of discrete bits of ("teacher-owned") information. Furthermore, as an internal classroom process, rarefaction came to socialize both student and teacher. By *socialize* I mean "a process of making people safe. This process acts selectively on the possibilities of a man's actions by creating through time a sense of inevitability of a given social arrangement, and through limiting the means of permitted change" (Bernstein 1988, 476). Indeed, rarefaction essentially operated as (a) a mechanism of self-censorship wherein the struggle between Mr. Albert and students essentially defined out points of controversy, i.e. differing interpretations of media practices, and (b) over time came to develop a "sense of inevitability" not only over *what* one discussed with regard to the media, but also *how* one was to interact with this information.

To illustrate this point I will focus on the last lesson in the technical orientation—the events that occurred after the film *Solo* was shown in class. The film documents a mountain climber, Mike Hover, in his journey to the top of the Grand Tetons. What was striking about this lesson was the fact that the discussion of the film was so congenial. Mr. Albert had asked students to identify various technical terms found in the film *Solo*. Student response to Mr. Albert was somewhat enthusiastic. For instance, at one point students debated, on their own, whether or not one shot in the film was a moving-camera shot. Given the prior gaps and struggles between Mr. Albert and the students, it was difficult to imagine that these same students were really as interested as they appeared to be in these particular topics. Why the sudden interest in identifying technical terms?

After reviewing the evolution of the discourse, the answer appeared to lie in the fact that *Solo* was, to a certain respect, the inevitable conclusion of the long hard struggle between Mr. Albert and the students. Lessons had come to the point where the discourse had been depleted to such an extent that, in order to avoid further confrontation, both students and teacher tacitly normalized relations. As in a chess game, both Mr. Albert and students had come to a stalemate. Mr. Albert wished to regain his audience, since teaching to a group of bored, restless students was no pleasant experience. To this end, Mr. Albert allowed students more time to discuss information presented in class. Interviews with students made it clear that they wished to pass the course. To this end, students avoided issues of opinions that led to conflict in the past (e.g., calling the film "dumb"). With all other avenues of discussion defined out of the agenda, the only safe move was to accept, though not necessarily believe in, the current state of affairs they had come to create.

To this extent, the discussion and interpretation of the movie had to remain at a surface level. While students may have found the content of the film enjoyable, which added to the congenial atmosphere, the point is that the discussion was construed within narrowly defined parameters. Within this context, it was not surprising, for example, that students did not pursue any issues beyond those asked by Mr. Albert. Note the following example:

> Mr. Albert: An instance of the long shot?
> Student: The side of the mountain, to show how small he was next to it.

This type of interrogation was all that was possible under these circumstances. Normalization, then, is indicative of the neutralization of conflict between student and teacher.

Here the constitution of a safe discussion was the result of real human concerns: concern on the part of the teacher to have a pleasant lesson and concern on the part of the students to pass the course. Rarefaction of the discourse, however, greatly reduced the options available for student and teacher interaction. It is interesting to note that it was the ability of student and teacher to act upon each other's actions that generated the rarefaction process. And through rarefaction, the discourse was rendered safe. No parent or administrator ever entered the media class. In a sense, the very social dynamic of the media class came to constitute its own form of censorship, its own form of containment to the extent that members of the media class limited their own possibilities for action.

TEACHER MOTIVATION

Keeping It Clean

This study presents a fairly clear picture as to the formation of a safe discourse, and the normalization of student-teacher relations. Throughout the study it became apparent that each attempted to control, and hence define, the informational environment of the classroom. The question that remains, however, is Why? *Why* did students tacitly attempt to control discussions? And *why* was Mr. Albert so afraid of losing control?

To a certain extent, student actions seem understandable when viewed from the perspective of the institutional constraints placed on them, for schools offer few avenues for students to include their knowledge into the official curriculum. Specifically, my investigation suggests that the struggle between students and Mr.

Albert did not appear to be motivated by a clash in personality types. Instead, the data suggests that student resistances were motivated by their attempt to speak in a situation in which student speech was normally kept to a minimum. Ultimately student attempts to speak must be viewed as an act of seizing power, seizing control over some aspect of daily life in school—in this case the discourse, where "the discourse is not simply that which translates struggle . . . but the theme for which and by which there is struggle, the discourse is the power which is to be seized" (Foucault 1981, 53). Concretely, these acts of struggle may take the very simple form of students stating an opinion when not asked to by the teacher, or expressing a point of view that contradicts school (teacher) information.

The actions by students then are understandable to the extent that they want control over some aspect of their school day. But why was Mr. Albert so afraid of losing control? Why, for instance, didn't he allow students to discuss Steichen's personal life if it legitimately pertained to the film? We know that Mr. Albert controlled discussions by keeping classroom information "clean," free of any controversial issues. But why?

In this context, "Keeping it clean" seems to refer to the moral imperatives permeating the school setting itself. Robert Everhart suggests that schools tacitly isolate adolescents from society. The development of middle and secondary education was premised in part on the notion that adolescence was a distinctive stage of life where "people came to see that handling the traumas of adolescence could best be achieved through the prolongation of innocence through a moratorium where the child was protected from adult duties, . . . nurtured, controlled and educated by parents, and most of all, by legions of professionals" (1983, 260–61).

Everhart's discussion provides a historic perspective on the moral function of secondary middle schools. It is interesting to note, however, that a residual element to this perspective on adolescence is still evident within the modern school structure. Mr. Albert's situation seems to be a case in point. Keeping it clean tacitly enables Mr. Albert to control discussions through the elimination of such topics as sex (as in the Steichen incident) and race (the events during the showing of *Harvest of Shame*). While control was certainly a key dimension of keeping it clean, it also imposes moral strictures on the parameters of legitimate knowledge.

To be sure, the study suggests that for Mr. Albert, keeping it clean not only acts as a mode of classroom control, but also may have represented his interpretation of those moral imperatives embedded in the institutional teaching of adolescents. Along similar lines, we note historic religious practices linking moral structure with "cleanness" in biblical text, such as Leviticus. Gordon Wenham (1979), for example, explores how in Leviticus the terms *holy, clean,* and *unclean* were used by priests to delimit and distinguish cultic practices and rituals associated with the sacred and the profane, and to thereby establish a sense of normality.

Can the micropolitics identified in Mr. Albert's class assume a similar dynamic? That is, can student knowledge/ways of knowing be framed as "unclean," and school knowledge/ways of knowing be framed by Mr. Albert as "clean" so that the classroom curriculum—that contested discourse—becomes the buffer zone between the holy and the unclean? The holy, in turn, is sanctified (normalized) knowledge as a result of the student-teacher struggle: the safe discourse (legitimate knowledge). That is, classroom processes can be diagrammed as follows:

normalization- - - - -rarefaction

holy (legitimate knowledge) - - clean (class knowledge) - - unclean (student knowledge)

profane use - - - - - polluted.

Conversely, the "fall" of legitimate knowledge is illustrated by the Steichen and *Harvest of Shame* incidents. In both instances, legitimate knowledge was appropriated (profane use) by students into classroom discussion. Once, within the classroom discourse, school knowledge became infused with student issues of sexuality or race—issues that Mr. Albert finds threatening to discuss in class. Hence, the class discussion becomes polluted, unclean, which in turn initiates the process of rarefaction.

Rarefaction and Terror

"What is so perilous," asks Foucault (1981), "in the fact that people speak, and that their discourse proliferates to infinity? Where is the danger in that?" (52). To define the discourse is to define the terrain of the informational environment for a situation in which the informational environment gives specific direction to the kinds of ideas, social attitudes, and definitions of knowledge available.

To this end, this study identified points of struggle that occurred over the social and communicative landscape of a single mass media course. It was found that over time this struggle led to the rarefaction of classroom discussions. That is, the content of discussions was stripped of its potential richness and what remained held little intrinsic value for students. Of importance was the discovery that even though the struggle between student and teacher did cause rarefaction in the content of the course, a "particular way of talking" about the media was nonetheless constituted; that is, a safe discourse came about. The *safe discourse* means that by the end of the course both student and teacher avoided the discussion of issues or topics that would fuel further conflict. Furthermore, the safe discourse came to define not only *what* was said between student and teacher, but also *how* it was to be said so as to avoid conflict. In the end, students and teacher normalized relations in order for each to attain their respective goals (i.e., pleasant lesson experience for the teacher, passing the course for the students).

What does this study suggest for present and future (interdisciplinary) mass media courses? It suggests that if we truly believe that students should gain a critical understanding of the media, how it shapes their lives and contributes to patterns of sexism, racism, and the unequal distribution of wealth, then our very *first* step must be to reverse the process of rarefaction. That is, we must put the media back into the study of media, so to speak. Instead of hiding from the media, the familiar media of the student, we must accept this as the given, and strive to aid students in their critical examination of this familiar knowledge. Here student knowledge serves as the primary content of the curriculum, where features of everyday life are isolated as themes of study.

The inclusion of student knowledge into the official course agenda means that we strive to expand, as opposed to contract, the parameters of legitimate classroom knowledge. This may mean that classroom discussions will become "unclean" when we consider the content presented on such stations as MTV. Furthermore, discussions are likely to become more lively—as students begin to perceive that their opinions and perceptions have validity. To my mind, the risks involved in a critical and open discussion of media are far more pedagogically desirable that the comfortable retreat to a safe discourse, the "normalization" of student-teacher relations, and the continuation of sexist and racist attitudes on the part of students.

We should not romanticize the risks involved in working with students as we attend to both implicit and explicit forms of racial discrimination. The challenges are as considerable as they are complex. Consider for a moment issues revolving around race in Mr. Albert's class. One question would be, Why are these middle-class white students making racists remarks in class? In part, as I have suggested, their responses are linked to student-felt conflicts, and are meant to antagonize Mr. Albert (who defines himself as liberal, and is perceived by students as a liberal). But this is surface stuff; there are other mitigating factors at play, and one I would like to consider here is money.

In a recent religious forum in Boston, "A Conversation on Race and Class," three theologians were asked to respond to the following statement made by African-American scholar Henry Louis Gates Jr.: "I think it's welcome to have the American public talk about racial differences and discrimination, but the real issue is scarcity. That's an economic issue masking itself, often in America as a racial issue. That's a conversation no one in America is ready to have. And class is as important—often it's more important—to one's daily life than race, even within the black community" (*World* 1998, 14).

One respondent to Gate's claim was the African-American theologian and scholar Thandeka. In her response she discussed her recent efforts to work with liberal, middle-class white Unitarian Universalist (UU) congregations on issues around race and white privilege. Thandeka states,

> "What are our racial wounds?" And the answer is that our racial wounds do not involve Euro-American UU's walking around saying "nigger" under their breath. Rather, these wounds have to do with class issues, family issues, and other kinds of *radical [economic] insecurity.* I've discovered in my theoretical work, as well as working with numerous UU congregations around the country, that the center of the white racial identity formation for Euro-Americans who don't define themselves as racists is not race but family disappointments, class, religious regrets, fears of being at risk. If we peel back the language of white-mindedness and look at its affective content, we find persons who feel extremely at risk.

What kinds of risk? First, middle-class poverty. Even though we say our congrega-
tion, our association is filled with well-to-do persons, all this means is that we happen to make a little more than the average Jane and Joe. Like most Euro-Americans,
no matter what we make, if we stop working, within a matter of months we'll be
impoverished. By that definition most Euro-Americans are poor. (*World* 1998, 19)

And how do we teachers reap this "harvest of shame" in the media classroom?
How do we begin to address the concrete realities of scarcity (both material and
psychological) as it pertains to racial issues? As Thandeka notes, the issues of
whiteness are historically constituted, and ought not be taken out of that context.
But for our purposes, note the possible linkages among identity, class, race, and
how student racism may come from "family economic trauma"—that is, "radical
economic insecurity" within the household. Thandeka suggests that working with
radical economic insecurity is not solely an intellectual problem, not something
that can be solved solely by intellectual, cognitive means. Some form of therapy
may be needed.

Indeed, we may have located a possible point of convergence between Mr.
Albert and his students: the trauma of middle-class, white social identities when
framed within the contexts of economic insecurity. We know that throughout this
study, Mr. Albert consciously veered away from controversial topics, topics in
which ironically, not only was he himself well-read, but also interested in discussing (e.g., issues of sexism and racism in film) for their moral and social
import. How, then, do we account for his action? Mr. Albert chose to "keep it
clean." I want to suggest that Mr. Albert was motivated, to a greater extent, to keep
it clean because of fear, the fear, simply, of losing his job. For him to expand the
parameters of legitimate knowledge would mean that classroom discussions
might become "unclean," particularly when we consider the ideological content
presented on such popular stations as MTV. Here the risk for a teacher like Mr.
Albert is that discussions may transgress the perceived boundary of school
morals, and this needs to be given serious consideration. Given the selective
moral traditions embedded within the fabric of schooling, the notion of an
"open"—interdisciplinary—discussion may be more difficult than we realize.

As such, for many teachers like Mr. Albert, the avoidance of risk-taking practices in classroom discussions may often be motivated by concerns over job security. In the United States, for example, educators are often reminded, by the
media, of unemployment statistics. If one's job security is tenuous (as Mr. Albert's
was), unemployment is a grim reminder of the possible future for the would-be
"rebel" teacher challenging the school's moral code. Indeed as Delaruelle and
McDonald (1984) tell us, "being first and foremost a means of social control,
work is also a means of threatening the potential rebel with the status that goes
with unemployment. Being neither free, nor captive, the unemployed lives in a
no-man's land. He/she is outlawed, condemned to symbolic death by an anonymous judgement, and therefore no longer exchangeable (desirable), transparent

to others, insignificant" (22). To be unemployed, to be rendered invisible, is frightening, and can evoke moments of terror.

In the United States the specter of a permanent class of unemployed individuals can hang over the teacher's head as a grim reminder of the consequences of challenging the system and losing. In a conservative political climate it is difficult for the (media) teacher to find support for curriculum reforms that challenge the moral traditions of the school (reforms such as an open discussion of the media). Within this moral/political climate it is easy to see why some teachers are too "terrorized" to have open—interdisciplinary—discussions with adolescents. There are many teachers who are knowledgeable in a number of disciplines and wish to engage in open/critical discussions with students. However, given political and moral pressures within the school context we can understand why they choose to normalize relations with students.

The real tragedy here is that for radical educators such as Paulo Freire (1997) learning about, say, issues of race in the media is a transformative experience. This process not only entails that the student (and teacher) reflects on self and society, but also the realization that as a human being he/she can actively participate in history as an agent of social and political change. However, this participation entails, in part, learning "moral courage," the courage it takes to stand up in the face of terror for what one considers to be just, right, and humane. Such courage comes about when students and teacher become connected as colearners and cocreators of knowledge—working together to better understand the historical context of the moral pressures and the concrete realities of our lives.

REFERENCES

Bernstein, B. 1988. "Social Class, Language and Socialization." In *Power and Ideology in Education,* edited by J. Karabel and A. H. Halsey. New York: Oxford University Press.

Bhabha, H. 1990 "The Third Space." In *Identity: Community, Culture, Difference,* edited by J. Rutherford. London: Lawrence and Wishart.

Delaruelle, J. , and J. McDonald. 1984. "Resistance and Submission." In *Seduced and Abandoned,* edited by A. Frankovits. New York: Semiotext(e) Inc.

Everhart, R. 1983. *Reading, Writing and Resistance.* Boston: Routledge and Kegan Paul.

Foucault, M. 1981. "The Order of the Discourse." In *Untying the Text,* edited by R. Young. Boston: Routledge and Kegan Paul.

Freire, P. 1997. *Pedagogy of the Oppressed.* New York: Continuum.

Gitlin, T. 1985. *Inside Prime Time.* New York: Pantheon Books.

Hudak, G. M. 1995. "Popular Media, Socialization, and Speech Codes in Education: The Media-Schooling Couplet." In *Knowledge and Pedagogy: The Sociology of Basil Bernstein,* edited by A. Sadovnik. Norwood, N.J.: Ablex.

Lusted, D. 1986. "Why Pedagogy?" *Screen* 27: 2–14.

Wenham, G. J. 1979. *The Book of Leviticus.* Grand Rapids, Mich.: W. B. Eerdmans.

World staff. 1998. "A Conversation on Race and Class." *World.* 12, no. 4: 12–23.

INDEX